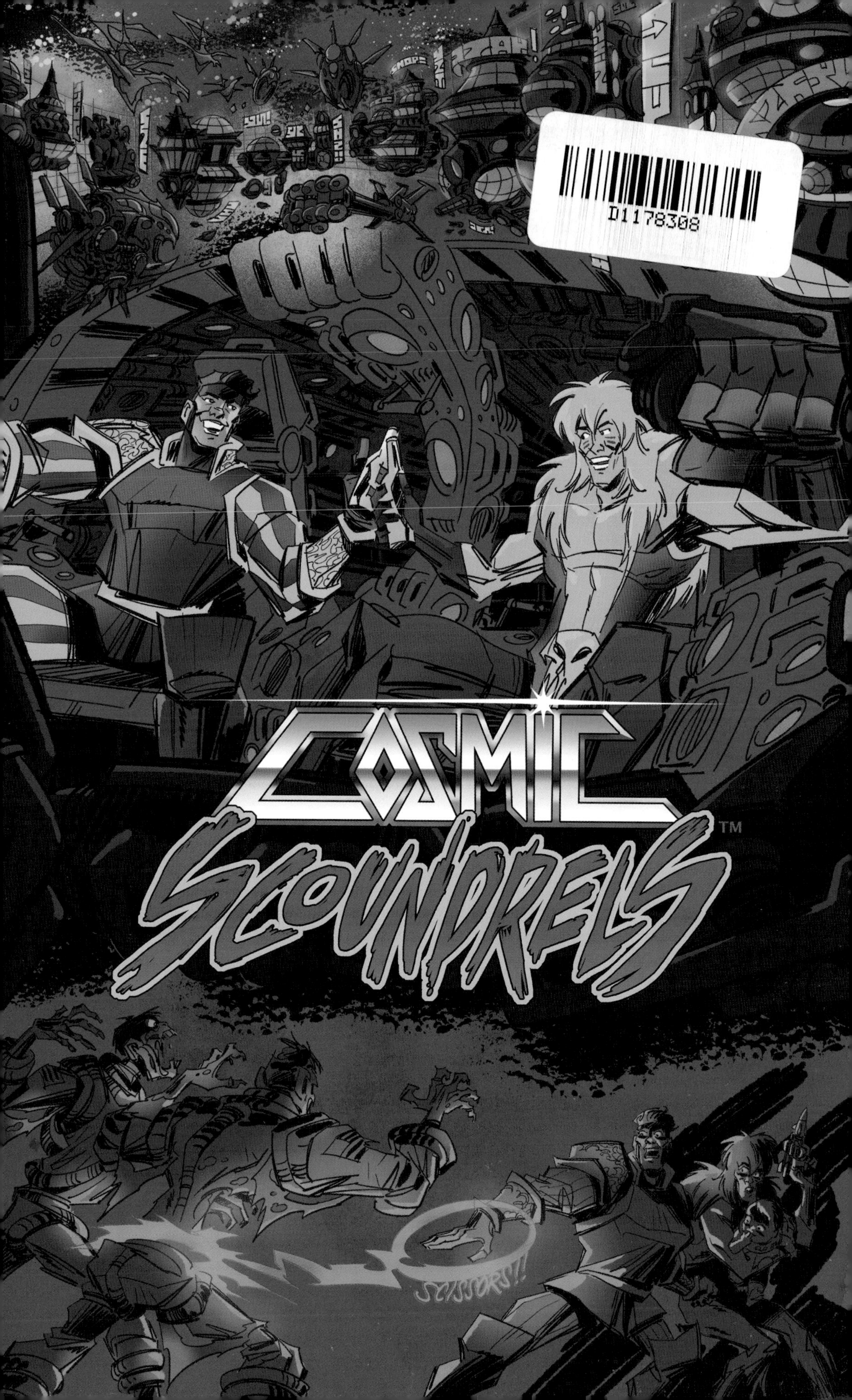
COSMIC SCOUNDRELS™
SCISSORS!!

COVERS....ANDY SURIANO

COVER VARIANTS.......ANDREW MACLEAN, WARWICK JOHNSON CADWELL, DAN MCDAID, ALEXIS ZIRITT, AARON CONLEY AND VERONICA FISH

COLLECTION EDITORS....JUSTIN EISINGER AND ALONZO SIMON

PUBLISHER: TED ADAMS

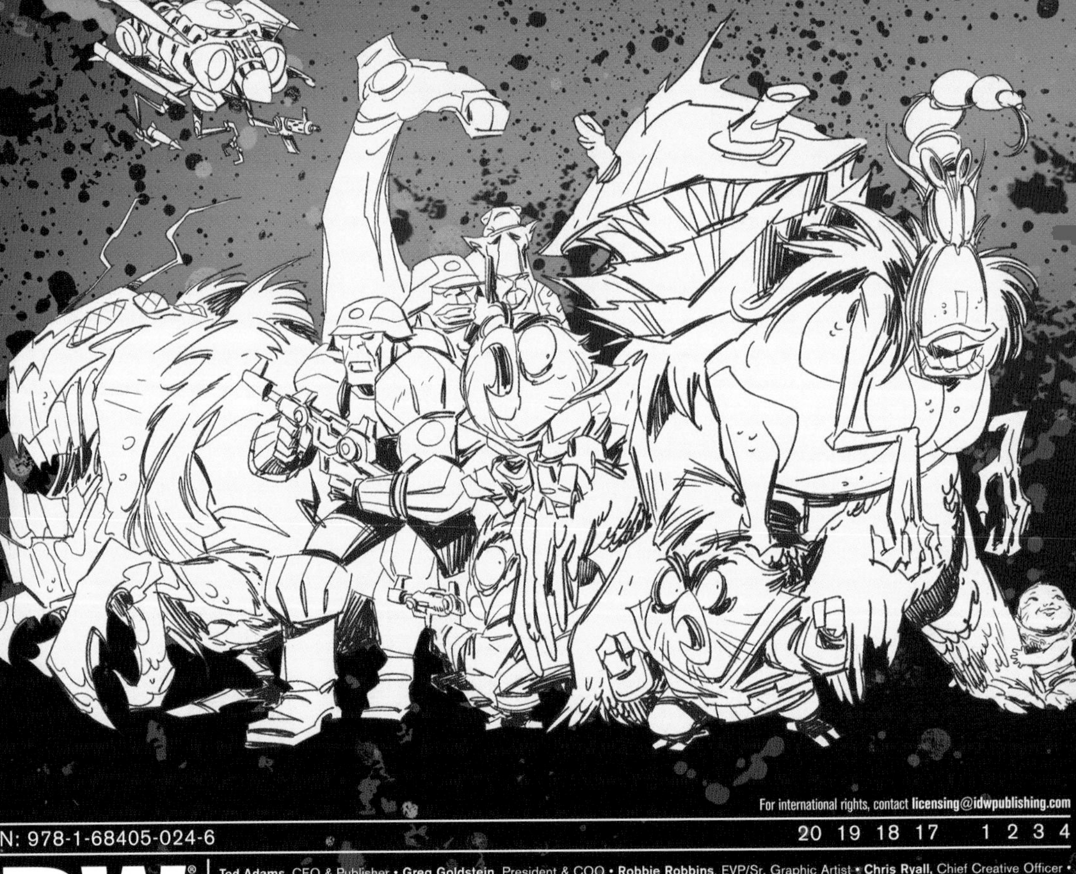

For international rights, contact **licensing@idwpublishing.com**

SBN: 978-1-68405-024-6

20 19 18 17   1 2 3 4

IDW®
www.IDWPUBLISHING.com

Ted Adams, CEO & Publisher • **Greg Goldstein**, President & COO • **Robbie Robbins**, EVP/Sr. Graphic Artist • **Chris Ryall**, Chief Creative Officer • **David Hedgecock**, Editor-in-Chief • **Laurie Windrow**, Senior Vice President of Sales & Marketing • **Matthew Ruzicka**, CPA, Chief Financial Officer • **Lorelei Bunjes**, VP of Digital Services • **Jerry Bennington**, VP of New Product Development

Facebook: **facebook.com/idwpublishing** • Twitter: **@idwpublishing** • YouTube: **youtube.com/idwpublishing**
Tumblr: **tumblr.idwpublishing.com** • Instagram: **instagram.com/idwpublishing**

WORDS AND STORY........MATT CHAPMAN

STORY AND ART............ANDY SURIANO

COLOR ASSISTS................T DANG

LETTERING....CHRISTA MIESNER
AND ANDY SURIANO

LOGO DESIGN.......JEFF SIMS

SERIES EDITS....SARAH GAYDOS

SERIES ASSISTANT EDITOR...CHASE MAROTZ

COSMIC SCOUNDRELS CREATED BY
ANDY SURIANO AND MATT CHAPMAN

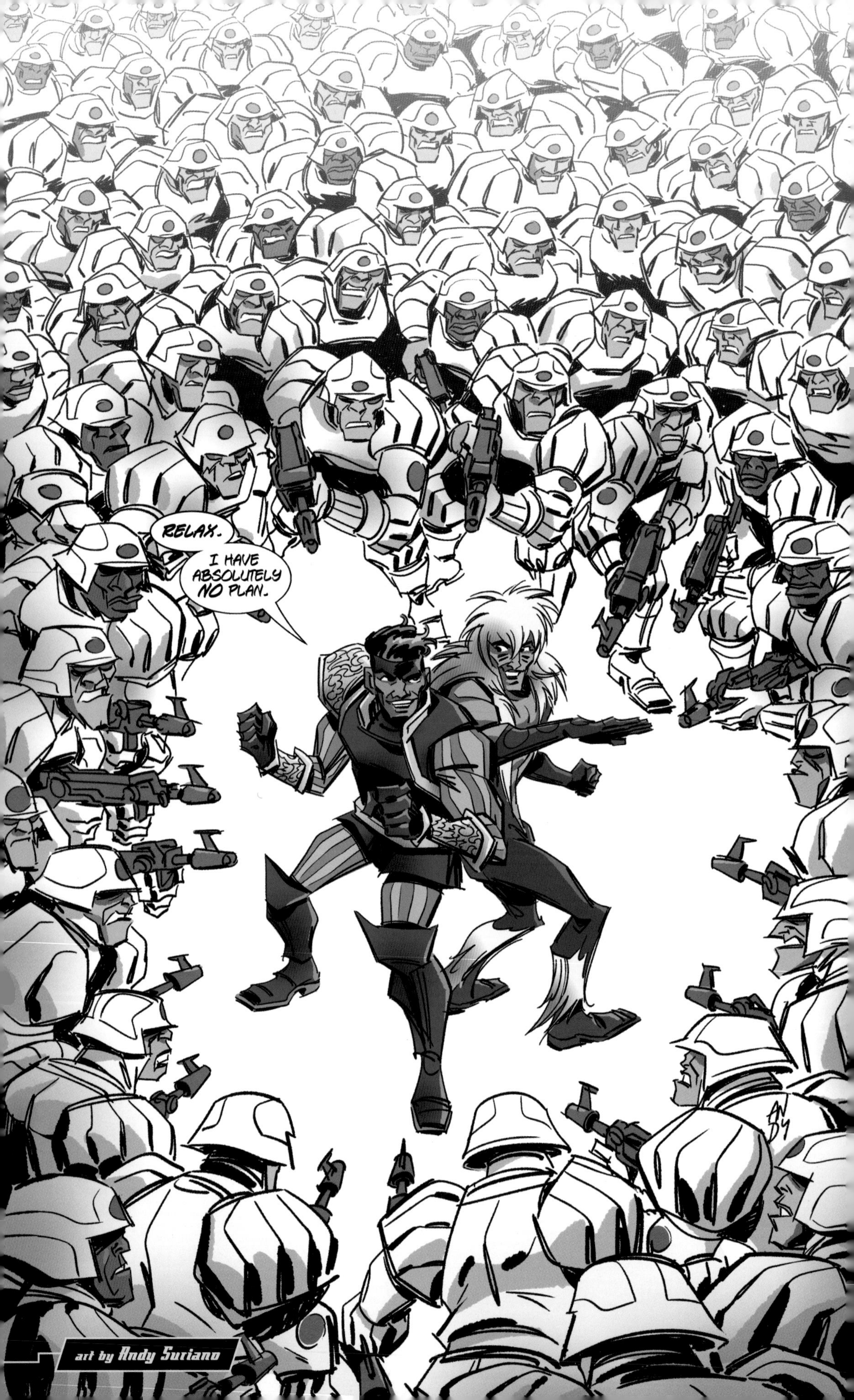
RELAX.
I HAVE ABSOLUTELY NO PLAN.

art by Andy Suriano

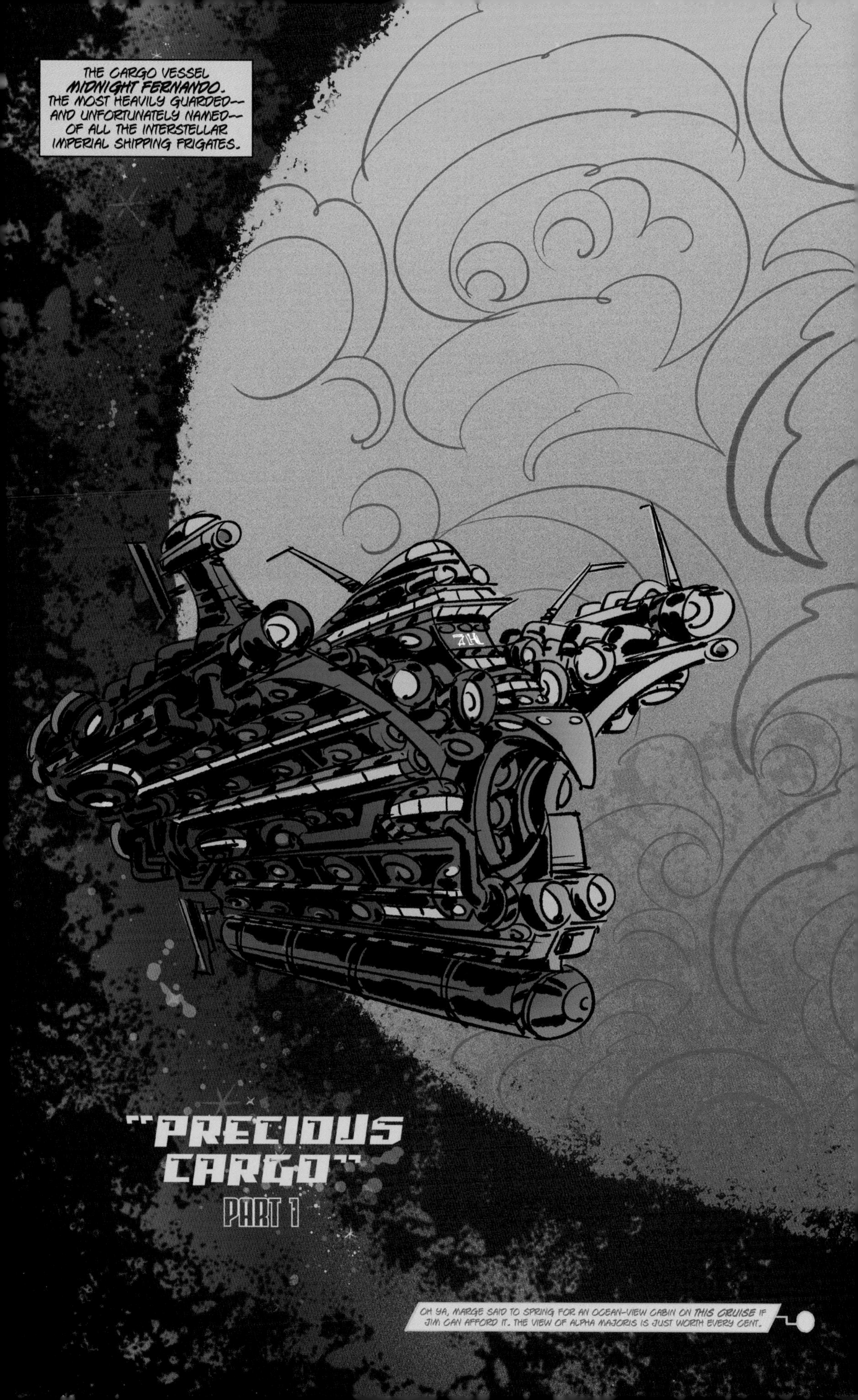
THE CARGO VESSEL ***MIDNIGHT FERNANDO***. THE MOST HEAVILY GUARDED-- AND UNFORTUNATELY NAMED-- OF ALL THE INTERSTELLAR IMPERIAL SHIPPING FRIGATES.
"PRECIOUS CARGO"
PART 1
OH YA, MARGE SAID TO SPRING FOR AN OCEAN-VIEW CABIN ON *THIS CRUISE* IF JIM CAN AFFORD IT. THE VIEW OF ALPHA MAJORIS IS JUST WORTH EVERY CENT.

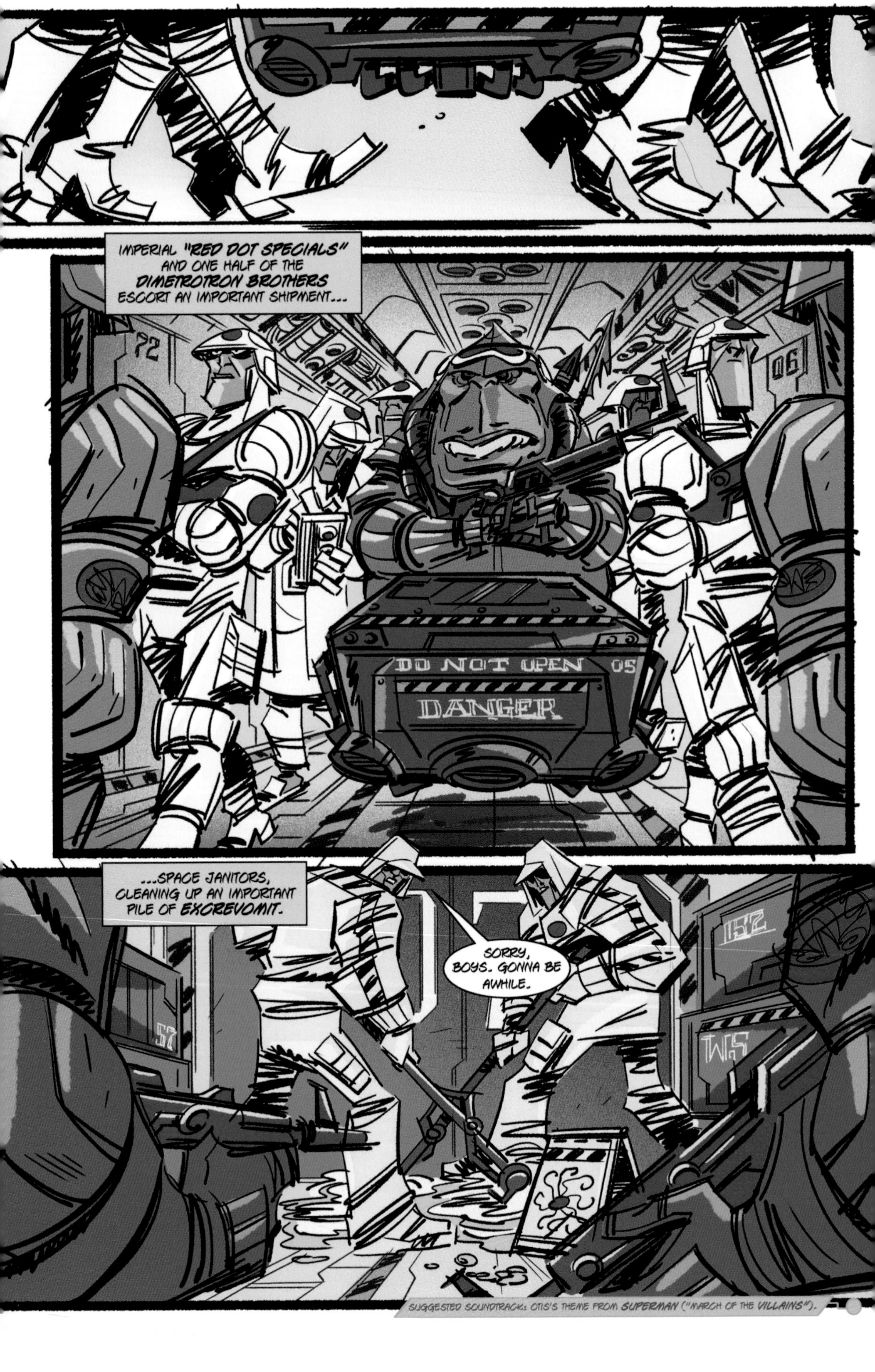
IMPERIAL "RED DOT SPECIALS" AND ONE HALF OF THE DIMETROTRON BROTHERS ESCORT AN IMPORTANT SHIPMENT...
72
06
DO NOT OPEN 05
DANGER
...SPACE JANITORS, CLEANING UP AN IMPORTANT PILE OF EXCREVOMIT.
SORRY, BOYS. GONNA BE AWHILE.

SUGGESTED SOUNDTRACK: OTIS'S THEME FROM *SUPERMAN* ("MARCH OF THE *VILLAINS*").

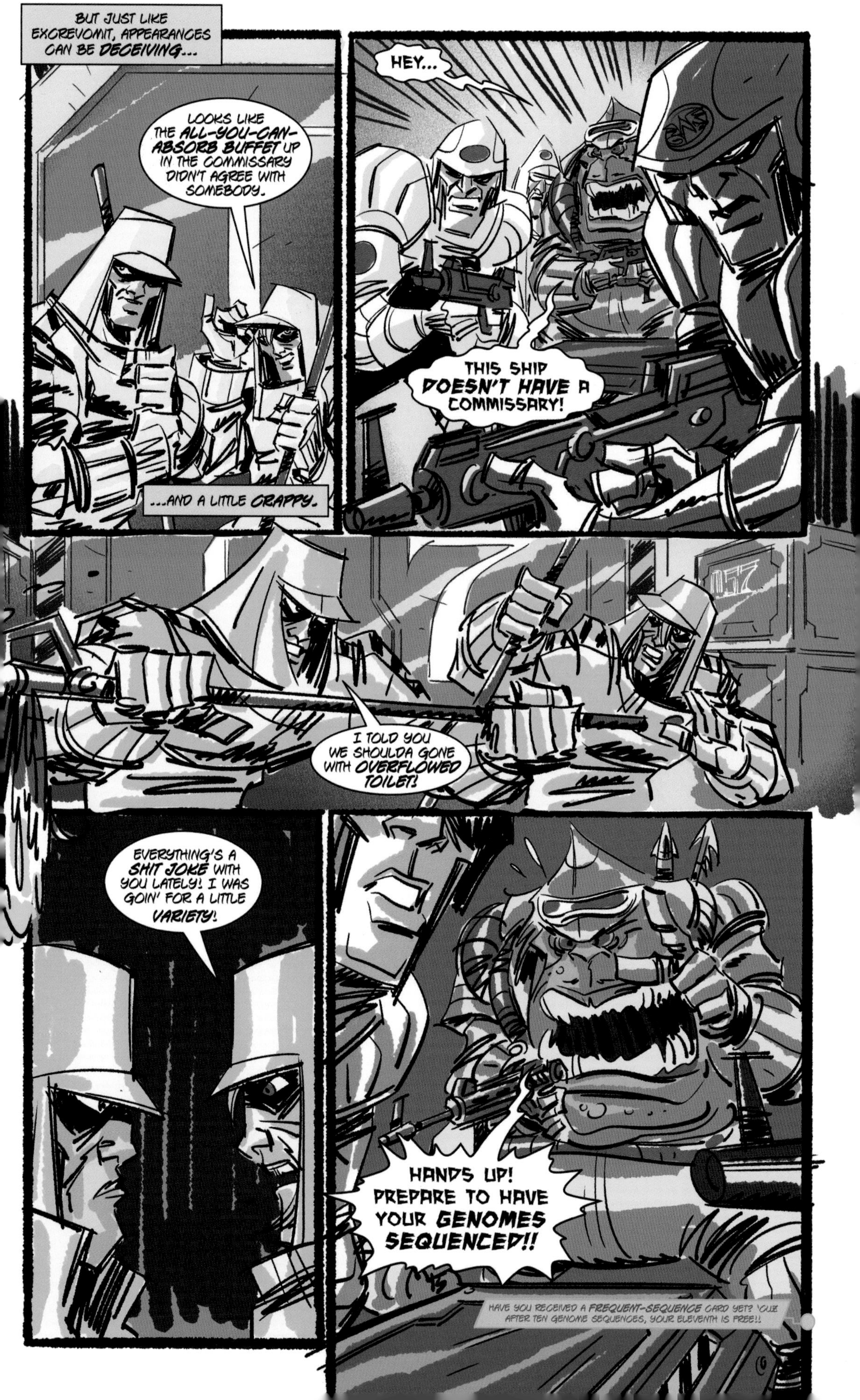
BUT JUST LIKE EXCREVOMIT, APPEARANCES CAN BE DECEIVING...
LOOKS LIKE THE ALL-YOU-CAN-ABSORB BUFFET UP IN THE COMMISSARY DIDN'T AGREE WITH SOMEBODY.
...AND A LITTLE CRAPPY.
HEY...
THIS SHIP DOESN'T HAVE A COMMISSARY!
I TOLD YOU WE SHOULDA GONE WITH OVERFLOWED TOILET!
EVERYTHING'S A SHIT JOKE WITH YOU LATELY! I WAS GOIN' FOR A LITTLE VARIETY!
HANDS UP! PREPARE TO HAVE YOUR GENOMES SEQUENCED!!
HAVE YOU RECEIVED A FREQUENT-SEQUENCE CARD YET? 'CUZ AFTER TEN GENOME SEQUENCES, YOUR ELEVENTH IS FREE!!

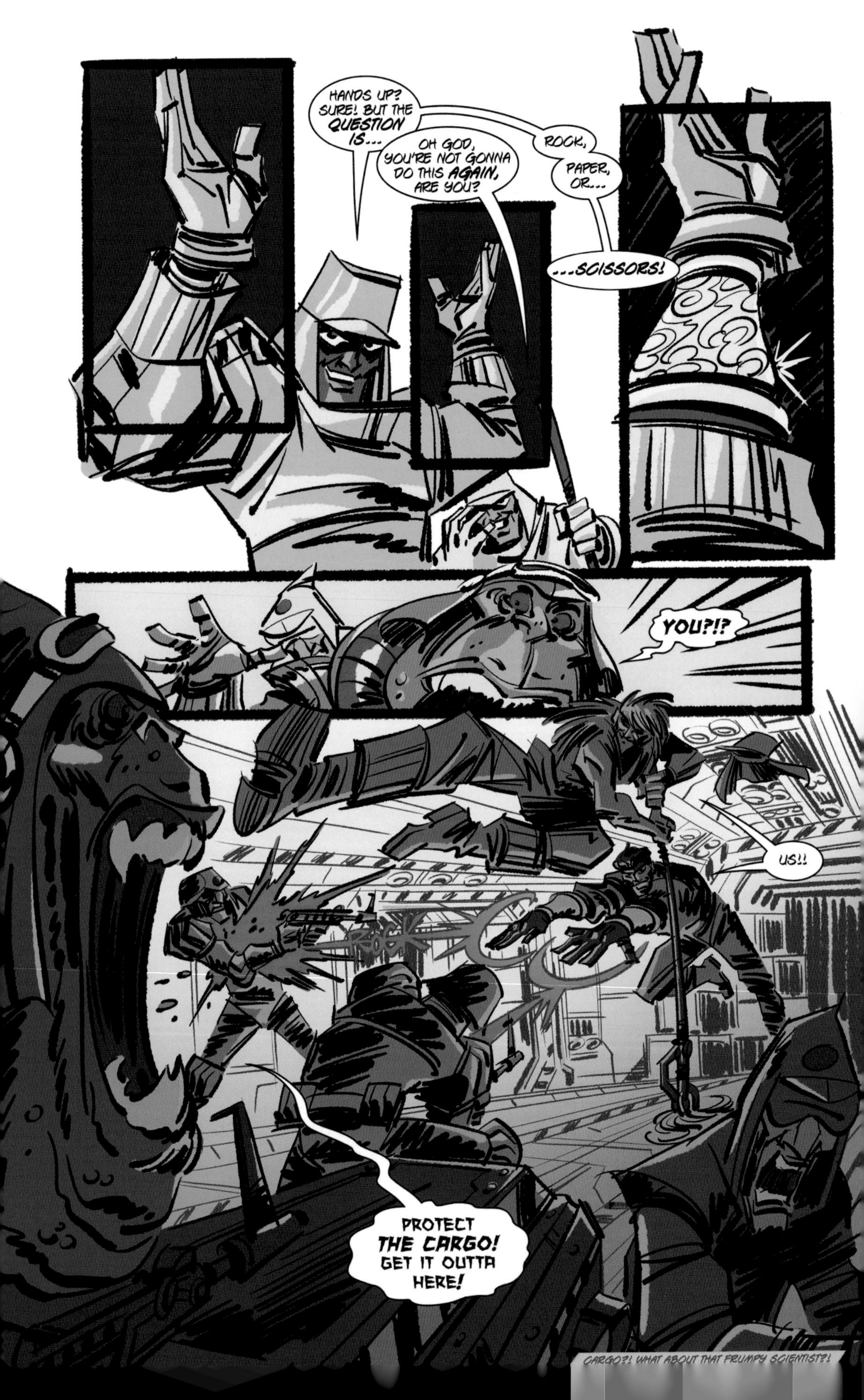
HANDS UP? SURE! BUT THE QUESTION IS...
OH GOD, YOU'RE NOT GONNA DO THIS AGAIN, ARE YOU?
ROCK,
PAPER, OR...
...SCISSORS!
YOU?!?
US!!
PROTECT THE CARGO! GET IT OUTTA HERE!
CARGO?! WHAT ABOUT THAT FRUMPY SCIENTIST?!

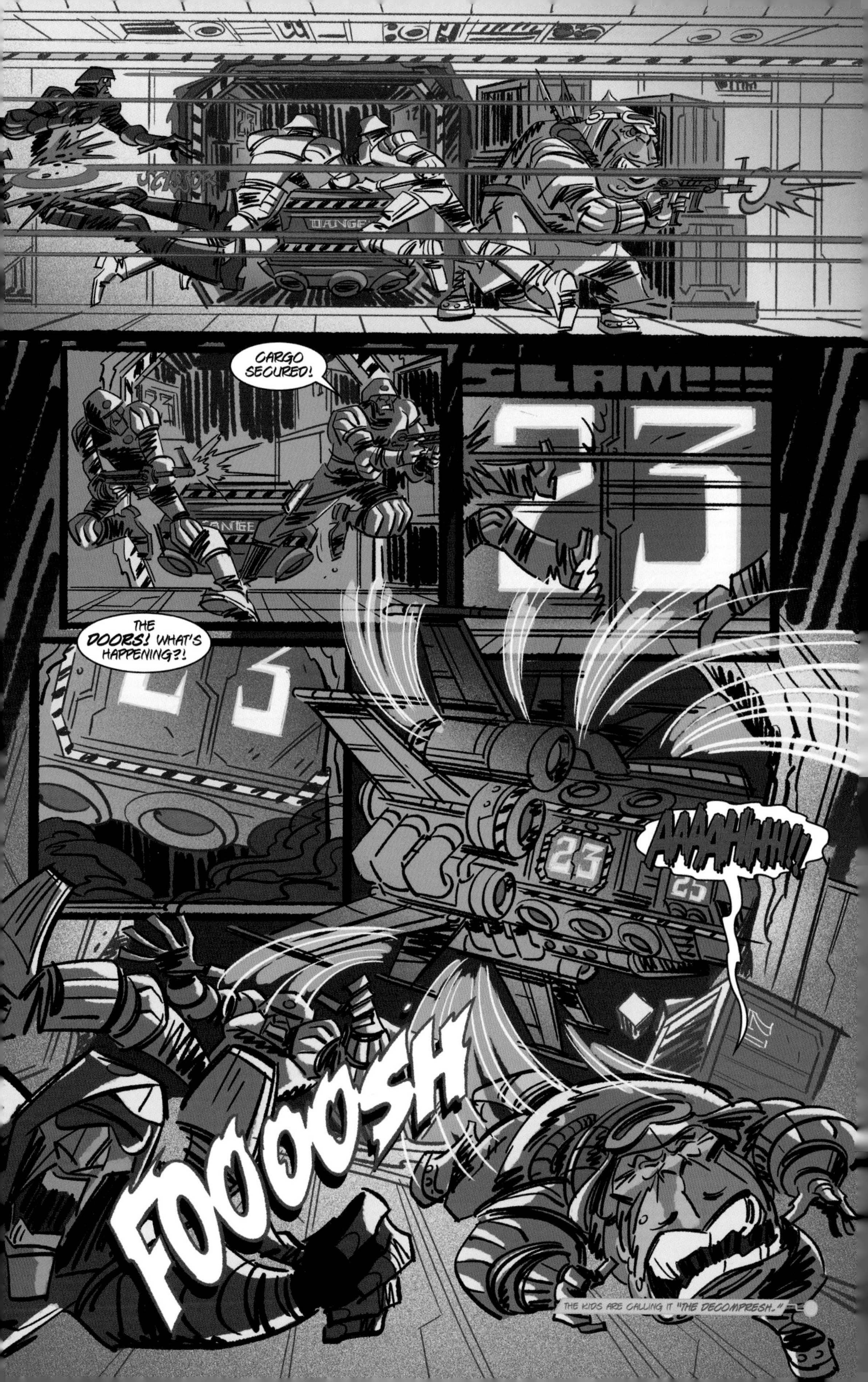
CARGO SECURED!
SLAM
THE DOORS! WHAT'S HAPPENING?!
AAAAHHHH!!!
FOOOOSH
THE KIDS ARE CALLING IT "THE DECOMPRESH."

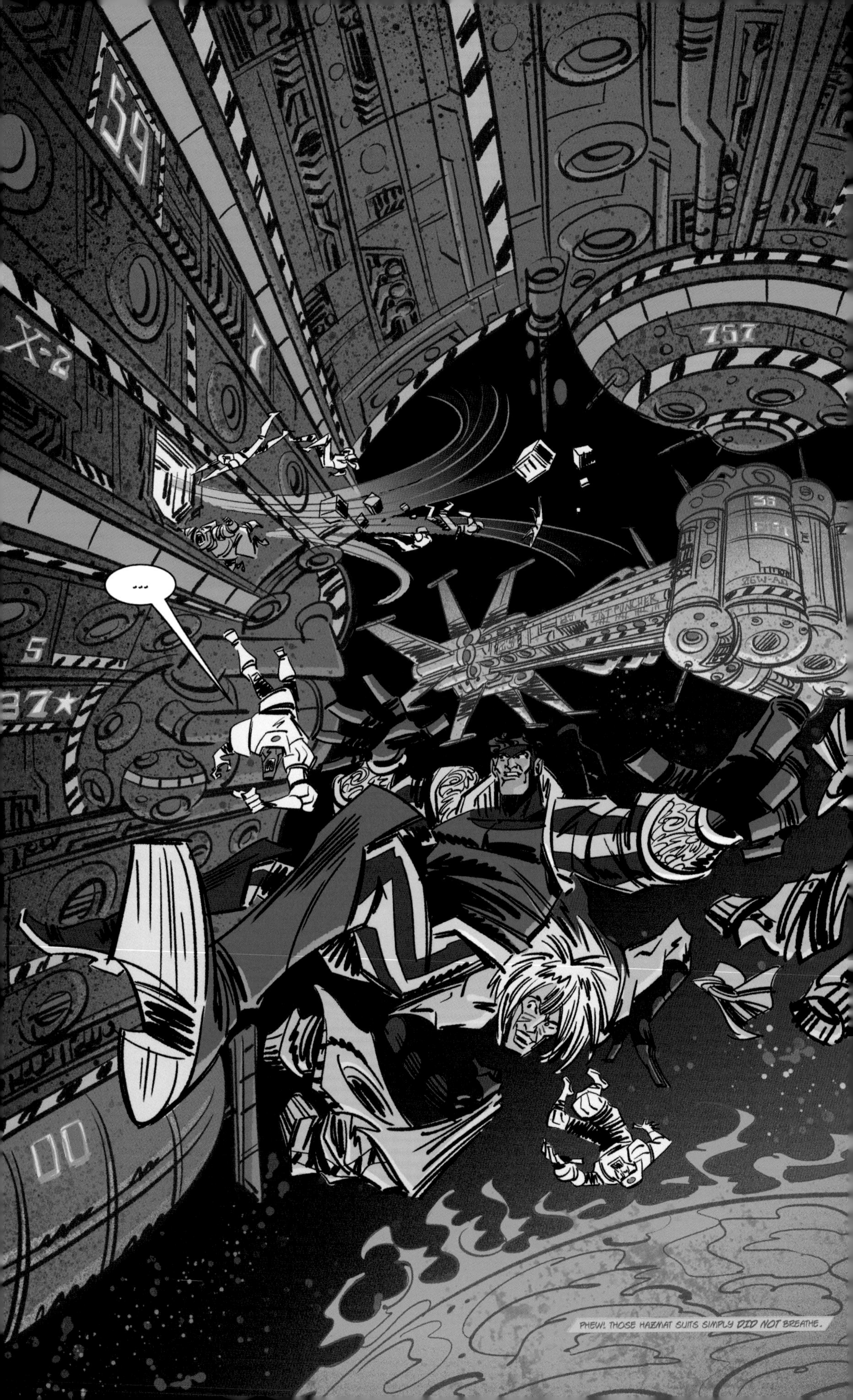
...
PHEW! THOSE HAZMAT SUITS SIMPLY *DID NOT* BREATHE.

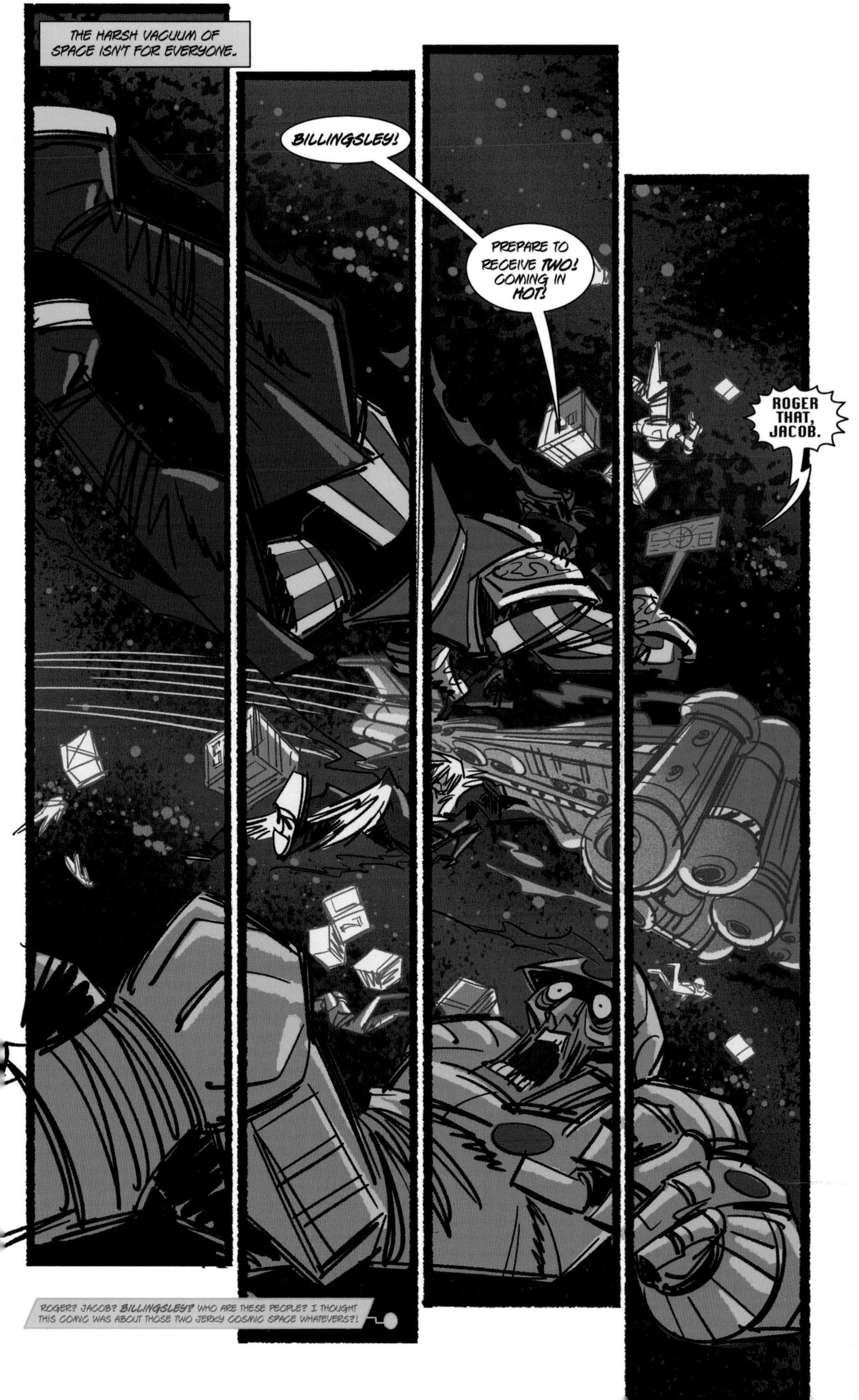
THE HARSH VACUUM OF SPACE ISN'T FOR EVERYONE.
BILLINGSLEY!
PREPARE TO RECEIVE TWO! COMING IN HOT!
ROGER THAT, JACOB.
ROGER? JACOB? BILLINGSLEY? WHO ARE THESE PEOPLE? I THOUGHT THIS COMIC WAS ABOUT THOSE TWO JERKY COSMIC SPACE WHATEVERS?!

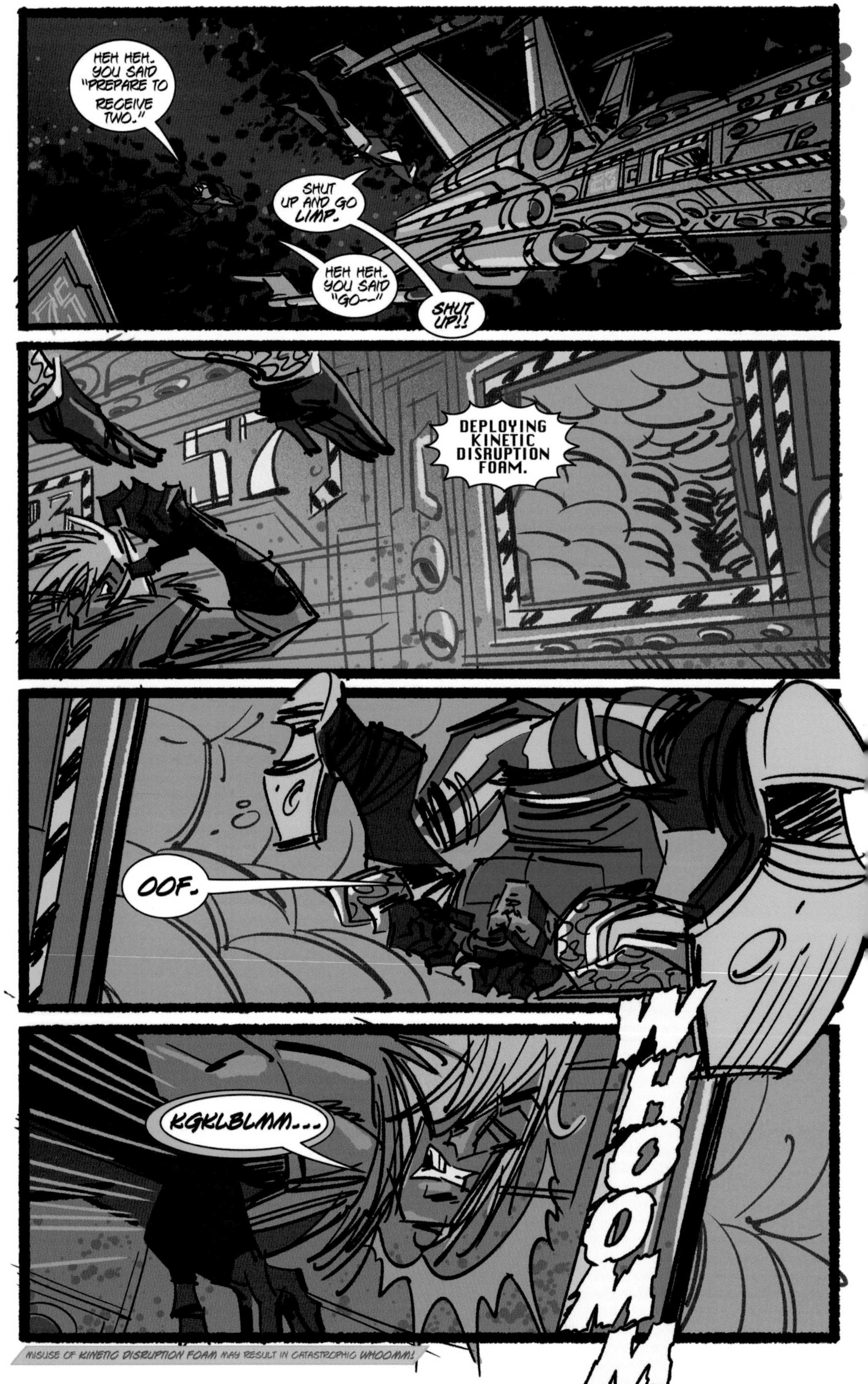
HEH HEH. YOU SAID "PREPARE TO RECEIVE TWO."
SHUT UP AND GO LIMP.
HEH HEH. YOU SAID "GO--"
SHUT UP!!
DEPLOYING KINETIC DISRUPTION FOAM.
OOF.
KGKLBLMM...
WHOOMM
MISUSE OF KINETIC DISRUPTION FOAM MAY RESULT IN CATASTROPHIC WHOOMM!

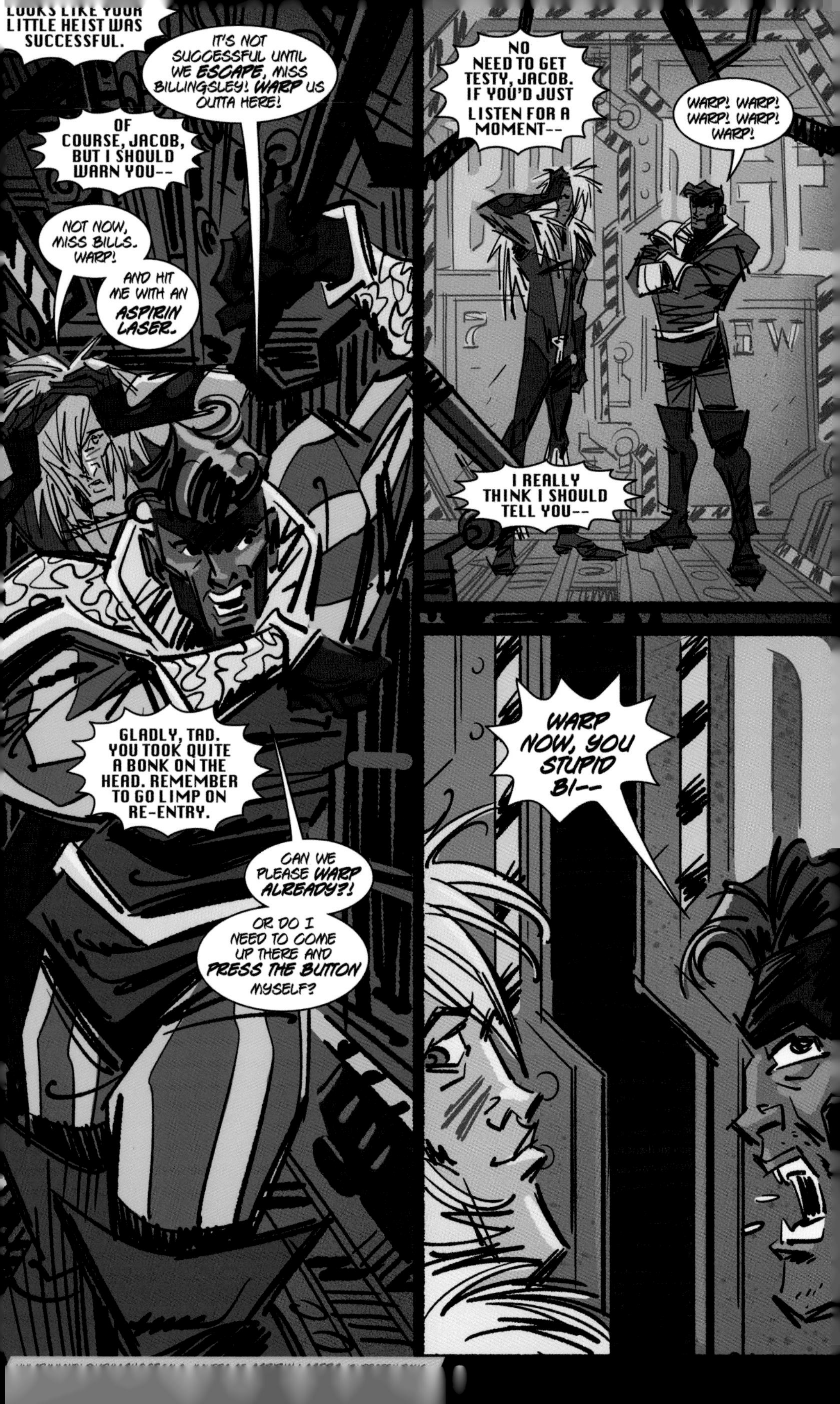

LOOKS LIKE YOUR LITTLE HEIST WAS SUCCESSFUL.
IT'S NOT SUCCESSFUL UNTIL WE ESCAPE, MISS BILLINGSLEY! WARP US OUTTA HERE!
OF COURSE, JACOB, BUT I SHOULD WARN YOU--
NOT NOW, MISS BILLS. WARP!
AND HIT ME WITH AN ASPIRIN LASER.
GLADLY, TAD. YOU TOOK QUITE A BONK ON THE HEAD. REMEMBER TO GO LIMP ON RE-ENTRY.
CAN WE PLEASE WARP ALREADY?!
OR DO I NEED TO COME UP THERE AND PRESS THE BUTTON MYSELF?
NO NEED TO GET TESTY, JACOB. IF YOU'D JUST LISTEN FOR A MOMENT--
WARP! WARP! WARP! WARP! WARP!
I REALLY THINK I SHOULD TELL YOU--
WARP NOW, YOU STUPID BI--

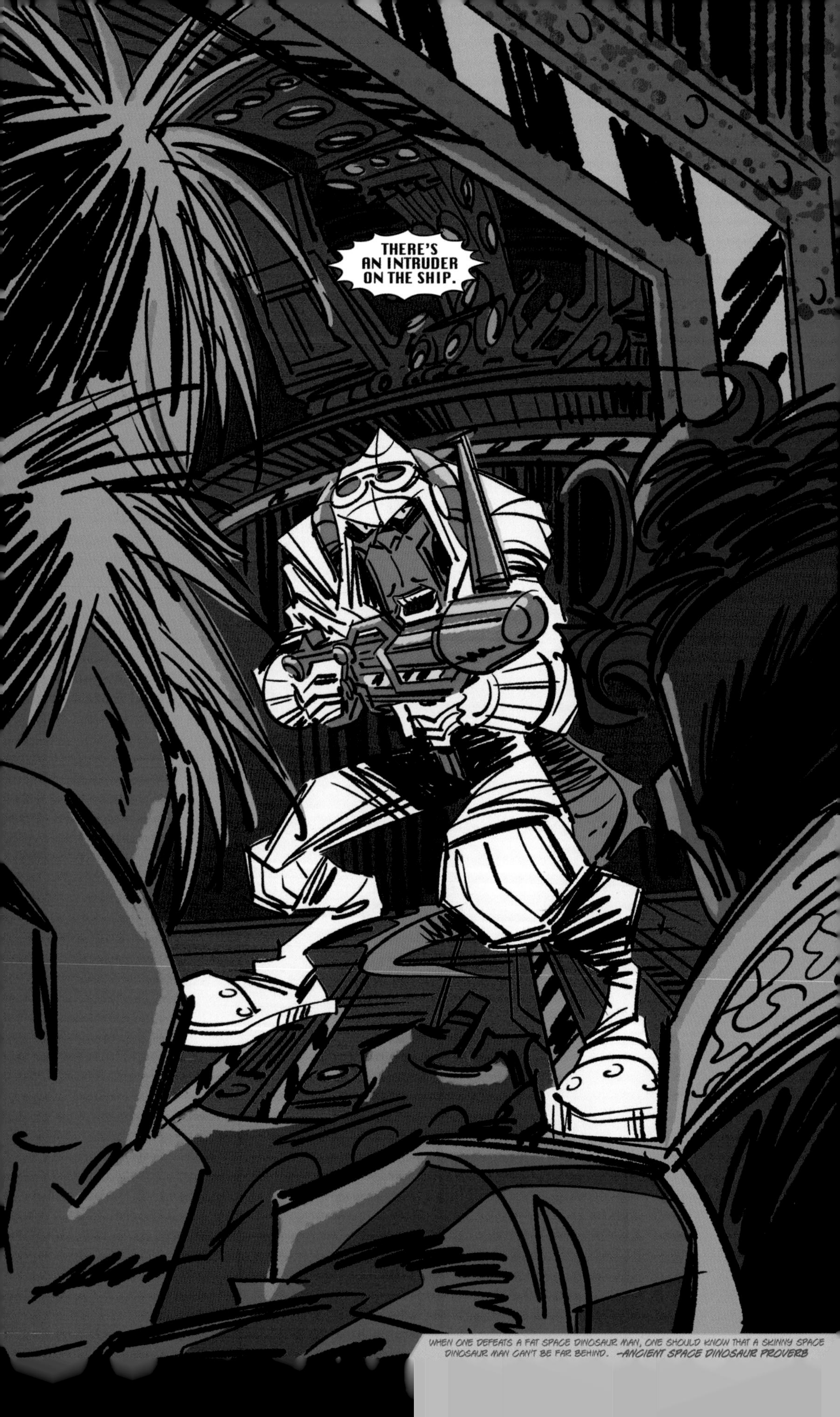
THERE'S AN INTRUDER ON THE SHIP.
WHEN ONE DEFEATS A FAT SPACE DINOSAUR MAN, ONE SHOULD KNOW THAT A SKINNY SPACE DINOSAUR MAN CAN'T BE FAR BEHIND. –ANCIENT SPACE DINOSAUR PROVERB

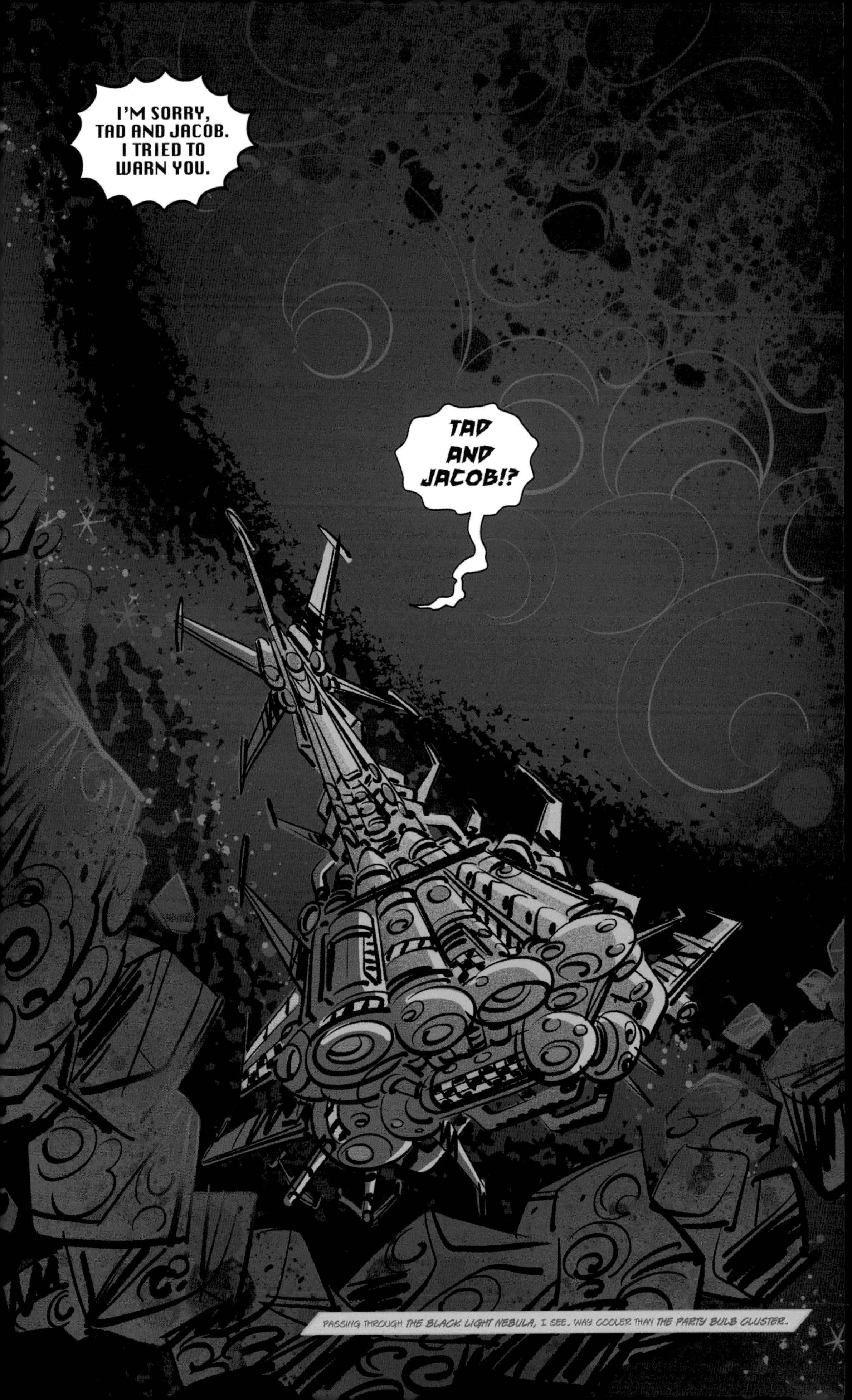
I'M SORRY, TAD AND JACOB. I TRIED TO WARN YOU.
TAD AND JACOB!?
PASSING THROUGH THE BLACK LIGHT NEBULA, I SEE. WAY COOLER THAN THE PARTY BULB CLUSTER.

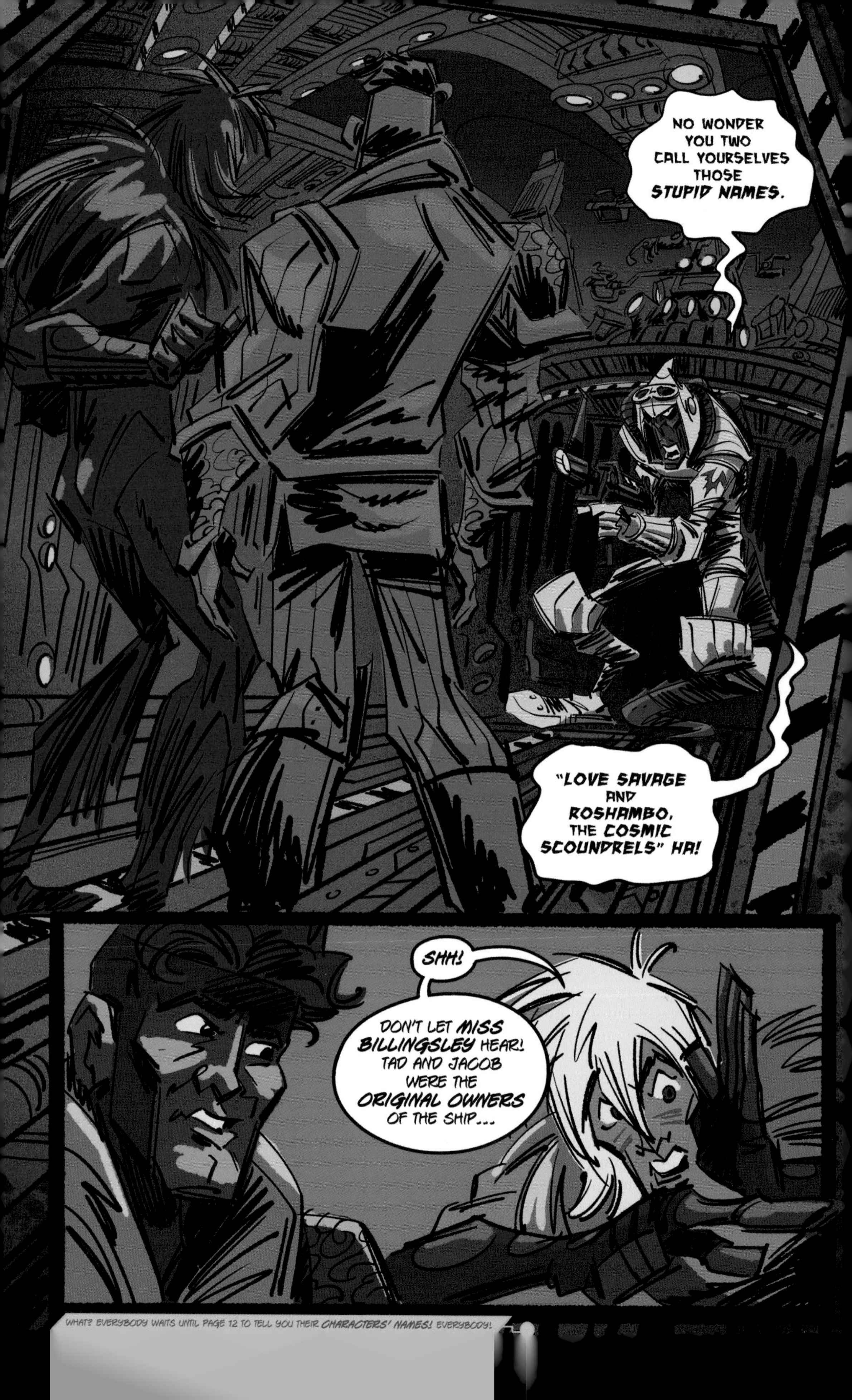
NO WONDER YOU TWO CALL YOURSELVES THOSE STUPID NAMES.
"LOVE SAVAGE AND ROSHAMBO, THE COSMIC SCOUNDRELS" HA!
SHH!
DON'T LET MISS BILLINGSLEY HEAR! TAD AND JACOB WERE THE ORIGINAL OWNERS OF THE SHIP...
WHAT? EVERYBODY WAITS UNTIL PAGE 12 TO TELL YOU THEIR CHARACTERS' NAMES! EVERYBODY!

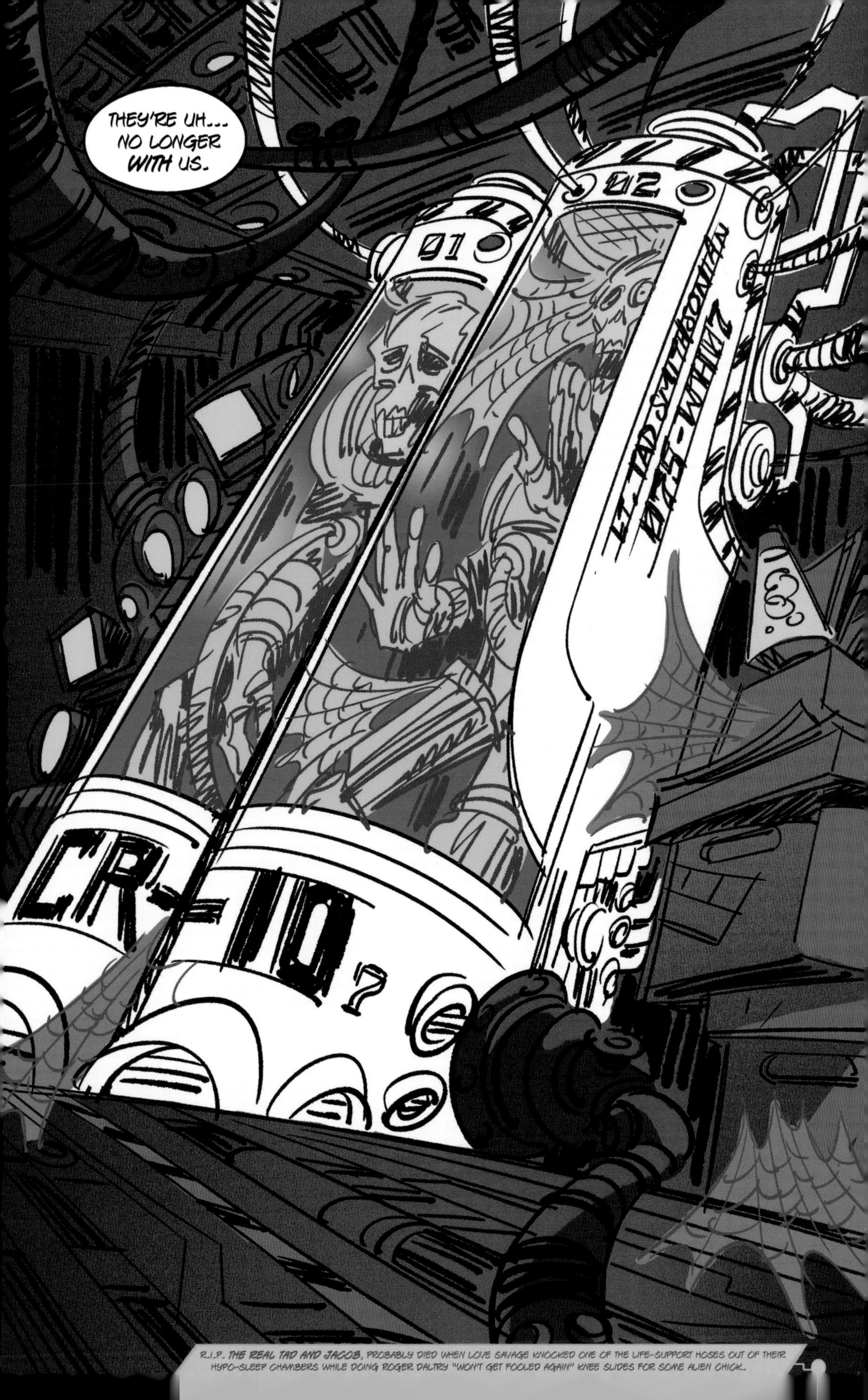
THEY'RE UH... NO LONGER WITH US.
02
01
LT. TAD SMITHSONIAN
CR-10
7
R.I.P. THE REAL TAD AND JACOB. PROBABLY DIED WHEN LOVE SAVAGE KNOCKED ONE OF THE LIFE-SUPPORT HOSES OUT OF THEIR HYPO-SLEEP CHAMBERS WHILE DOING ROGER DALTRY "WON'T GET FOOLED AGAIN" KNEE SLIDES FOR SOME ALIEN CHICK.

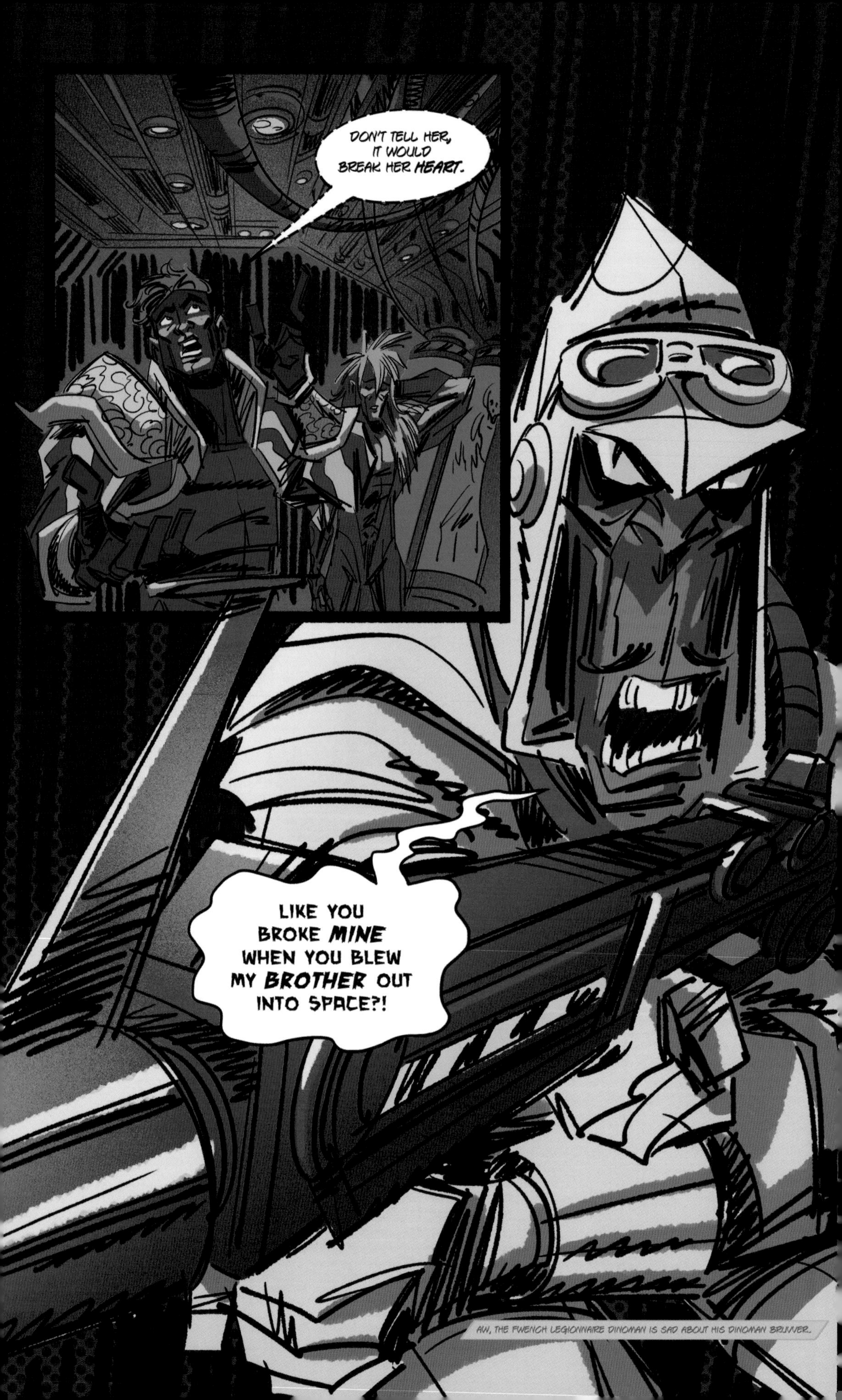
DON'T TELL HER, IT WOULD BREAK HER **HEART**.
LIKE YOU BROKE ***MINE*** WHEN YOU BLEW MY ***BROTHER*** OUT INTO SPACE?!
AW, THE FWENCH LEGIONNAIRE DINOMAN IS SAD ABOUT HIS DINOMAN BRUVVER.

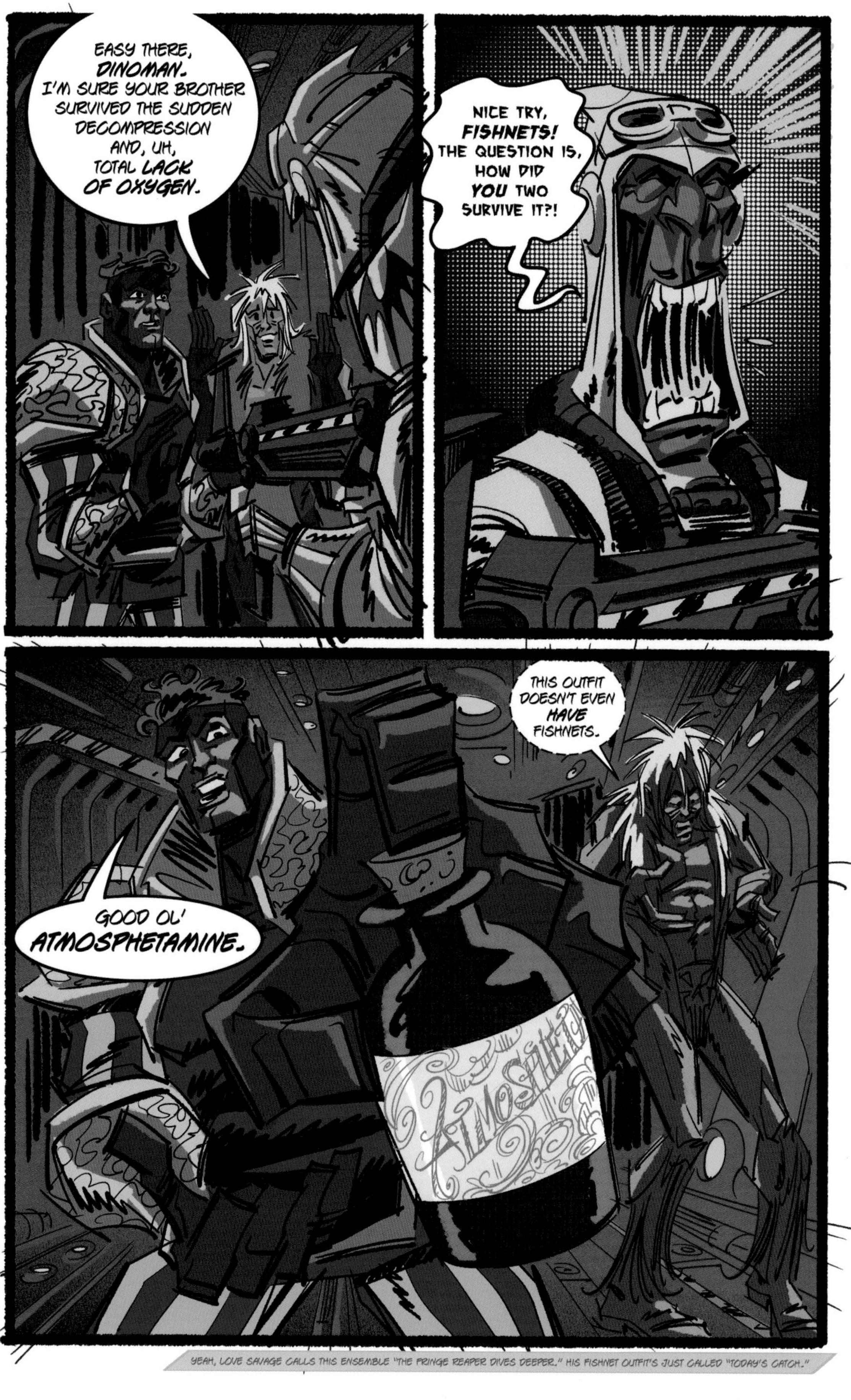
EASY THERE, DINOMAN. I'M SURE YOUR BROTHER SURVIVED THE SUDDEN DECOMPRESSION AND, UH, TOTAL LACK OF OXYGEN.
NICE TRY, FISHNETS! THE QUESTION IS, HOW DID YOU TWO SURVIVE IT?!
THIS OUTFIT DOESN'T EVEN HAVE FISHNETS.
GOOD OL' ATMOSPHETAMINE.
YEAH, LOVE SAVAGE CALLS THIS ENSEMBLE "THE FRINGE REAPER DIVES DEEPER." HIS FISHNET OUTFIT'S JUST CALLED "TODAY'S CATCH."

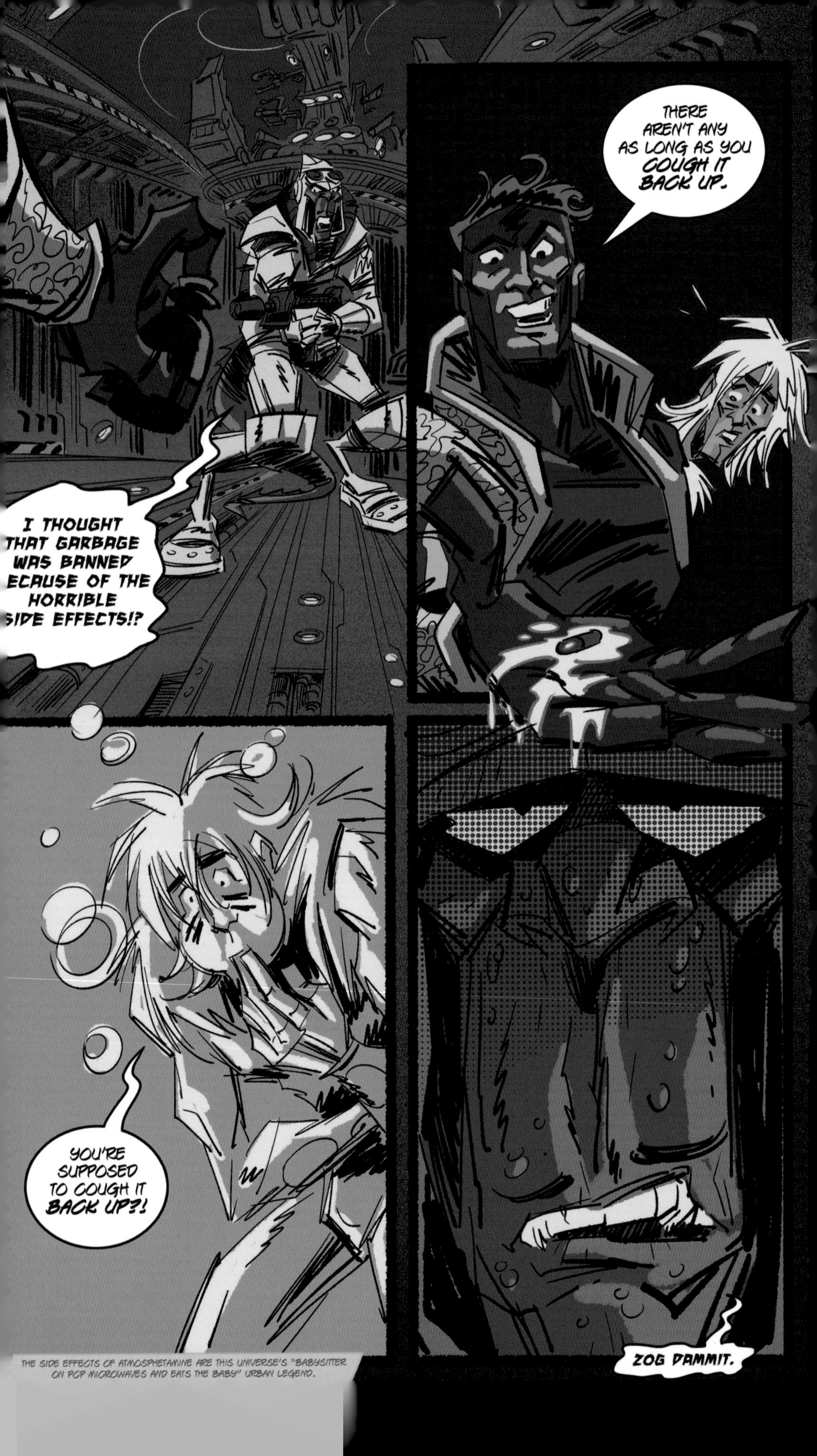
I THOUGHT THAT GARBAGE WAS BANNED ECAUSE OF THE HORRIBLE SIDE EFFECTS!?
THERE AREN'T ANY AS LONG AS YOU COUGH IT BACK UP.
YOU'RE SUPPOSED TO COUGH IT BACK UP?!
ZOG DAMMIT.
THE SIDE EFFECTS OF ATMOSPHETAMINE ARE THIS UNIVERSE'S "BABYSITTER ON PCP MICROWAVES AND EATS THE BABY" URBAN LEGEND.

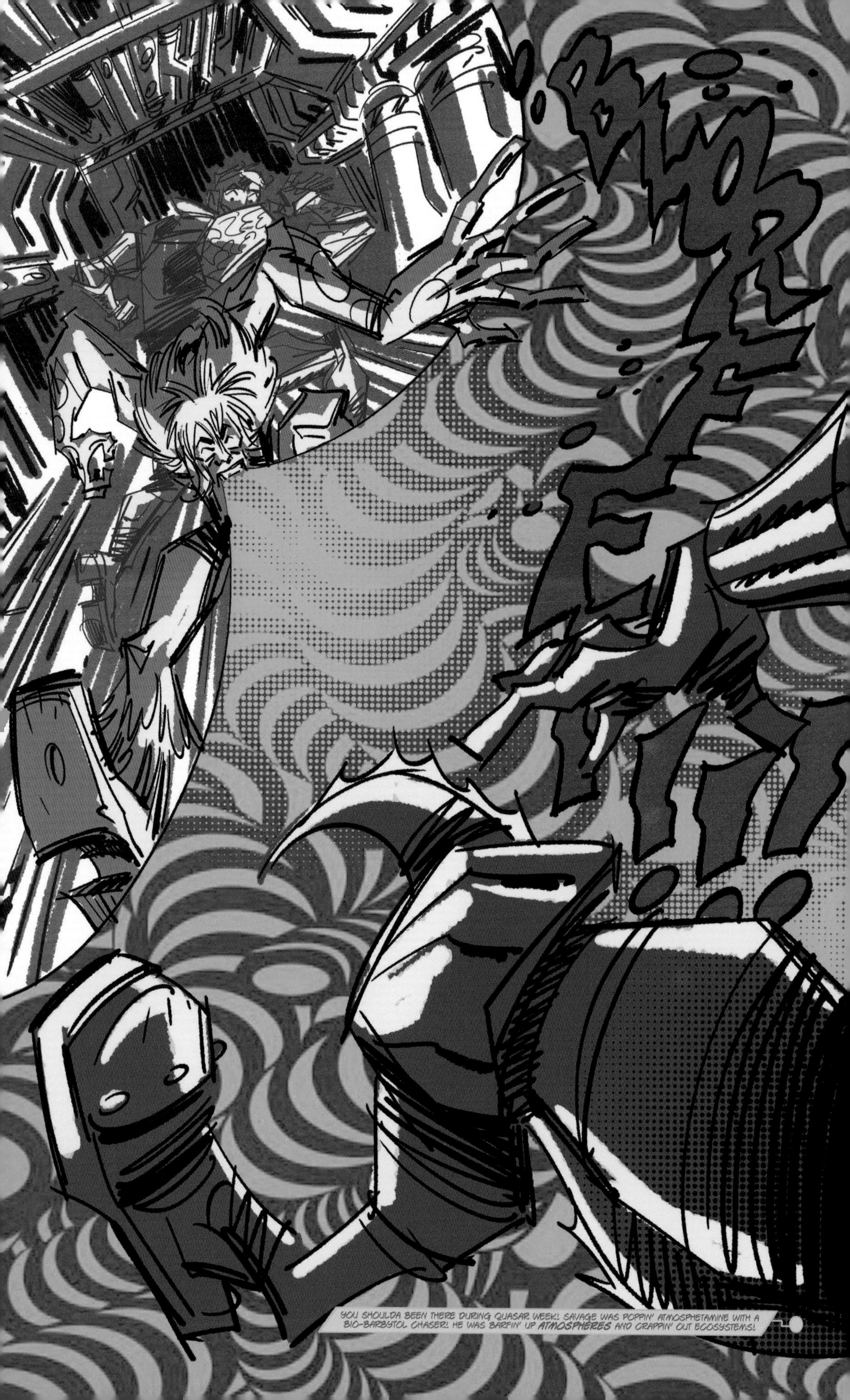
BLORRFFFF!!!
YOU SHOULDA BEEN THERE DURING QUASAR WEEK! SAVAGE WAS POPPIN' ATMOSPHETAMINE WITH A BIO-BARBYTOL CHASER! HE WAS BARFIN' UP *ATMOSPHERES* AND CRAPPIN' OUT ECOSYSTEMS!

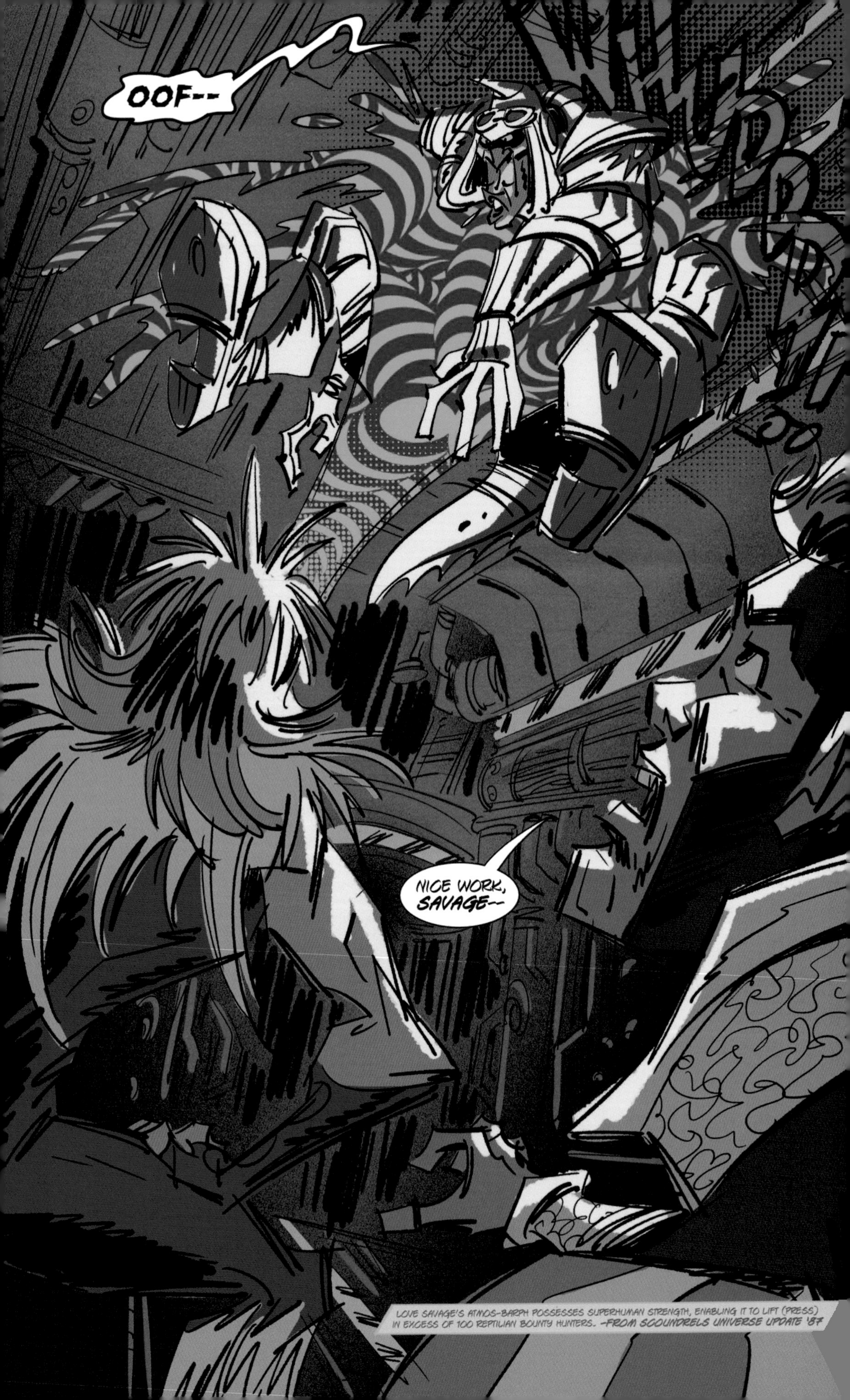
OOF--
NICE WORK, SAVAGE--
LOVE SAVAGE'S ATMOS-BARPH POSSESSES SUPERHUMAN STRENGTH, ENABLING IT TO LIFT (PRESS) IN EXCESS OF 100 REPTILIAN BOUNTY HUNTERS. -FROM SCOUNDRELS UNIVERSE UPDATE '87

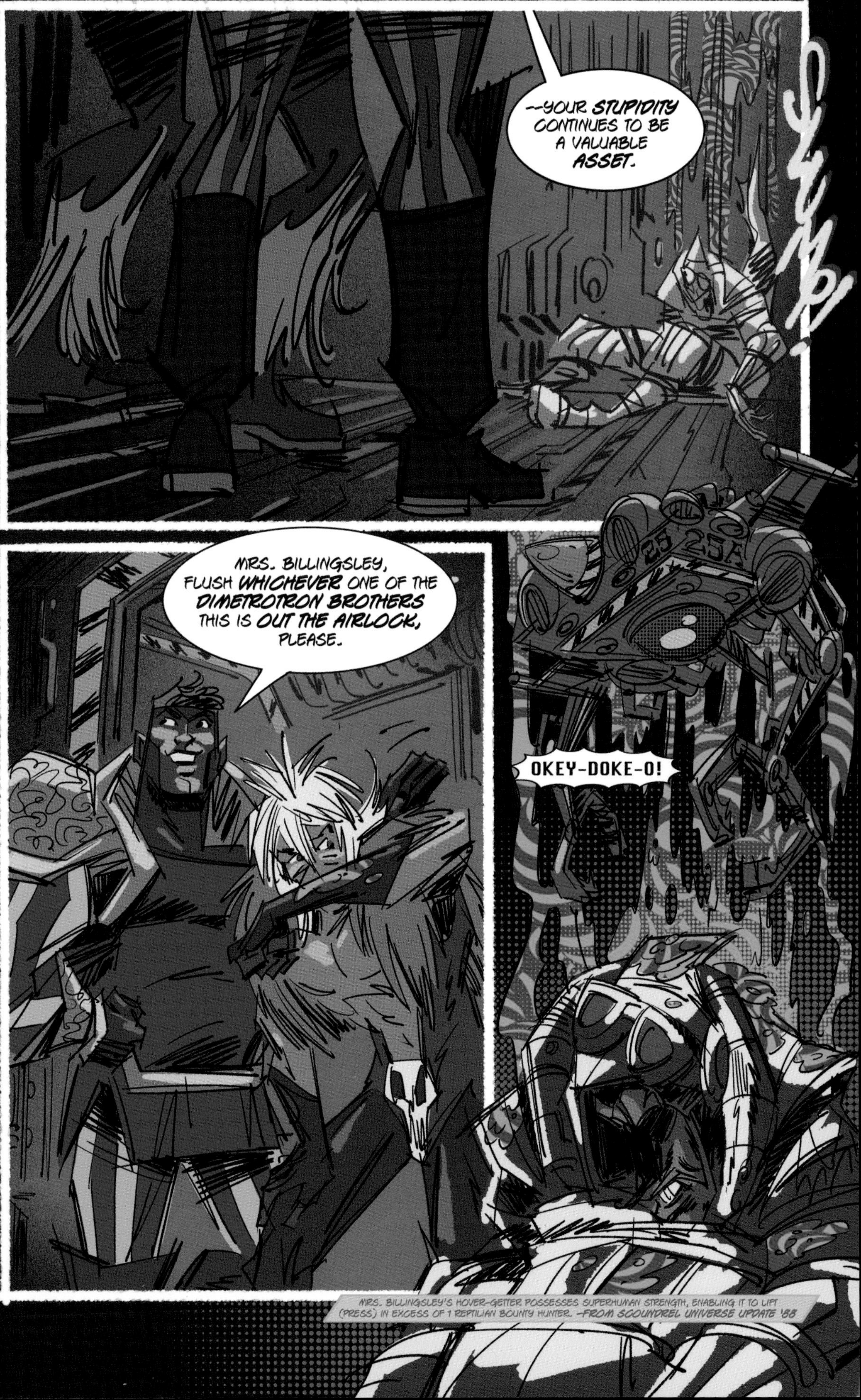
--YOUR STUPIDITY CONTINUES TO BE A VALUABLE ASSET.
SLUMP!
MRS. BILLINGSLEY, FLUSH WHICHEVER ONE OF THE DIMETROTRON BROTHERS THIS IS OUT THE AIRLOCK, PLEASE.
OKEY-DOKE-O!
MRS. BILLINGSLEY'S HOVER-GETTER POSSESSES SUPERHUMAN STRENGTH, ENABLING IT TO LIFT (PRESS) IN EXCESS OF 1 REPTILIAN BOUNTY HUNTER. -FROM SCOUNDREL UNIVERSE UPDATE '88

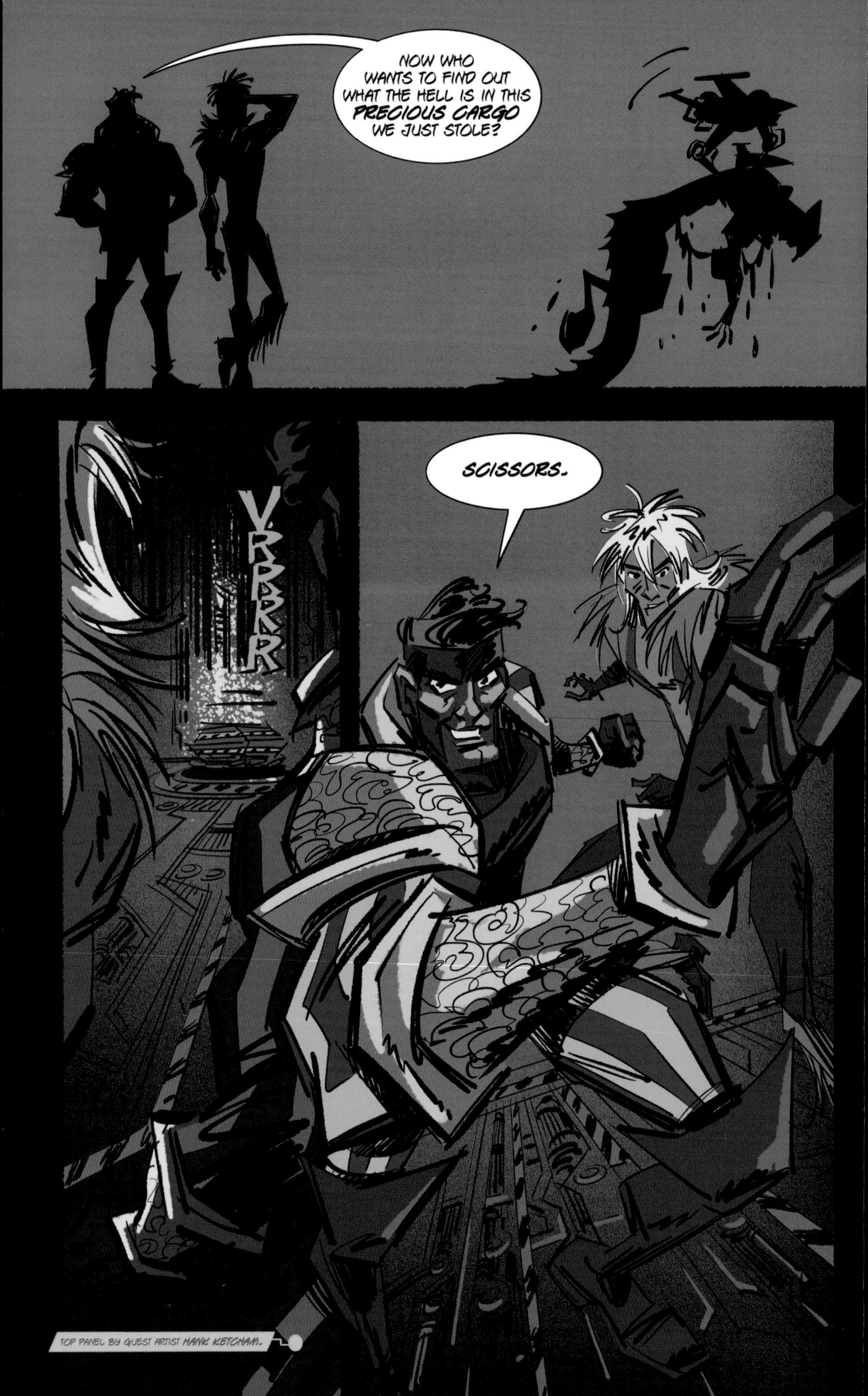
NOW WHO WANTS TO FIND OUT WHAT THE HELL IS IN THIS PRECIOUS CARGO WE JUST STOLE?
VRRRRR
SCISSORS.
TOP PANEL BY GUEST ARTIST HANK KETCHAM.

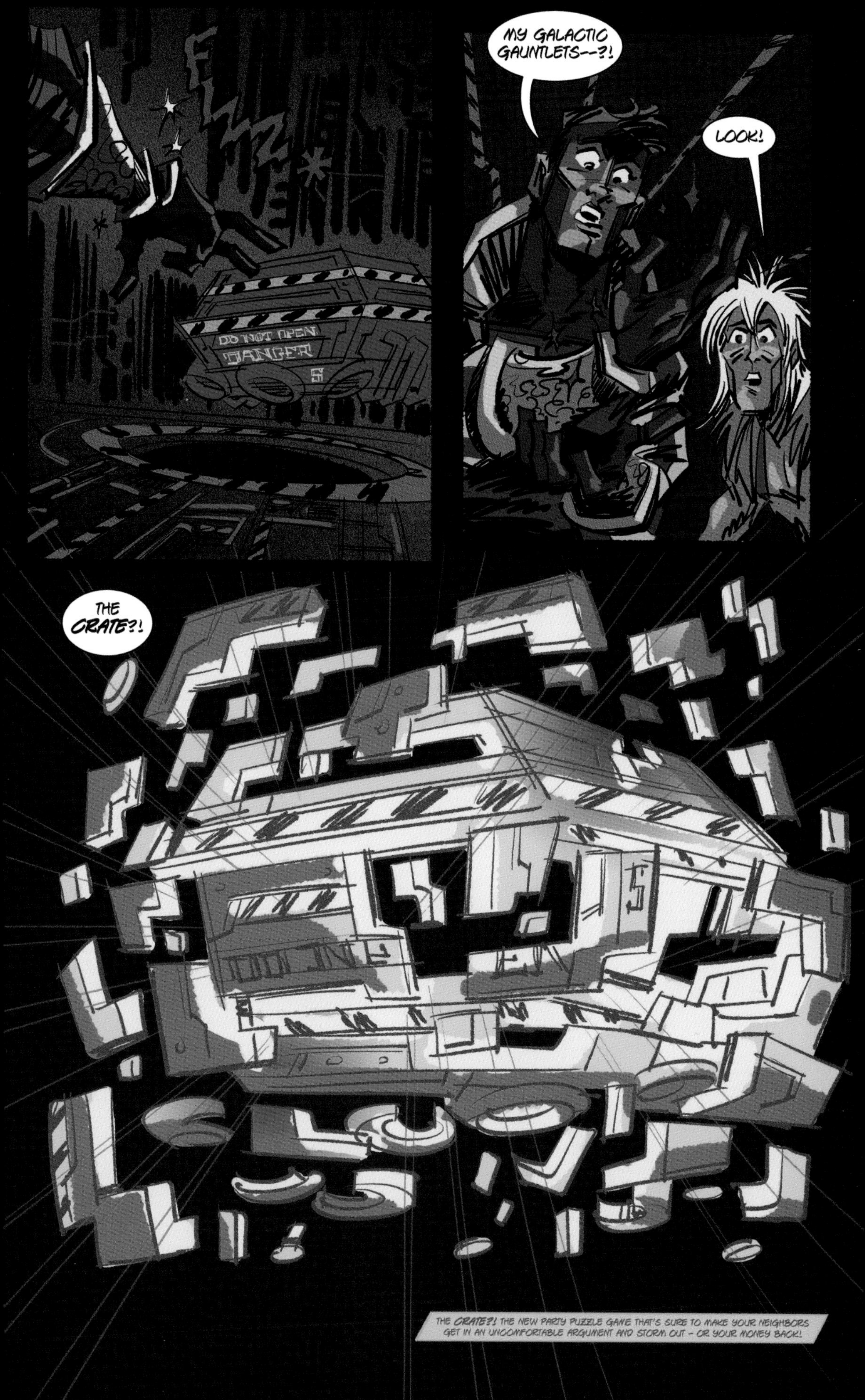
DO NOT OPEN
DANGER
MY GALACTIC GAUNTLETS--?!
LOOK!
THE CRATE?!
THE CRATE?! THE NEW PARTY PUZZLE GAME THAT'S SURE TO MAKE YOUR NEIGHBORS GET IN AN UNCOMFORTABLE ARGUMENT AND STORM OUT - OR YOUR MONEY BACK!

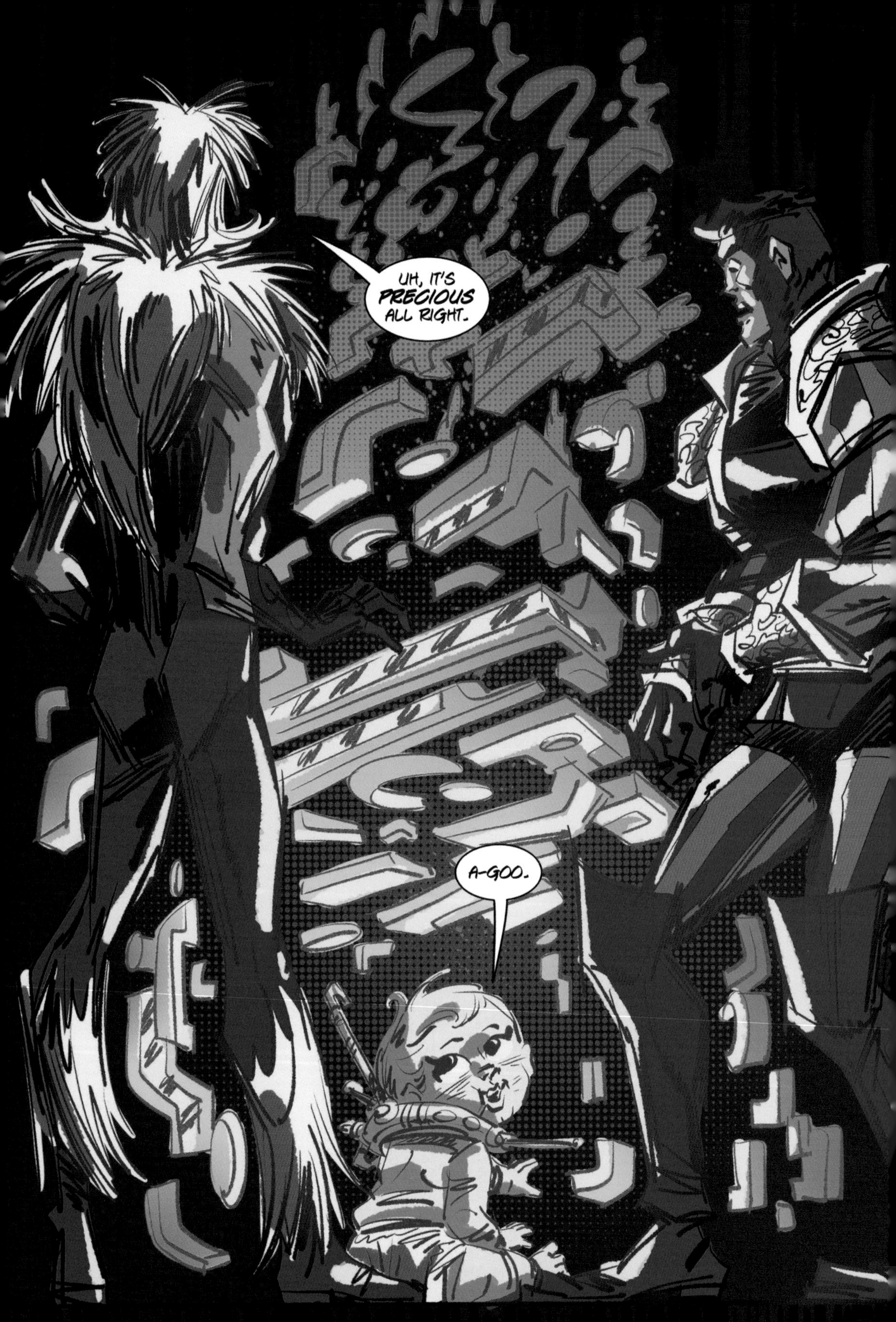
UH, IT'S **PRECIOUS** ALL RIGHT.
A-GOO.

OH MAN! IS THAT BABY WEARING A ***RUNNING MAN***-STYLE ***EXPLOSIVE SLAVE COLLAR?*** THAT'S MESSED UP, RICHARD DAWSON!

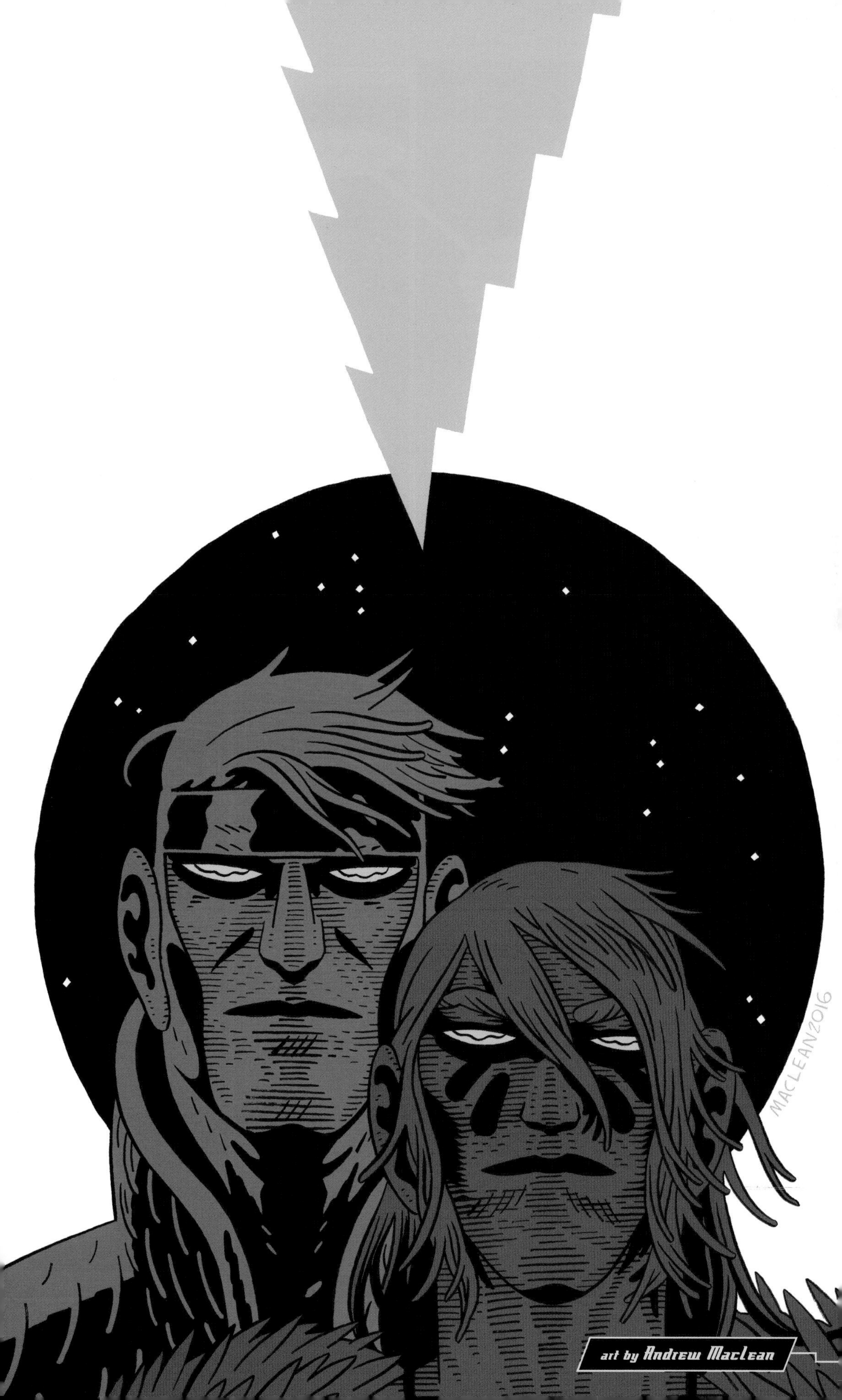
MACLEAN2016

art by Andrew MacLean

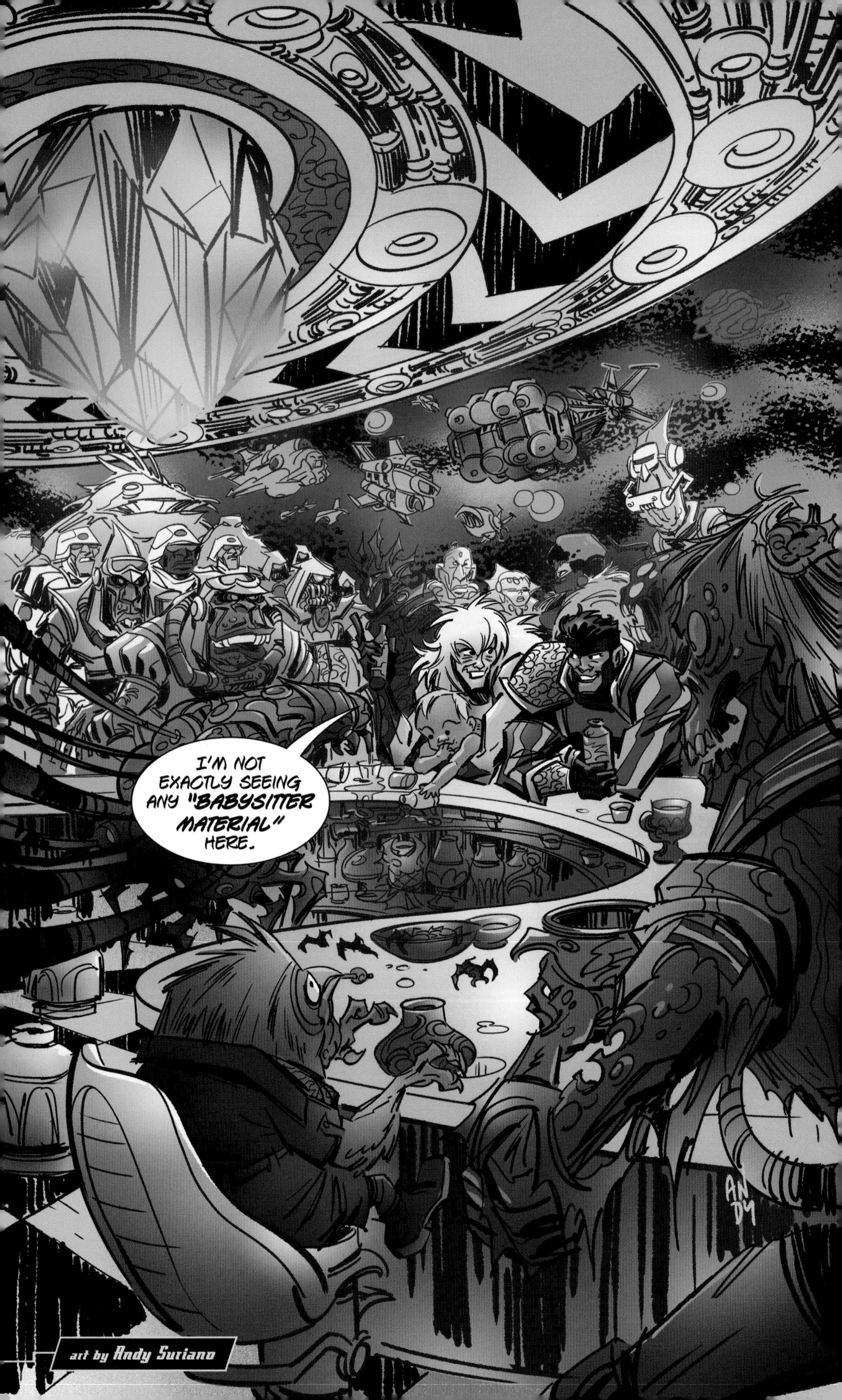
I'M NOT EXACTLY SEEING ANY "BABYSITTER MATERIAL" HERE.
ANDY
art by Andy Suriano

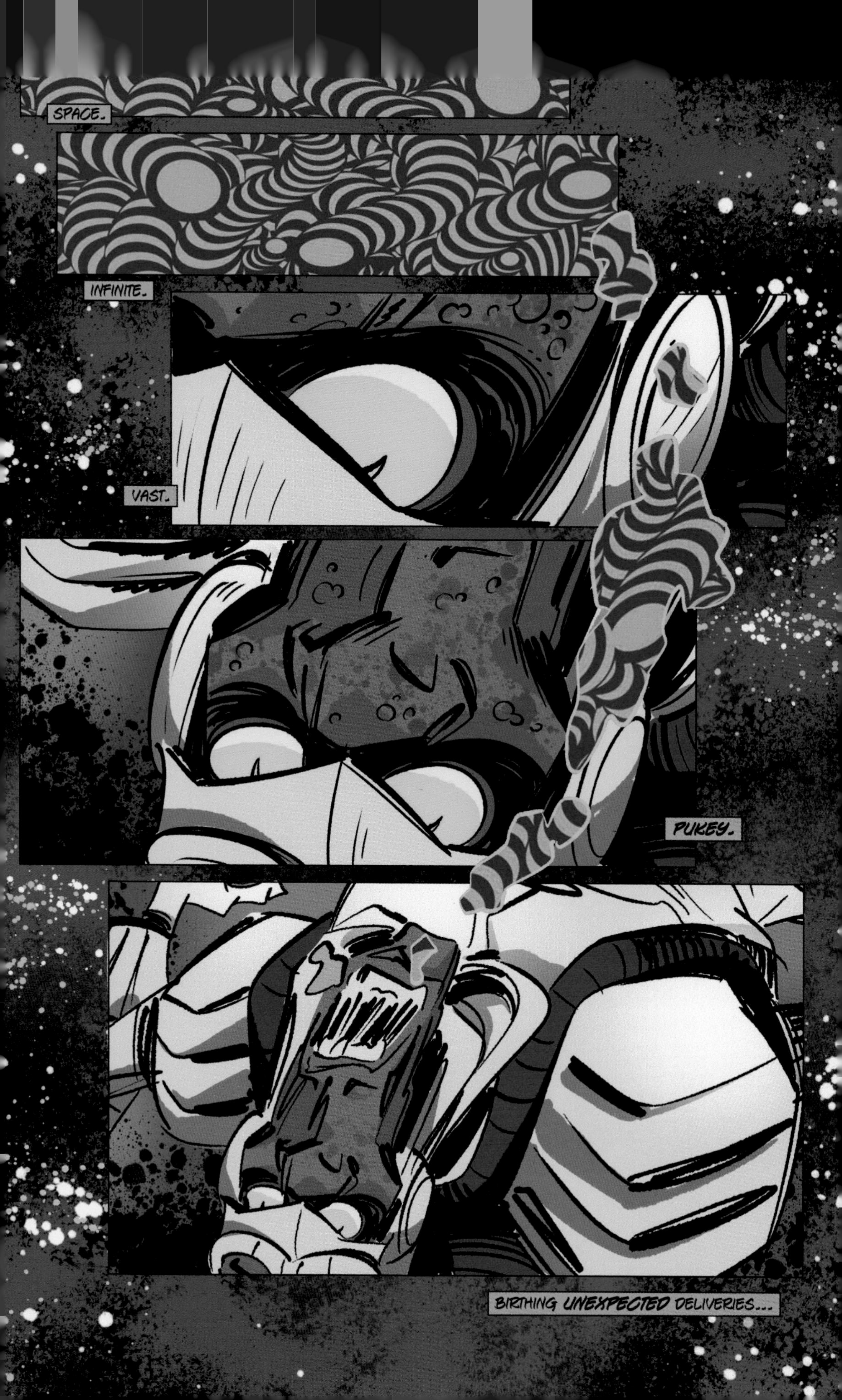
SPACE.
INFINITE.
VAST.
PUKEY.
BIRTHING *UNEXPECTED* DELIVERIES...

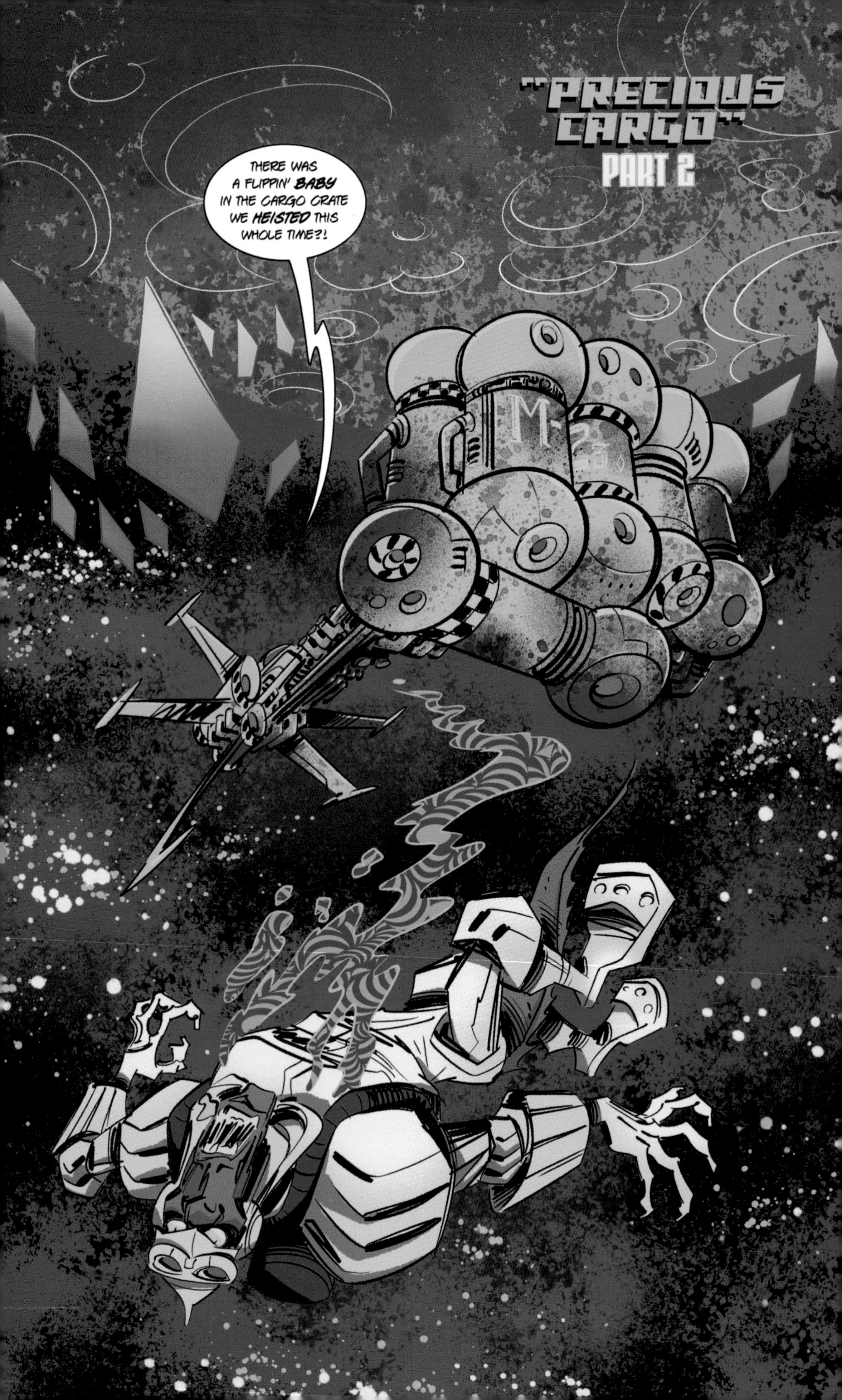
"PRECIOUS CARGO"
PART 2
THERE WAS A FLIPPIN' BABY IN THE CARGO CRATE WE HEISTED THIS WHOLE TIME?!

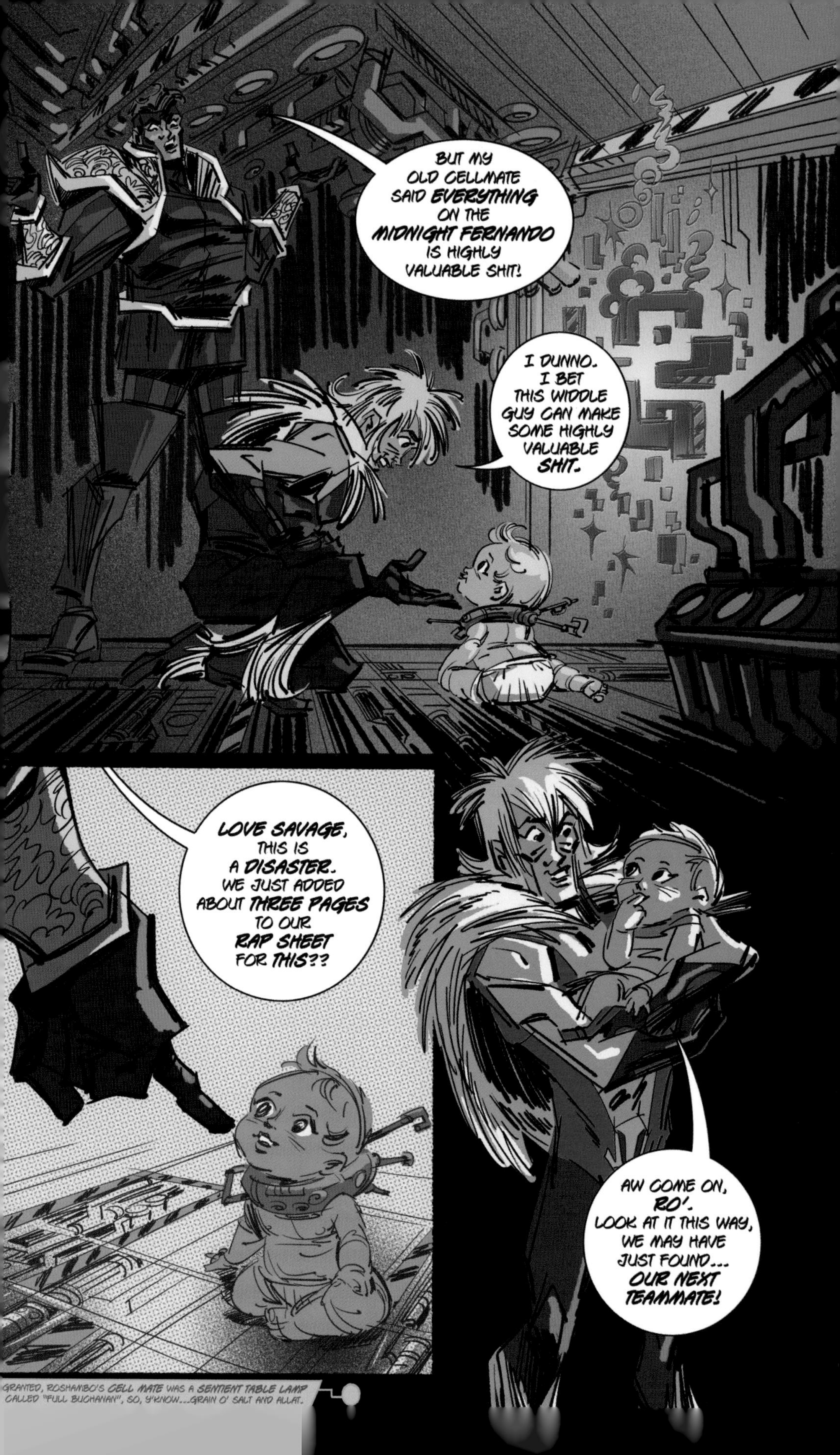
BUT MY OLD CELLMATE SAID EVERYTHING ON THE MIDNIGHT FERNANDO IS HIGHLY VALUABLE SHIT!
I DUNNO. I BET THIS WIDDLE GUY CAN MAKE SOME HIGHLY VALUABLE SHIT.
LOVE SAVAGE, THIS IS A DISASTER. WE JUST ADDED ABOUT THREE PAGES TO OUR RAP SHEET FOR THIS??
AW COME ON, RO'. LOOK AT IT THIS WAY, WE MAY HAVE JUST FOUND... OUR NEXT TEAMMATE!
GRANTED, ROSHAMBO'S CELL MATE WAS A SENTIENT TABLE LAMP CALLED "FULL BUCHANAN", SO, Y'KNOW... GRAIN O' SALT AND ALLAT.

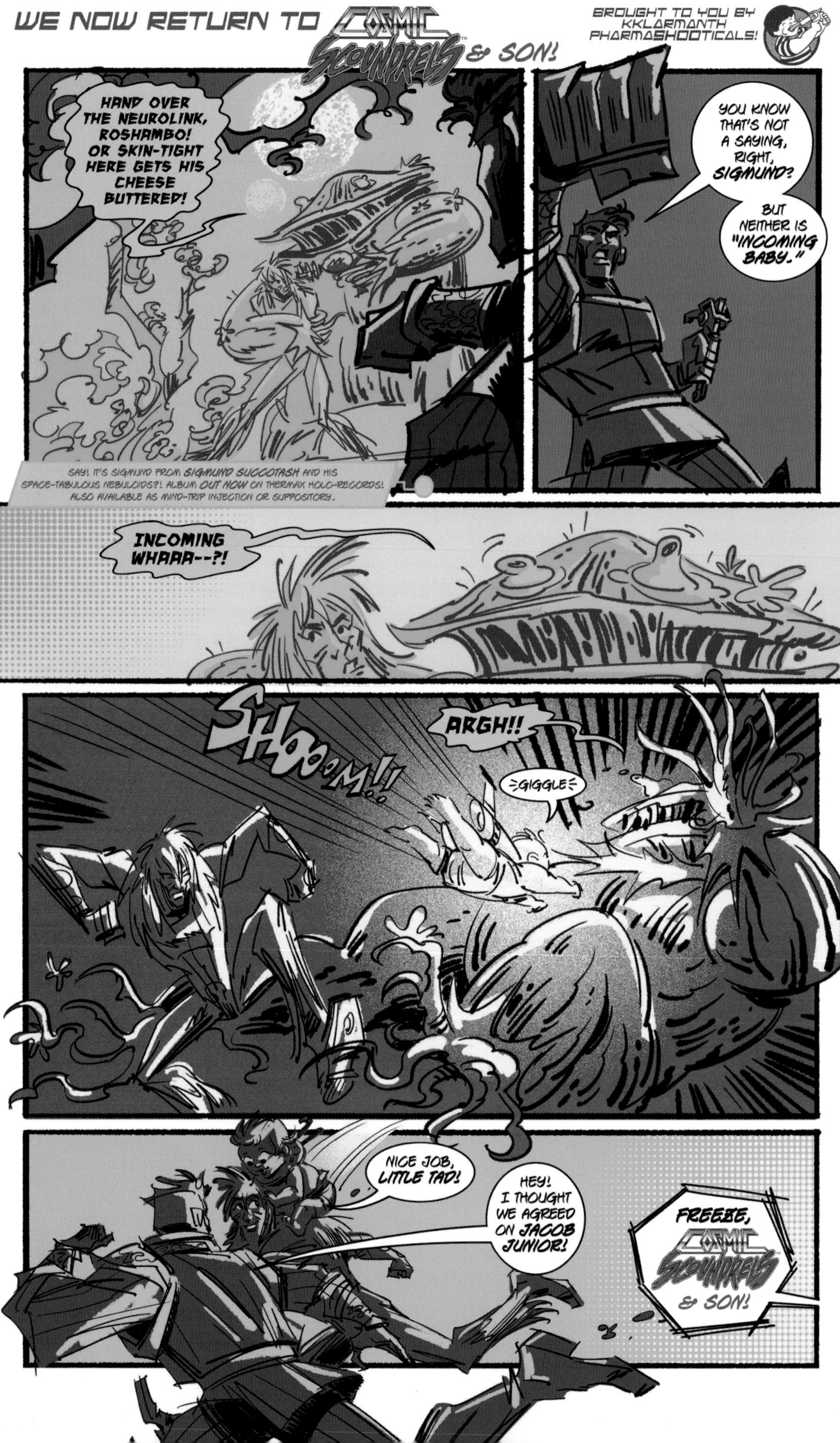
WE NOW RETURN TO COSMIC SCOUNDRELS & SON!
BROUGHT TO YOU BY KKLARMANTH PHARMASHOOTICALS!
HAND OVER THE NEUROLINK, ROSHAMBO! OR SKIN-TIGHT HERE GETS HIS CHEESE BUTTERED!
YOU KNOW THAT'S NOT A SAYING, RIGHT, SIGMUND?
BUT NEITHER IS "INCOMING BABY."
SAY! IT'S SIGMUND FROM SIGMUND SUCCOTASH AND HIS SPACE-TABULOUS NEBULOIDS?! ALBUM OUT NOW ON THERMAX HOLO-RECORDS! ALSO AVAILABLE AS MIND-TRIP INJECTION OR SUPPOSITORY.
INCOMING WHAAA--?!
SHOOOOM!!
ARGH!!
GIGGLE
NICE JOB, LITTLE TAD!
HEY! I THOUGHT WE AGREED ON JACOB JUNIOR!
FREEZE, COSMIC SCOUNDRELS & SON!

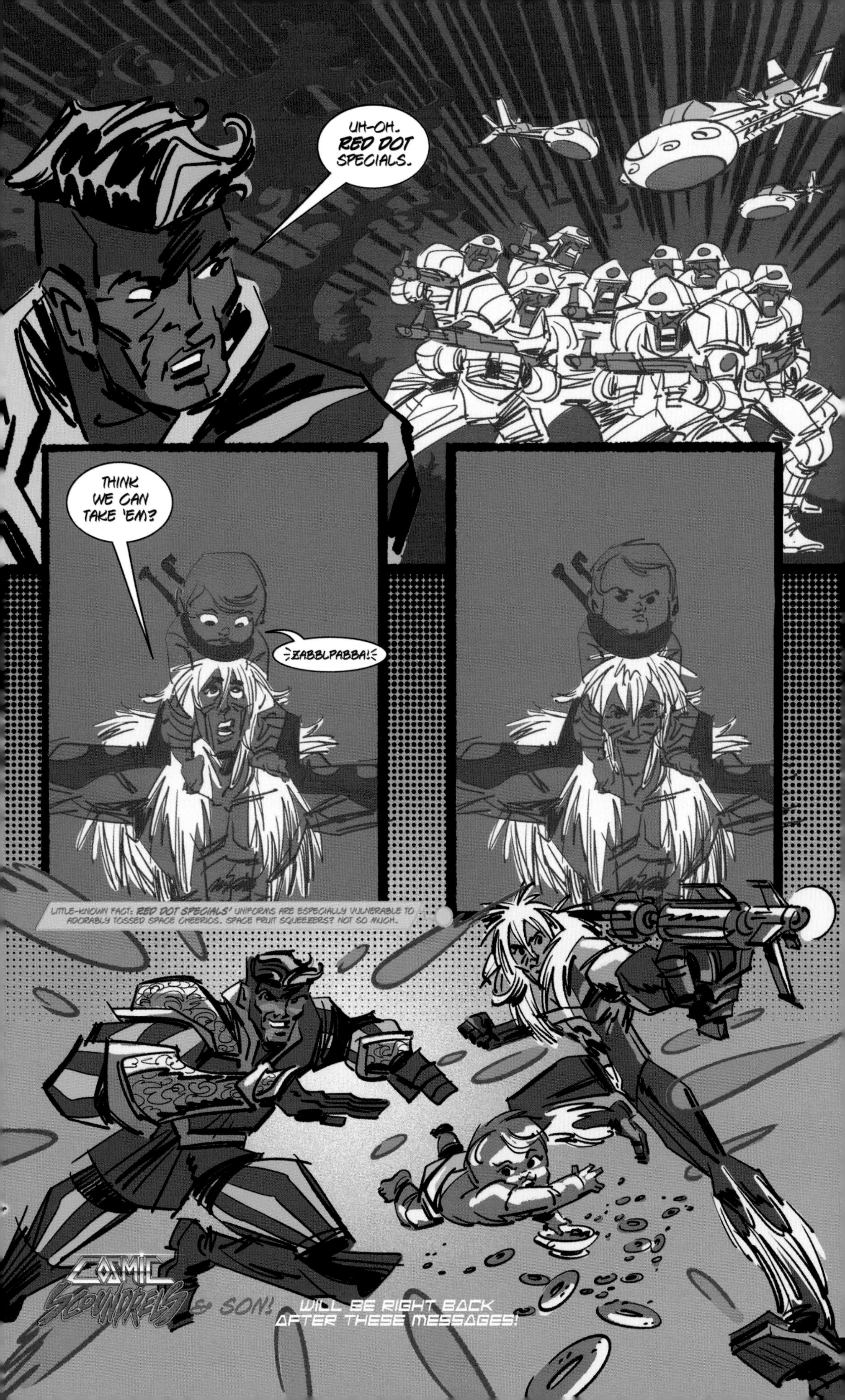
UH-OH. **RED DOT** SPECIALS.
THINK WE CAN TAKE 'EM?
ZABBLPABBA!
LITTLE-KNOWN FACT: ***RED DOT SPECIALS'*** UNIFORMS ARE ESPECIALLY VULNERABLE TO ADORABLY TOSSED SPACE CHEERIOS. SPACE FRUIT SQUEEZERS? NOT SO MUCH.
COSMIC SCOUNDRELS & SON! WILL BE RIGHT BACK AFTER THESE MESSAGES!

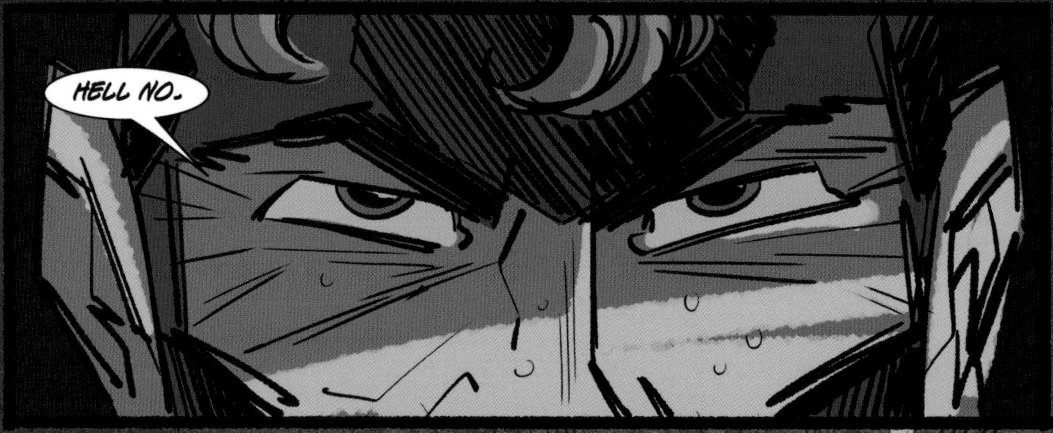
HELL NO.

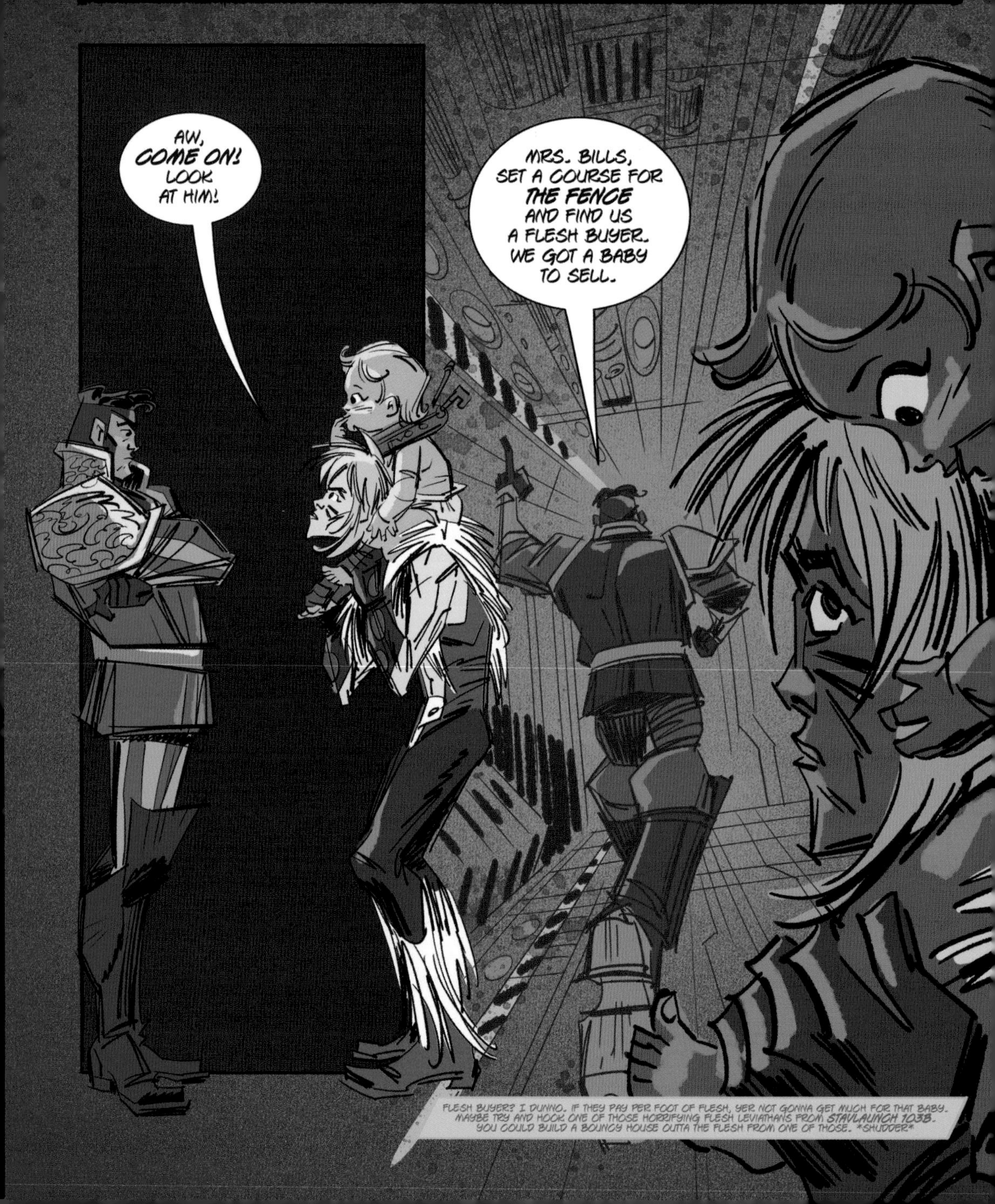
AW, **COME ON!** LOOK AT HIM!
MRS. BILLS, SET A COURSE FOR ***THE FENCE*** AND FIND US A FLESH BUYER. WE GOT A BABY TO SELL.
FLESH BUYER? I DUNNO. IF THEY PAY PER FOOT OF FLESH, YER NOT GONNA GET MUCH FOR THAT BABY. MAYBE TRY AND HOOK ONE OF THOSE HORRIFYING FLESH LEVIATHANS FROM ***STAVLAUNCH 103B.*** YOU COULD BUILD A BOUNCY HOUSE OUTTA THE FLESH FROM ONE OF THOSE. *SHUDDER*

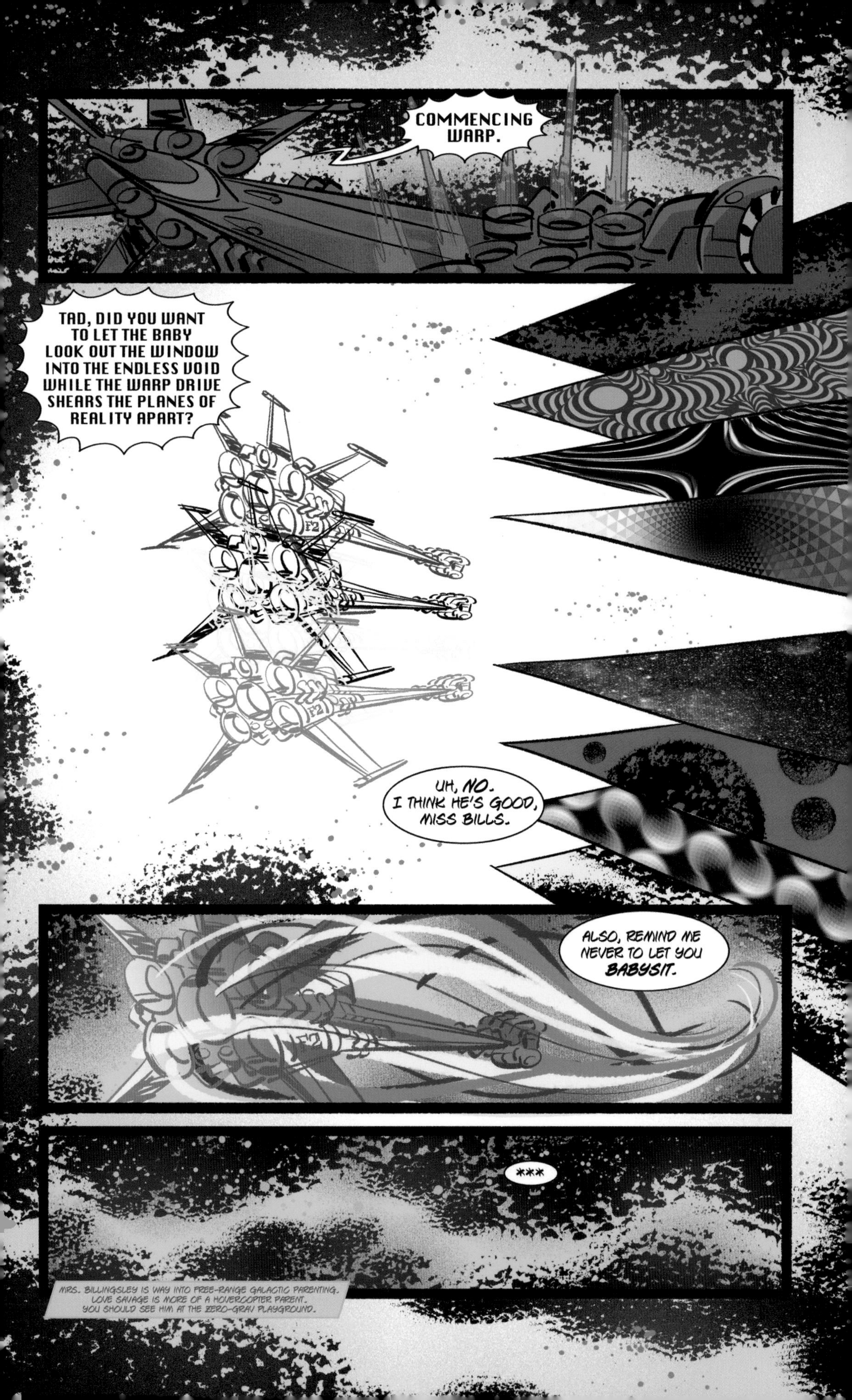
COMMENCING WARP.
TAD, DID YOU WANT TO LET THE BABY LOOK OUT THE WINDOW INTO THE ENDLESS VOID WHILE THE WARP DRIVE SHEARS THE PLANES OF REALITY APART?
UH, NO. I THINK HE'S GOOD, MISS BILLS.
ALSO, REMIND ME NEVER TO LET YOU BABYSIT.
***
MRS. BILLINGSLEY IS WAY INTO FREE-RANGE GALACTIC PARENTING. LOVE SAVAGE IS MORE OF A HOVERCOPTER PARENT. YOU SHOULD SEE HIM AT THE ZERO-GRAV PLAYGROUND.

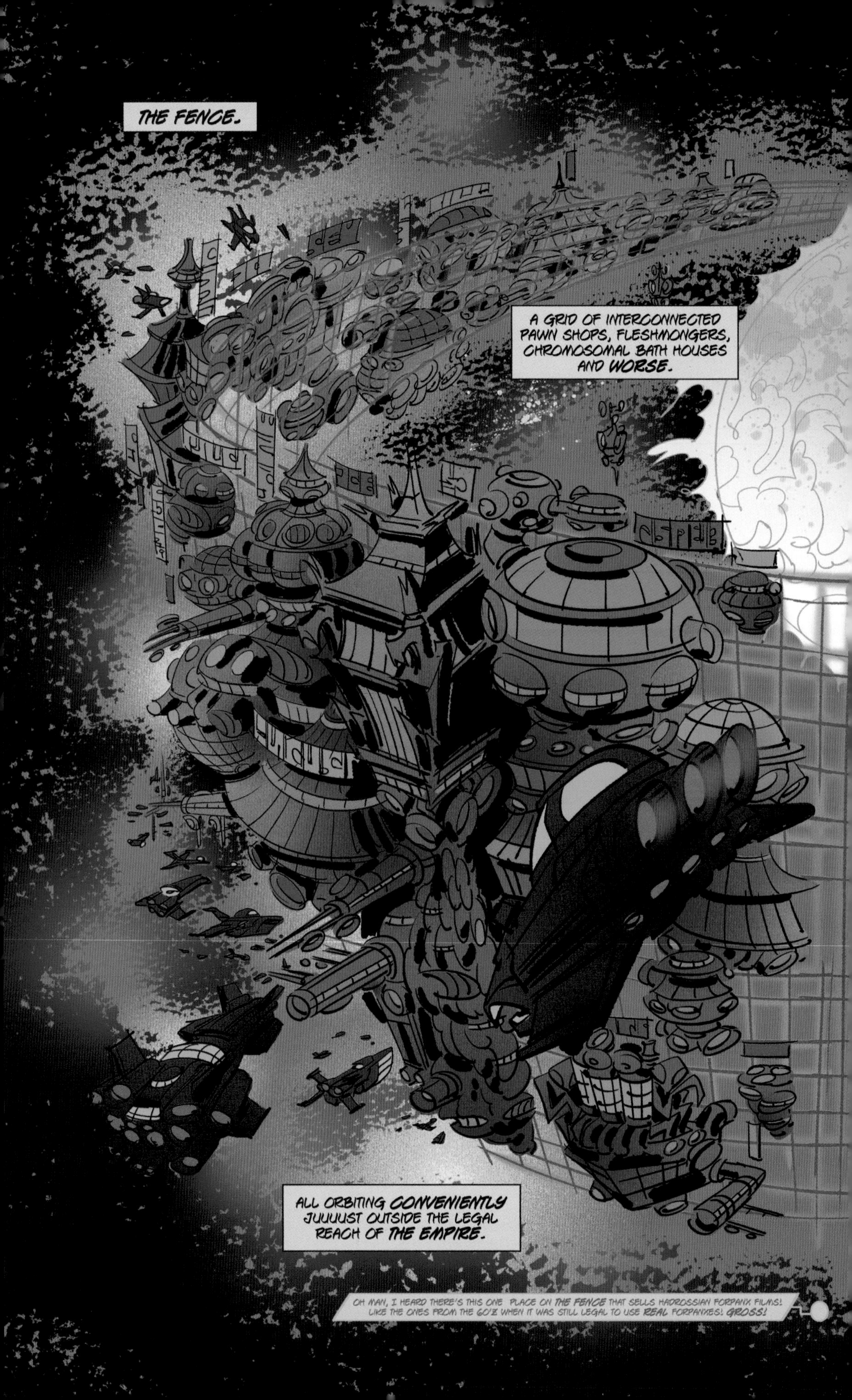
THE FENCE.
A GRID OF INTERCONNECTED PAWN SHOPS, FLESHMONGERS, CHROMOSOMAL BATH HOUSES AND WORSE.
ALL ORBITING CONVENIENTLY JUUUUST OUTSIDE THE LEGAL REACH OF THE EMPIRE.
OH MAN, I HEARD THERE'S THIS ONE PLACE ON THE FENCE THAT SELLS HADROSSIAN FORPANX FILMS! LIKE THE ONES FROM THE 60'Z WHEN IT WAS STILL LEGAL TO USE REAL FORPANXES! GROSS!

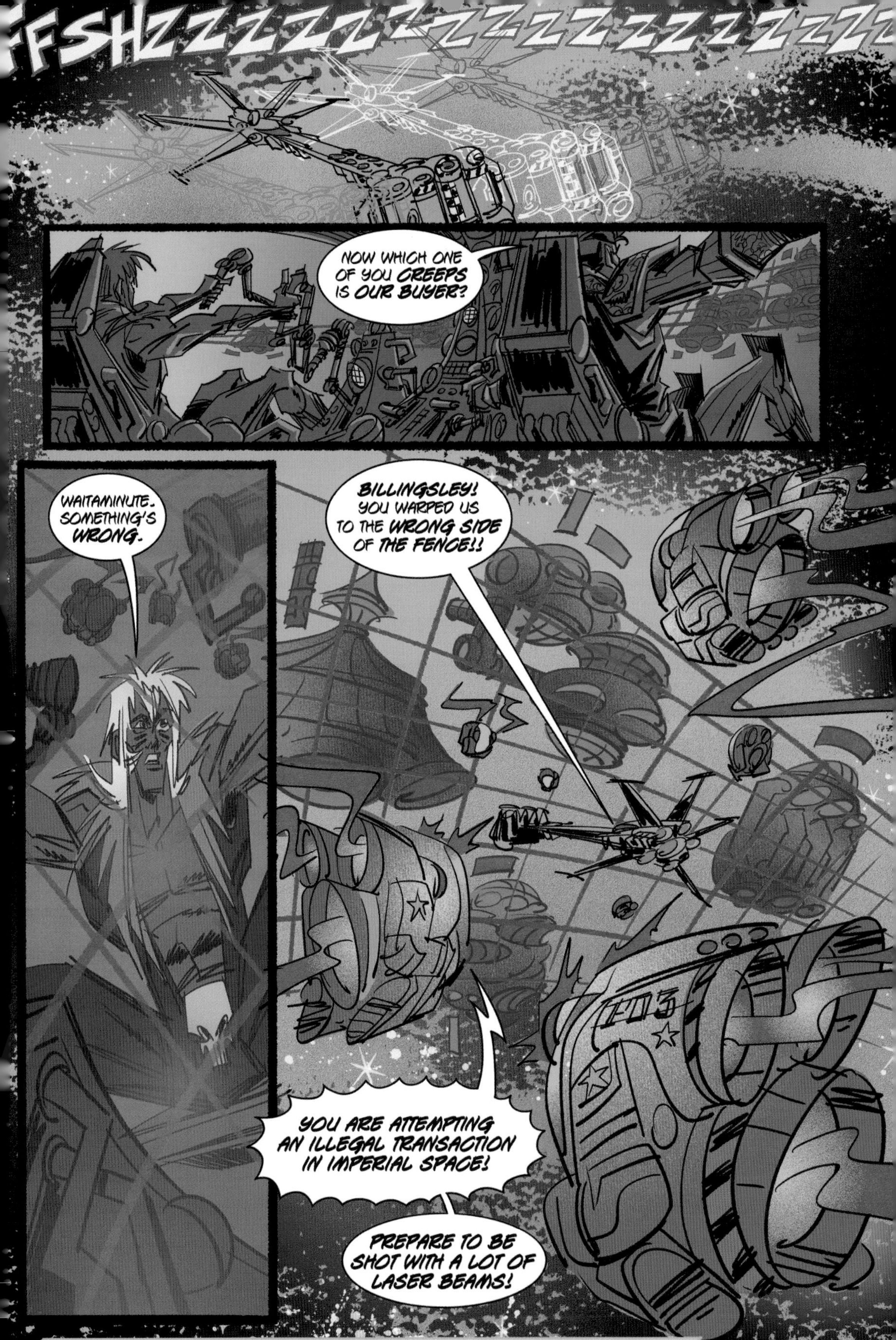
FFSHZZZZZZZZZZZZZZZZZ
NOW WHICH ONE OF YOU CREEPS IS OUR BUYER?
WAITAMINUTE. SOMETHING'S WRONG.
BILLINGSLEY! YOU WARPED US TO THE WRONG SIDE OF THE FENCE!!
YOU ARE ATTEMPTING AN ILLEGAL TRANSACTION IN IMPERIAL SPACE!
PREPARE TO BE SHOT WITH A LOT OF LASER BEAMS!

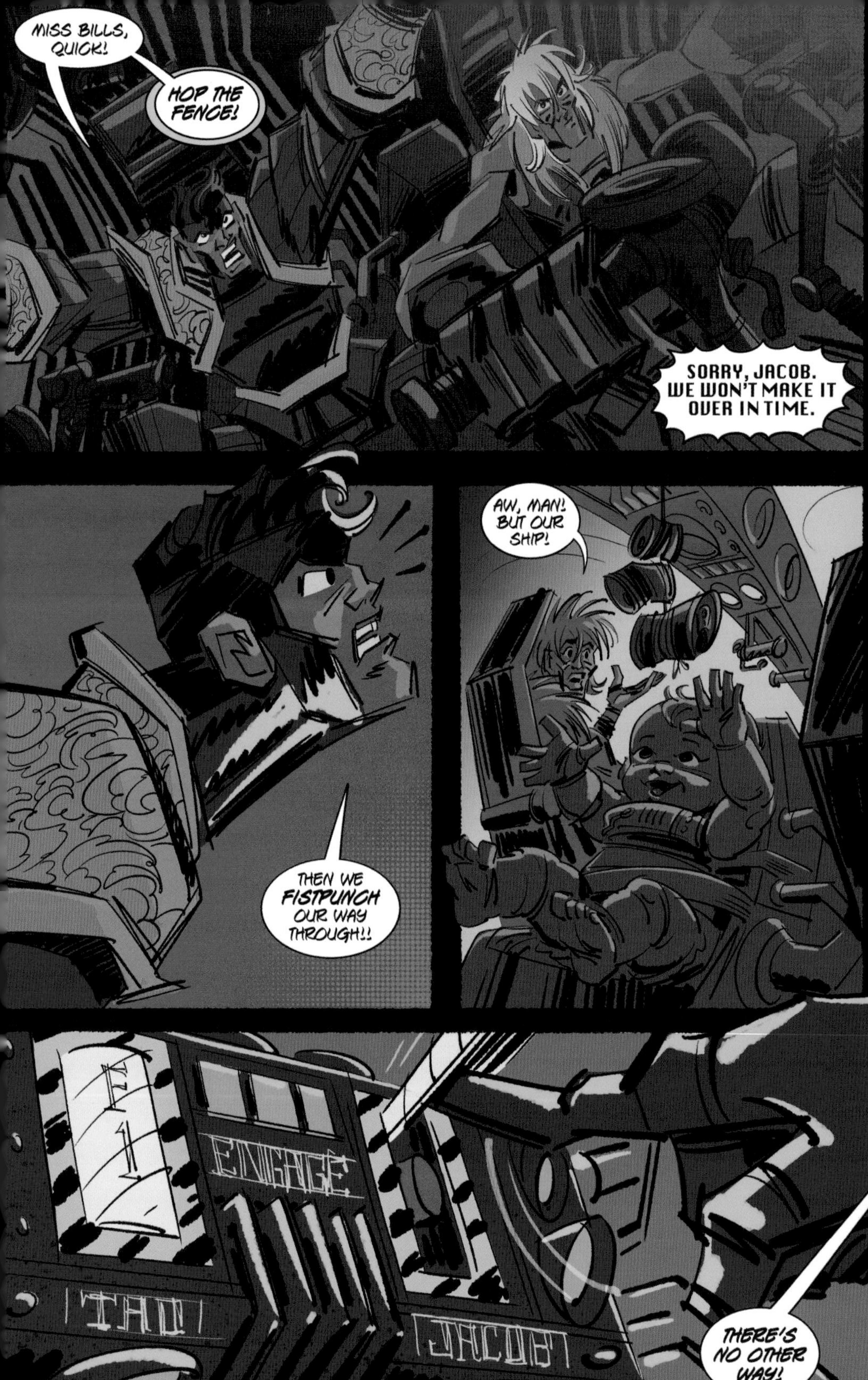
MISS BILLS, QUICK!
HOP THE FENCE!
SORRY, JACOB. WE WON'T MAKE IT OVER IN TIME.
THEN WE FISTPUNCH OUR WAY THROUGH!!
AW, MAN! BUT OUR SHIP!
ENGAGE
TAD
JACOB
THERE'S NO OTHER WAY!

MAKERDADS! JUST STRING THREE CANS OF YOUR FAV HYDROZORBIC CRAFT BEER TOGETHER AND *VIOLA!* INSTANT DISTRACTION FOR BABY IN THE COCKPIT! AND HEY, IF THERE'S STILL BEER IN THE CANS, EVEN BETTER! *NAPTIME!*

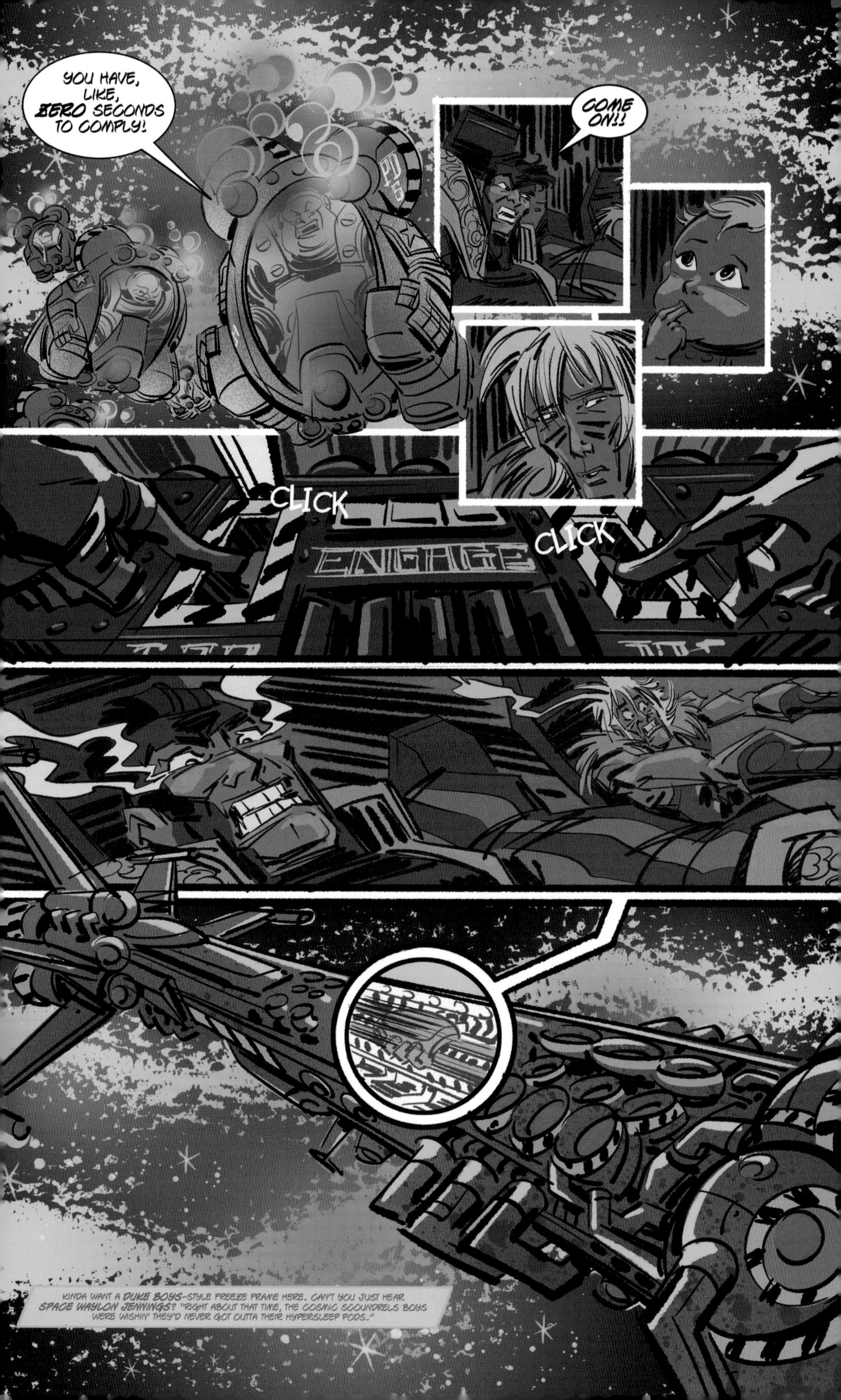
YOU HAVE, LIKE, **ZERO** SECONDS TO COMPLY!
COME ON!!
CLICK
ENGAGE
CLICK
KINDA WANT A ***DUKE BOYS***-STYLE FREEZE FRAME HERE. CAN'T YOU JUST HEAR ***SPACE WAYLON JENNINGS***? "RIGHT ABOUT THAT TIME, THE COSMIC SCOUNDRELS BOYS WERE WISHIN' THEY'D NEVER GOT OUTTA THEIR HYPERSLEEP PODS."

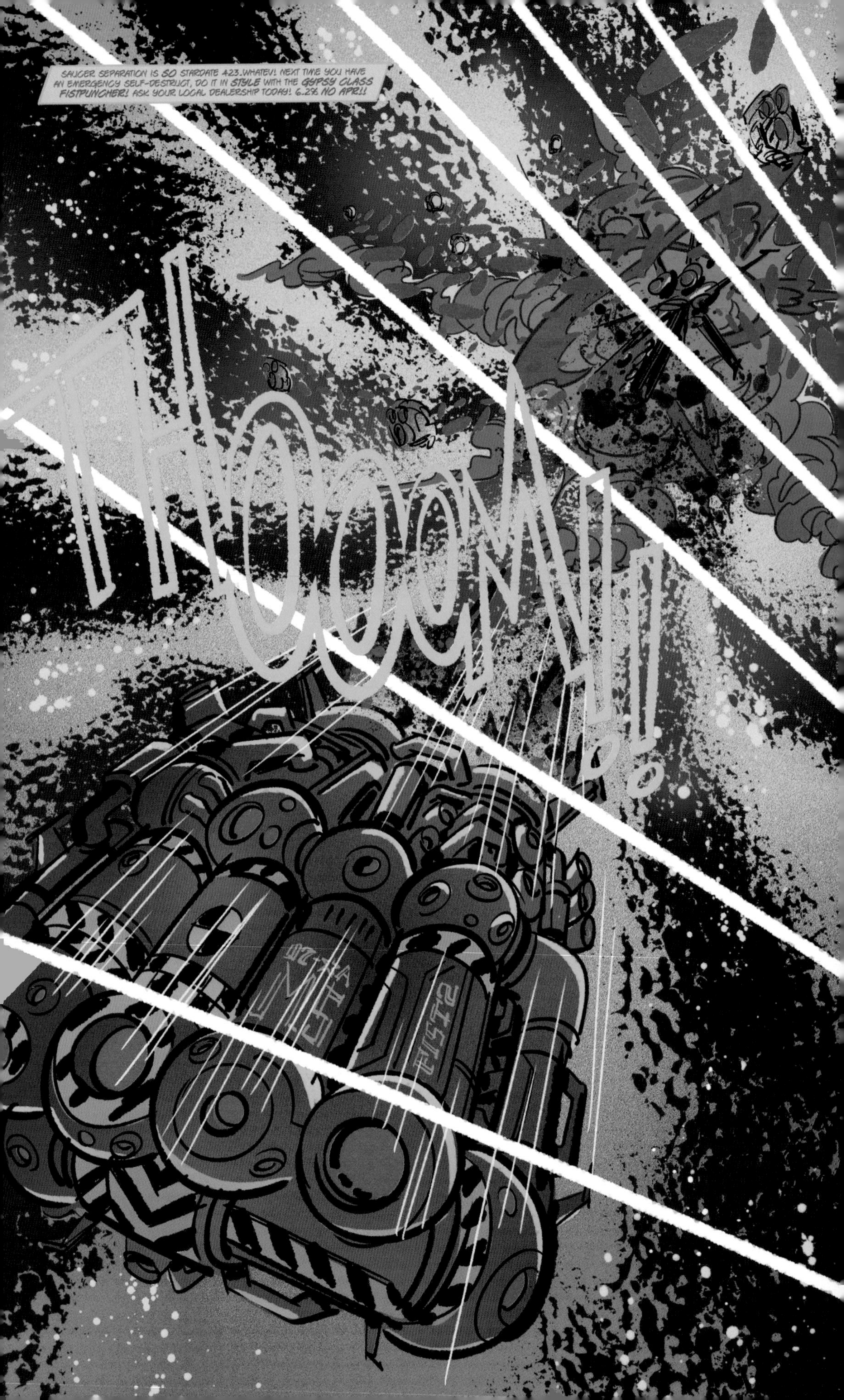
SAUCER SEPARATION IS SO STARDATE 423.WHATEV! NEXT TIME YOU HAVE AN EMERGENCY SELF-DESTRUCT, DO IT IN STYLE WITH THE GYPSY CLASS FISTPUNCHER! ASK YOUR LOCAL DEALERSHIP TODAY! 6.2% NO APR!!
THOOOM!!

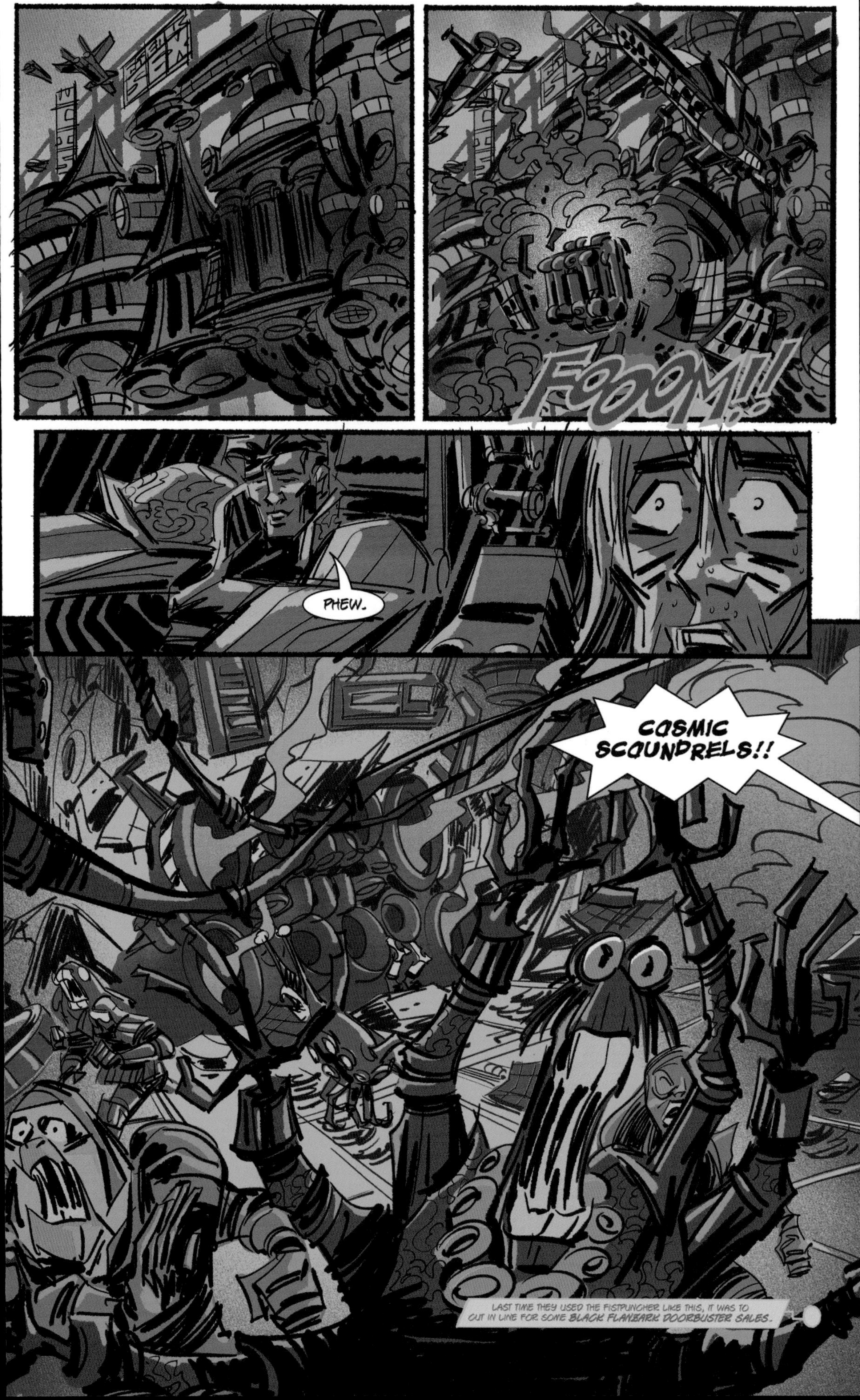
SEX
FOOOM!!
PHEW.
COSMIC SCOUNDRELS!!
LAST TIME THEY USED THE FISTPUNCHER LIKE THIS, IT WAS TO CUT IN LINE FOR SOME BLACK FLANBARK DOORBUSTER SALES.

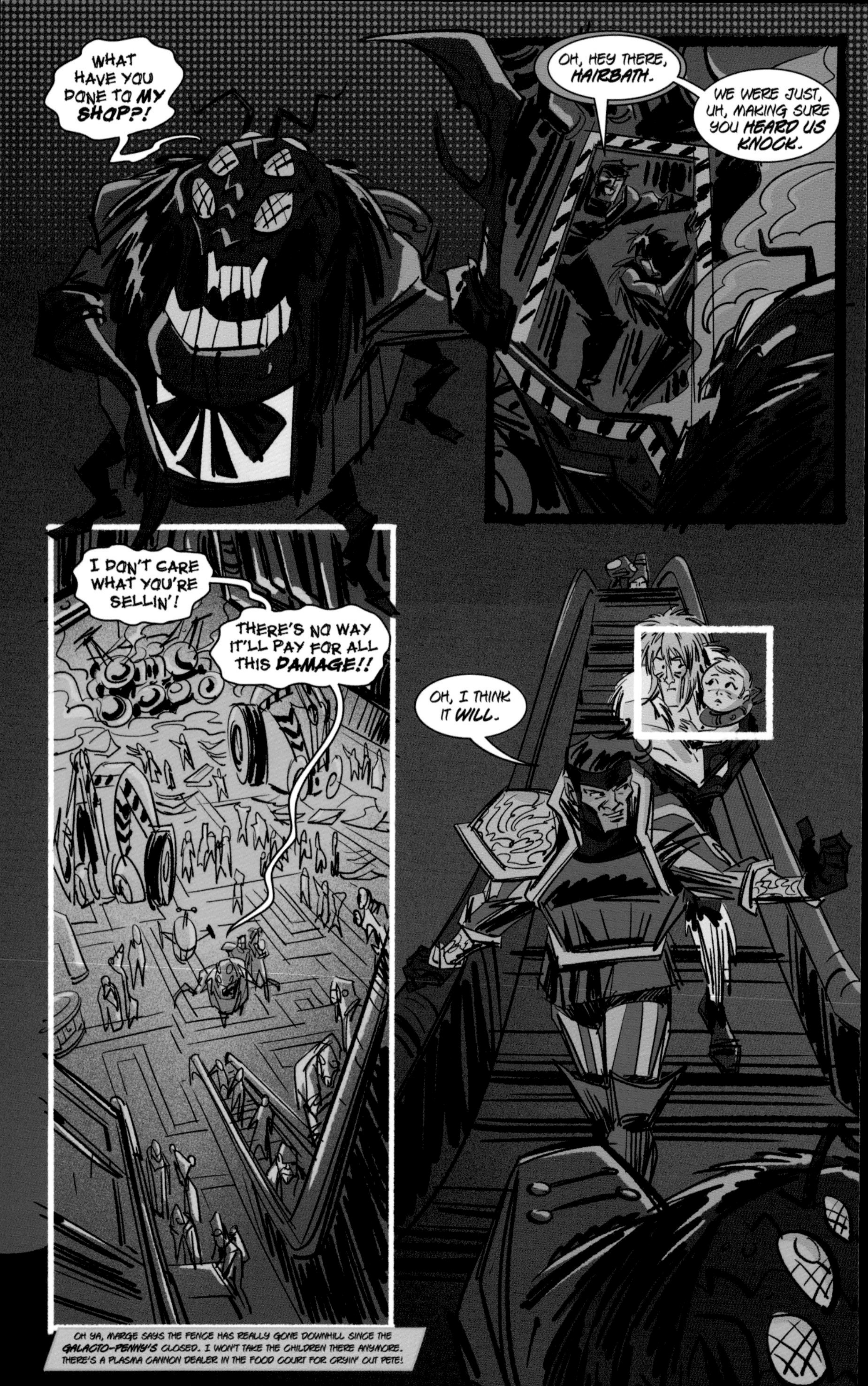
WHAT HAVE YOU DONE TO **MY SHOP?!**
OH, HEY THERE, **HAIRBATH.**
WE WERE JUST, UH, MAKING SURE YOU **HEARD US KNOCK.**
I DON'T CARE WHAT YOU'RE SELLIN'!
THERE'S NO WAY IT'LL PAY FOR ALL THIS **DAMAGE!!**
OH, I THINK IT **WILL.**
OH YA, MARGE SAYS THE FENCE HAS REALLY GONE DOWNHILL SINCE THE **GALACTO-PENNY'S** CLOSED. I WON'T TAKE THE CHILDREN THERE ANYMORE. THERE'S A PLASMA CANNON DEALER IN THE FOOD COURT FOR CRYIN' OUT PETE!

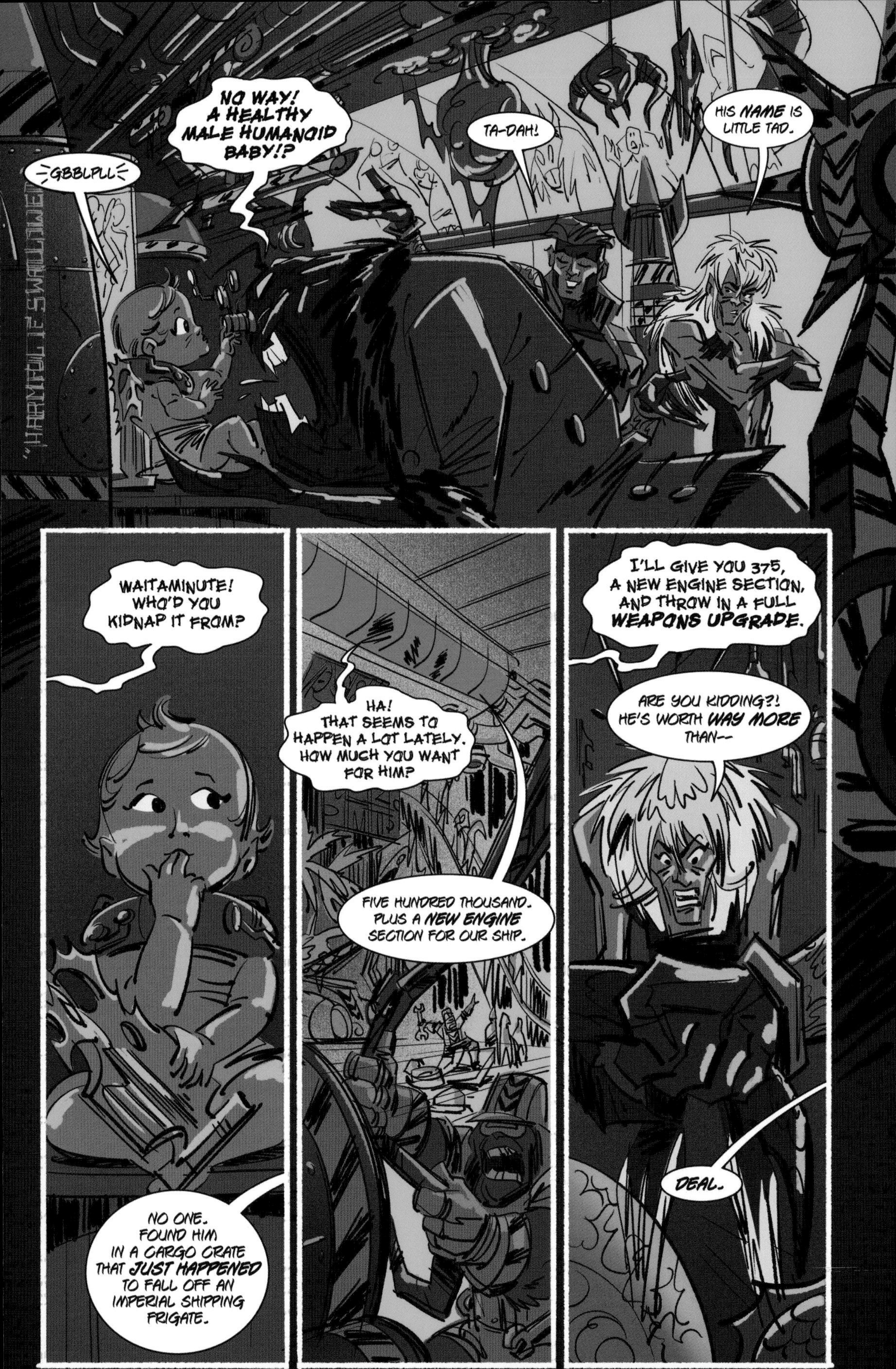
"HARMFUL IF SWALLOWED
GBBLPLL
NO WAY! A HEALTHY MALE HUMANOID BABY!?
TA-DAH!
HIS NAME IS LITTLE TAD.
WAITAMINUTE! WHO'D YOU KIDNAP IT FROM?
NO ONE. FOUND HIM IN A CARGO CRATE THAT JUST HAPPENED TO FALL OFF AN IMPERIAL SHIPPING FRIGATE.
HA! THAT SEEMS TO HAPPEN A LOT LATELY. HOW MUCH YOU WANT FOR HIM?
FIVE HUNDRED THOUSAND. PLUS A NEW ENGINE SECTION FOR OUR SHIP.
I'LL GIVE YOU 375, A NEW ENGINE SECTION, AND THROW IN A FULL WEAPONS UPGRADE.
ARE YOU KIDDING?! HE'S WORTH WAY MORE THAN--
DEAL.

THEY SHOULD REALLY CHECK IF THERE ARE ANY ***RECALLS*** ON THAT THING LITTLE TAD'S PLAYING WITH. I NEVER TRUST PUTRESCO PRODUCTS. WE'RE A SPACE GRACO FAMILY.

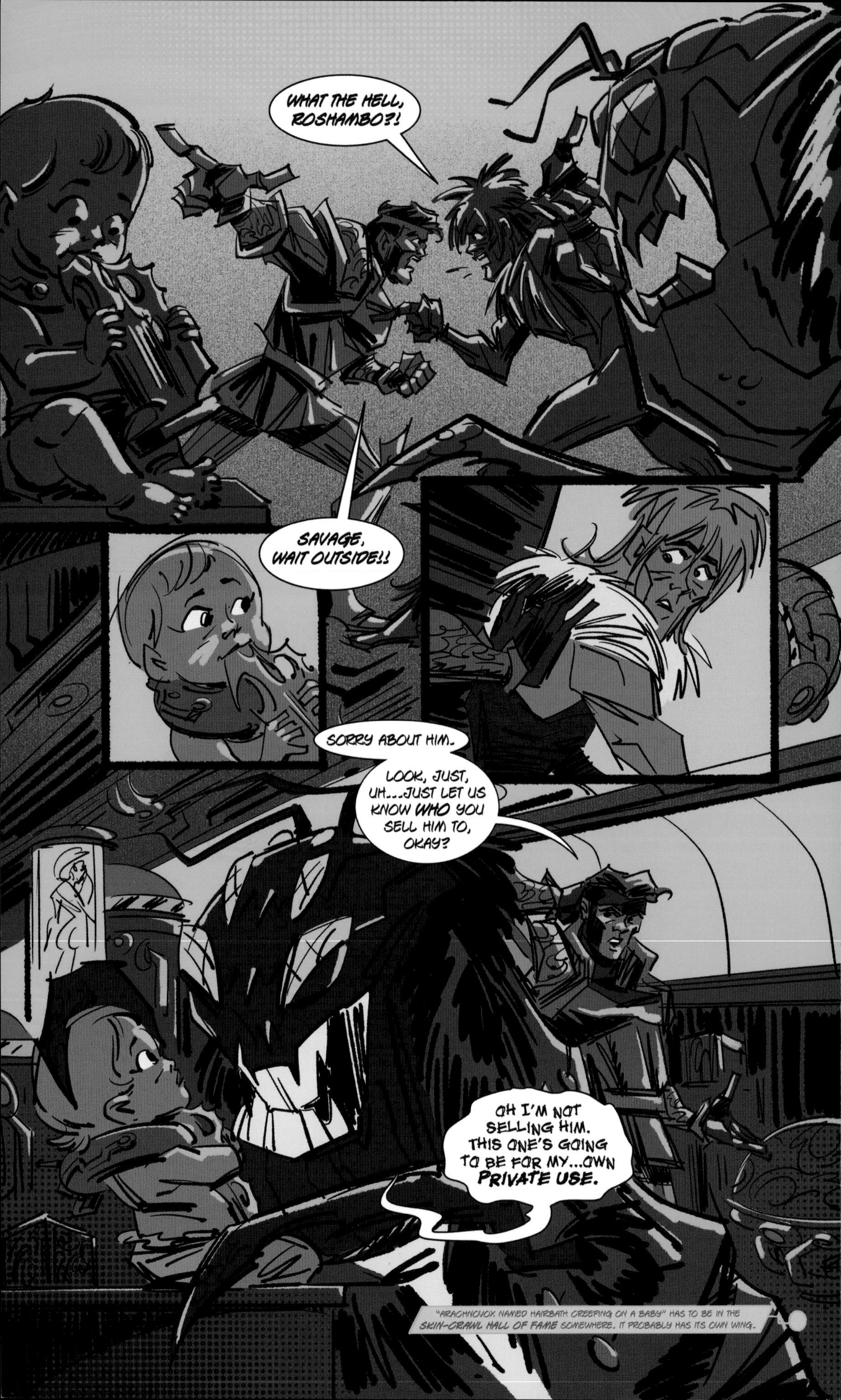
WHAT THE HELL, ROSHAMBO?!
SAVAGE, WAIT OUTSIDE!!
SORRY ABOUT HIM.
LOOK, JUST, UH...JUST LET US KNOW WHO YOU SELL HIM TO, OKAY?
OH I'M NOT SELLING HIM. THIS ONE'S GOING TO BE FOR MY...OWN PRIVATE USE.
"ARACHNOVOX NAMED HAIRBATH CREEPING ON A BABY" HAS TO BE IN THE SKIN-CRAWL HALL OF FAME SOMEWHERE. IT PROBABLY HAS ITS OWN WING.

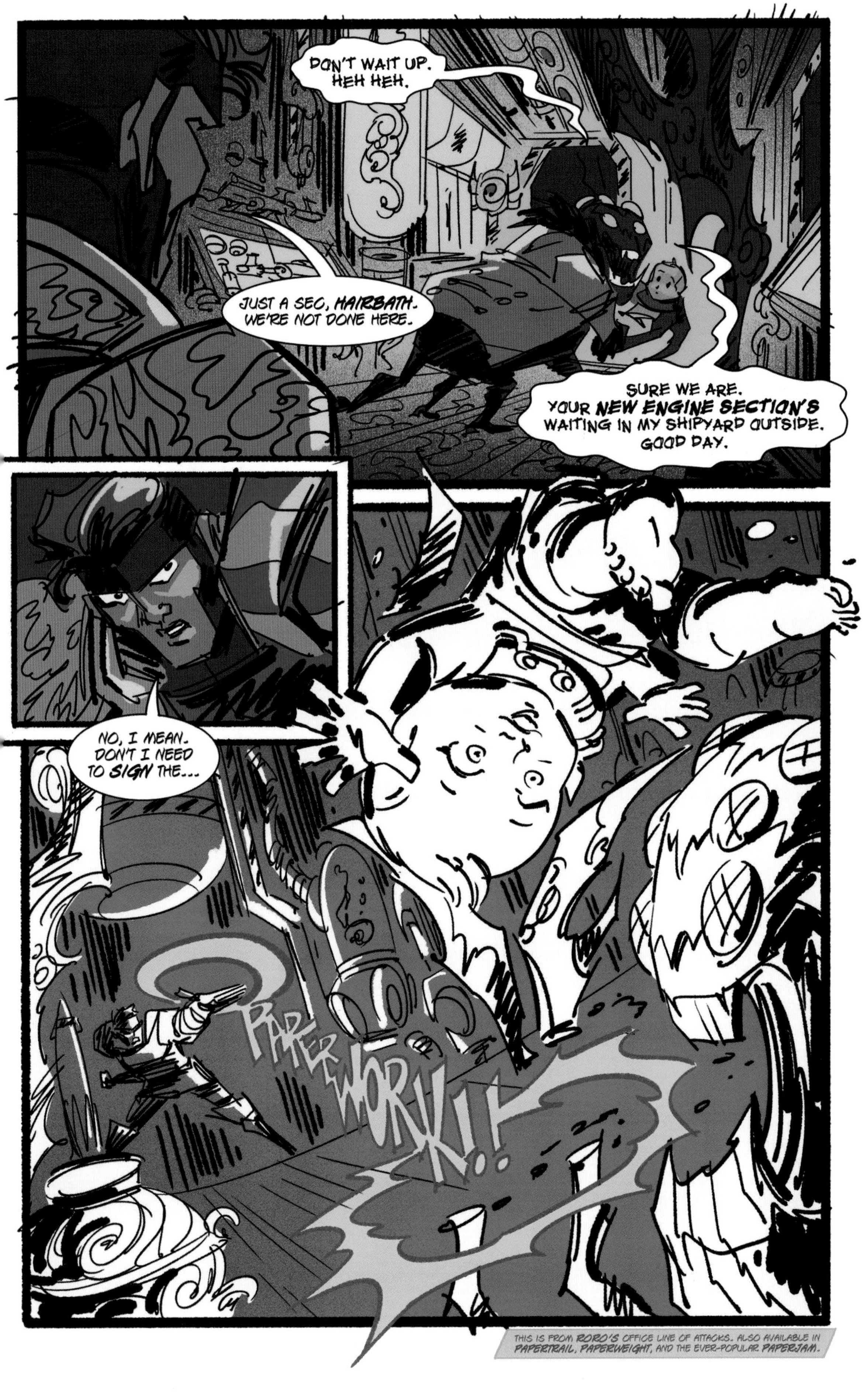
DON'T WAIT UP. HEH HEH.
JUST A SEC, HAIRBATH. WE'RE NOT DONE HERE.
SURE WE ARE. YOUR NEW ENGINE SECTION'S WAITING IN MY SHIPYARD OUTSIDE. GOOD DAY.
NO, I MEAN. DON'T I NEED TO SIGN THE...
PAPERWORK!!

THIS IS FROM RORO'S OFFICE LINE OF ATTACKS. ALSO AVAILABLE IN PAPERTRAIL, PAPERWEIGHT, AND THE EVER-POPULAR PAPERJAM.

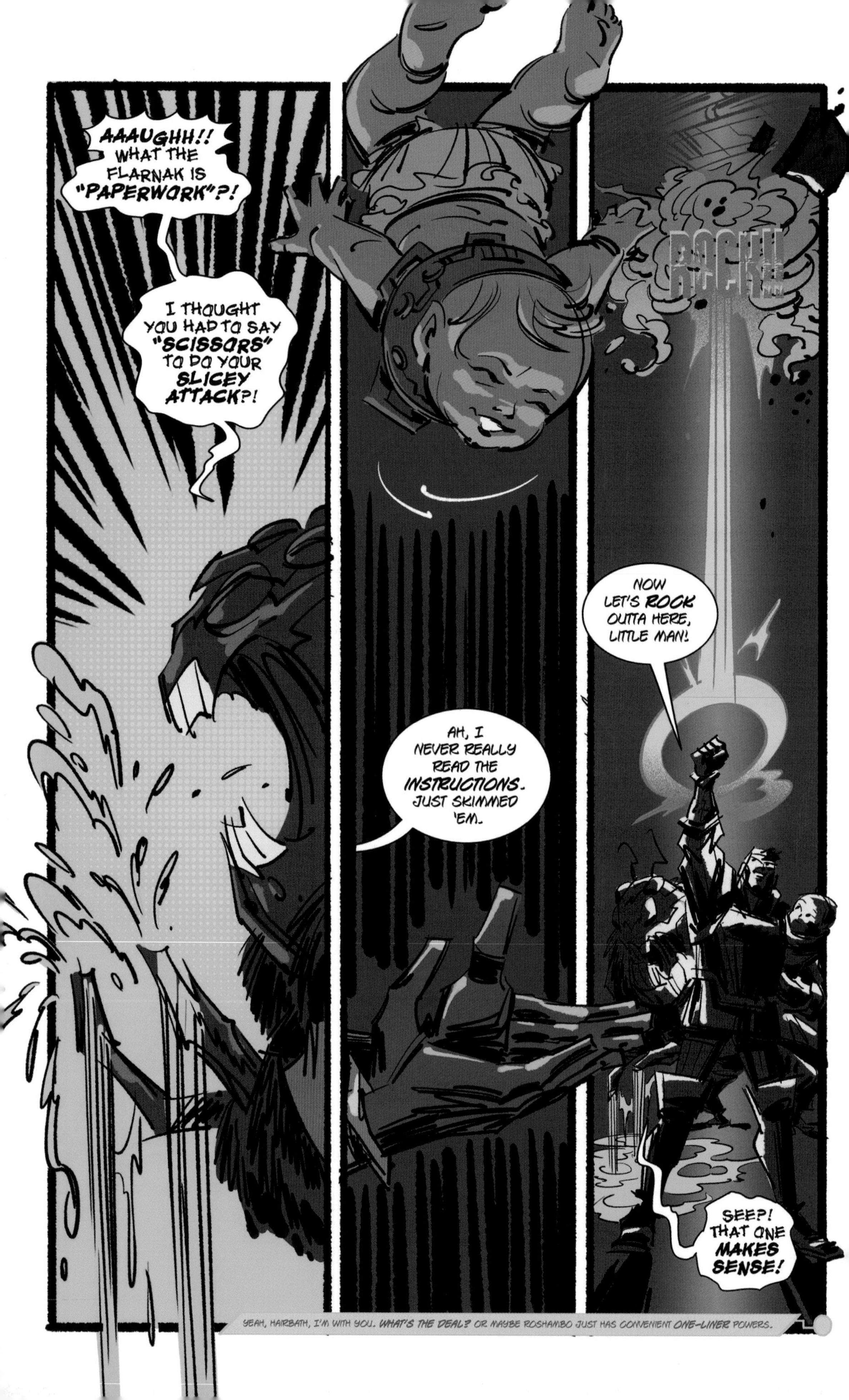
AAAUGHH!! WHAT THE FLARNAK IS "PAPERWORK"?!
I THOUGHT YOU HAD TO SAY "SCISSORS" TO DO YOUR SLICEY ATTACK?!
AH, I NEVER REALLY READ THE INSTRUCTIONS. JUST SKIMMED 'EM.
ROCK!!
NOW LET'S ROCK OUTTA HERE, LITTLE MAN!
SEE?! THAT ONE MAKES SENSE!
YEAH, HAIRBATH, I'M WITH YOU. WHAT'S THE DEAL? OR MAYBE ROSHAMBO JUST HAS CONVENIENT ONE-LINER POWERS.

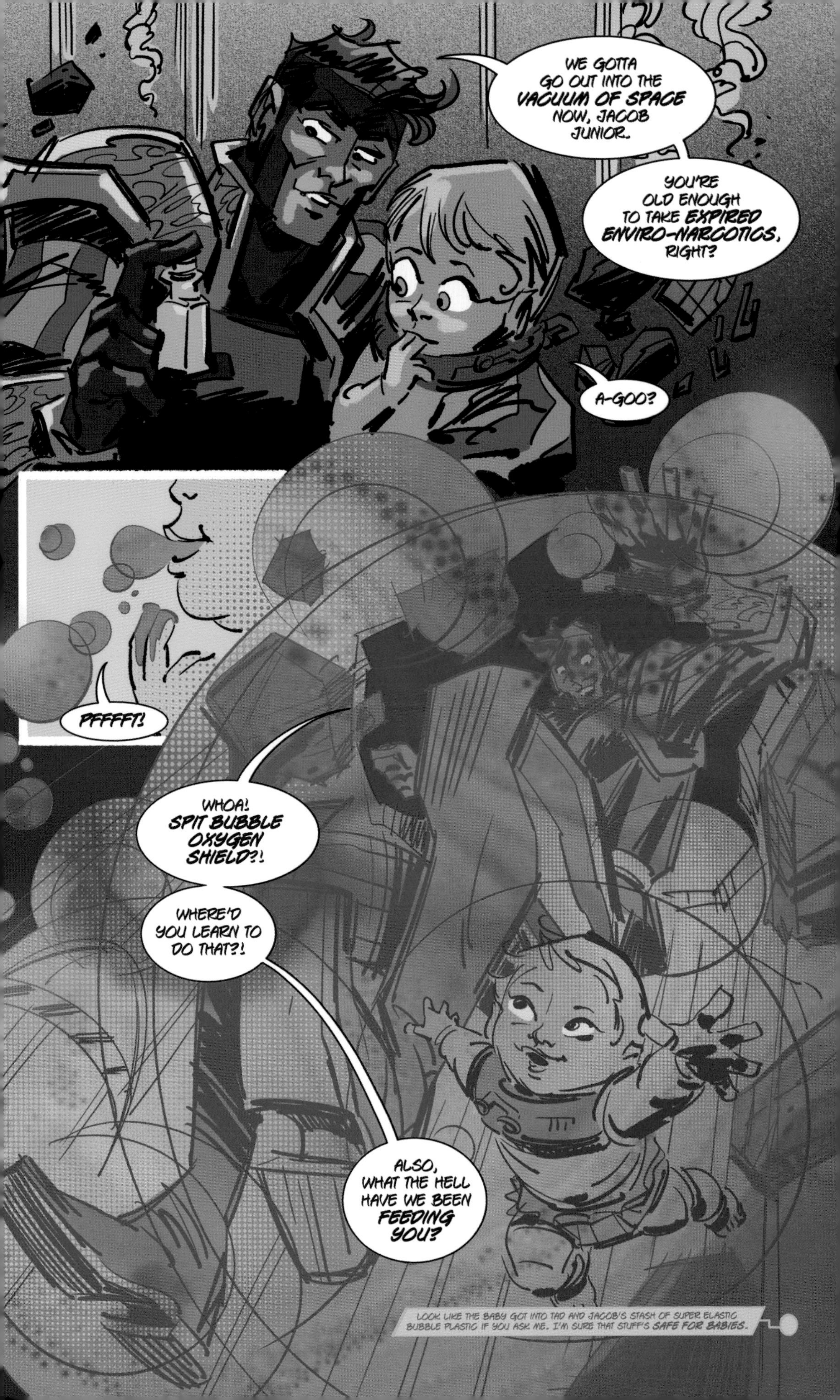
WE GOTTA GO OUT INTO THE VACUUM OF SPACE NOW, JACOB JUNIOR.
YOU'RE OLD ENOUGH TO TAKE EXPIRED ENVIRO-NARCOTICS, RIGHT?
A-GOO?
PFFFFT!
WHOA! SPIT BUBBLE OXYGEN SHIELD?!
WHERE'D YOU LEARN TO DO THAT?!
ALSO, WHAT THE HELL HAVE WE BEEN FEEDING YOU?
LOOK LIKE THE BABY GOT INTO TAD AND JACOB'S STASH OF SUPER ELASTIC BUBBLE PLASTIC IF YOU ASK ME. I'M SURE THAT STUFF'S SAFE FOR BABIES.

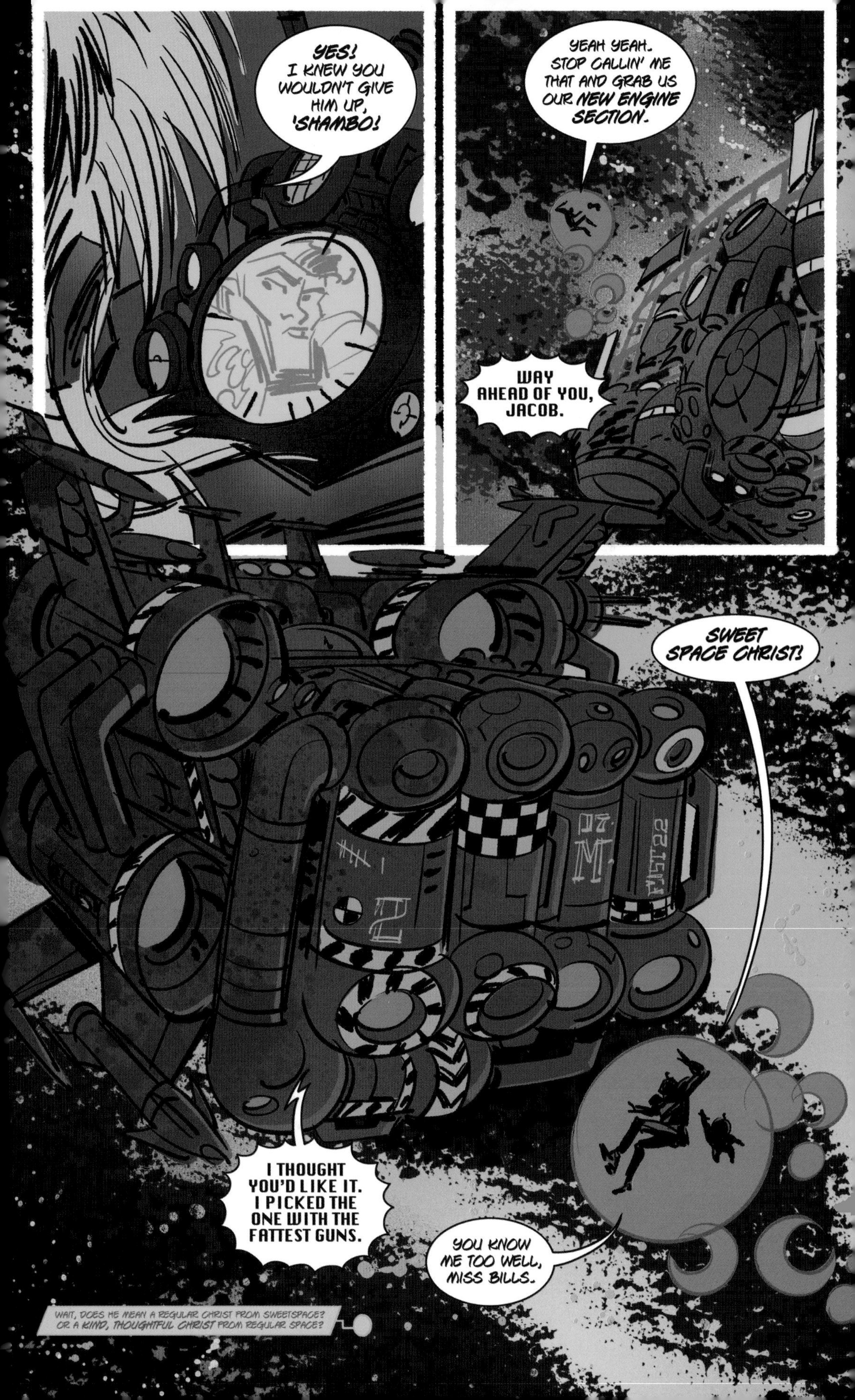
YES! I KNEW YOU WOULDN'T GIVE HIM UP, 'SHAMBO!
YEAH YEAH. STOP CALLIN' ME THAT AND GRAB US OUR NEW ENGINE SECTION.
WAY AHEAD OF YOU, JACOB.
SWEET SPACE CHRIST!
I THOUGHT YOU'D LIKE IT. I PICKED THE ONE WITH THE FATTEST GUNS.
YOU KNOW ME TOO WELL, MISS BILLS.
WAIT, DOES HE MEAN A REGULAR CHRIST FROM SWEETSPACE? OR A KIND, THOUGHTFUL CHRIST FROM REGULAR SPACE?

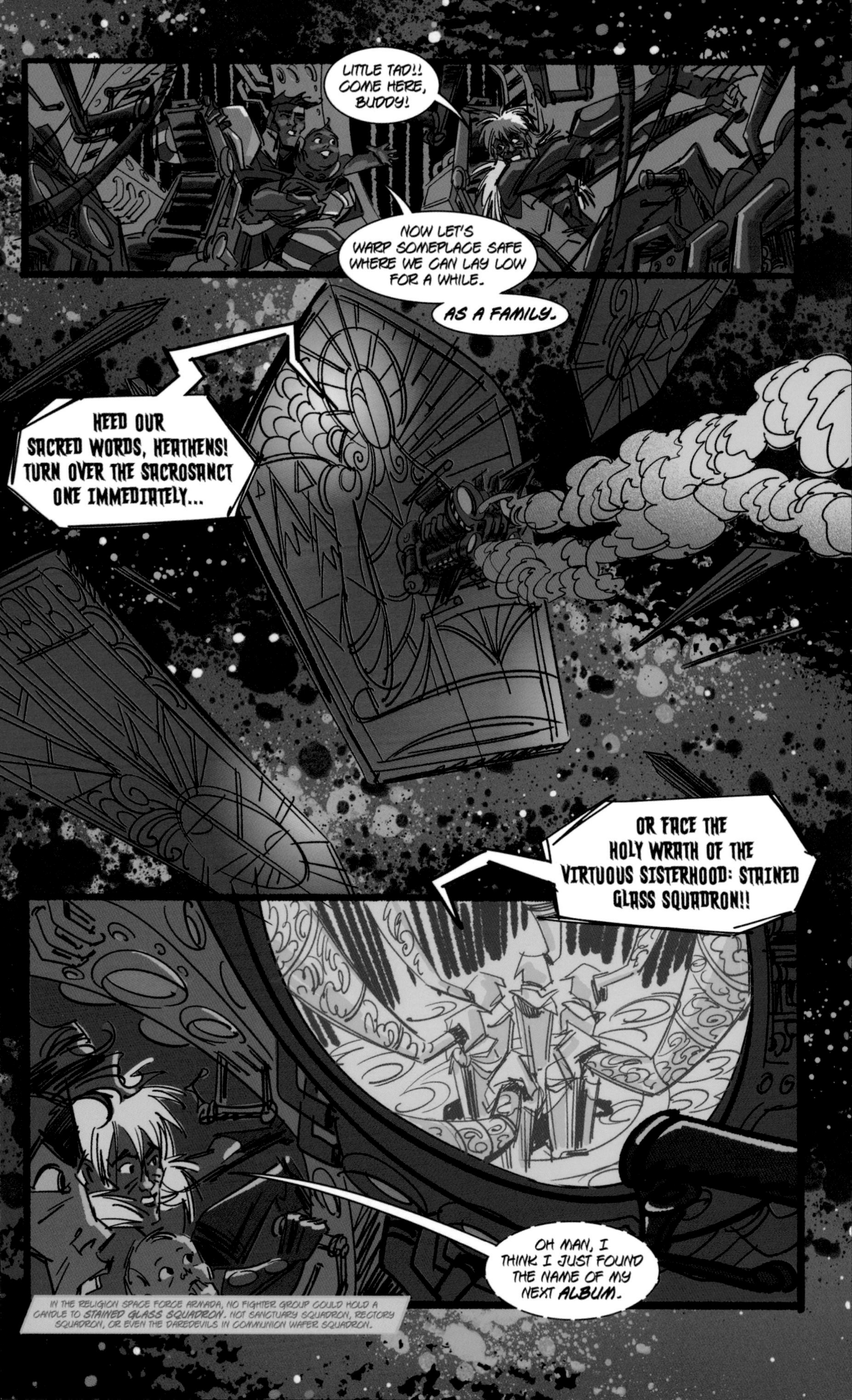
LITTLE TAD!! COME HERE, BUDDY!
NOW LET'S WARP SOMEPLACE SAFE WHERE WE CAN LAY LOW FOR A WHILE.
AS A FAMILY.
HEED OUR SACRED WORDS, HEATHENS! TURN OVER THE SACROSANCT ONE IMMEDIATELY...
OR FACE THE HOLY WRATH OF THE VIRTUOUS SISTERHOOD: STAINED GLASS SQUADRON!!
OH MAN, I THINK I JUST FOUND THE NAME OF MY NEXT **ALBUM**.
IN THE RELIGION SPACE FORCE ARMADA, NO FIGHTER GROUP COULD HOLD A CANDLE TO **STAINED GLASS SQUADRON**. NOT SANCTUARY SQUADRON, RECTORY SQUADRON, OR EVEN THE DAREDEVILS IN COMMUNION WAFER SQUADRON.

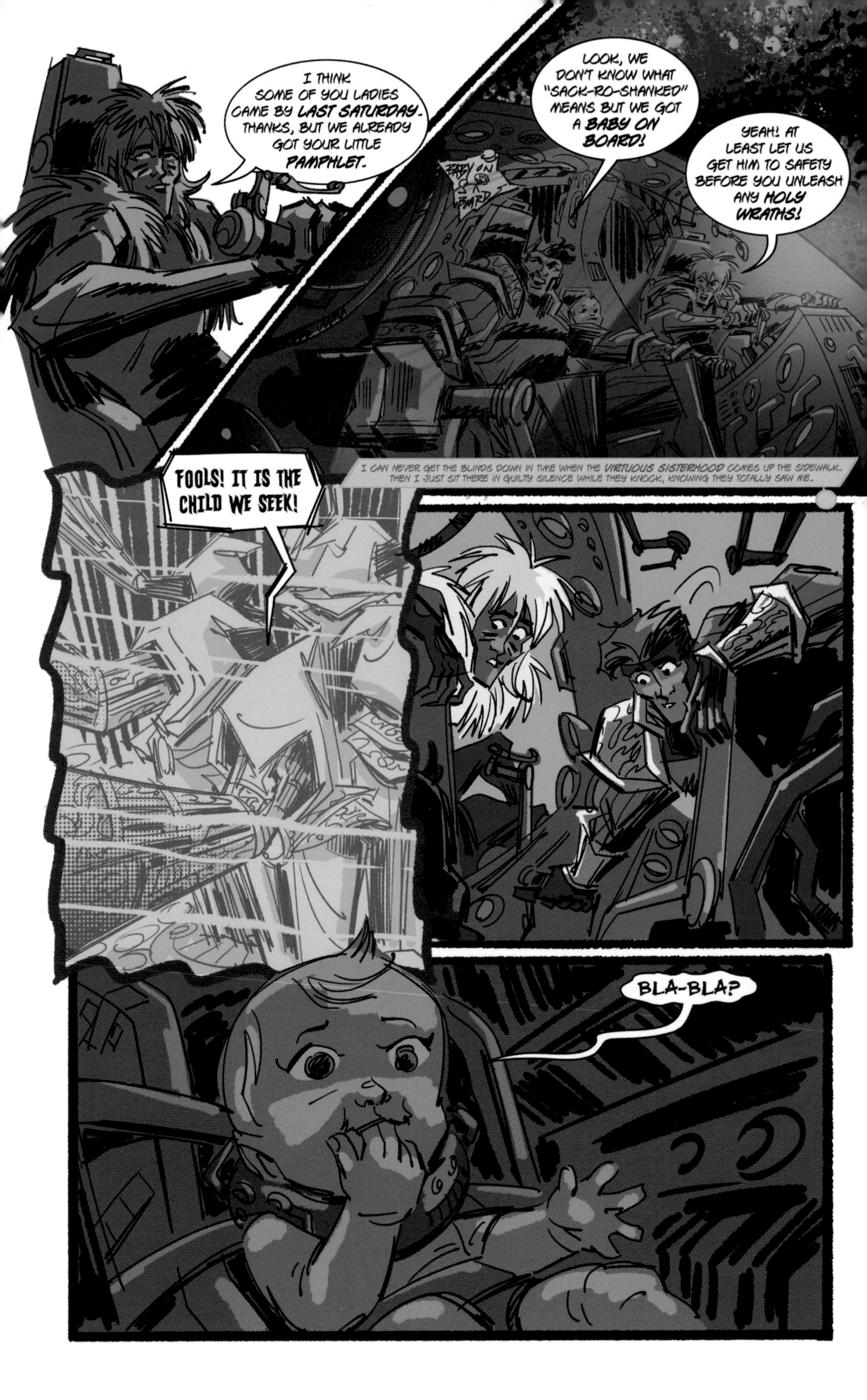
I THINK SOME OF YOU LADIES CAME BY LAST SATURDAY. THANKS, BUT WE ALREADY GOT YOUR LITTLE PAMPHLET.
LOOK, WE DON'T KNOW WHAT "SACK-RO-SHANKED" MEANS BUT WE GOT A BABY ON BOARD!
BABY ON BOARD
YEAH! AT LEAST LET US GET HIM TO SAFETY BEFORE YOU UNLEASH ANY HOLY WRATHS!
I CAN NEVER GET THE BLINDS DOWN IN TIME WHEN THE VIRTUOUS SISTERHOOD COMES UP THE SIDEWALK. THEN I JUST SIT THERE IN GUILTY SILENCE WHILE THEY KNOCK, KNOWING THEY TOTALLY SAW ME.
FOOLS! IT IS THE CHILD WE SEEK!
BLA-BLA?

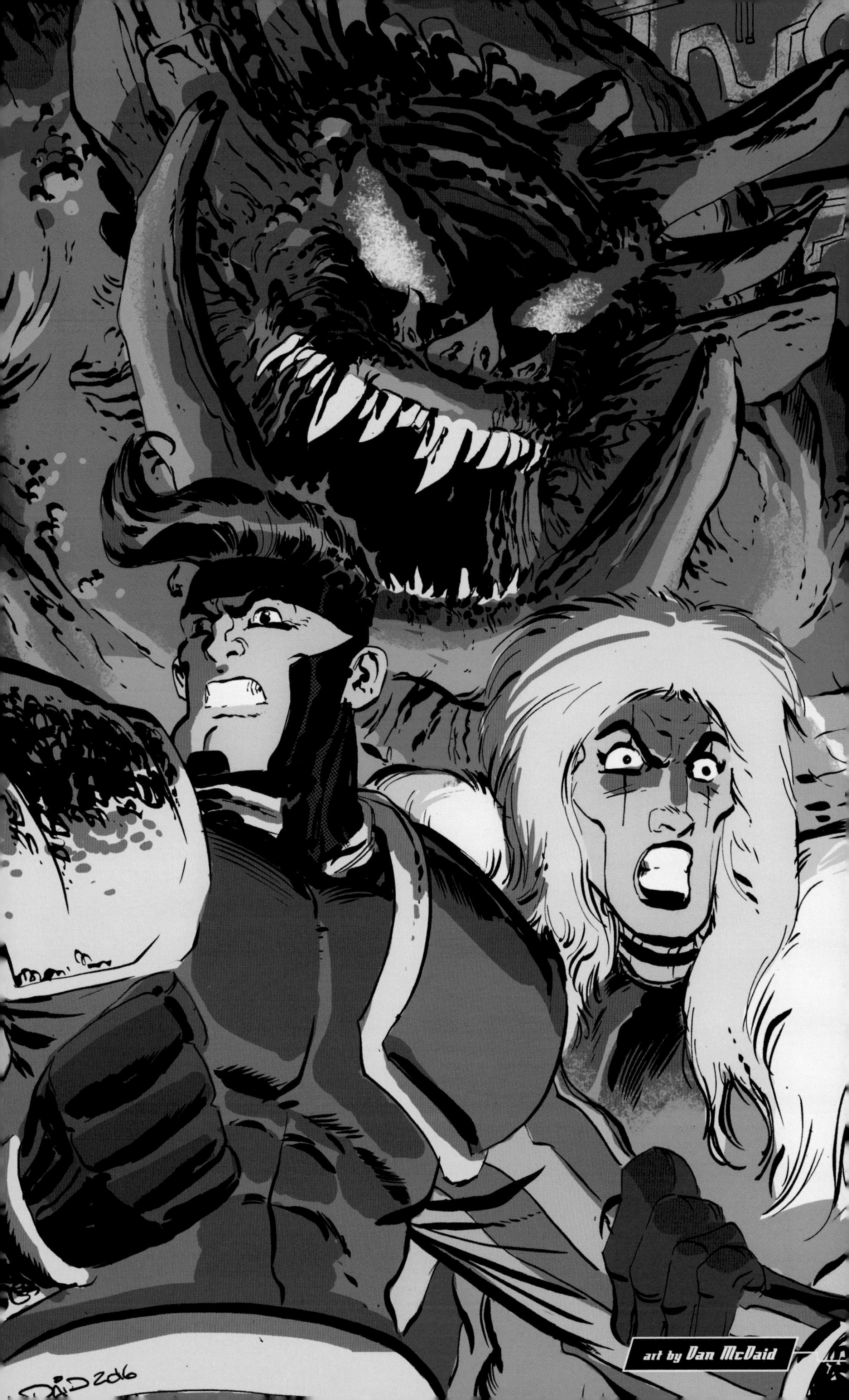
art by Dan McDaid

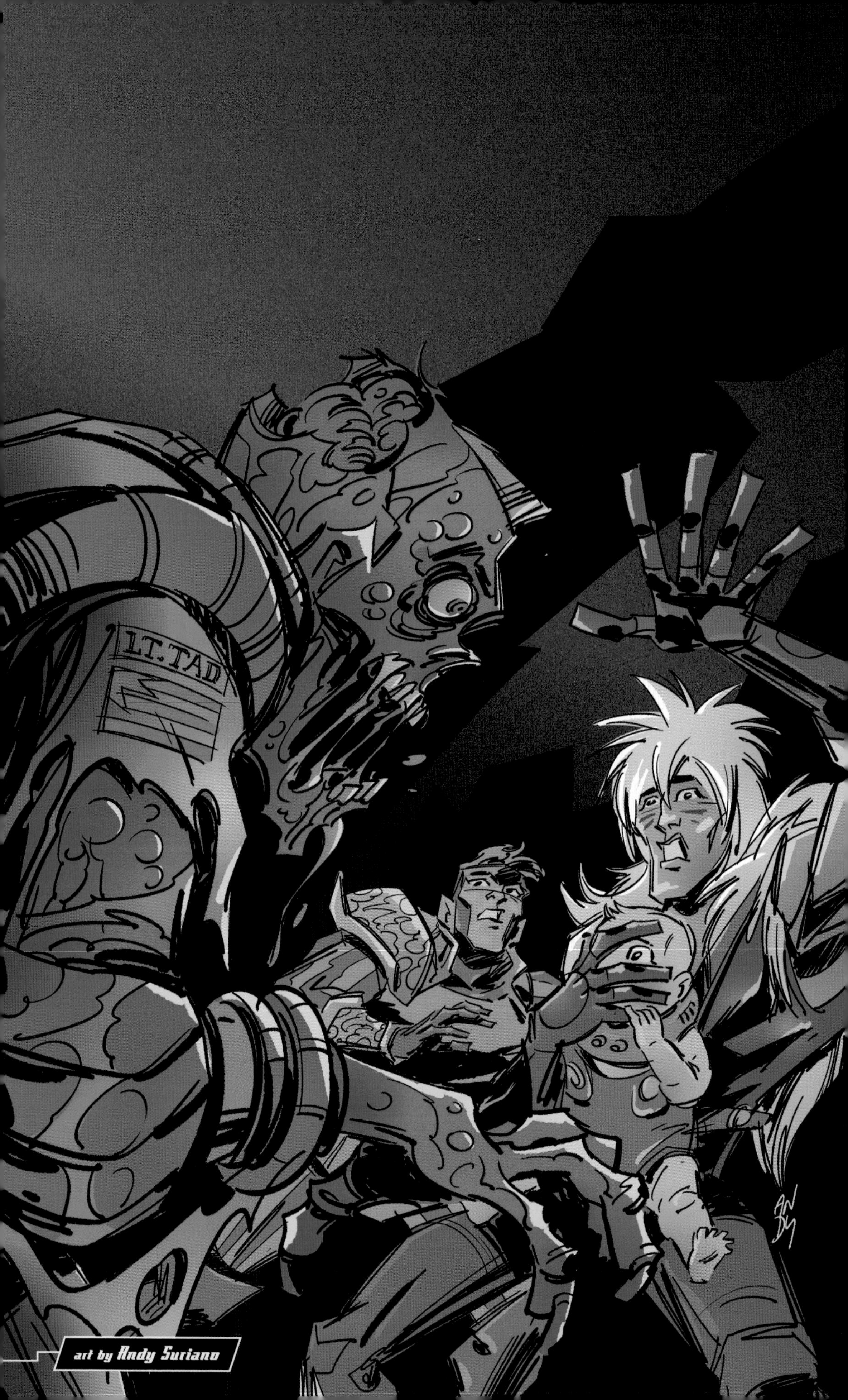
LT. TAD

art by Andy Suriano

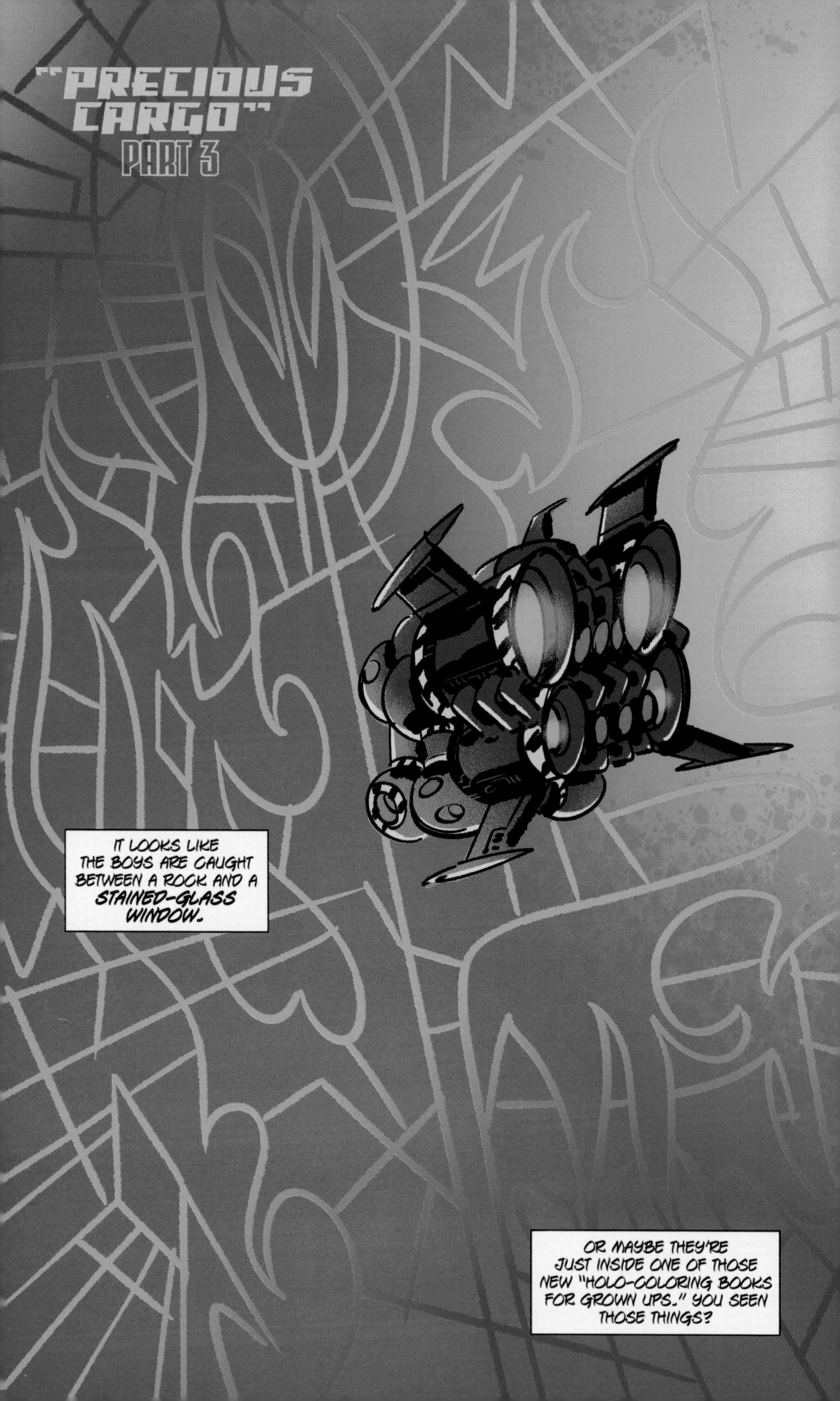
"PRECIOUS CARGO"
PART 3
IT LOOKS LIKE THE BOYS ARE CAUGHT BETWEEN A ROCK AND A STAINED-GLASS WINDOW.
OR MAYBE THEY'RE JUST INSIDE ONE OF THOSE NEW "HOLO-COLORING BOOKS FOR GROWN UPS." YOU SEEN THOSE THINGS?

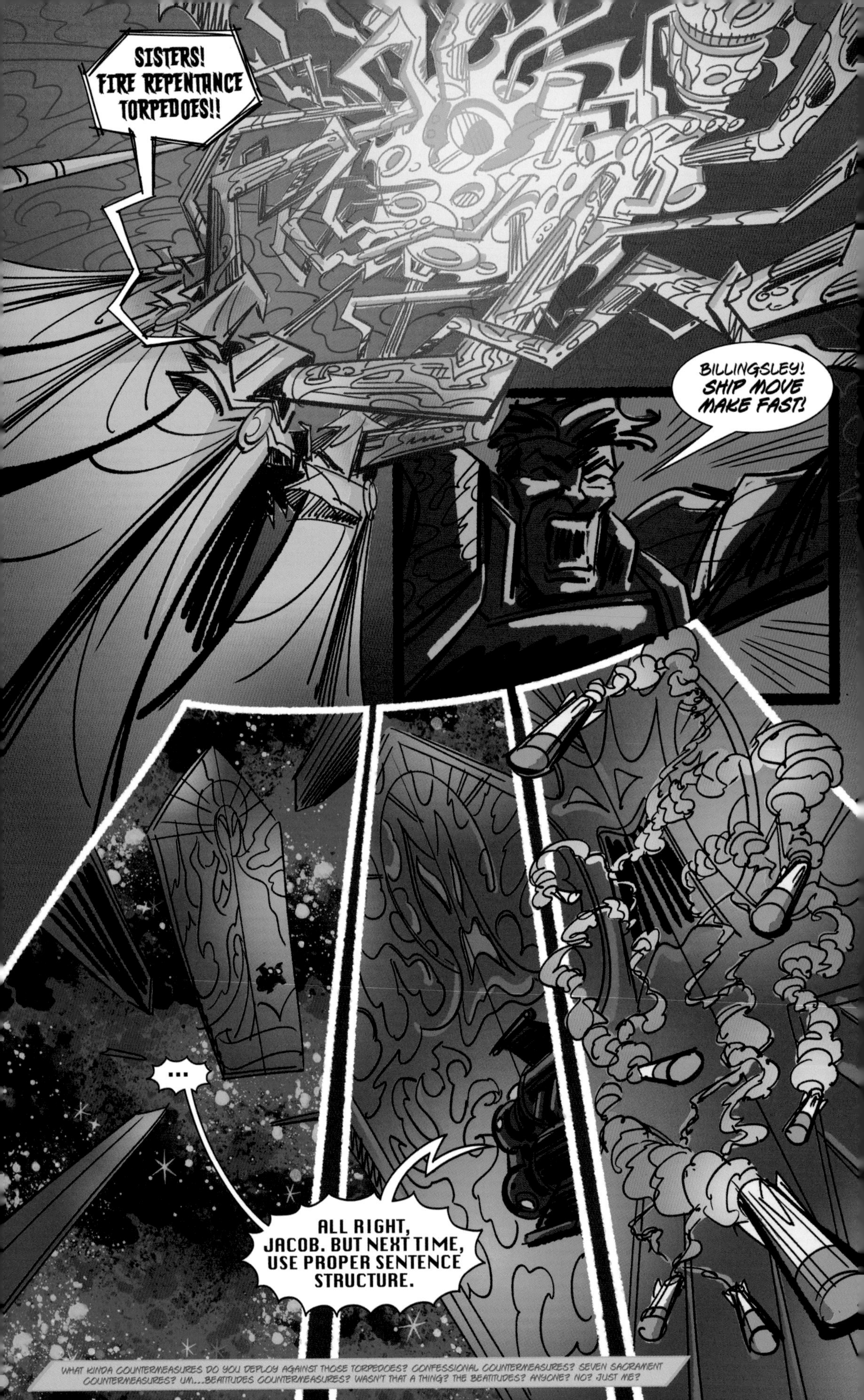
SISTERS! FIRE REPENTANCE TORPEDOES!!
BILLINGSLEY! SHIP MOVE MAKE FAST!
...
ALL RIGHT, JACOB. BUT NEXT TIME, USE PROPER SENTENCE STRUCTURE.
WHAT KINDA COUNTERMEASURES DO YOU DEPLOY AGAINST THOSE TORPEDOES? CONFESSIONAL COUNTERMEASURES? SEVEN SACRAMENT COUNTERMEASURES? UM...BEATITUDES COUNTERMEASURES? WASN'T THAT A THING? THE BEATITUDES? ANYONE? NO? JUST ME?

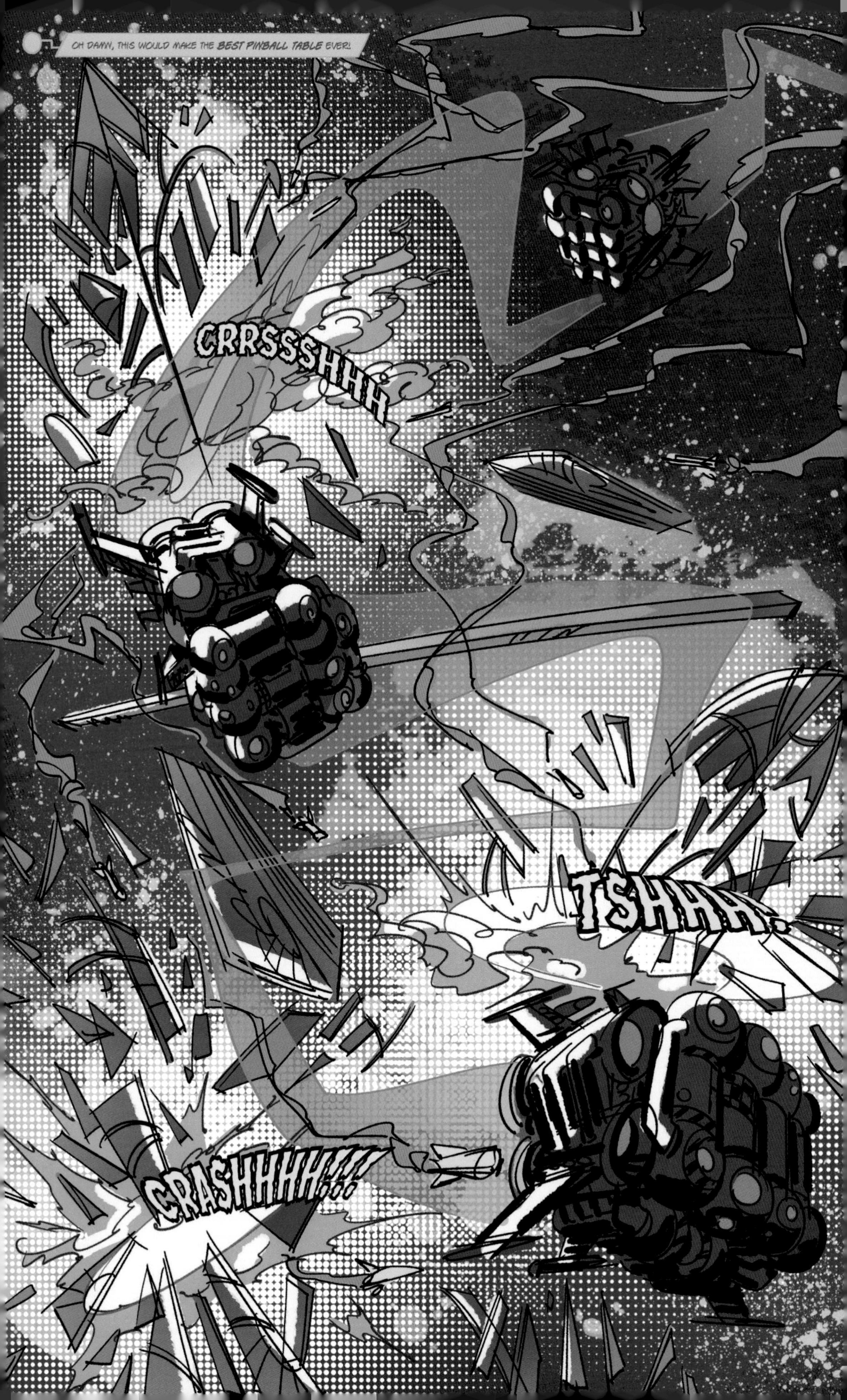
OH DAMN, THIS WOULD MAKE THE BEST PINBALL TABLE EVER!
CRRSSSHHH
TSHHH!
CRASHHHH!!!

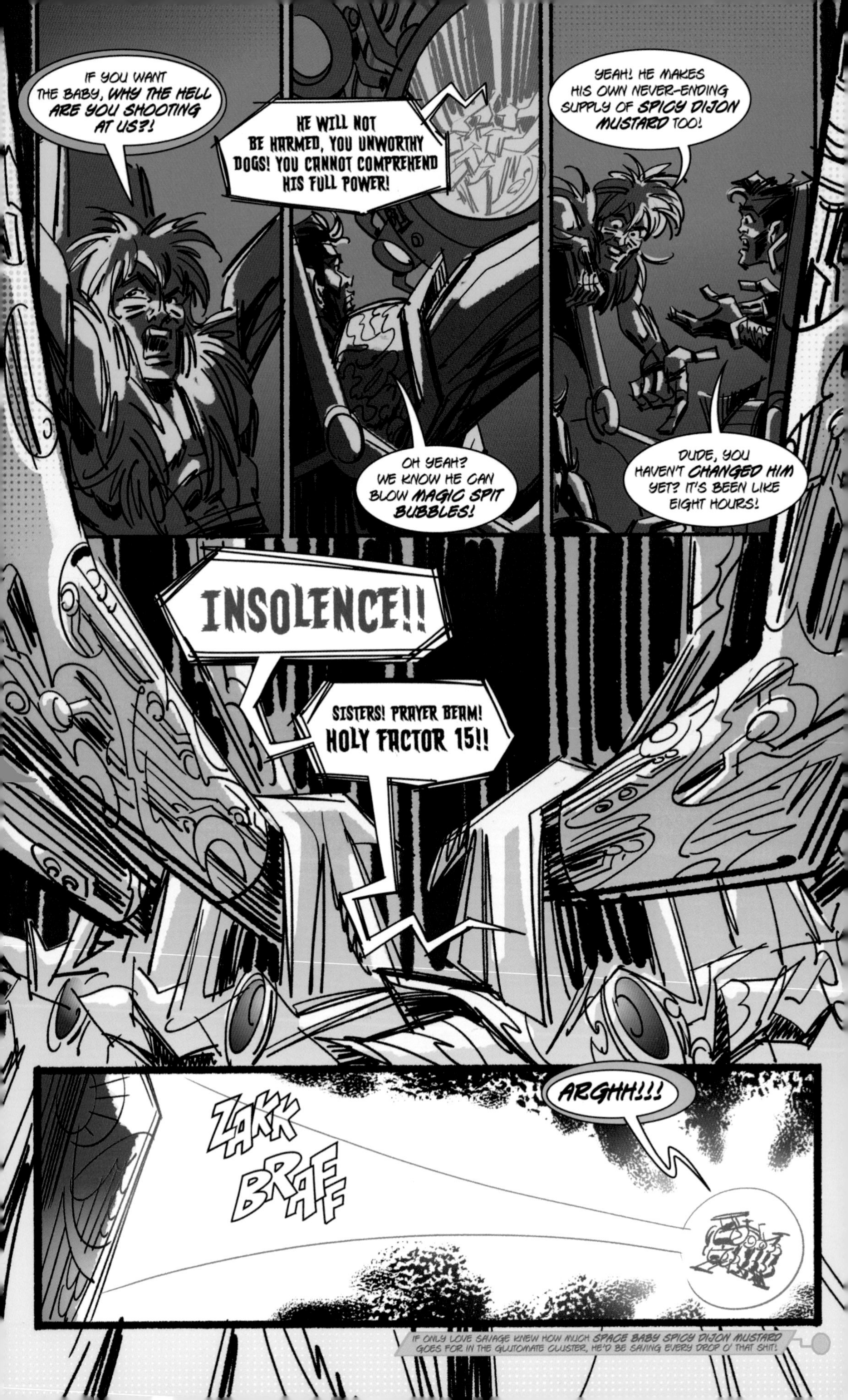
IF YOU WANT THE BABY, *WHY THE HELL ARE YOU SHOOTING AT US?!*
HE WILL NOT BE HARMED, YOU UNWORTHY DOGS! YOU CANNOT COMPREHEND HIS FULL POWER!
OH YEAH? WE KNOW HE CAN BLOW *MAGIC SPIT BUBBLES!*
YEAH! HE MAKES HIS OWN NEVER-ENDING SUPPLY OF *SPICY DIJON MUSTARD* TOO!
DUDE, YOU HAVEN'T *CHANGED HIM* YET? IT'S BEEN LIKE EIGHT HOURS!
INSOLENCE!!
SISTERS! PRAYER BEAM! HOLY FACTOR 15!!
ZAKK
BRAFF
ARGHH!!!
IF ONLY LOVE SAVAGE KNEW HOW MUCH *SPACE BABY SPICY DIJON MUSTARD* GOES FOR IN THE GLUTOMATE CLUSTER, HE'D BE SAVING EVERY DROP O' THAT SHIT!

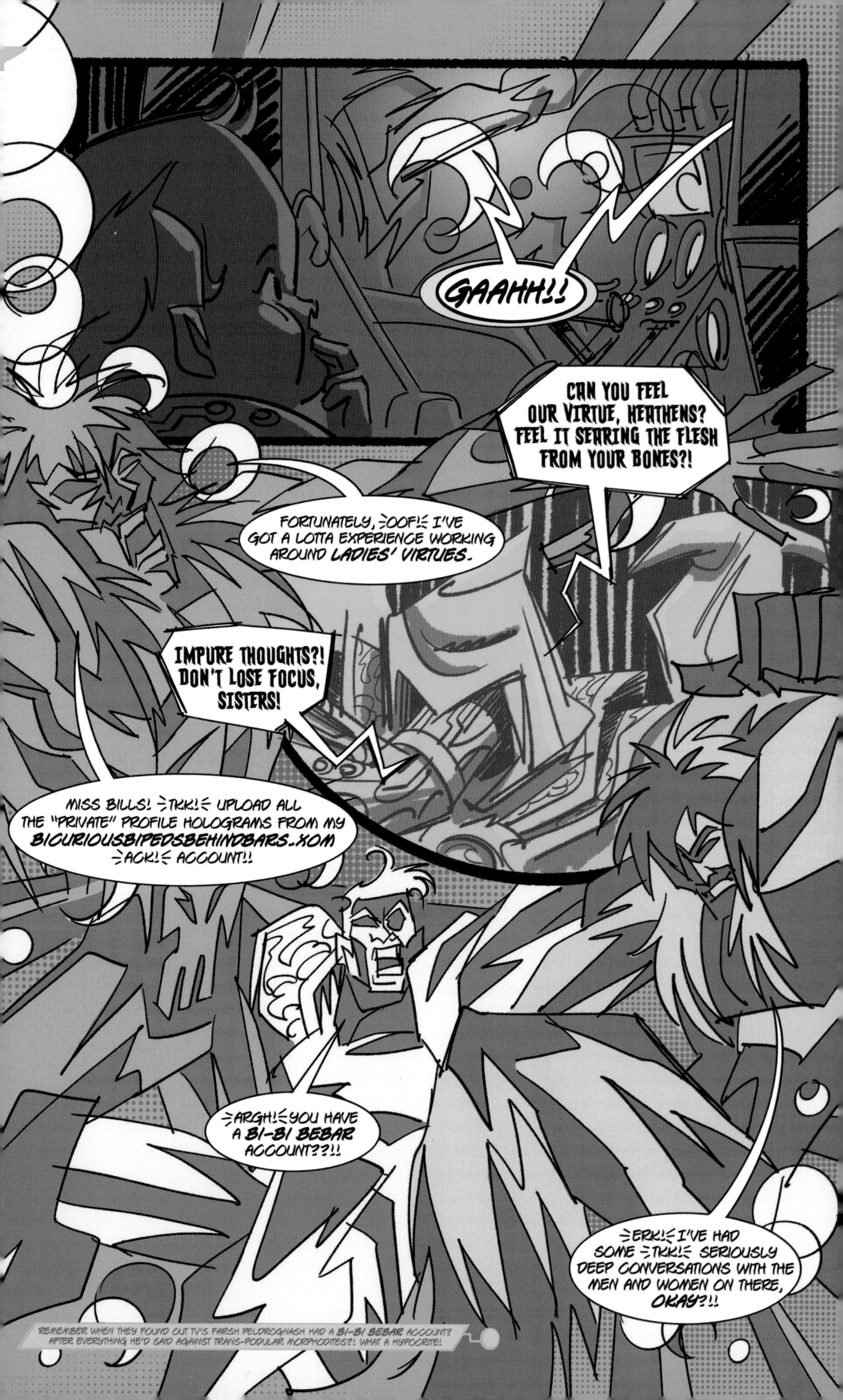
GAAHH!!
CAN YOU FEEL OUR VIRTUE, HEATHENS? FEEL IT SEARING THE FLESH FROM YOUR BONES?!
FORTUNATELY, =OOF!= I'VE GOT A LOTTA EXPERIENCE WORKING AROUND ***LADIES' VIRTUES***.
IMPURE THOUGHTS?! DON'T LOSE FOCUS, SISTERS!
MISS BILLS! =TKK!= UPLOAD ALL THE "PRIVATE" PROFILE HOLOGRAMS FROM MY ***BICURIOUSBIPEDSBEHINDBARS.XOM*** =ACK!= ACCOUNT!!
=ARGH!= YOU HAVE A ***BI-BI BEBAR*** ACCOUNT??!!
=ERK!= I'VE HAD SOME =TKK!= SERIOUSLY DEEP CONVERSATIONS WITH THE MEN AND WOMEN ON THERE, ***OKAY***?!!
REMEMBER WHEN THEY FOUND OUT TV'S FARSH PELDROGNASH HAD A ***BI-BI BEBAR*** ACCOUNT? AFTER EVERYTHING HE'D SAID AGAINST TRANS-PODULAR MORPHODITES?! WHAT A HYPOCRITE!

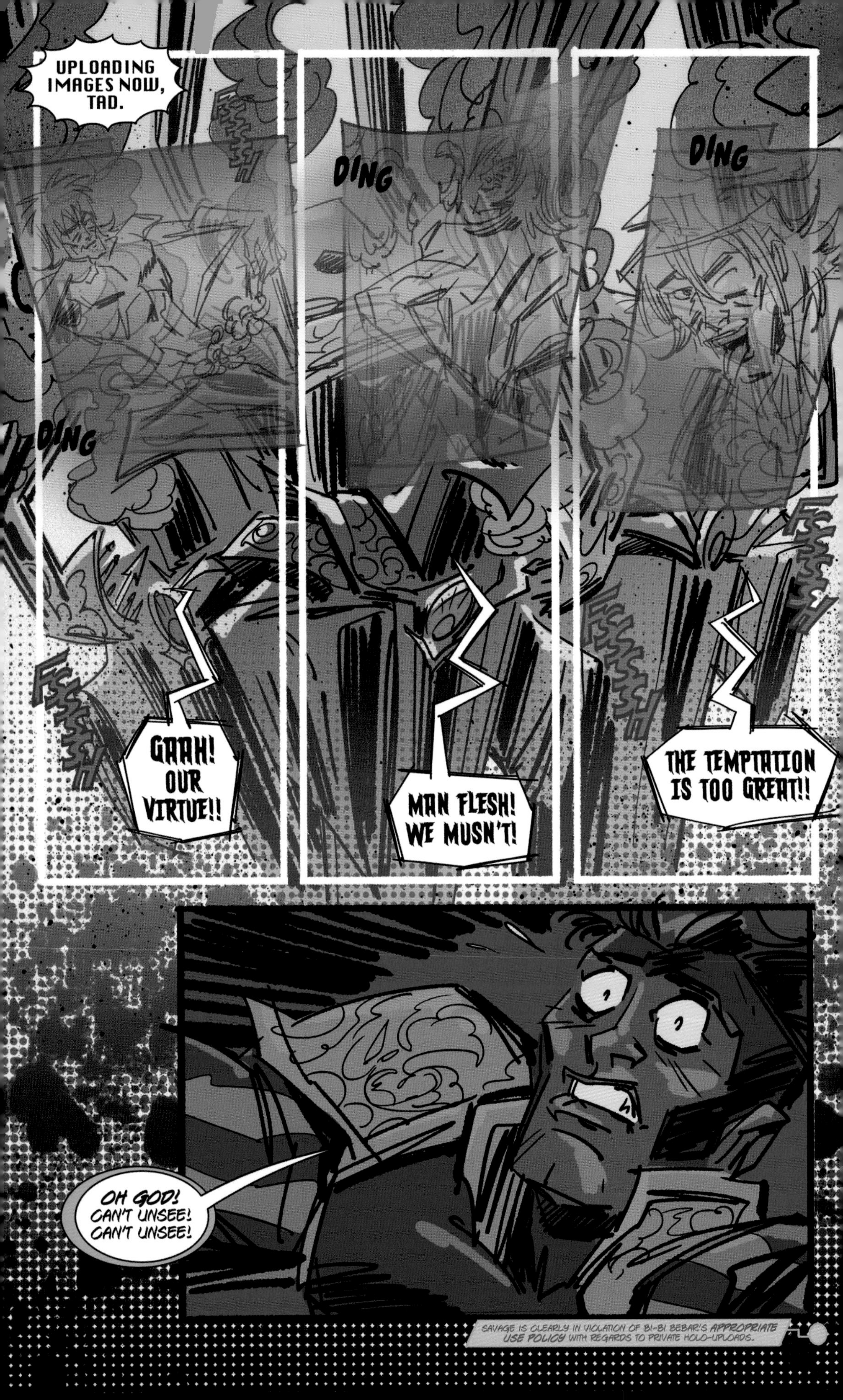
UPLOADING IMAGES NOW, TAD.
DING
GAAH! OUR VIRTUE!!
DING
MAN FLESH! WE MUSN'T!
DING
THE TEMPTATION IS TOO GREAT!!
OH GOD! CAN'T UNSEE! CAN'T UNSEE!
SAVAGE IS CLEARLY IN VIOLATION OF BI-BI BEBAR'S APPROPRIATE USE POLICY WITH REGARDS TO PRIVATE HOLO-UPLOADS.

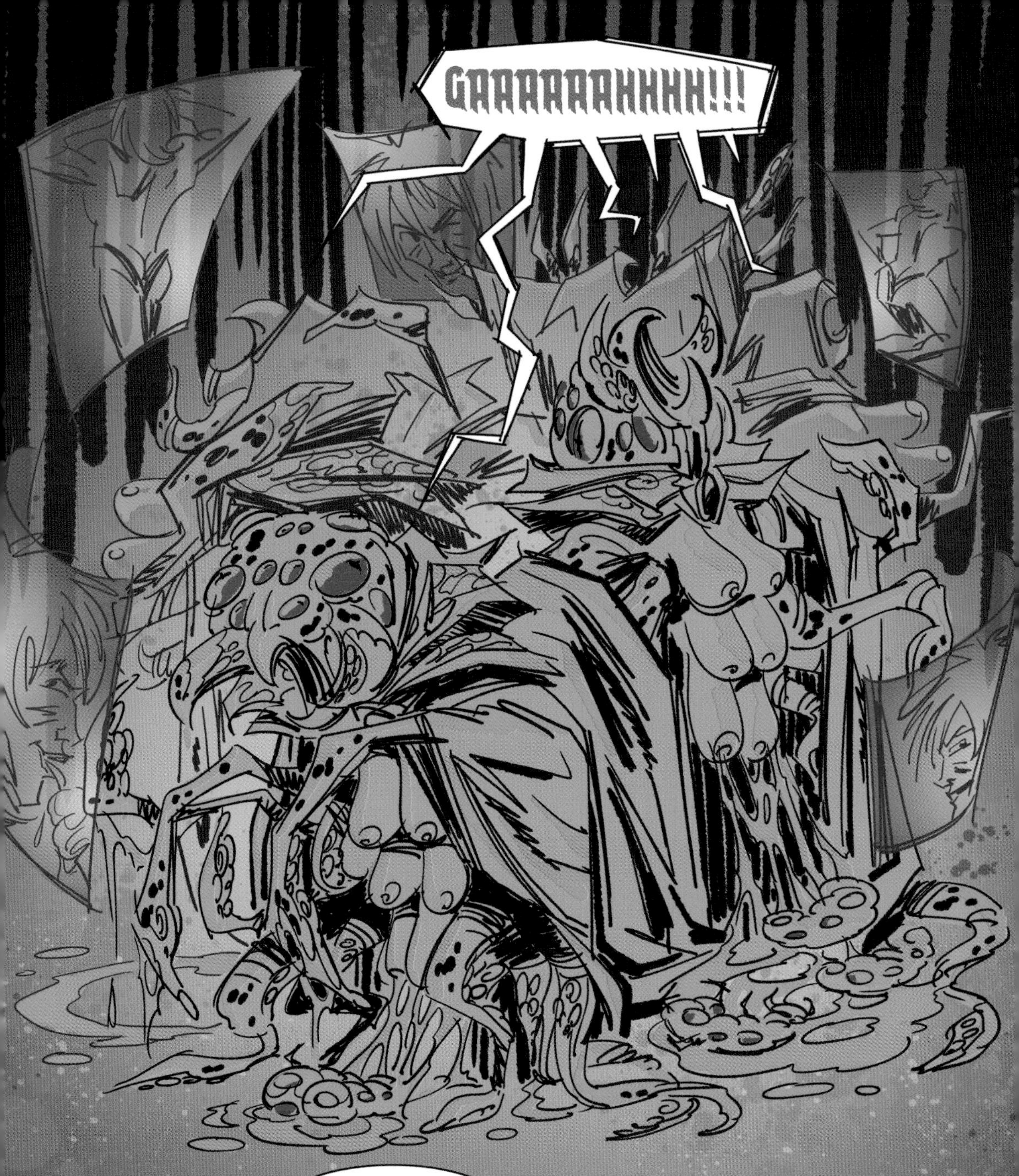
GAAAAAAHHHH!!!

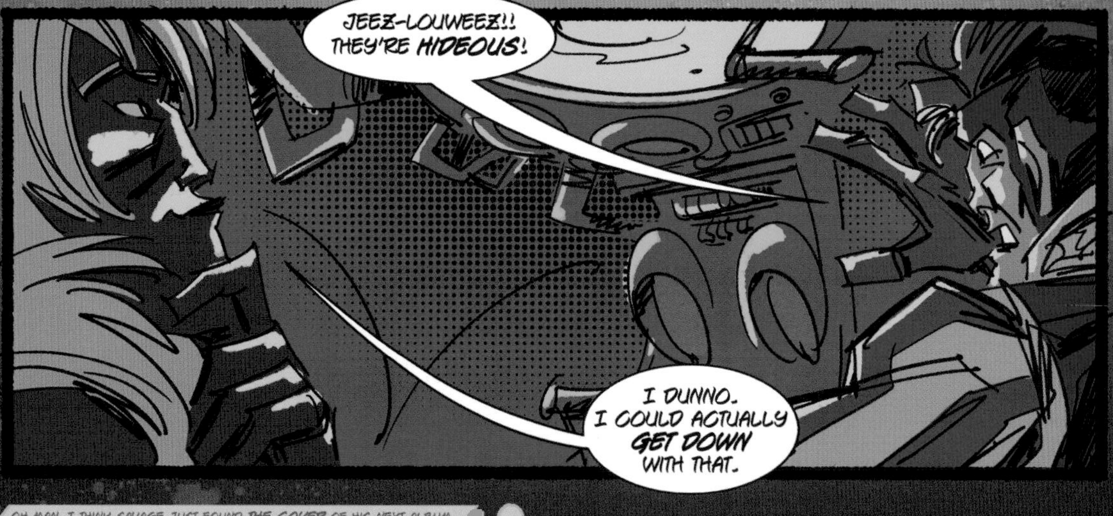
JEEZ-LOUWEEZ!! THEY'RE **HIDEOUS**!
I DUNNO. I COULD ACTUALLY **GET DOWN** WITH THAT.

OH MAN, I THINK SAVAGE JUST FOUND *THE COVER* OF HIS NEXT ALBUM.

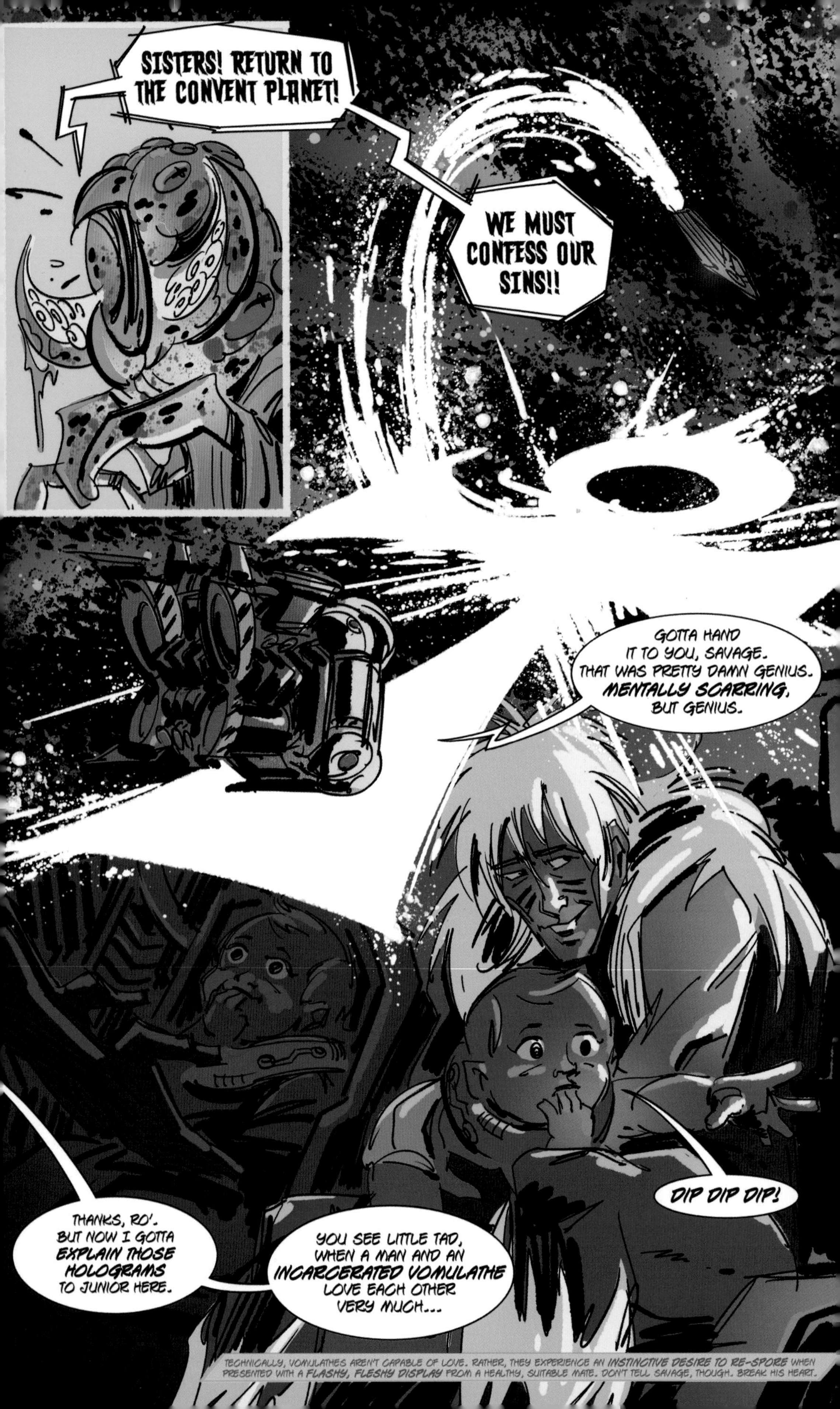
SISTERS! RETURN TO THE CONVENT PLANET!
WE MUST CONFESS OUR SINS!!
GOTTA HAND IT TO YOU, SAVAGE. THAT WAS PRETTY DAMN GENIUS. ***MENTALLY SCARRING,*** BUT GENIUS.
THANKS, RO'. BUT NOW I GOTTA ***EXPLAIN THOSE HOLOGRAMS*** TO JUNIOR HERE.
YOU SEE LITTLE TAD, WHEN A MAN AND AN ***INCARCERATED VOMULATHE*** LOVE EACH OTHER VERY MUCH...
DIP DIP DIP!
TECHNICALLY, VOMULATHES AREN'T CAPABLE OF LOVE. RATHER, THEY EXPERIENCE AN ***INSTINCTIVE DESIRE TO RE-SPORE*** WHEN PRESENTED WITH A ***FLASHY, FLESHY DISPLAY*** FROM A HEALTHY, SUITABLE MATE. DON'T TELL SAVAGE, THOUGH. BREAK HIS HEART.

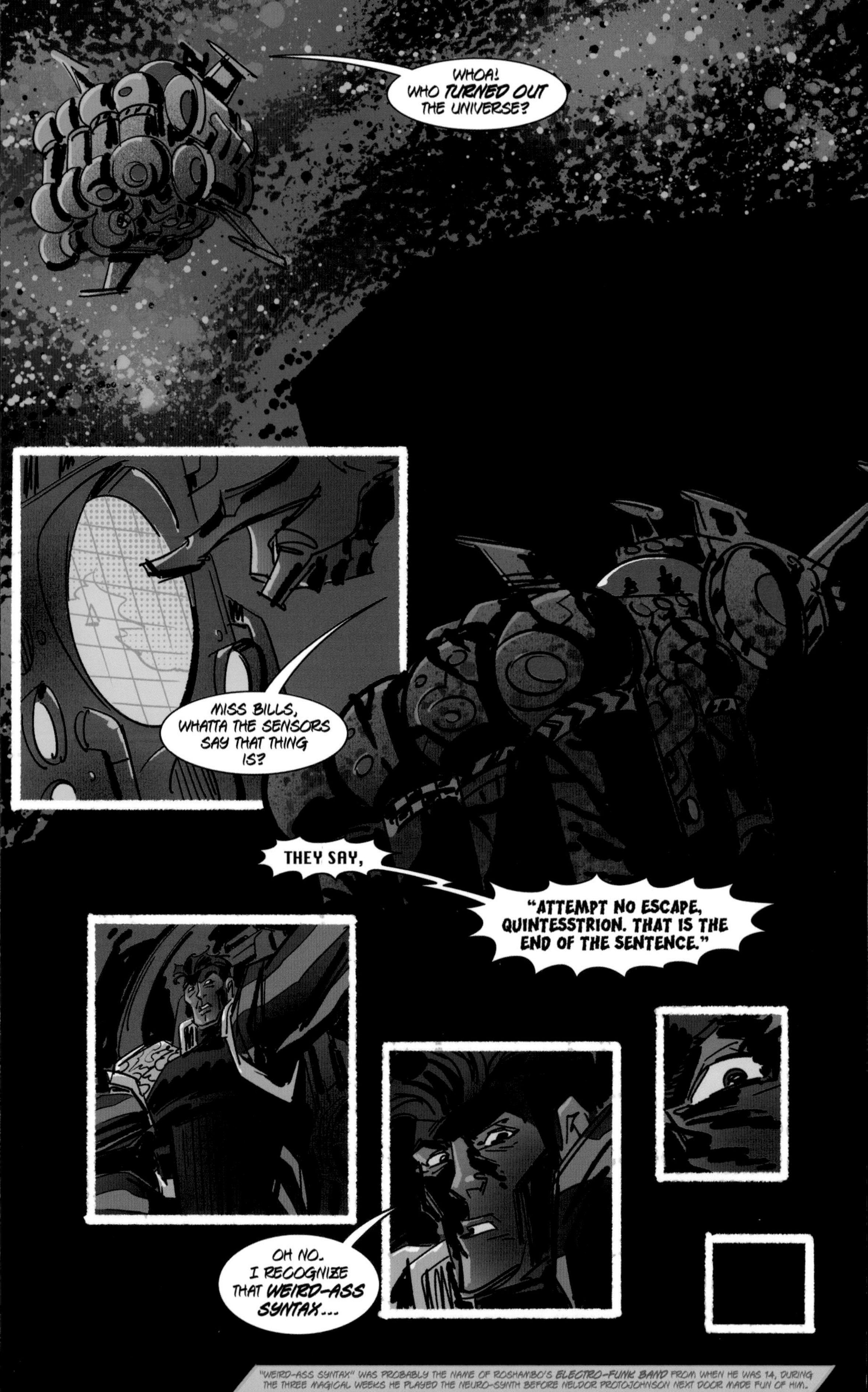
WHOA! WHO TURNED OUT THE UNIVERSE?
MISS BILLS, WHATTA THE SENSORS SAY THAT THING IS?
THEY SAY,
"ATTEMPT NO ESCAPE, QUINTESSTRION. THAT IS THE END OF THE SENTENCE."
OH NO. I RECOGNIZE THAT WEIRD-ASS SYNTAX...
"WEIRD-ASS SYNTAX" WAS PROBABLY THE NAME OF ROSHAMBO'S ELECTRO-FUNK BAND FROM WHEN HE WAS 14, DURING THE THREE MAGICAL WEEKS HE PLAYED THE NEURO-SYNTH BEFORE NELDOR PROTOJOHNSON NEXT DOOR MADE FUN OF HIM.

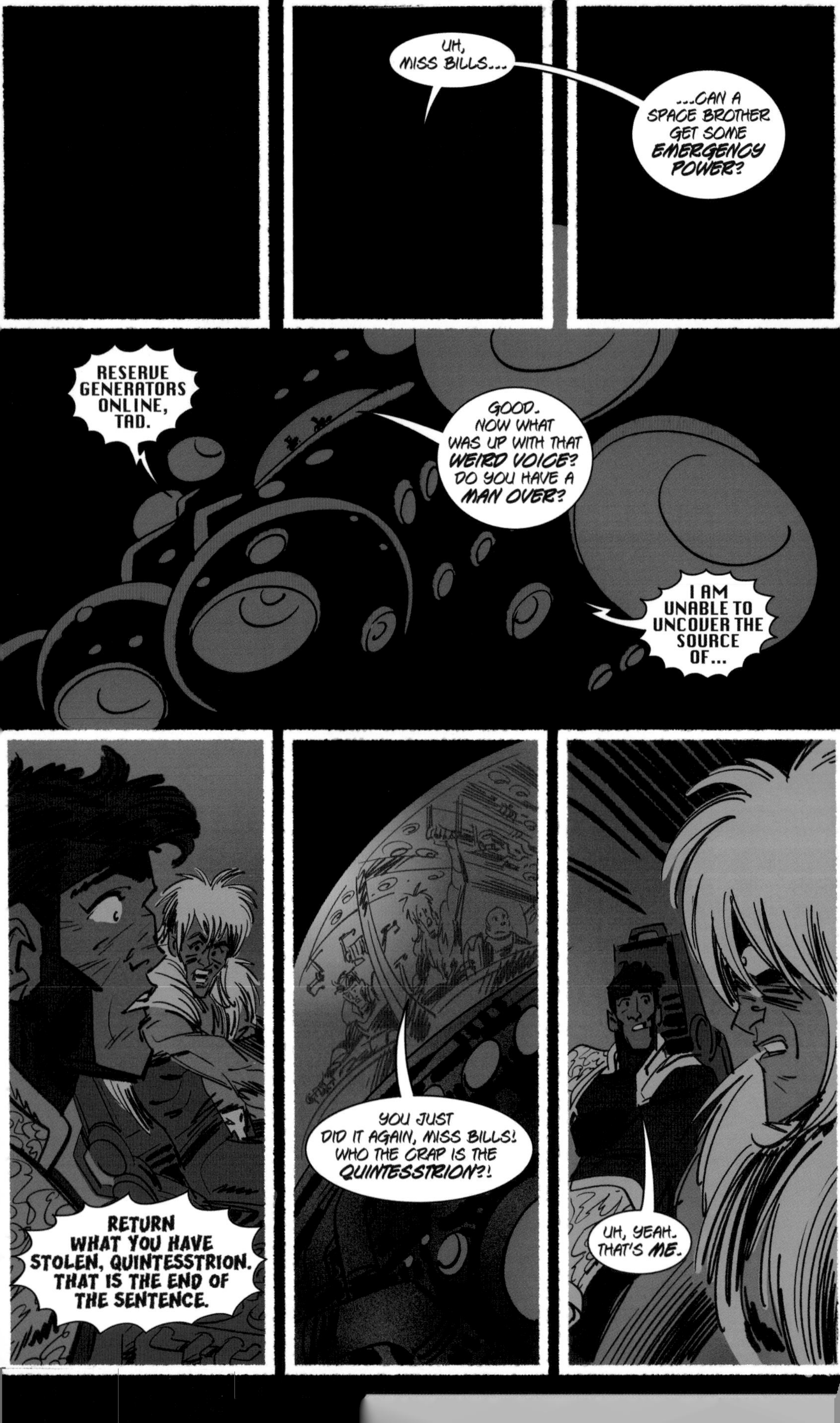
UH, MISS BILLS...
...CAN A SPACE BROTHER GET SOME EMERGENCY POWER?
RESERVE GENERATORS ONLINE, TAD.
GOOD. NOW WHAT WAS UP WITH THAT WEIRD VOICE? DO YOU HAVE A MAN OVER?
I AM UNABLE TO UNCOVER THE SOURCE OF...
RETURN WHAT YOU HAVE STOLEN, QUINTESSTRION. THAT IS THE END OF THE SENTENCE.
YOU JUST DID IT AGAIN, MISS BILLS! WHO THE CRAP IS THE QUINTESSTRION?!
UH, YEAH. THAT'S ME.

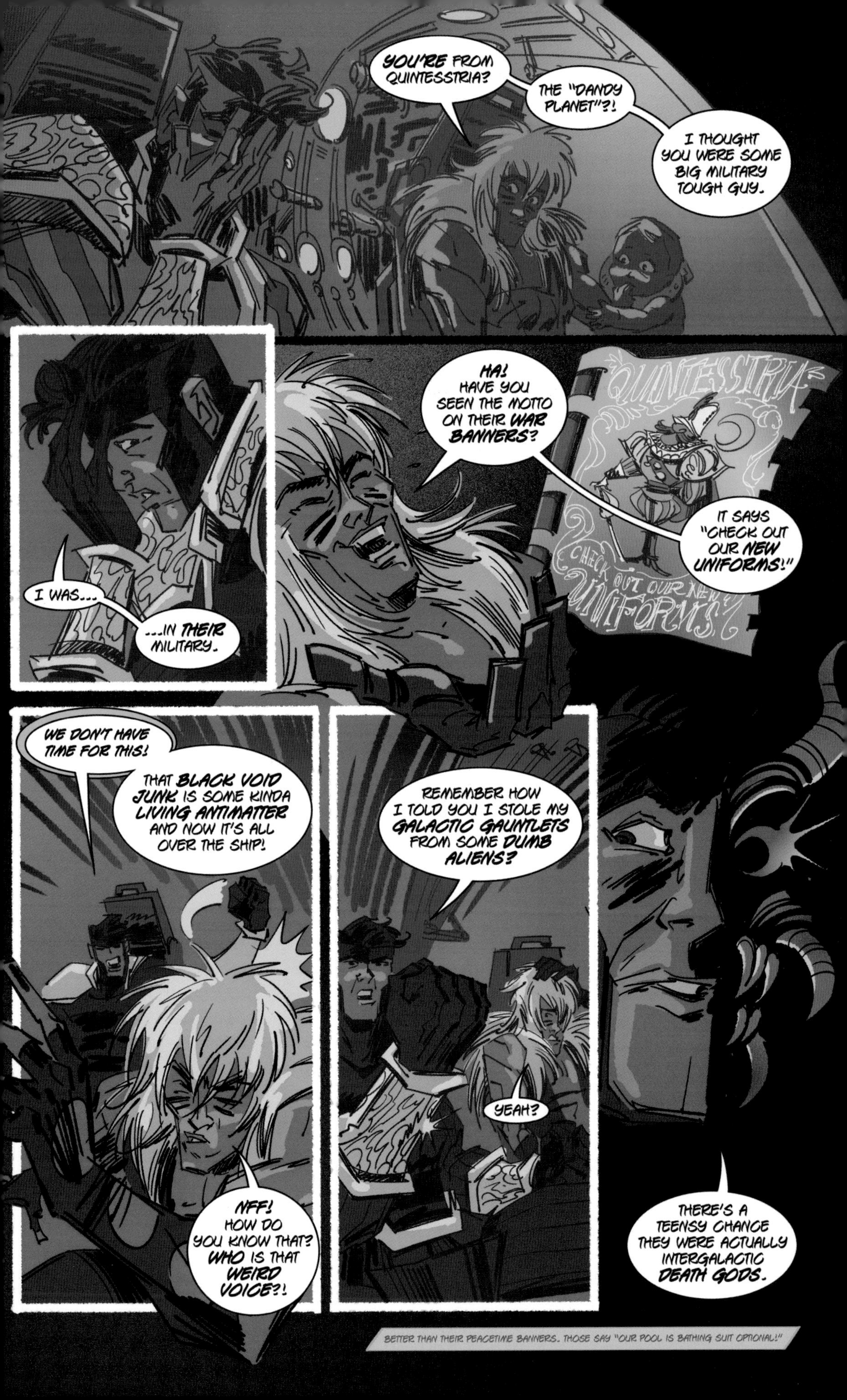
YOU'RE FROM QUINTESSTRIA?
THE "DANDY PLANET"?!
I THOUGHT YOU WERE SOME BIG MILITARY TOUGH GUY.
I WAS...
...IN THEIR MILITARY.
HA! HAVE YOU SEEN THE MOTTO ON THEIR WAR BANNERS?
QUINTESSTRIA
CHECK OUT OUR NEW UNIFORMS!
IT SAYS "CHECK OUT OUR NEW UNIFORMS!"
WE DON'T HAVE TIME FOR THIS!
THAT BLACK VOID JUNK IS SOME KINDA LIVING ANTIMATTER AND NOW IT'S ALL OVER THE SHIP!
NFF! HOW DO YOU KNOW THAT? WHO IS THAT WEIRD VOICE?!
REMEMBER HOW I TOLD YOU I STOLE MY GALACTIC GAUNTLETS FROM SOME DUMB ALIENS?
YEAH?
THERE'S A TEENSY CHANCE THEY WERE ACTUALLY INTERGALACTIC DEATH GODS.
BETTER THAN THEIR PEACETIME BANNERS. THOSE SAY "OUR POOL IS BATHING SUIT OPTIONAL!"

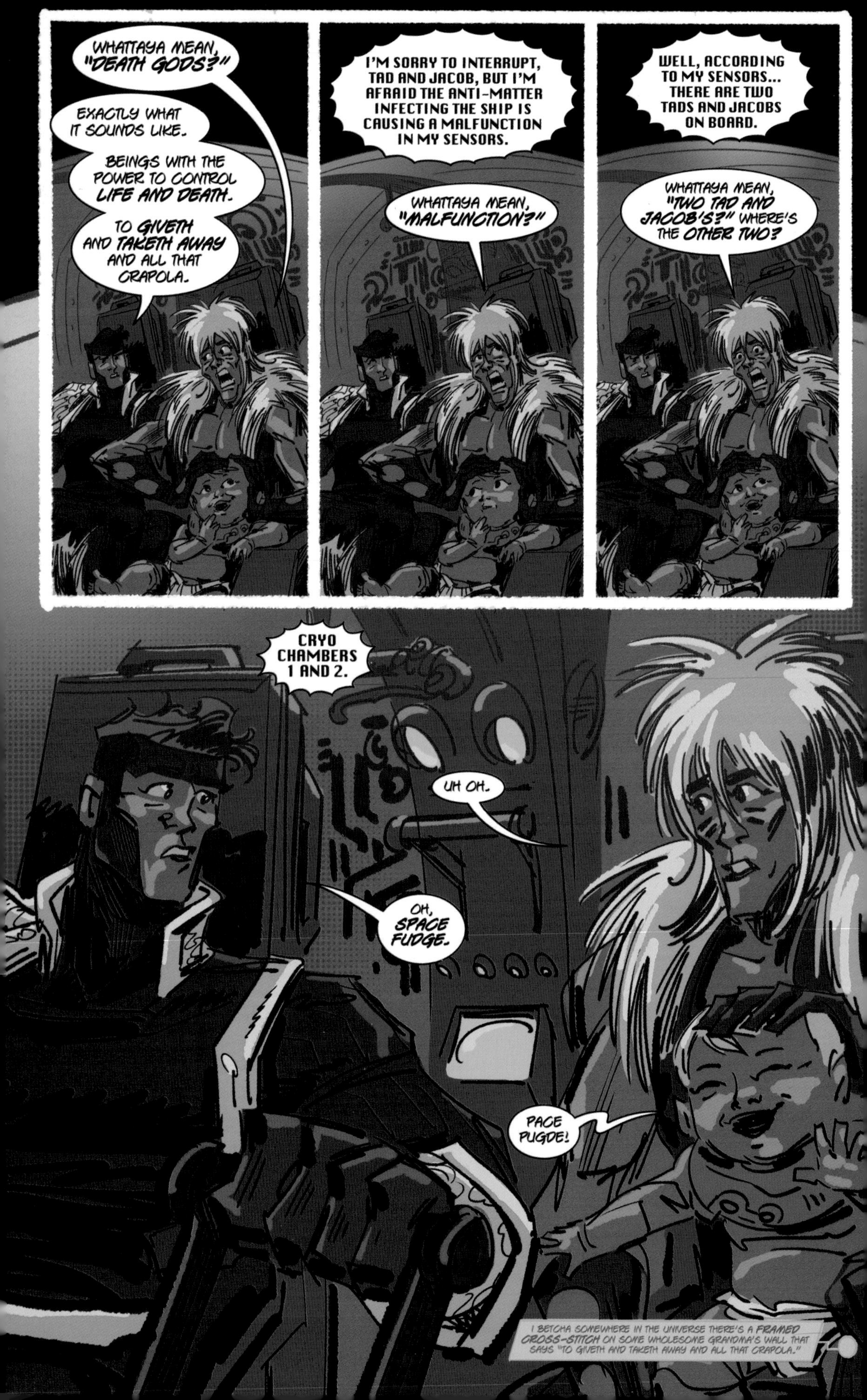
WHATTAYA MEAN, "DEATH GODS?"
EXACTLY WHAT IT SOUNDS LIKE.
BEINGS WITH THE POWER TO CONTROL LIFE AND DEATH.
TO GIVETH AND TAKETH AWAY AND ALL THAT CRAPOLA.
I'M SORRY TO INTERRUPT, TAD AND JACOB, BUT I'M AFRAID THE ANTI-MATTER INFECTING THE SHIP IS CAUSING A MALFUNCTION IN MY SENSORS.
WHATTAYA MEAN, "MALFUNCTION?"
WELL, ACCORDING TO MY SENSORS... THERE ARE TWO TADS AND JACOBS ON BOARD.
WHATTAYA MEAN, "TWO TAD AND JACOB'S?" WHERE'S THE OTHER TWO?
CRYO CHAMBERS 1 AND 2.
UH OH.
OH, SPACE FUDGE.
PACE PUGDE!
I BETCHA SOMEWHERE IN THE UNIVERSE THERE'S A FRAMED CROSS-STITCH ON SOME WHOLESOME GRANDMA'S WALL THAT SAYS "TO GIVETH AND TAKETH AWAY AND ALL THAT CRAPOLA."

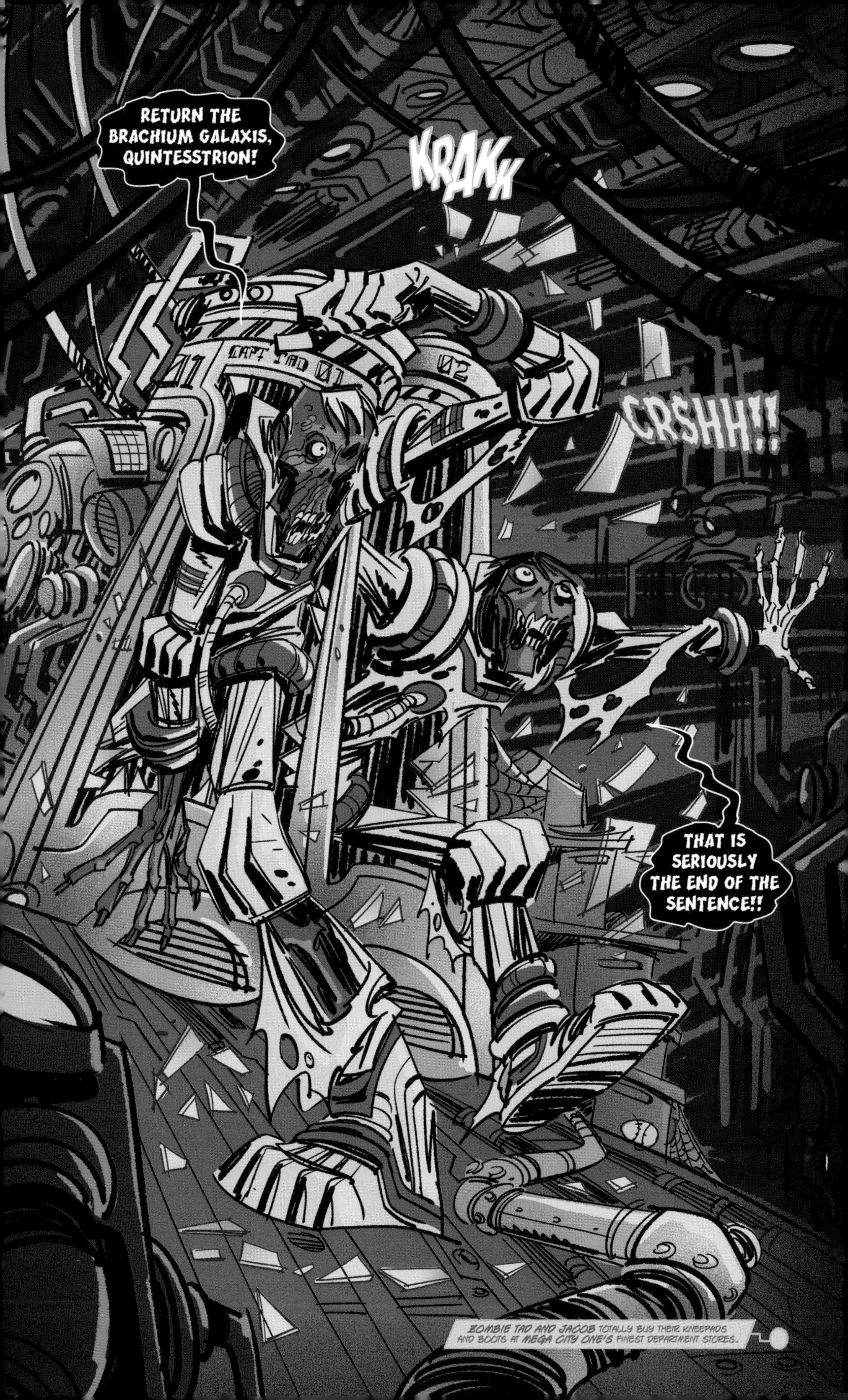
RETURN THE BRACHIUM GALAXIS, QUINTESSTRION!
KRAKK
CAPT TAD 01
CRSHH!!
THAT IS SERIOUSLY THE END OF THE SENTENCE!!
ZOMBIE TAD AND JACOB TOTALLY BUY THEIR KNEEPADS AND BOOTS AT MEGA CITY ONE'S FINEST DEPARTMENT STORES.

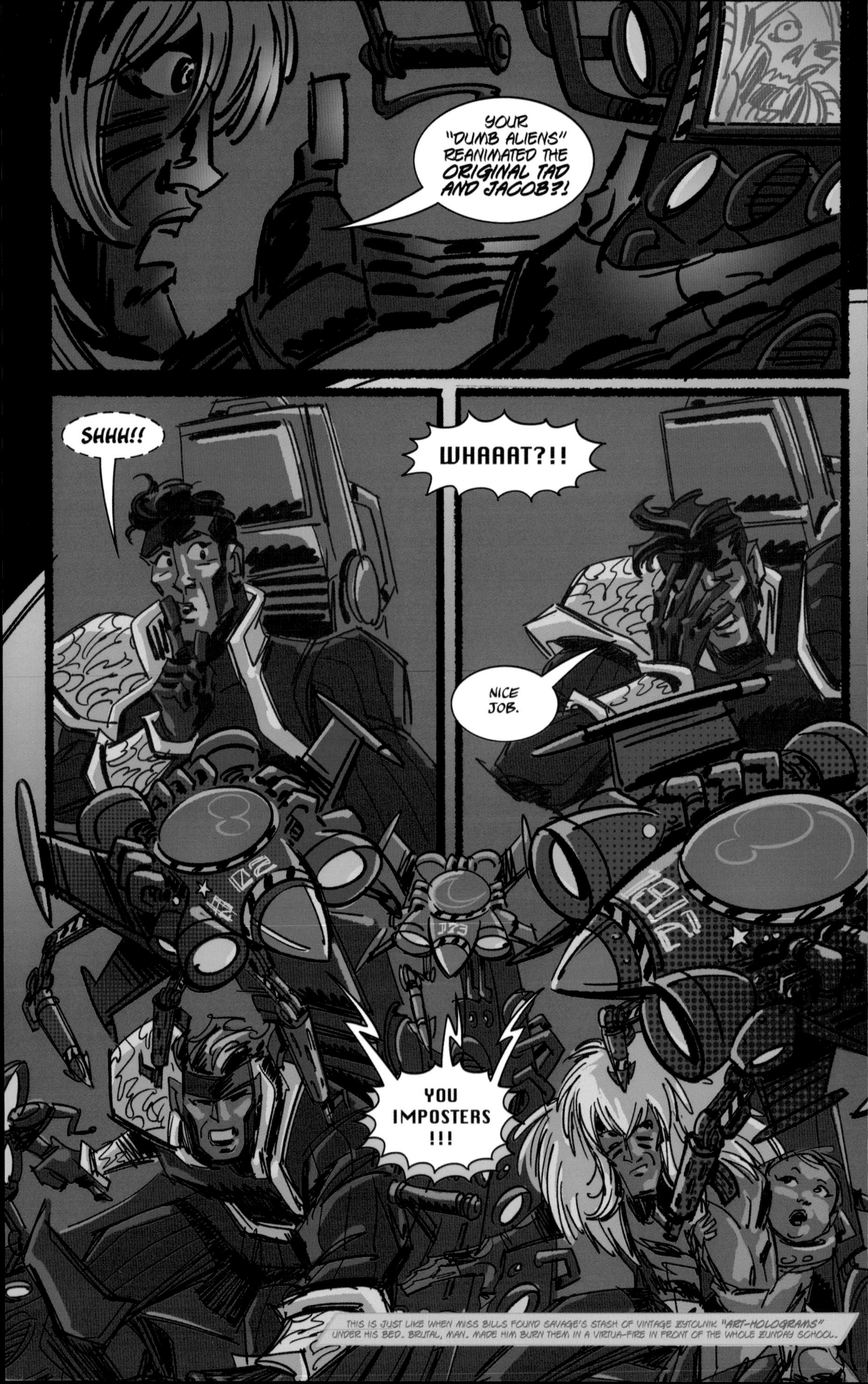
YOUR "DUMB ALIENS" REANIMATED THE ORIGINAL TAD AND JACOB?!
SHHH!!
WHAAAT?!!
NICE JOB.
YOU IMPOSTERS !!!
THIS IS JUST LIKE WHEN MISS BILLS FOUND SAVAGE'S STASH OF VINTAGE ZYTOLNIK "ART-HOLOGRAMS" UNDER HIS BED. BRUTAL, MAN. MADE HIM BURN THEM IN A VIRTUA-FIRE IN FRONT OF THE WHOLE ZUNDAY SCHOOL.

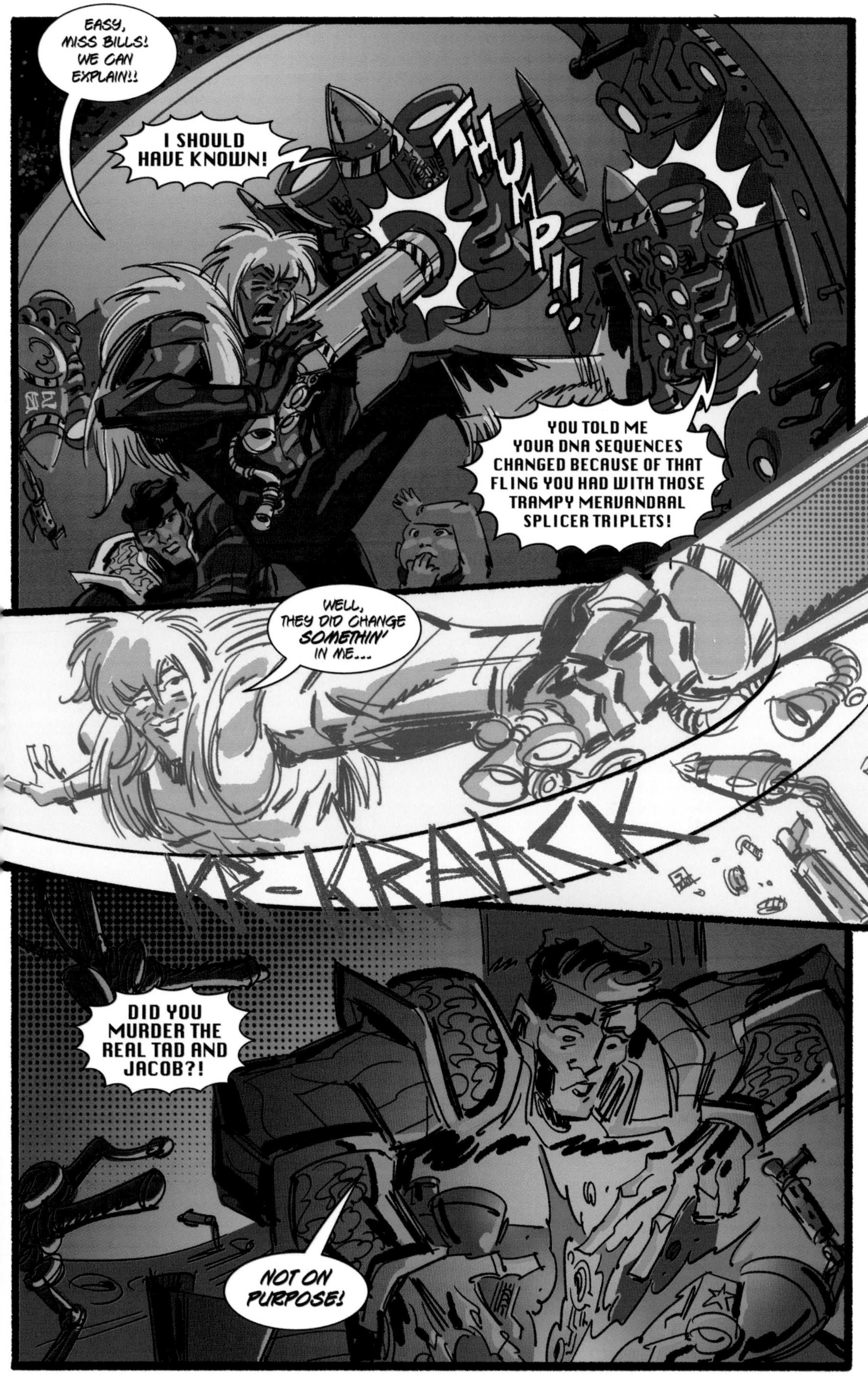
EASY, MISS BILLS! WE CAN EXPLAIN!!
I SHOULD HAVE KNOWN!
THUMP!!
YOU TOLD ME YOUR DNA SEQUENCES CHANGED BECAUSE OF THAT FLING YOU HAD WITH THOSE TRAMPY MERVANDRAL SPLICER TRIPLETS!
WELL, THEY DID CHANGE SOMETHIN' IN ME...
KR-KRAACK
DID YOU MURDER THE REAL TAD AND JACOB?!
NOT ON PURPOSE!

MISS BILLS *KNEW* THOSE *SPLICER TRIPLETS* WERE BAD NEWS.. WITH THEIR RIPPED JEANS AND THEIR LOOSE TALK.. WHO KNOWS *WHAT* KIND OF COMET-HIVE-MIND THEY WERE RAISED BY?!

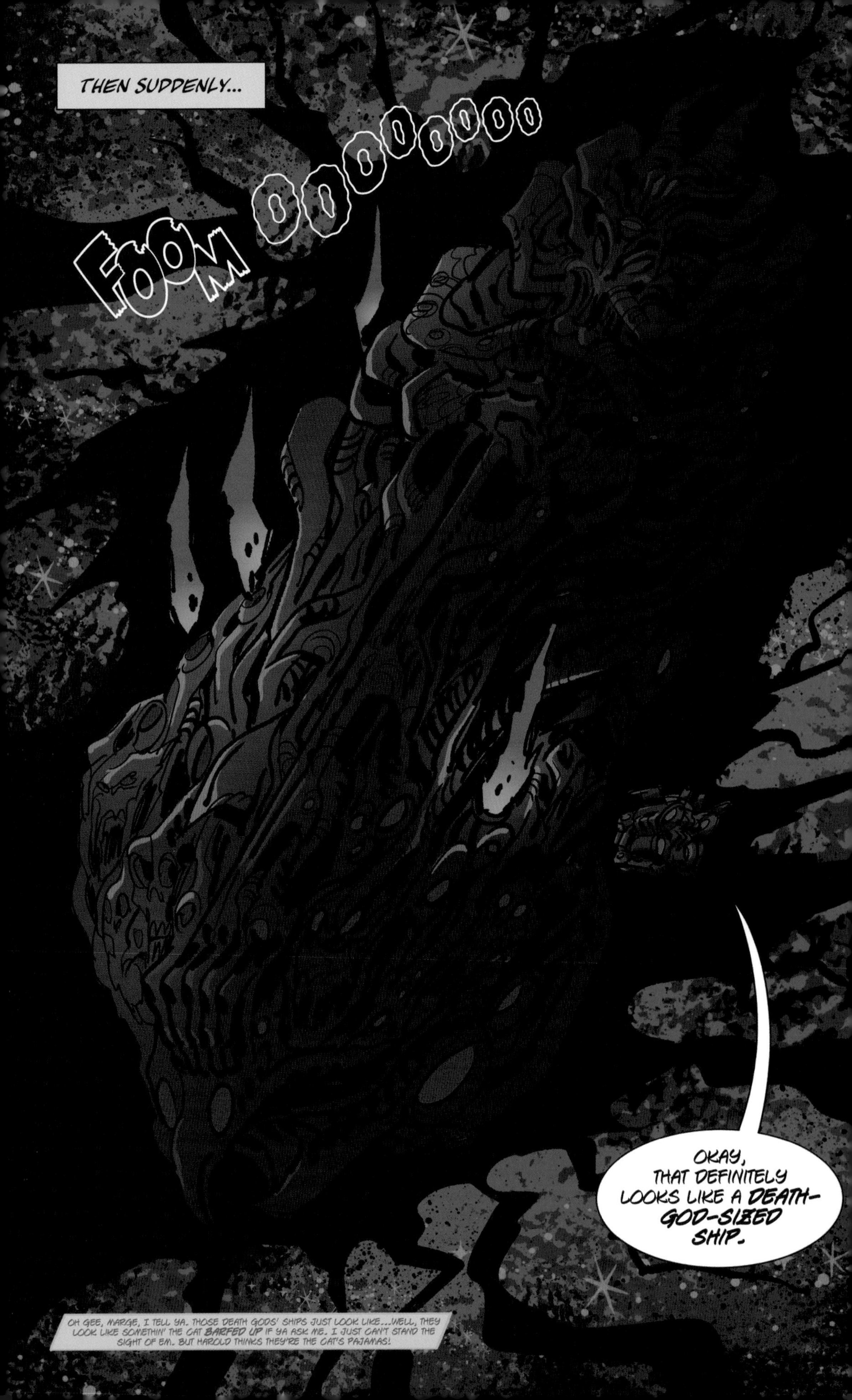
THEN SUDDENLY...
FOOM OOOOOOOOO
OKAY, THAT DEFINITELY LOOKS LIKE A **DEATH-GOD-SIZED SHIP.**
OH GEE, MARGE, I TELL YA. THOSE DEATH GODS' SHIPS JUST LOOK LIKE...WELL, THEY LOOK LIKE SOMETHIN' THE CAT **BARFED UP** IF YA ASK ME. I JUST CAN'T STAND THE SIGHT OF EM. BUT HAROLD THINKS THEY'RE THE CAT'S PAJAMAS!

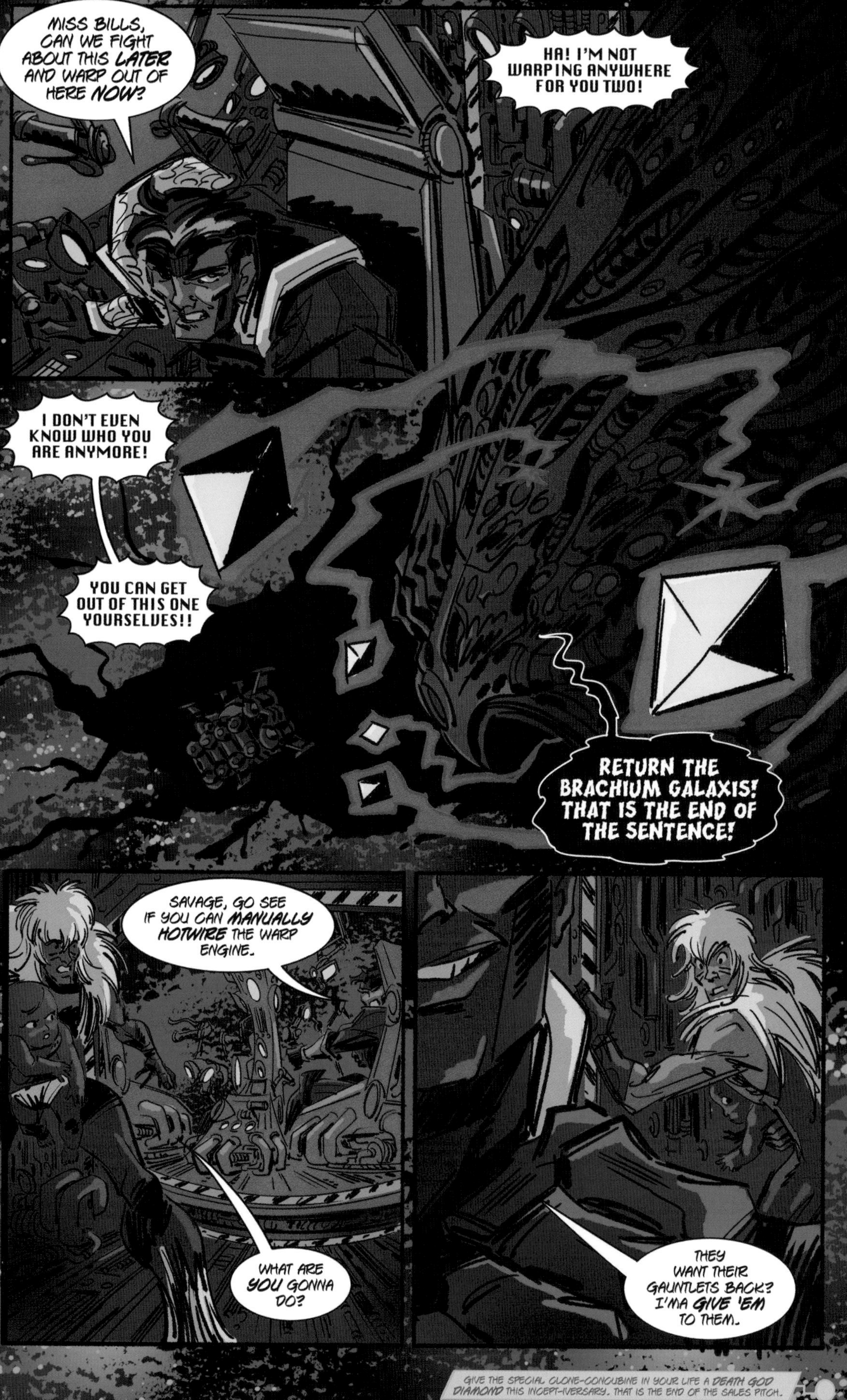
MISS BILLS, CAN WE FIGHT ABOUT THIS LATER AND WARP OUT OF HERE NOW?
HA! I'M NOT WARPING ANYWHERE FOR YOU TWO!
I DON'T EVEN KNOW WHO YOU ARE ANYMORE!
YOU CAN GET OUT OF THIS ONE YOURSELVES!!
RETURN THE BRACHIUM GALAXIS! THAT IS THE END OF THE SENTENCE!
SAVAGE, GO SEE IF YOU CAN MANUALLY HOTWIRE THE WARP ENGINE.
WHAT ARE YOU GONNA DO?
THEY WANT THEIR GAUNTLETS BACK? I'MA GIVE 'EM TO THEM.

GIVE THE SPECIAL CLONE-CONCUBINE IN YOUR LIFE A DEATH GOD DIAMOND THIS INCEPT-IVERSARY. THAT IS THE END OF THE SALES PITCH.

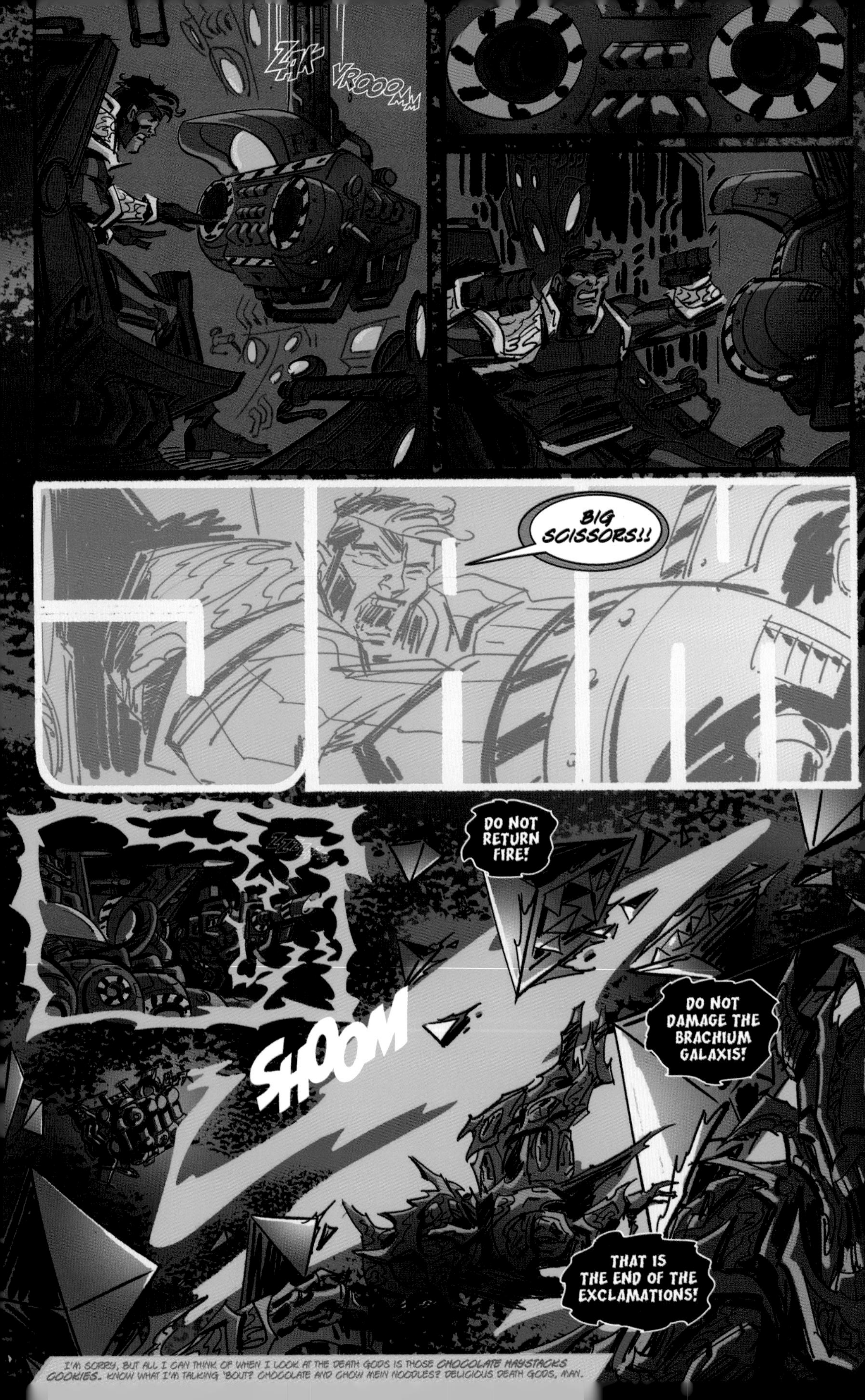
ZAK
VROOOMMM
BIG SCISSORS!!
DO NOT RETURN FIRE!
SHOOM
DO NOT DAMAGE THE BRACHIUM GALAXIS!
THAT IS THE END OF THE EXCLAMATIONS!
I'M SORRY, BUT ALL I CAN THINK OF WHEN I LOOK AT THE DEATH GODS IS THOSE CHOCOLATE HAYSTACKS COOKIES. KNOW WHAT I'M TALKING 'BOUT? CHOCOLATE AND CHOW MEIN NOODLES? DELICIOUS DEATH GODS, MAN.

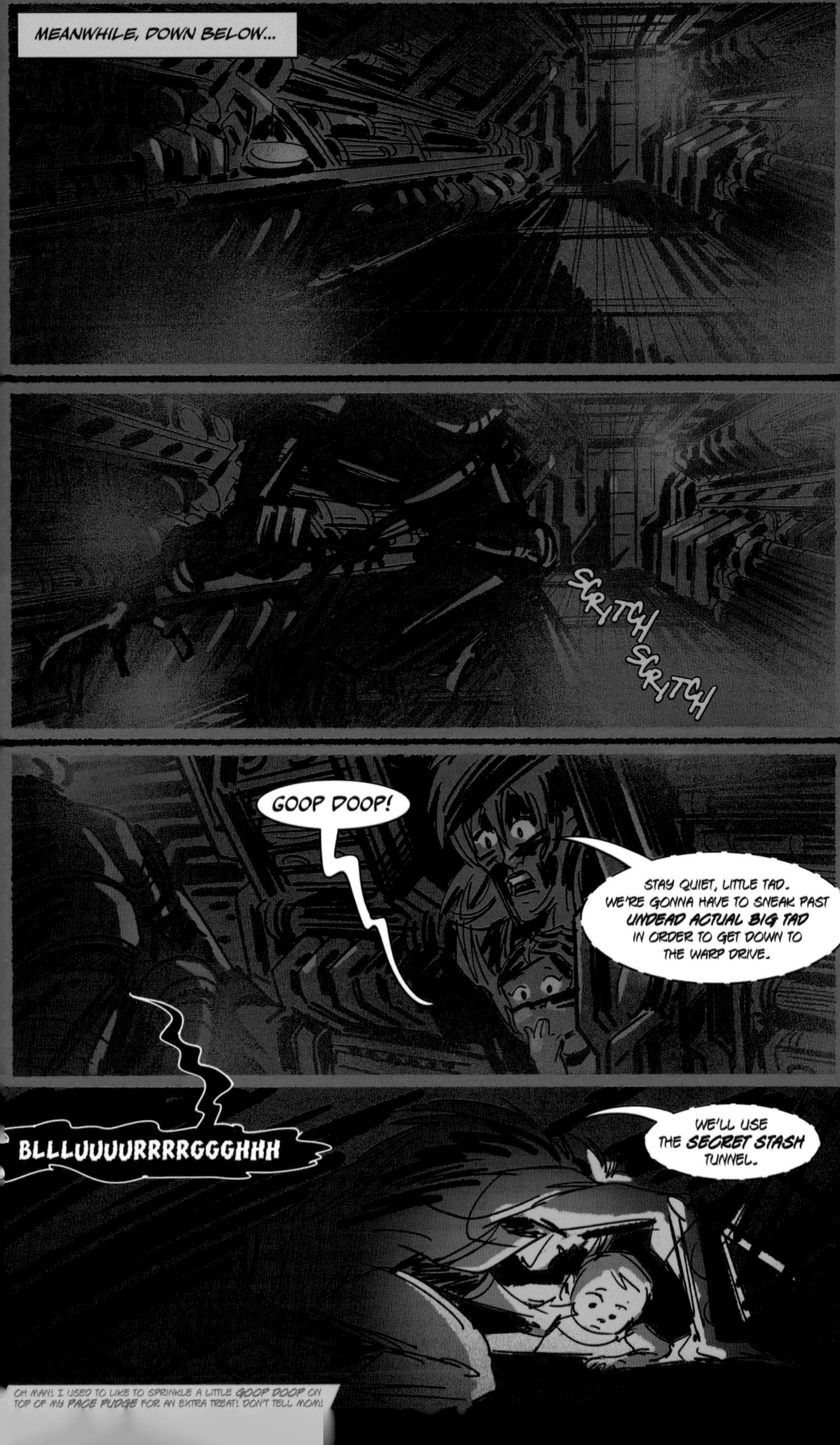
MEANWHILE, DOWN BELOW...
SCRITCH SCRITCH
GOOP DOOP!
STAY QUIET, LITTLE TAD. WE'RE GONNA HAVE TO SNEAK PAST UNDEAD ACTUAL BIG TAD IN ORDER TO GET DOWN TO THE WARP DRIVE.
BLLLUUUURRRRGGGHHH
WE'LL USE THE SECRET STASH TUNNEL.
OH MAN! I USED TO LIKE TO SPRINKLE A LITTLE GOOP DOOP ON TOP OF MY PACE PUDGE FOR AN EXTRA TREAT! DON'T TELL MOM!

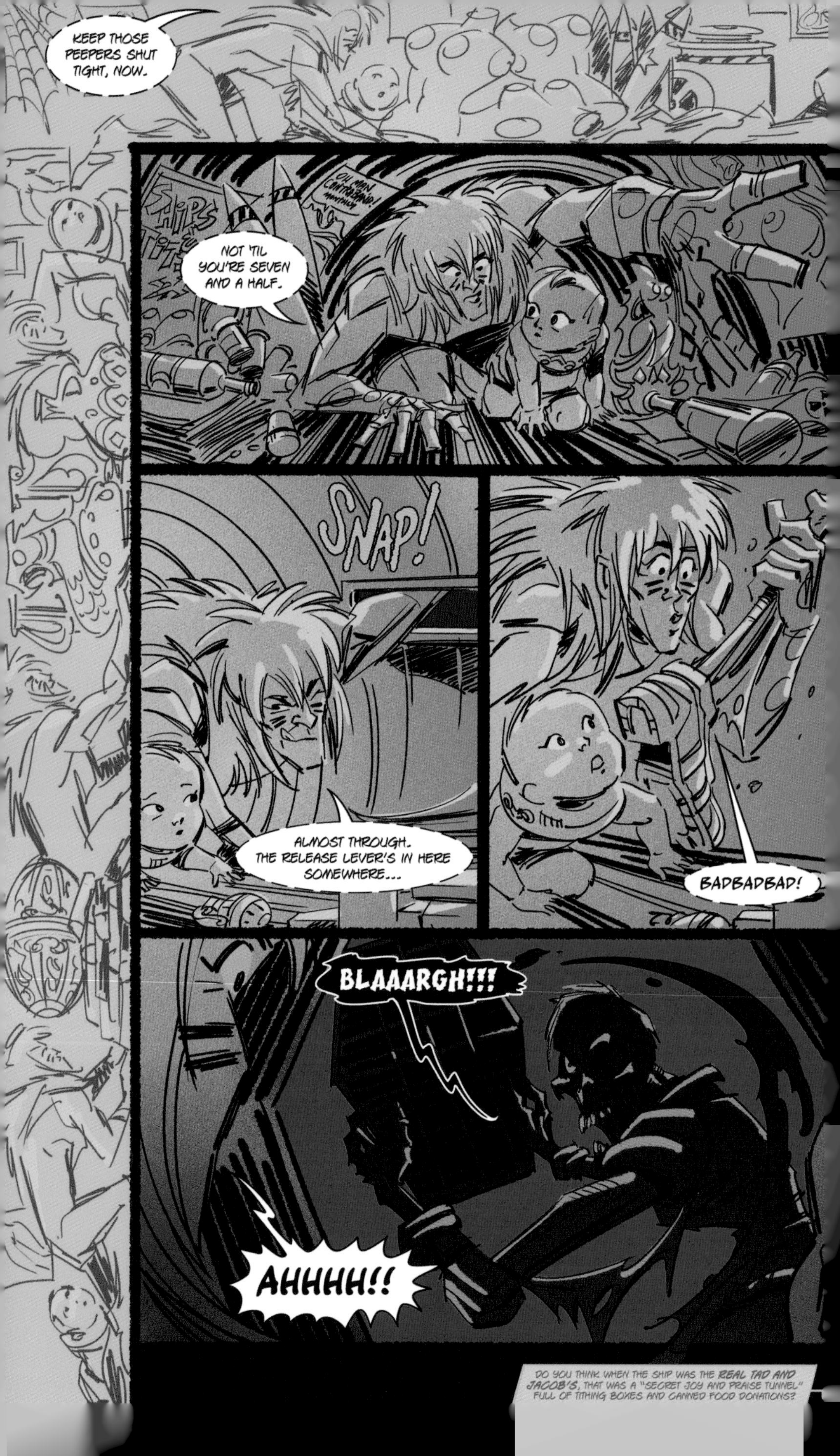
KEEP THOSE PEEPERS SHUT TIGHT, NOW.
NOT 'TIL YOU'RE SEVEN AND A HALF.
SNAP!
ALMOST THROUGH. THE RELEASE LEVER'S IN HERE SOMEWHERE...
BADBADBAD!
BLAAARGH!!!
AHHHH!!
DO YOU THINK WHEN THE SHIP WAS THE REAL TAD AND JACOB'S, THAT WAS A "SECRET JOY AND PRAISE TUNNEL" FULL OF TITHING BOXES AND CANNED FOOD DONATIONS?

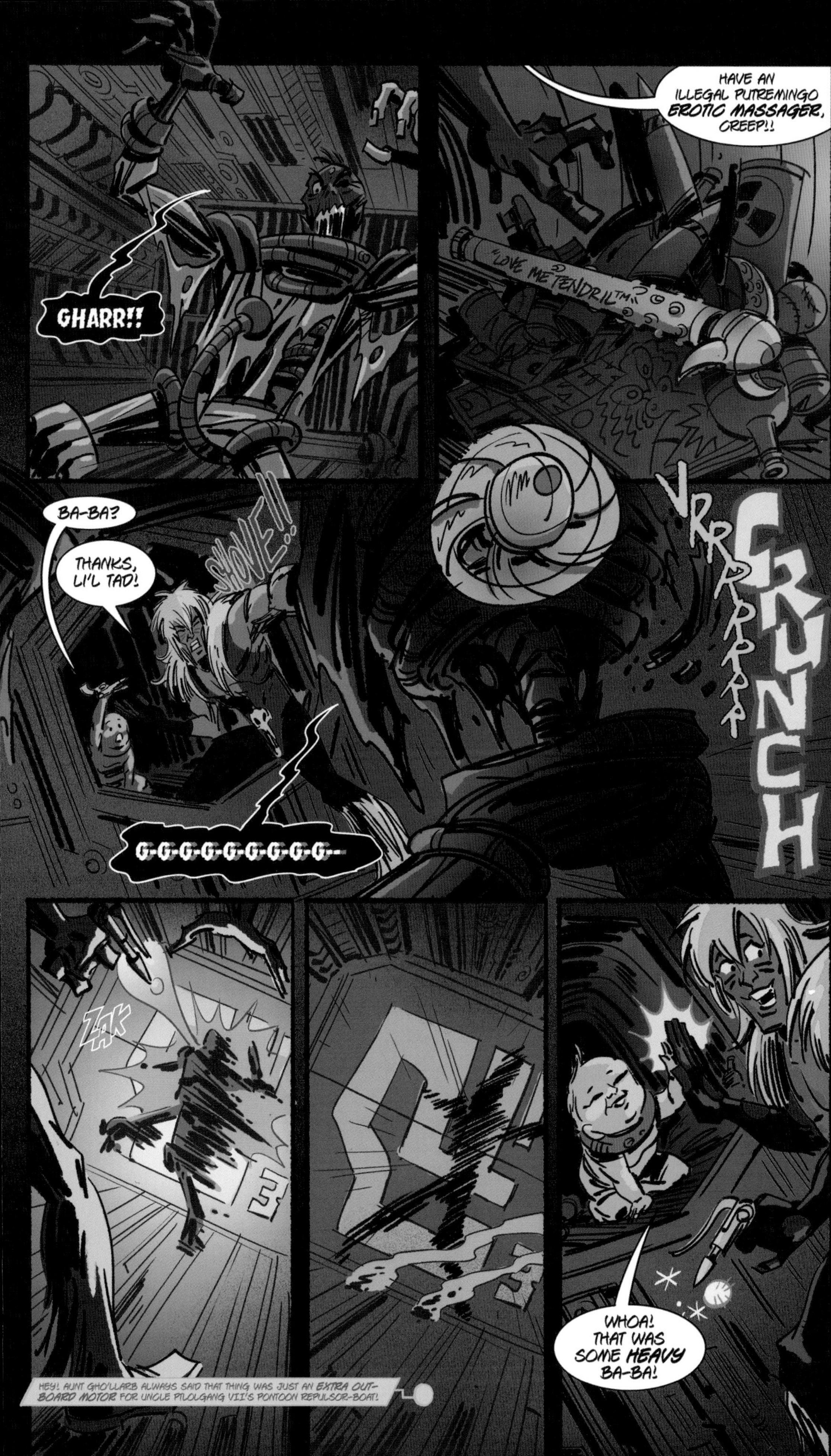
GHARR!!
HAVE AN ILLEGAL PUTREMINGO EROTIC MASSAGER, CREEP!!
"LOVE ME TENDRIL™"
BA-BA?
THANKS, LI'L TAD!
SHOVE!!
G-G-G-G-G-G-G-G-G--
VRRRRRRRR
CRUNCH
ZAK
HEY! AUNT GHO'LLARB ALWAYS SAID THAT THING WAS JUST AN EXTRA OUT-BOARD MOTOR FOR UNCLE PILOLGANG VII'S PONTOON REPULSOR-BOAT!
WHOA! THAT WAS SOME HEAVY BA-BA!

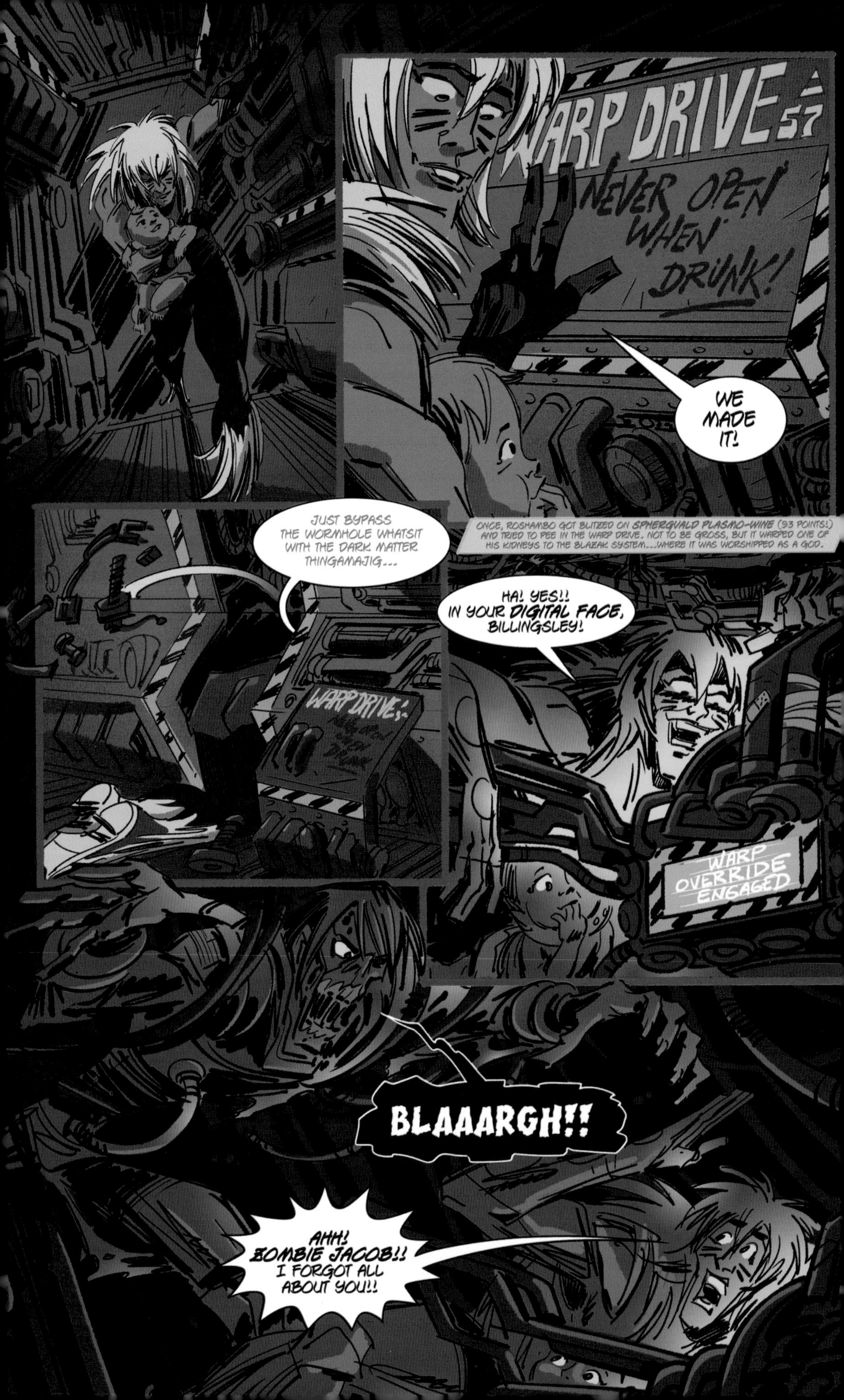
WARP DRIVE 57
NEVER OPEN WHEN DRUNK!
WE MADE IT!
JUST BYPASS THE WORMHOLE WHATSIT WITH THE DARK MATTER THINGAMAJIG...
WARP DRIVE
ONCE, ROSHAMBO GOT BLITZED ON *SPHERGVALD PLASMO-WINE* (93 POINTS!) AND TRIED TO PEE IN THE WARP DRIVE. NOT TO BE GROSS, BUT IT WARPED ONE OF HIS KIDNEYS TO THE BLAZAK SYSTEM...WHERE IT WAS WORSHIPPED AS A GOD.
HA! YES!! IN YOUR ***DIGITAL FACE,*** BILLINGSLEY!
WARP OVERRIDE ENGAGED
BLAARGH!!
AHH! ***ZOMBIE JACOB!!*** I FORGOT ALL ABOUT YOU!!

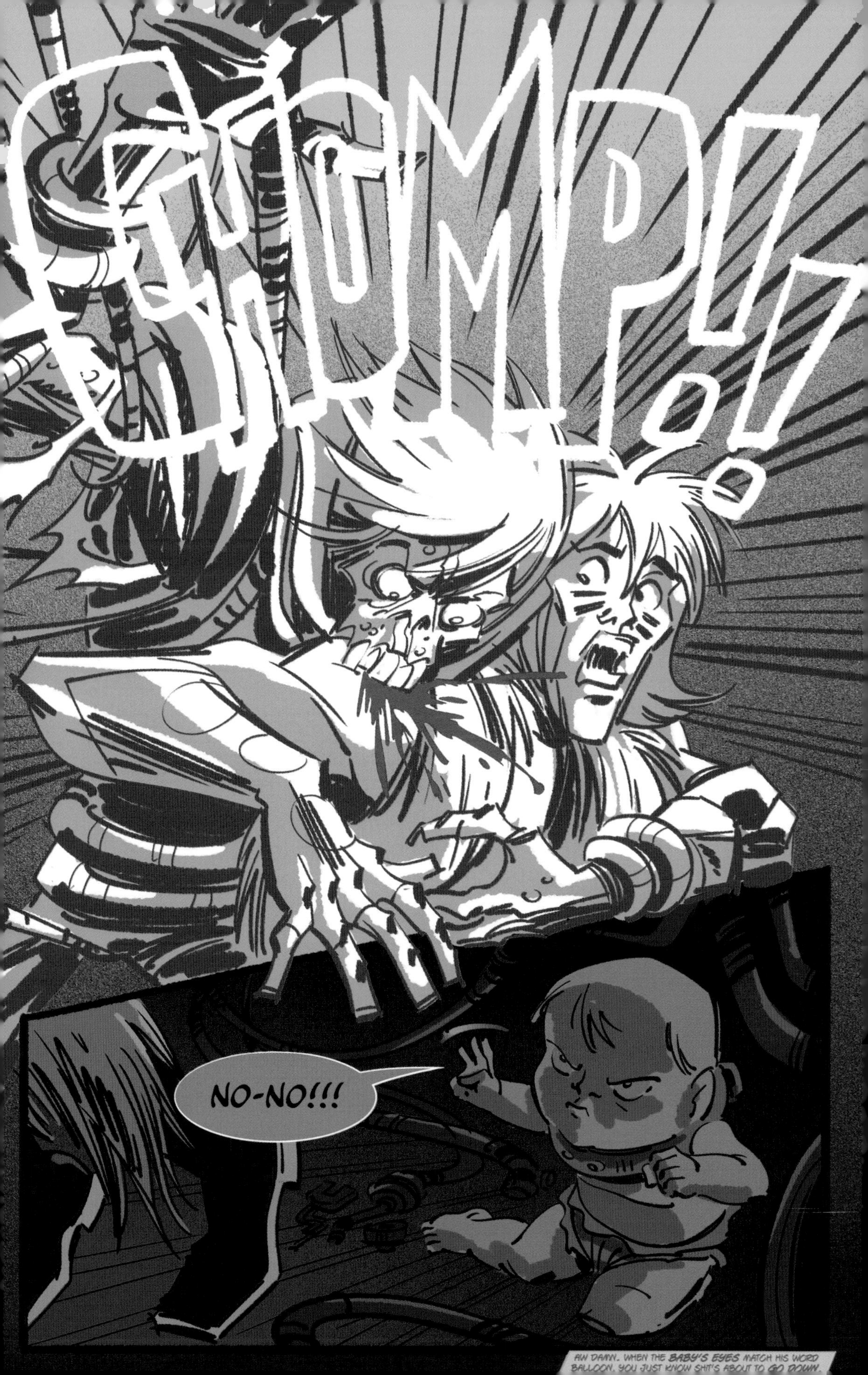
CHOMP!!
NO-NO!!!
AW DAMN. WHEN THE BABY'S EYES MATCH HIS WORD BALLOON, YOU JUST KNOW SHIT'S ABOUT TO GO DOWN.

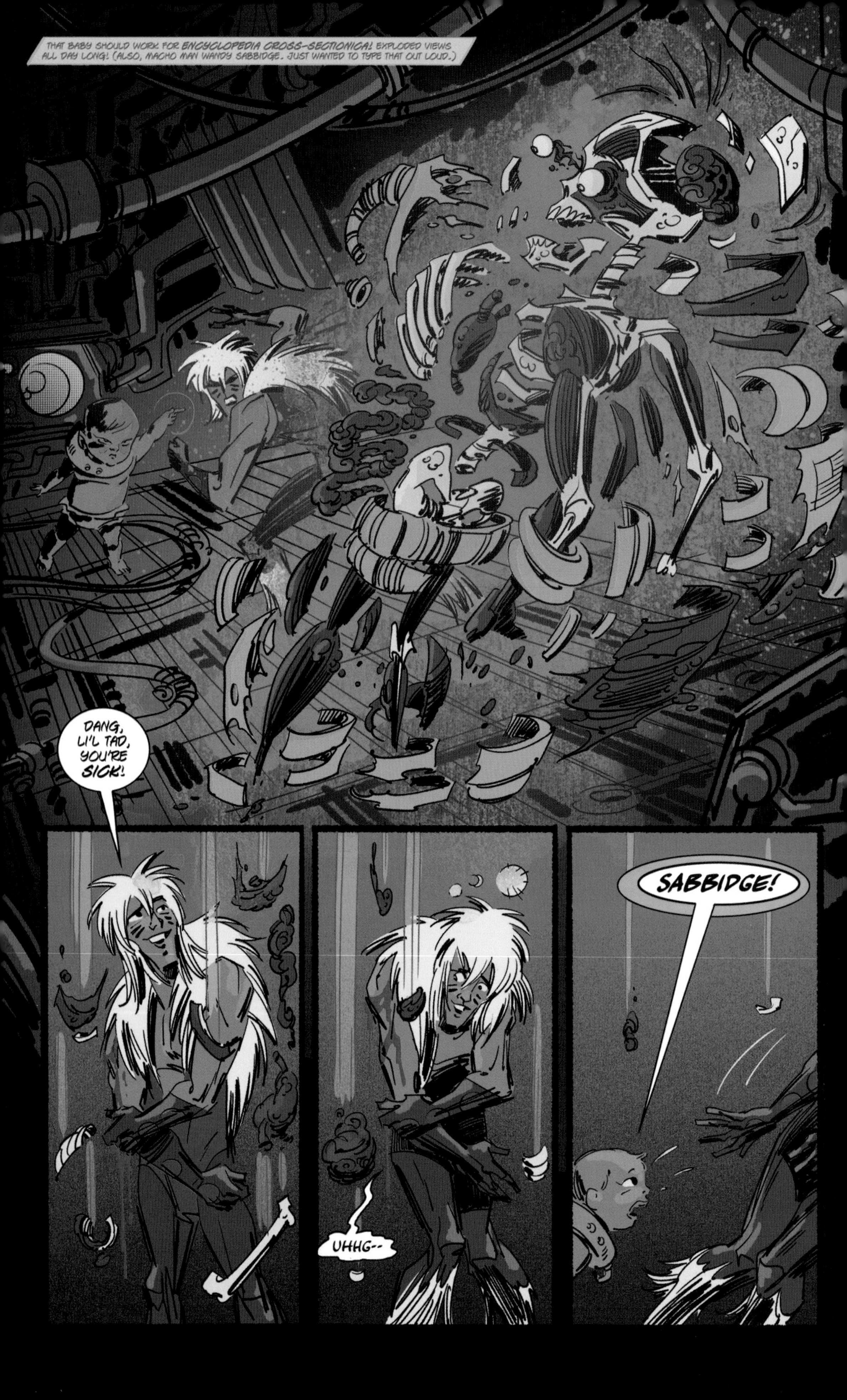
THAT BABY SHOULD WORK FOR ENCYCLOPEDIA CROSS-SECTIONICA! EXPLODED VIEWS ALL DAY LONG! (ALSO, MACHO MAN WANDY SABBIDGE. JUST WANTED TO TYPE THAT OUT LOUD.)
DANG, LI'L TAD, YOU'RE SICK!
UHHG--
SABBIDGE!

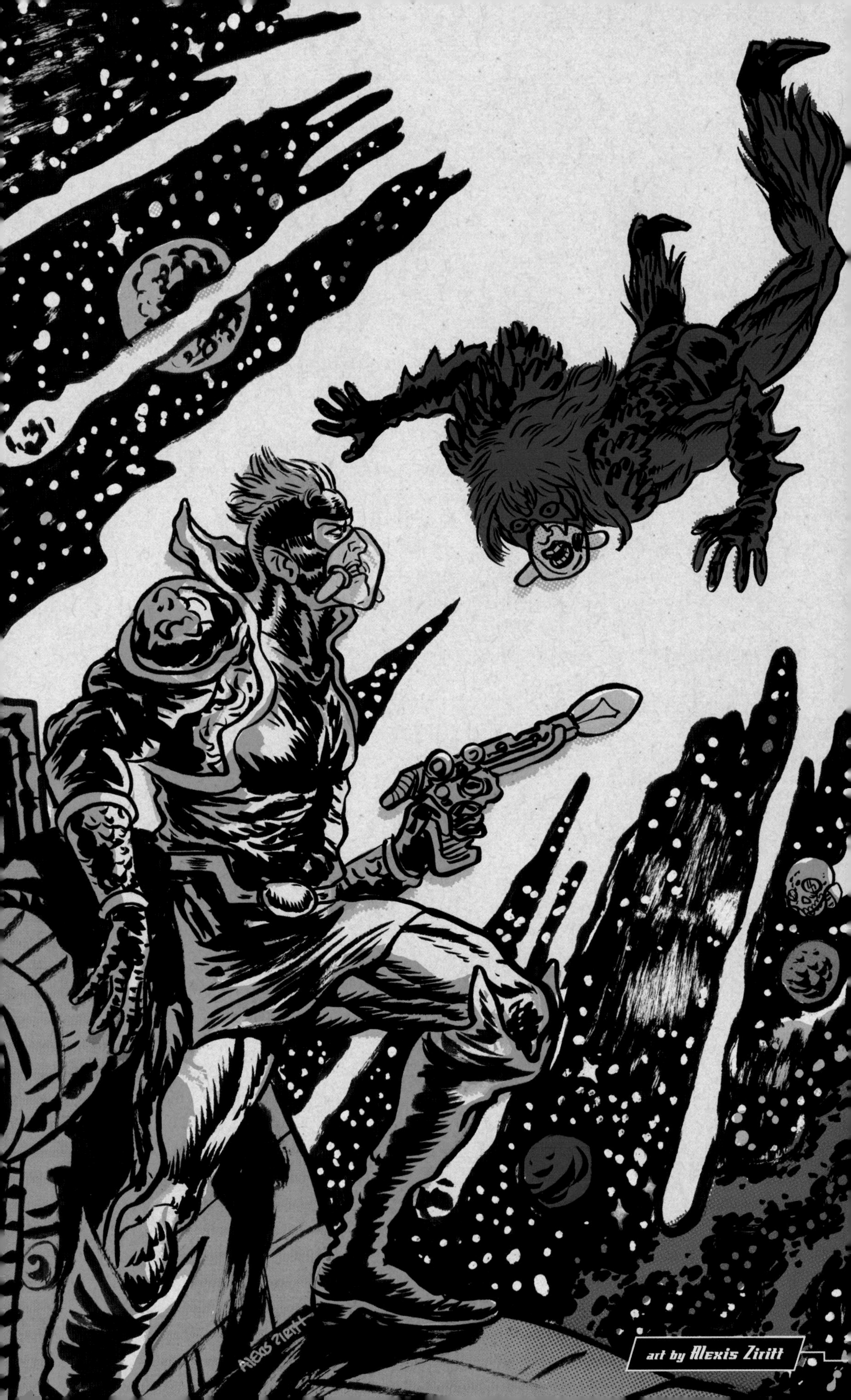

art by Alexis Ziritt

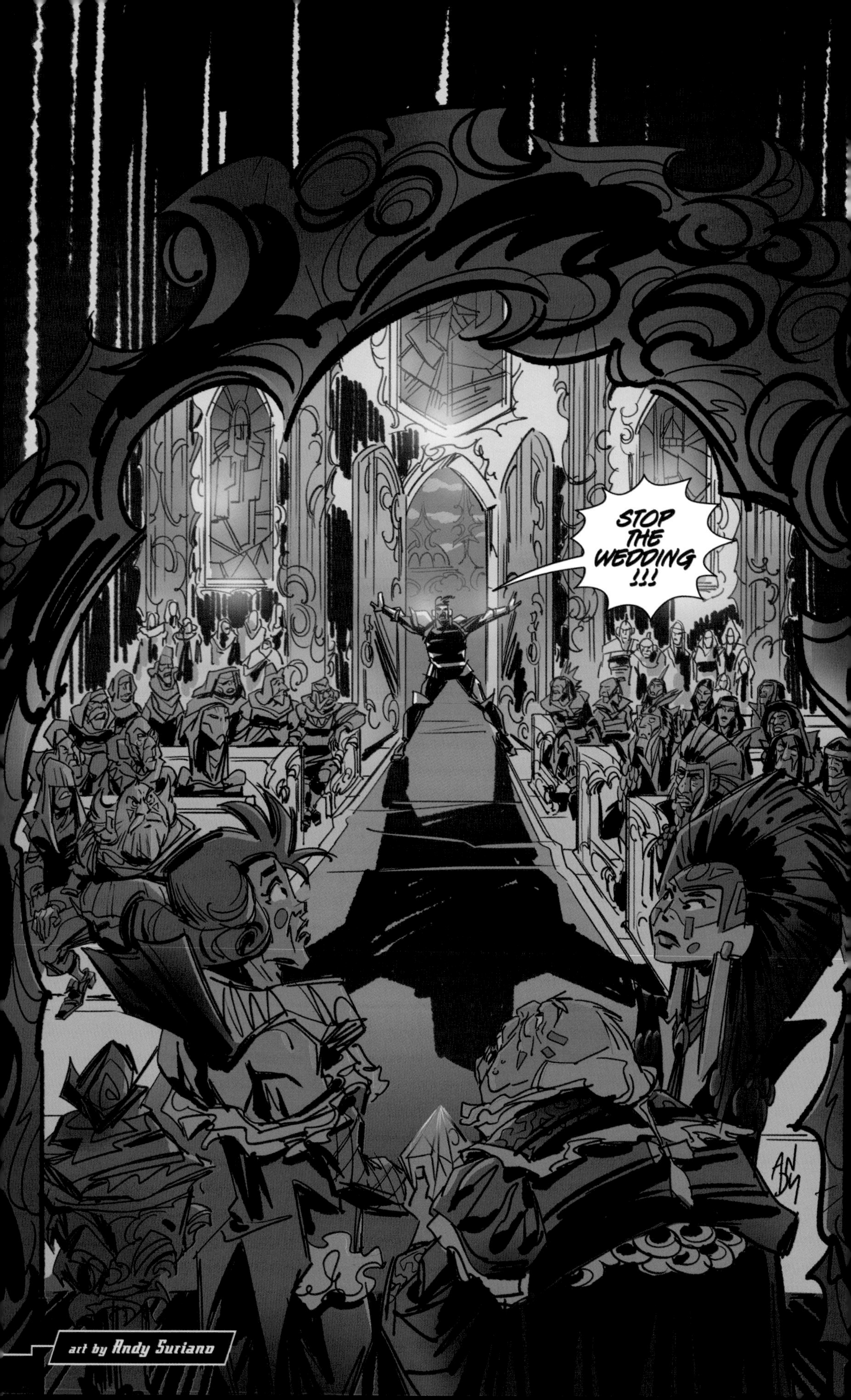
STOP THE WEDDING !!!
ANDY

art by Andy Suriano

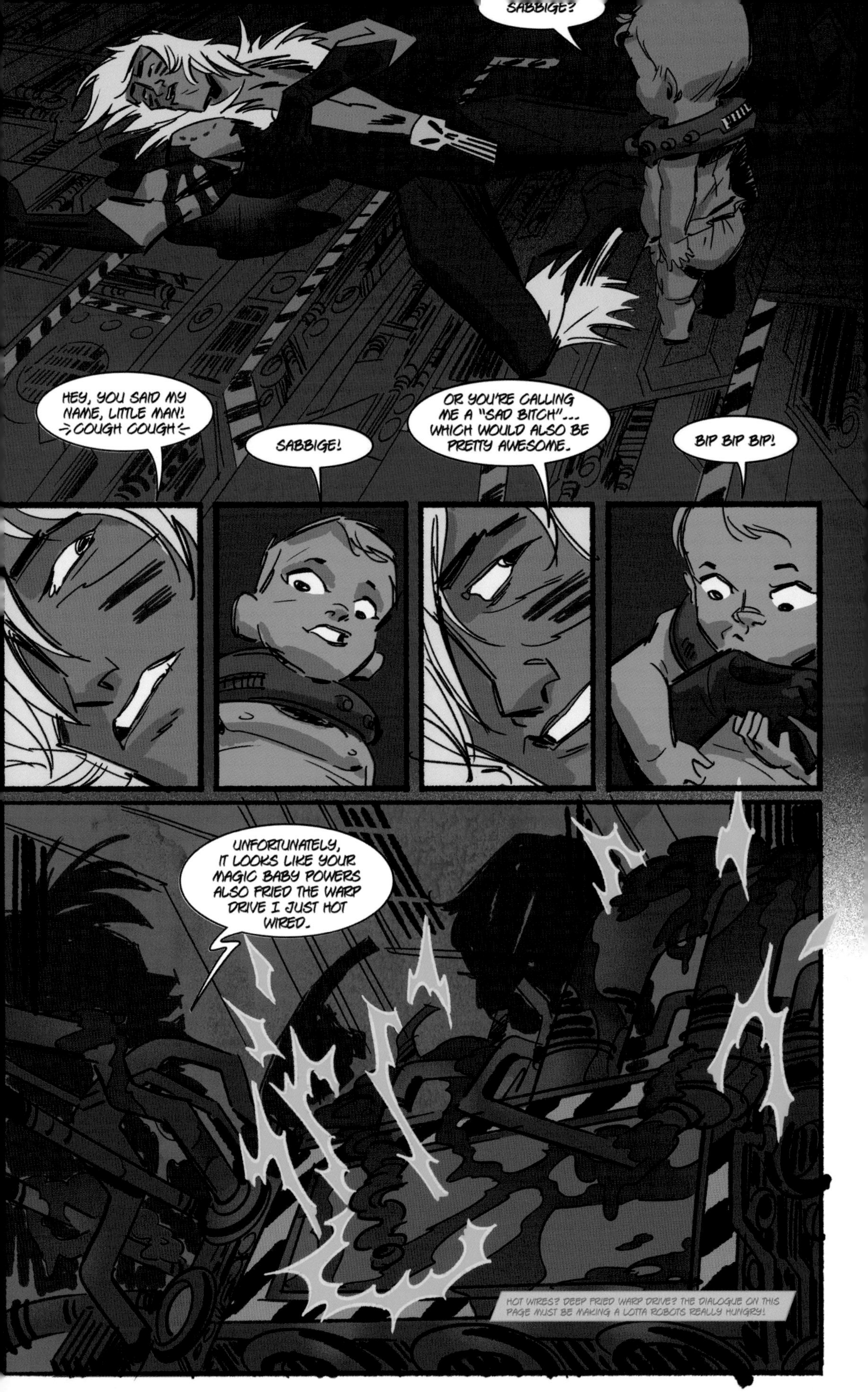
SABBIGE?
HEY, YOU SAID MY NAME, LITTLE MAN! *COUGH COUGH*
SABBIGE!
OR YOU'RE CALLING ME A "SAD BITCH"... WHICH WOULD ALSO BE PRETTY AWESOME.
BIP BIP BIP!
UNFORTUNATELY, IT LOOKS LIKE YOUR MAGIC BABY POWERS ALSO FRIED THE WARP DRIVE I JUST HOT WIRED.
HOT WIRES? DEEP FRIED WARP DRIVE? THE DIALOGUE ON THIS PAGE MUST BE MAKING A LOTTA ROBOTS REALLY HUNGRY!

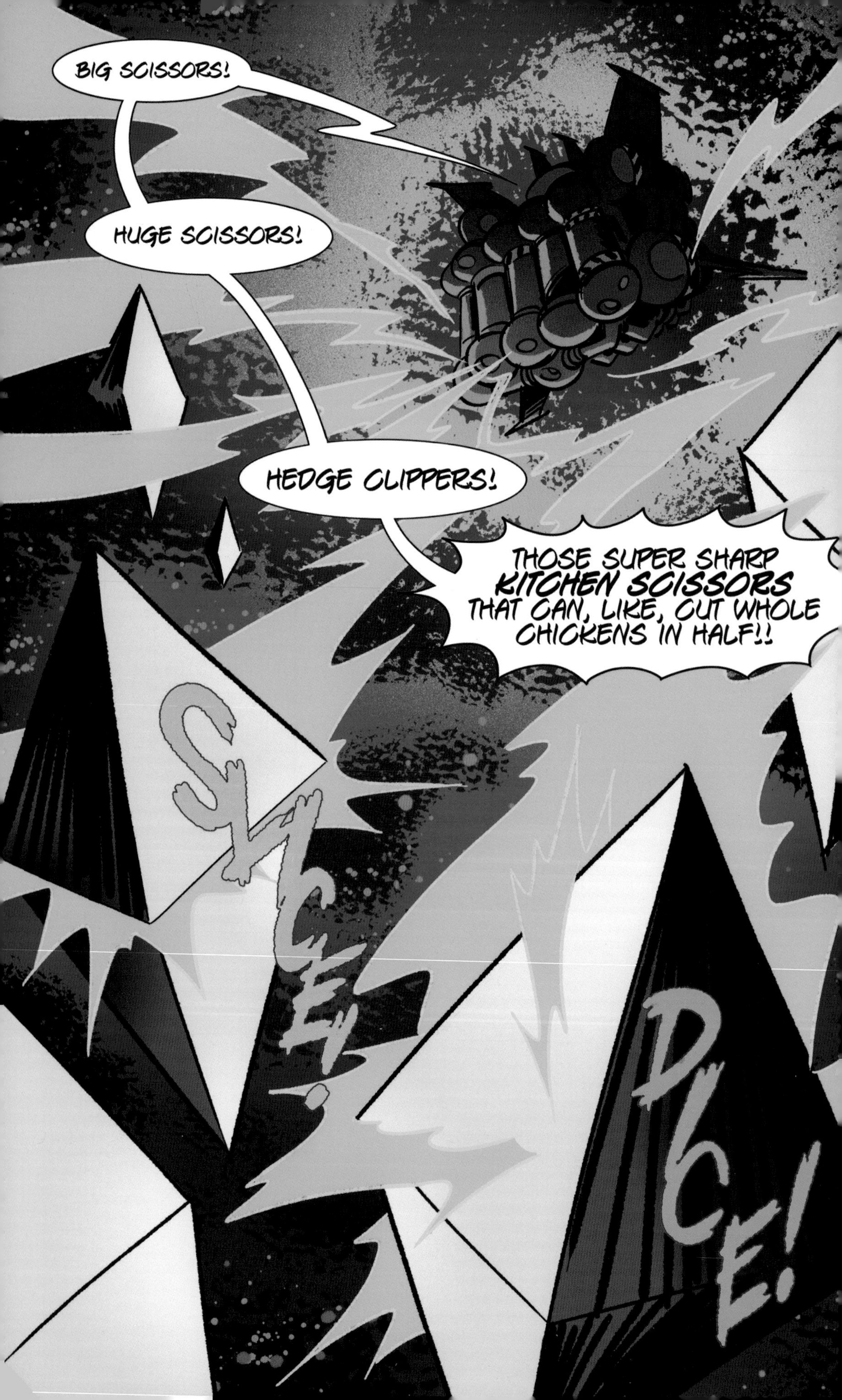
BIG SCISSORS!
HUGE SCISSORS!
HEDGE CLIPPERS!
THOSE SUPER SHARP **KITCHEN SCISSORS** THAT CAN, LIKE, CUT WHOLE CHICKENS IN HALF!!
SNCH!
DICE!

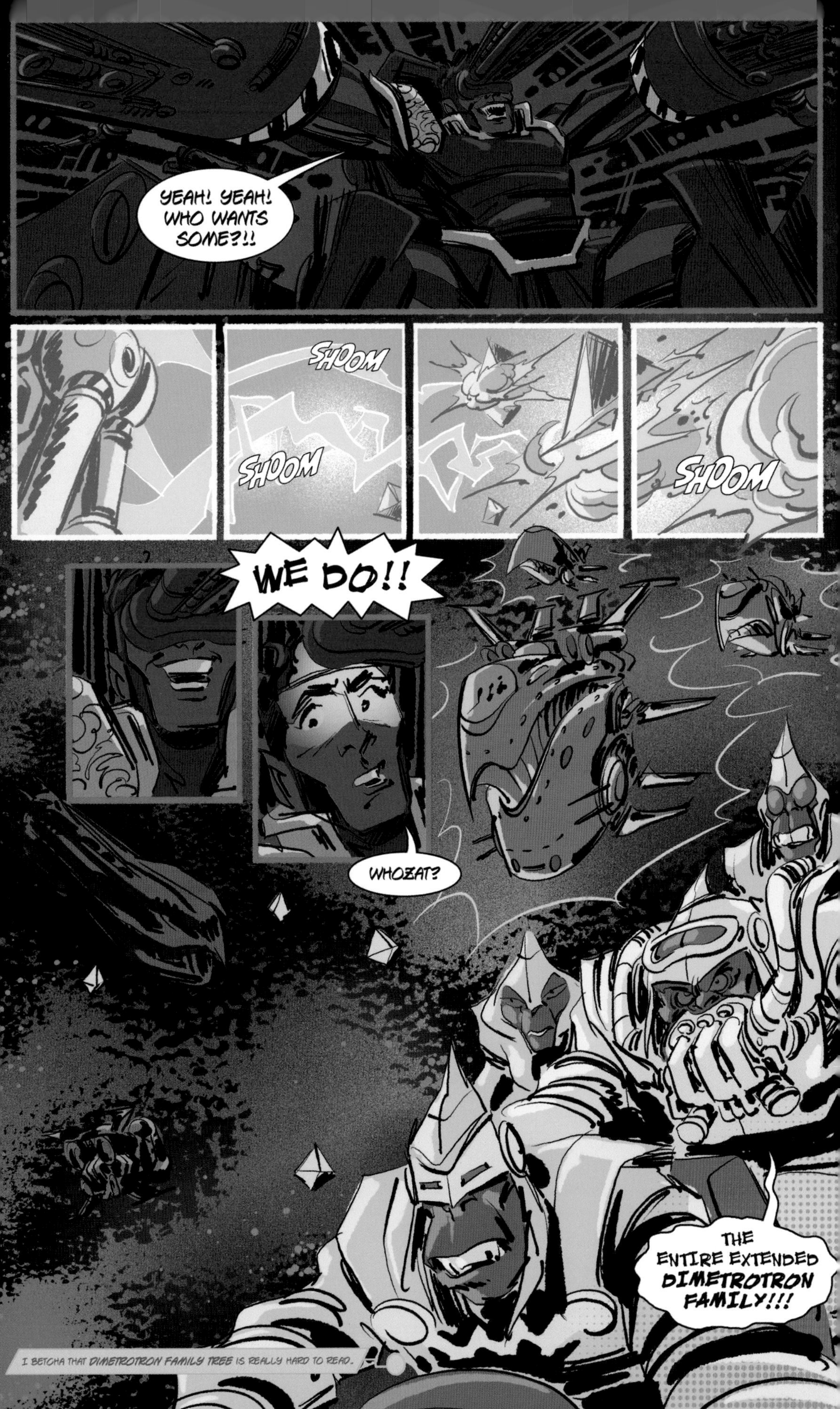
YEAH! YEAH! WHO WANTS SOME?!!
SHOOM
SHOOM
SHOOM
WE DO!!
WHOZAT?
THE ENTIRE EXTENDED DIMETROTRON FAMILY!!!
I BETCHA THAT DIMETROTRON FAMILY TREE IS REALLY HARD TO READ.

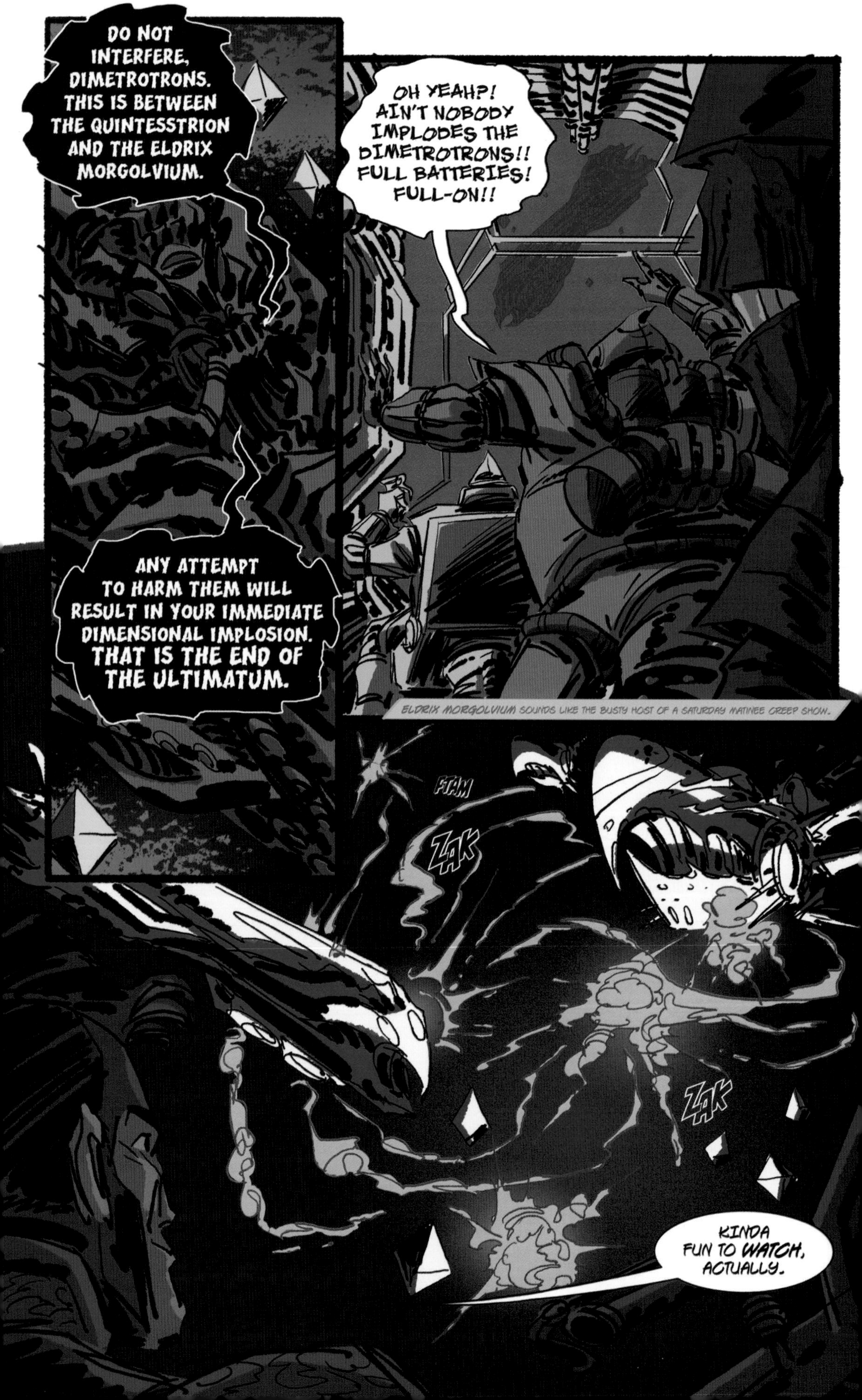
DO NOT INTERFERE, DIMETROTRONS. THIS IS BETWEEN THE QUINTESSTRION AND THE ELDRIX MORGOLVIUM.
OH YEAH?! AIN'T NOBODY IMPLODES THE DIMETROTRONS!! FULL BATTERIES! FULL-ON!!
ANY ATTEMPT TO HARM THEM WILL RESULT IN YOUR IMMEDIATE DIMENSIONAL IMPLOSION. THAT IS THE END OF THE ULTIMATUM.
ELDRIX MORGOLVIUM SOUNDS LIKE THE BUSTY HOST OF A SATURDAY MATINEE CREEP SHOW.
FTAM
ZAK
ZAK
KINDA FUN TO WATCH, ACTUALLY.

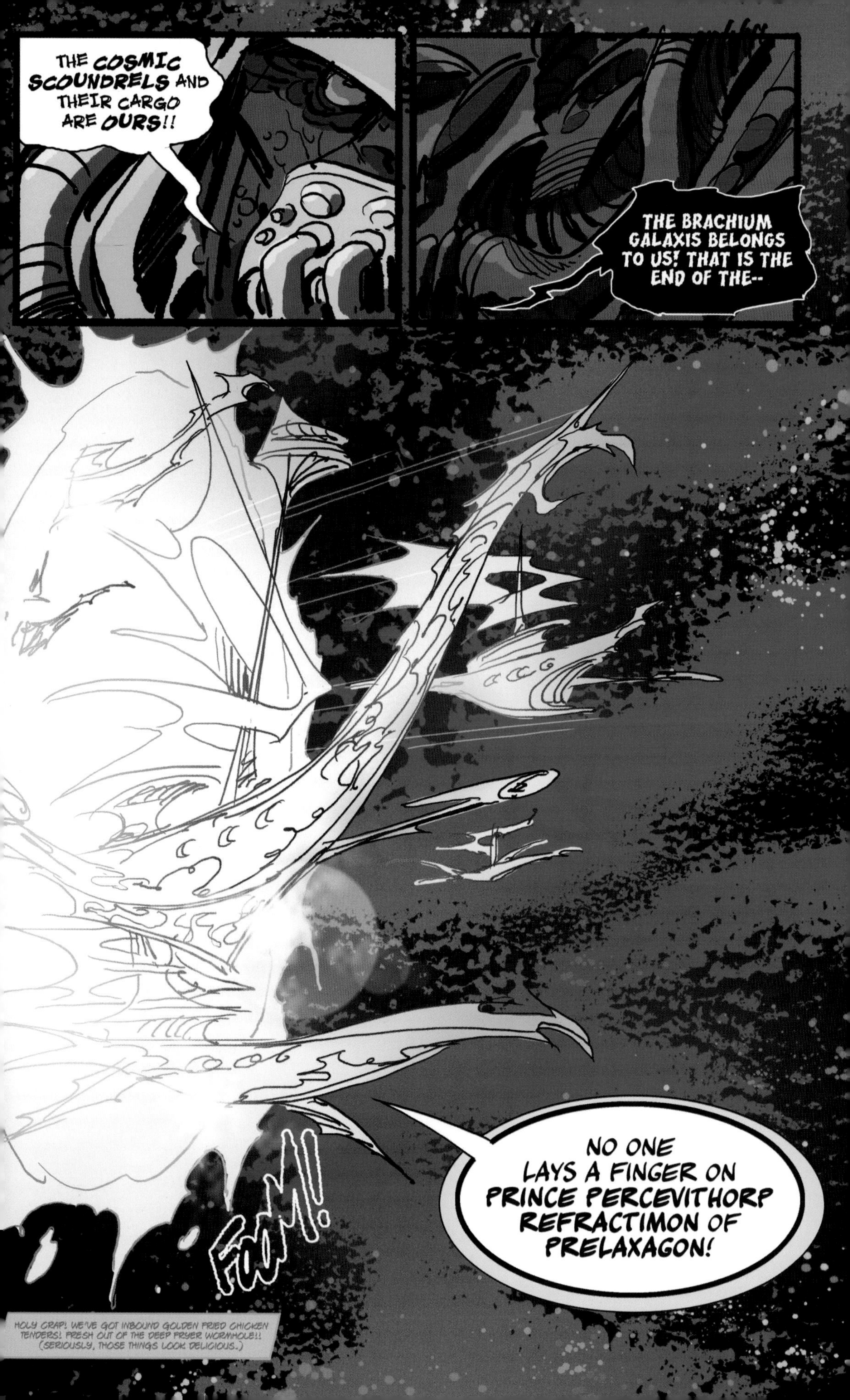
THE COSMIC SCOUNDRELS AND THEIR CARGO ARE OURS!!
THE BRACHIUM GALAXIS BELONGS TO US! THAT IS THE END OF THE--
FOOM!
NO ONE LAYS A FINGER ON PRINCE PERCEVITHORP REFRACTIMON OF PRELAXAGON!
HOLY CRAP! WE'VE GOT INBOUND GOLDEN FRIED CHICKEN TENDERS! FRESH OUT OF THE DEEP FRYER WORMHOLE!! (SERIOUSLY, THOSE THINGS LOOK DELICIOUS.)

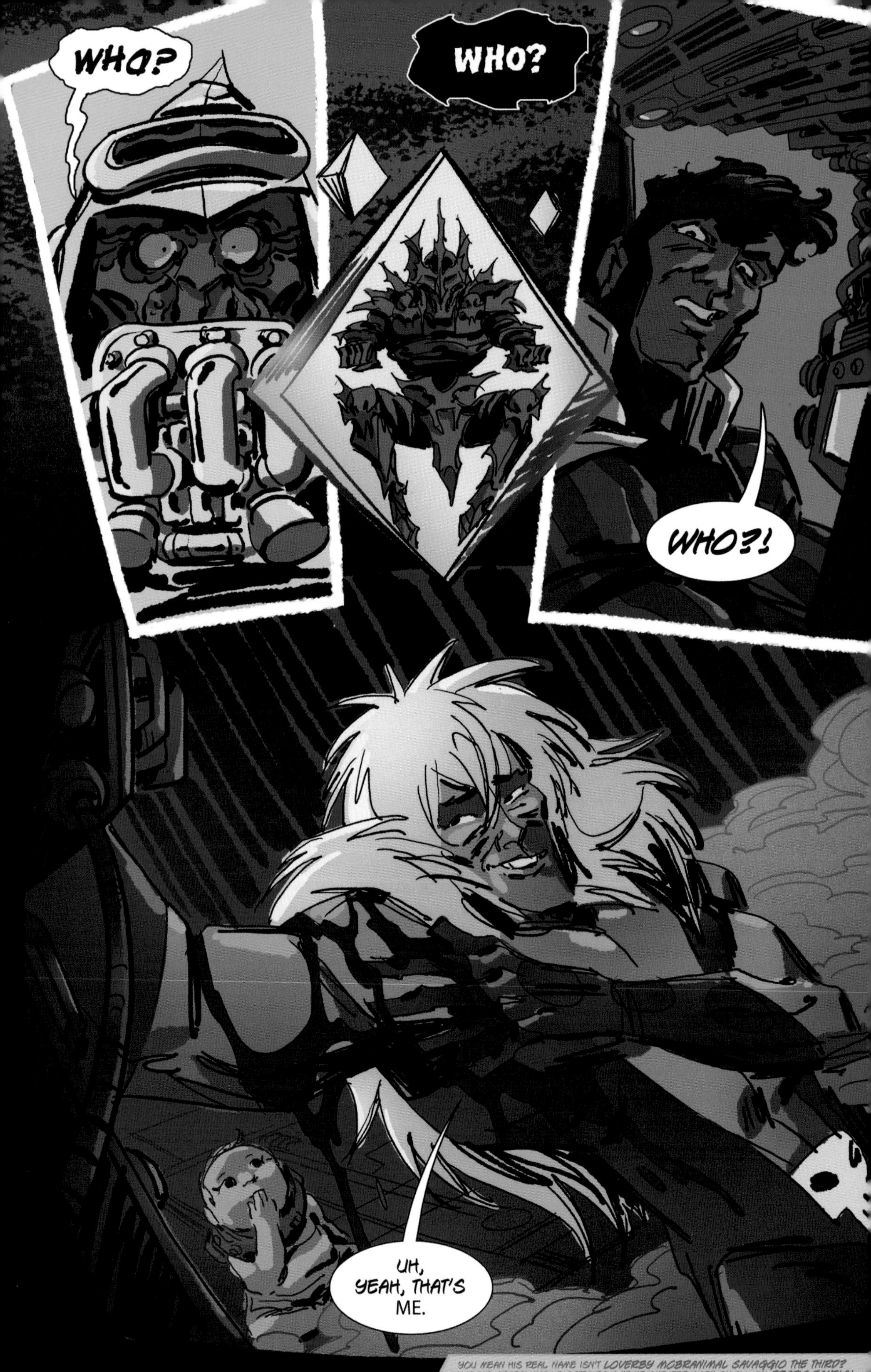
WHO?
WHO?
WHO?!
UH, YEAH, THAT'S ME.

YOU MEAN HIS REAL NAME ISN'T *LOVERBY MCBRANIMAL SAVAGGIO THE THIRD*? WHAT THE CRAP?! NOW I GOTTA DO A "FIND AND REPLACE" ON ALL MY *EROTIC FANFIC*!

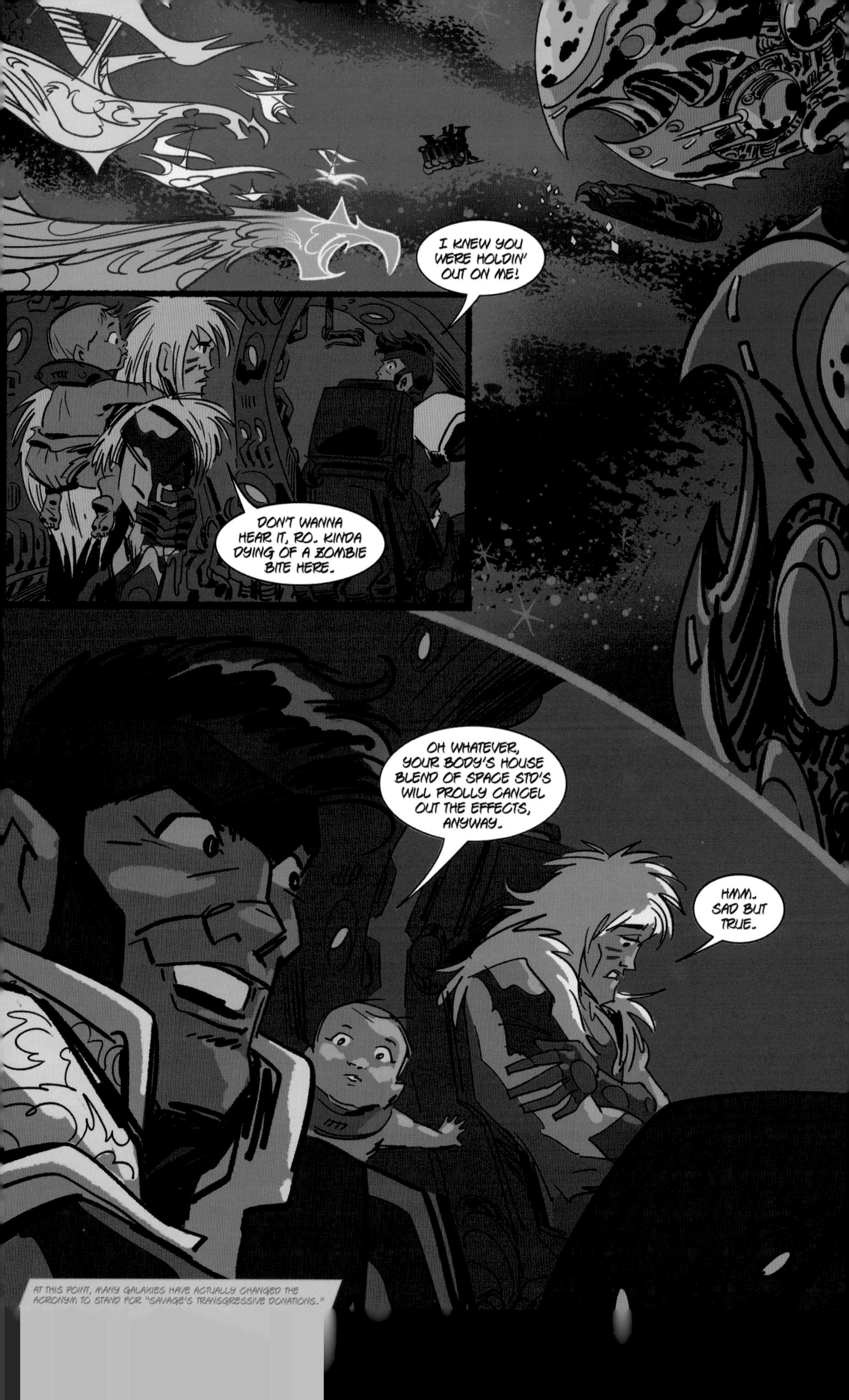
I KNEW YOU WERE HOLDIN' OUT ON ME!
DON'T WANNA HEAR IT, RO. KINDA DYING OF A ZOMBIE BITE HERE.
OH WHATEVER, YOUR BODY'S HOUSE BLEND OF SPACE STD'S WILL PROLLY CANCEL OUT THE EFFECTS, ANYWAY.
HMM. SAD BUT TRUE.
AT THIS POINT, MANY GALAXIES HAVE ACTUALLY CHANGED THE ACRONYM TO STAND FOR "SAVAGE'S TRANSGRESSIVE DONATIONS."

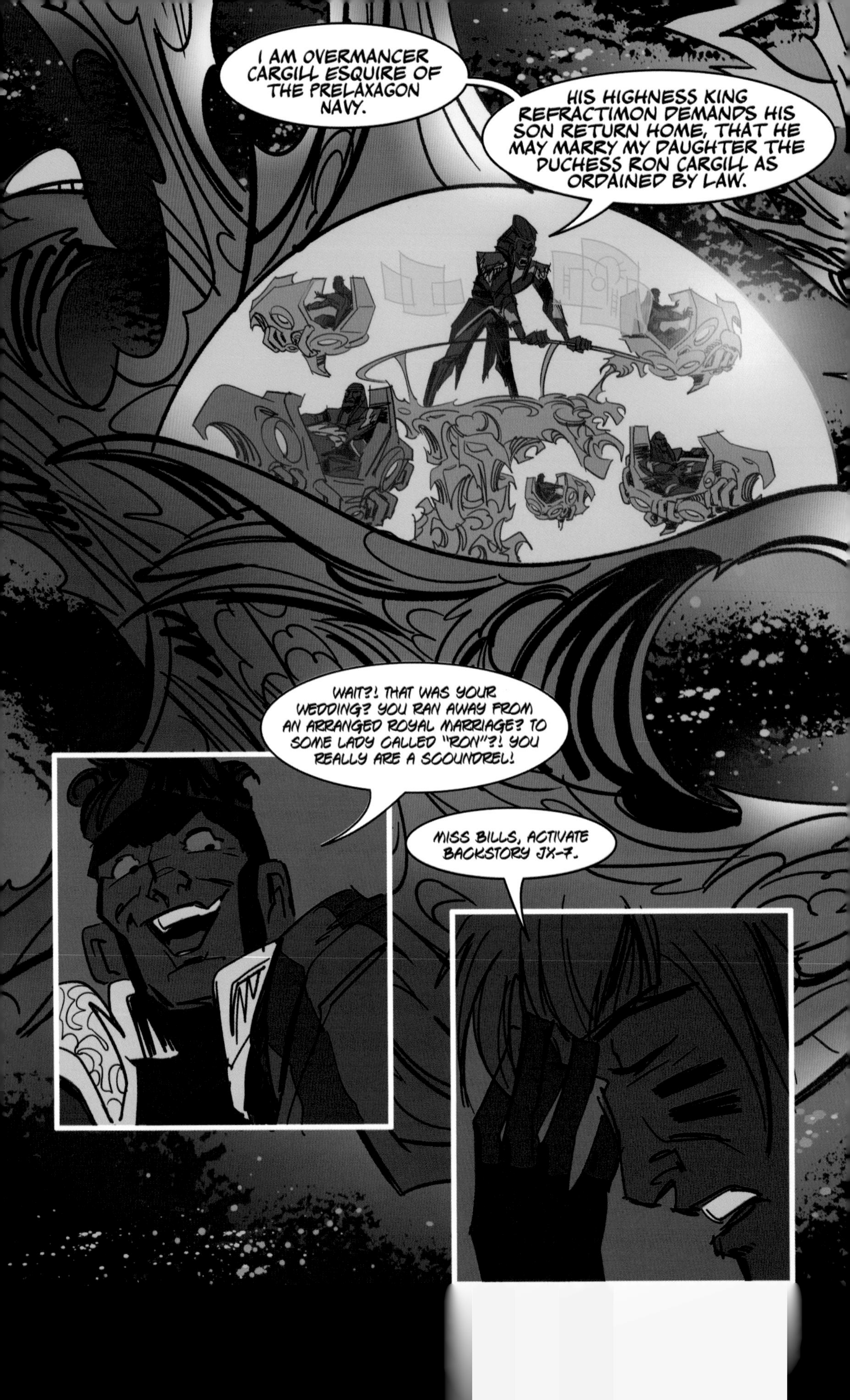
I AM OVERMANCER CARGILL ESQUIRE OF THE PRELAXAGON NAVY.
HIS HIGHNESS KING REFRACTIMON DEMANDS HIS SON RETURN HOME, THAT HE MAY MARRY MY DAUGHTER THE DUCHESS RON CARGILL AS ORDAINED BY LAW.
WAIT?! THAT WAS YOUR WEDDING? YOU RAN AWAY FROM AN ARRANGED ROYAL MARRIAGE? TO SOME LADY CALLED "RON"?! YOU REALLY ARE A SCOUNDREL!
MISS BILLS, ACTIVATE BACKSTORY JX-7.

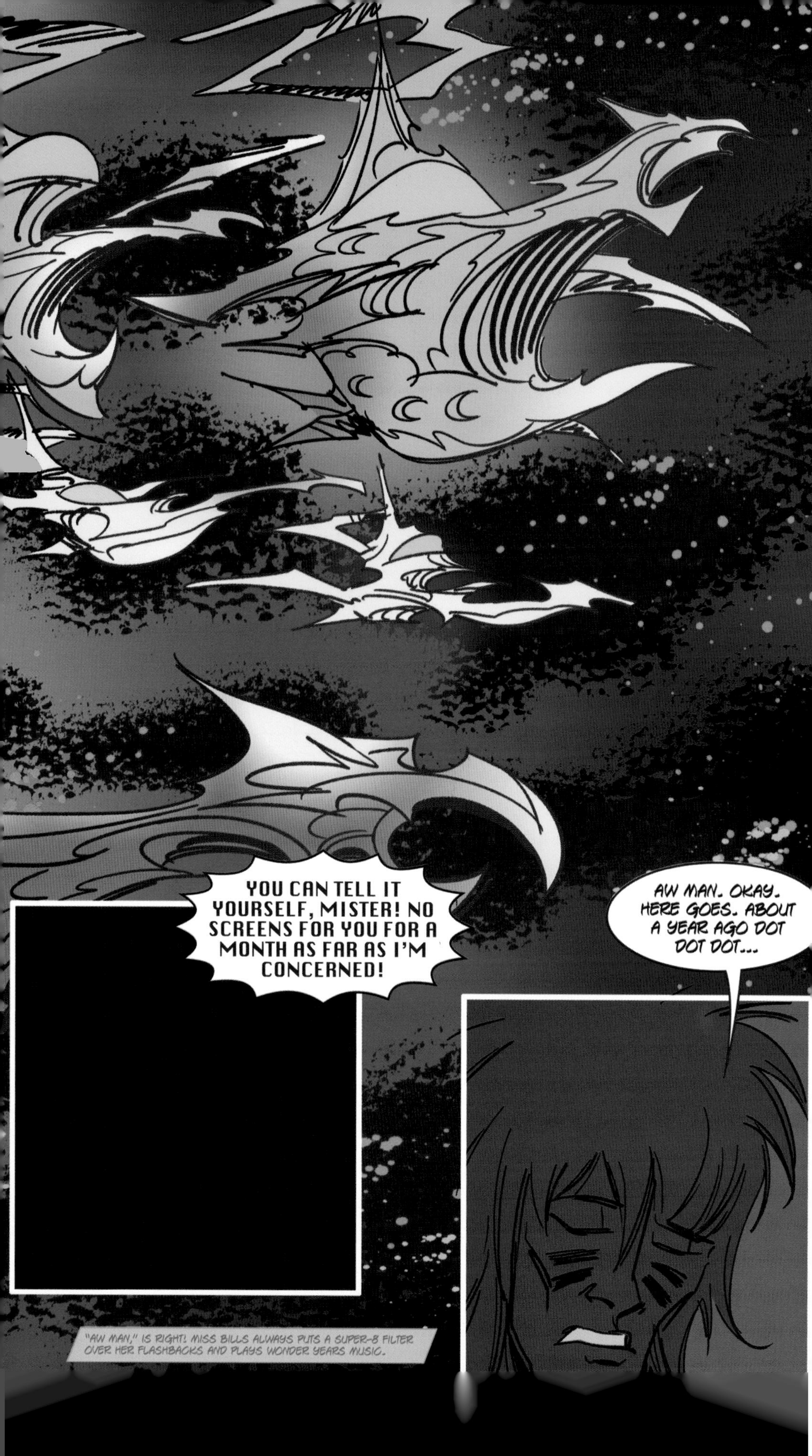
YOU CAN TELL IT YOURSELF, MISTER! NO SCREENS FOR YOU FOR A MONTH AS FAR AS I'M CONCERNED!
AW MAN. OKAY. HERE GOES. ABOUT A YEAR AGO DOT DOT DOT...
"AW MAN," IS RIGHT! MISS BILLS ALWAYS PUTS A SUPER-8 FILTER OVER HER FLASHBACKS AND PLAYS WONDER YEARS MUSIC.

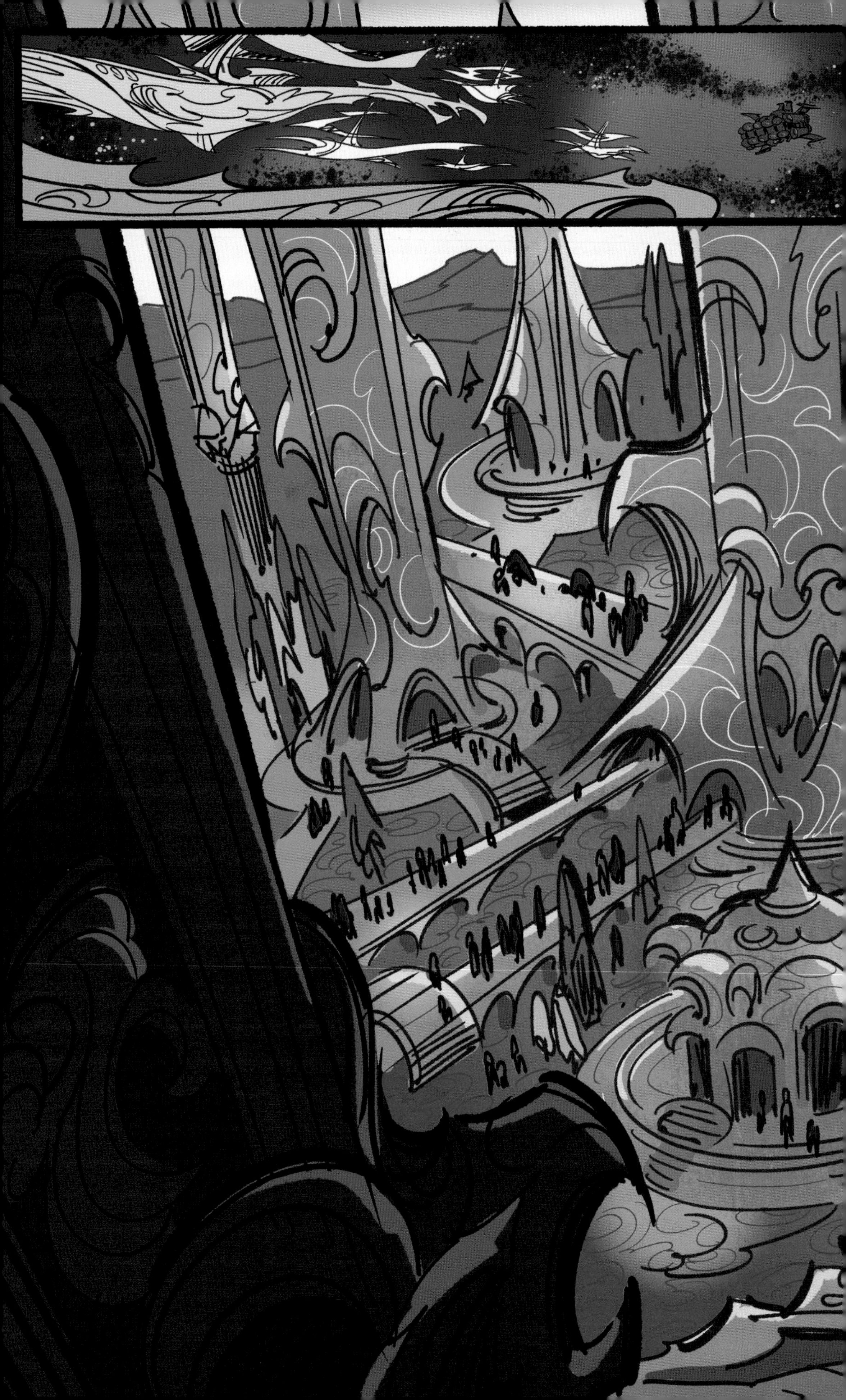

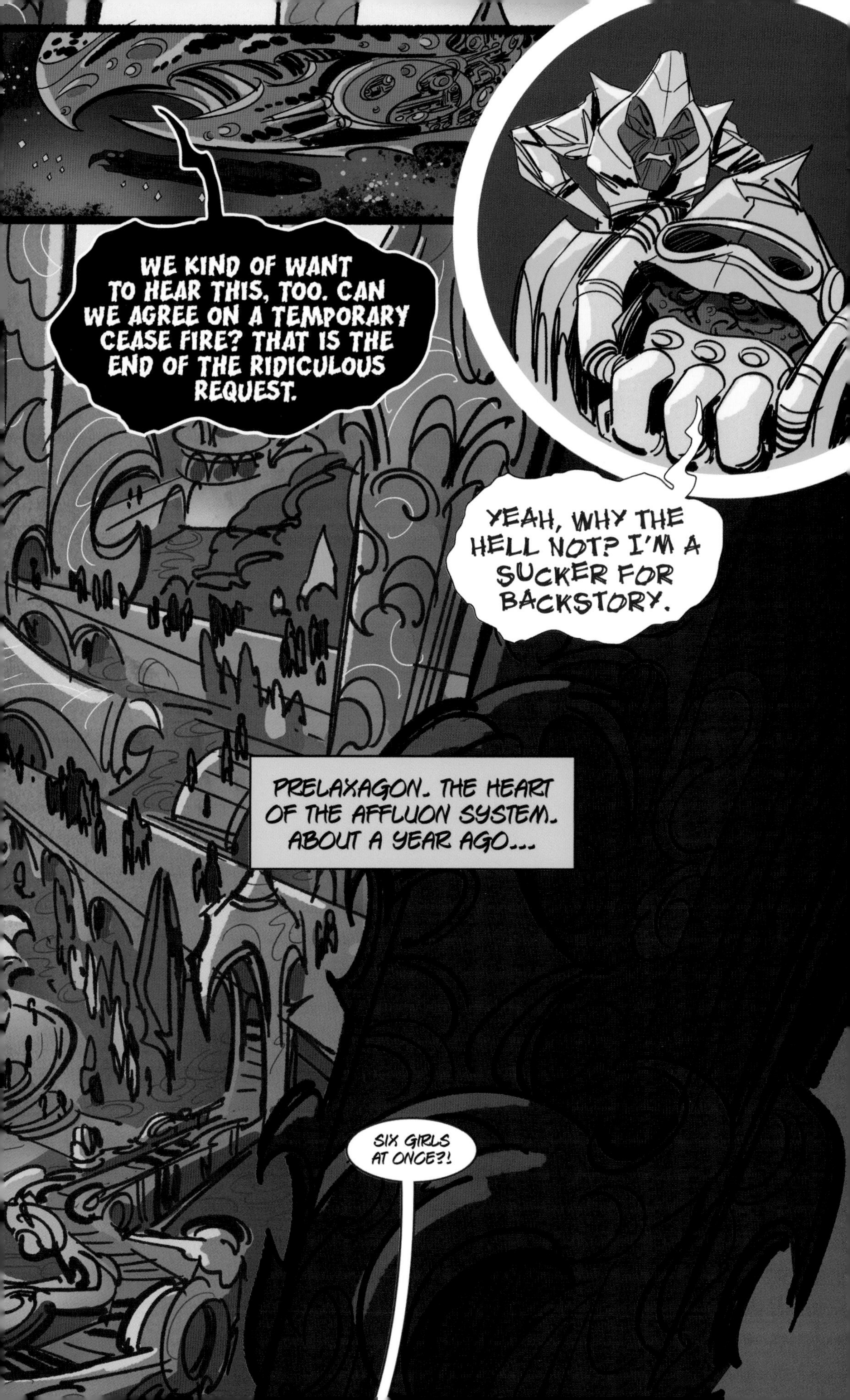
WE KIND OF WANT TO HEAR THIS, TOO. CAN WE AGREE ON A TEMPORARY CEASE FIRE? THAT IS THE END OF THE RIDICULOUS REQUEST.
YEAH, WHY THE HELL NOT? I'M A SUCKER FOR BACKSTORY.
PRELAXAGON. THE HEART OF THE AFFLUON SYSTEM. ABOUT A YEAR AGO...
SIX GIRLS AT ONCE?!

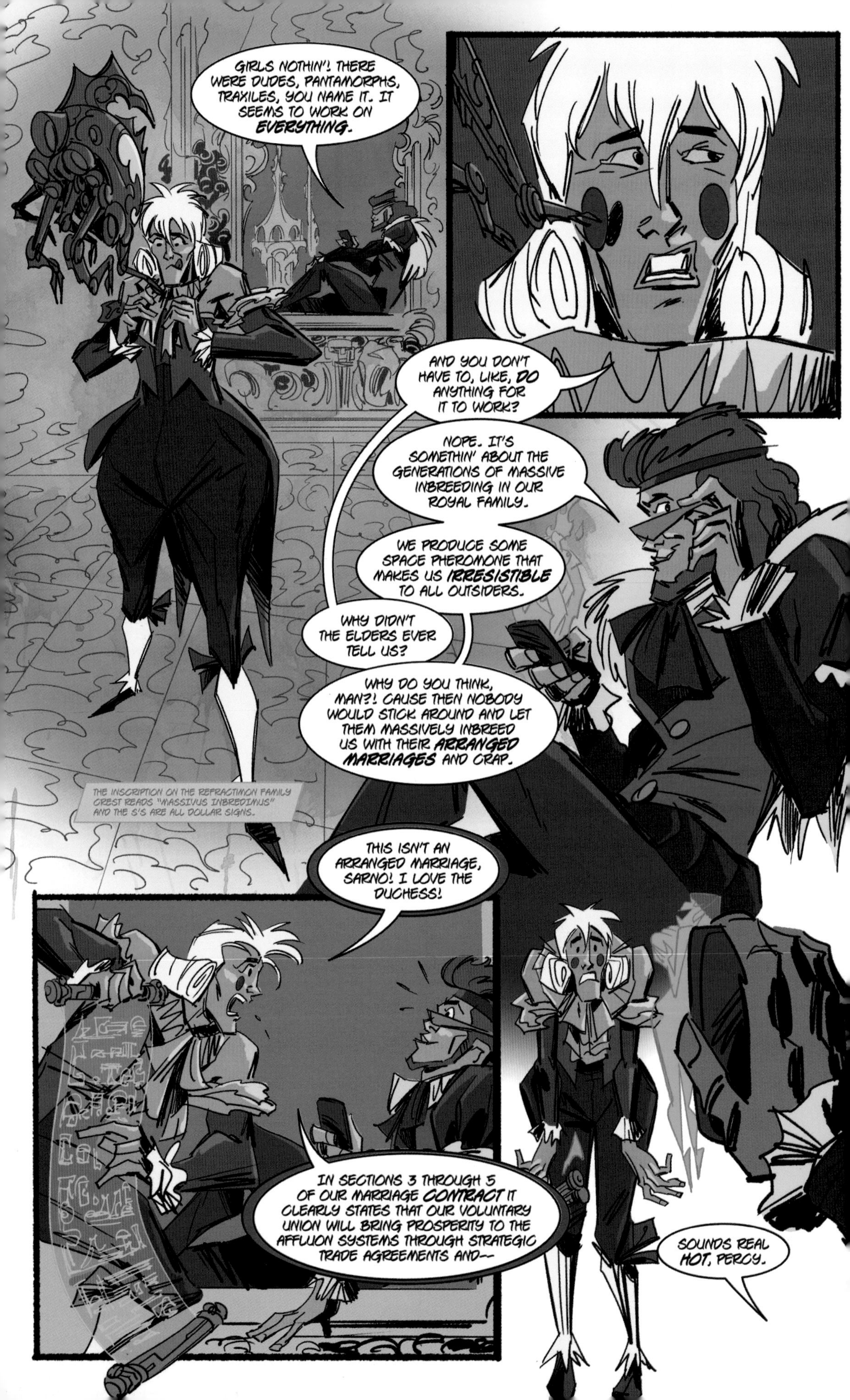
GIRLS NOTHIN'! THERE WERE DUDES, PANTAMORPHS, TRAXILES, YOU NAME IT. IT SEEMS TO WORK ON **EVERYTHING**.
AND YOU DON'T HAVE TO, LIKE, **DO** ANYTHING FOR IT TO WORK?
NOPE. IT'S SOMETHIN' ABOUT THE GENERATIONS OF MASSIVE INBREEDING IN OUR ROYAL FAMILY.
WE PRODUCE SOME SPACE PHEROMONE THAT MAKES US **IRRESISTIBLE** TO ALL OUTSIDERS.
WHY DIDN'T THE ELDERS EVER TELL US?
WHY DO YOU THINK, MAN?! CAUSE THEN NOBODY WOULD STICK AROUND AND LET THEM MASSIVELY INBREED US WITH THEIR **ARRANGED MARRIAGES** AND CRAP.
THE INSCRIPTION ON THE REFRACTIMON FAMILY CREST READS "MASSIVUS INBREDIMUS" AND THE S'S ARE ALL DOLLAR SIGNS.
THIS ISN'T AN ARRANGED MARRIAGE, SARNO! I LOVE THE DUCHESS!
IN SECTIONS 3 THROUGH 5 OF OUR MARRIAGE **CONTRACT** IT CLEARLY STATES THAT OUR VOLUNTARY UNION WILL BRING PROSPERITY TO THE AFFLUON SYSTEMS THROUGH STRATEGIC TRADE AGREEMENTS AND--
SOUNDS REAL **HOT**, PERCY.

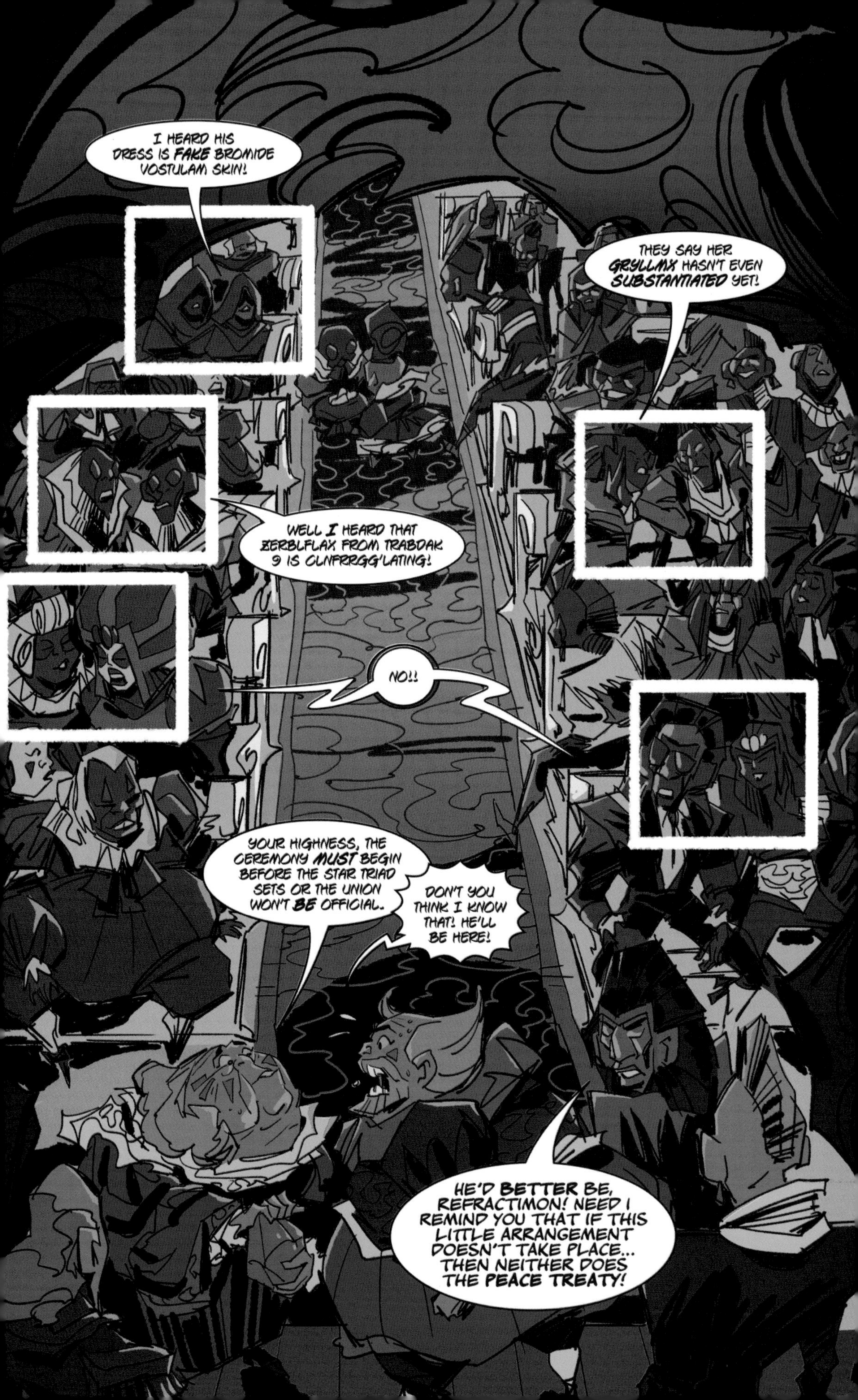
I HEARD HIS DRESS IS FAKE BROMIDE VOSTULAM SKIN!
THEY SAY HER GRYLLMX HASN'T EVEN SUBSTANTIATED YET!
WELL I HEARD THAT ZERBLFLAX FROM TRABDAK 9 IS OLNFRRGG'LATING!
NO!!
YOUR HIGHNESS, THE CEREMONY MUST BEGIN BEFORE THE STAR TRIAD SETS OR THE UNION WON'T BE OFFICIAL.
DON'T YOU THINK I KNOW THAT! HE'LL BE HERE!
HE'D BETTER BE, REFRACTIMON! NEED I REMIND YOU THAT IF THIS LITTLE ARRANGEMENT DOESN'T TAKE PLACE... THEN NEITHER DOES THE PEACE TREATY!

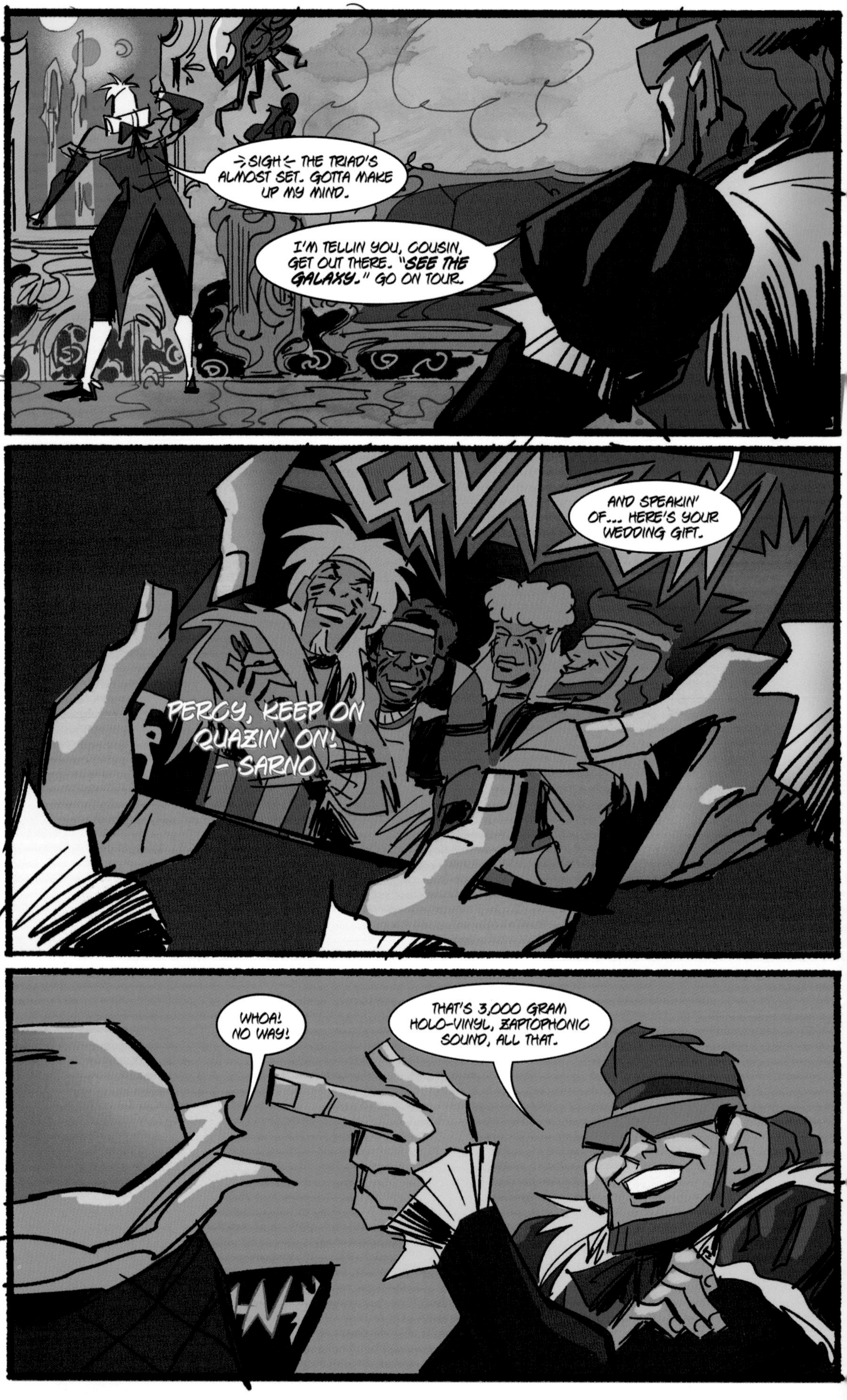

⇒SIGH⇐ THE TRIAD'S ALMOST SET. GOTTA MAKE UP MY MIND.
I'M TELLIN YOU, COUSIN, GET OUT THERE. "**SEE THE GALAXY.**" GO ON TOUR.
AND SPEAKIN' OF... HERE'S YOUR WEDDING GIFT.
PERCY, KEEP ON QUAZIN' ON! - SARNO
WHOA! NO WAY!
THAT'S 3,000 GRAM HOLO-VINYL, ZAPTOPHONIC SOUND, ALL THAT.

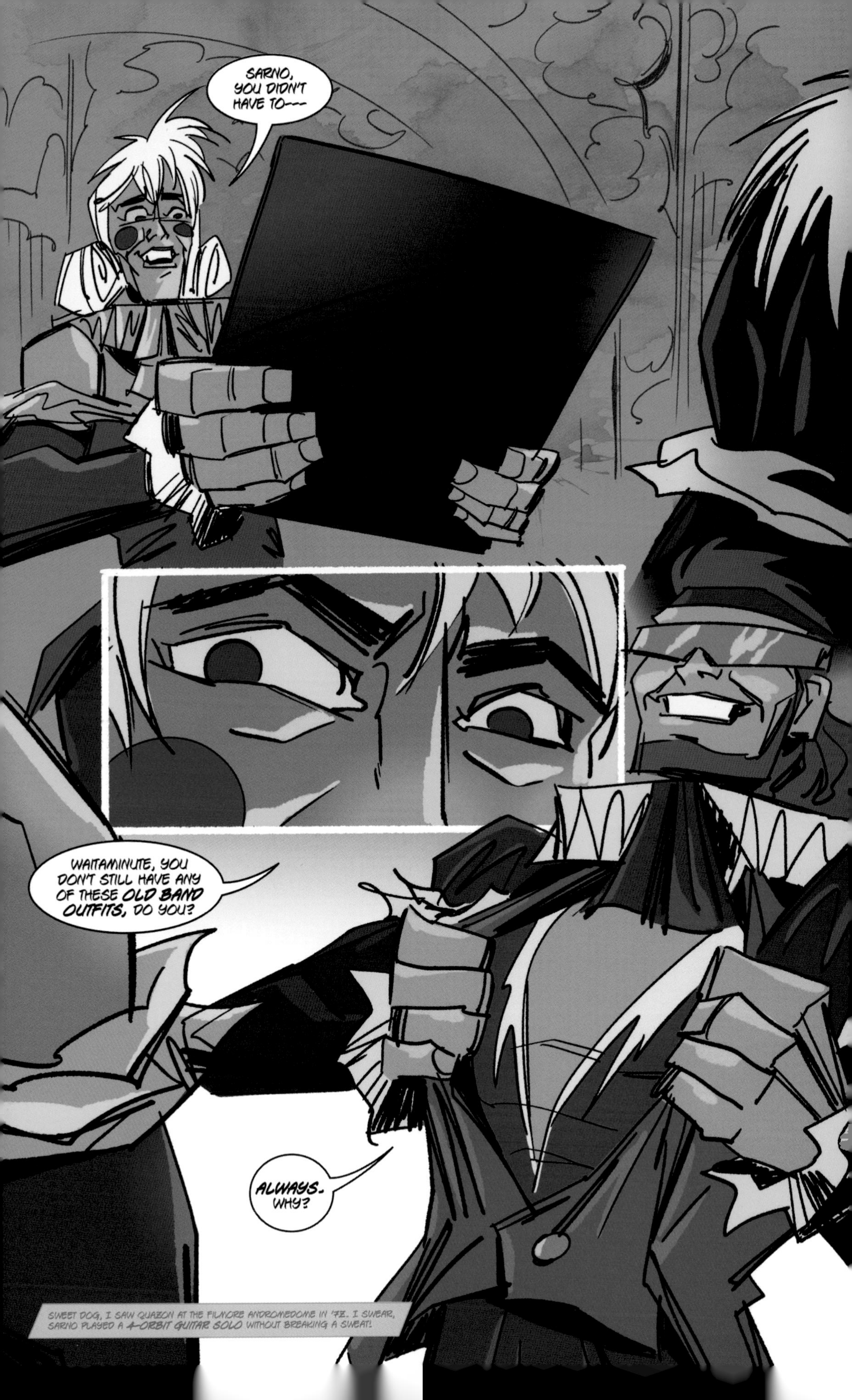
SARNO, YOU DIDN'T HAVE TO---
WAITAMINUTE, YOU DON'T STILL HAVE ANY OF THESE **OLD BAND OUTFITS,** DO YOU?
ALWAYS. WHY?
SWEET DOG, I SAW QUAZON AT THE FILMORE ANDROMEDOME IN '7Z. I SWEAR, SARNO PLAYED A **4-ORBIT GUITAR SOLO** WITHOUT BREAKING A SWEAT!

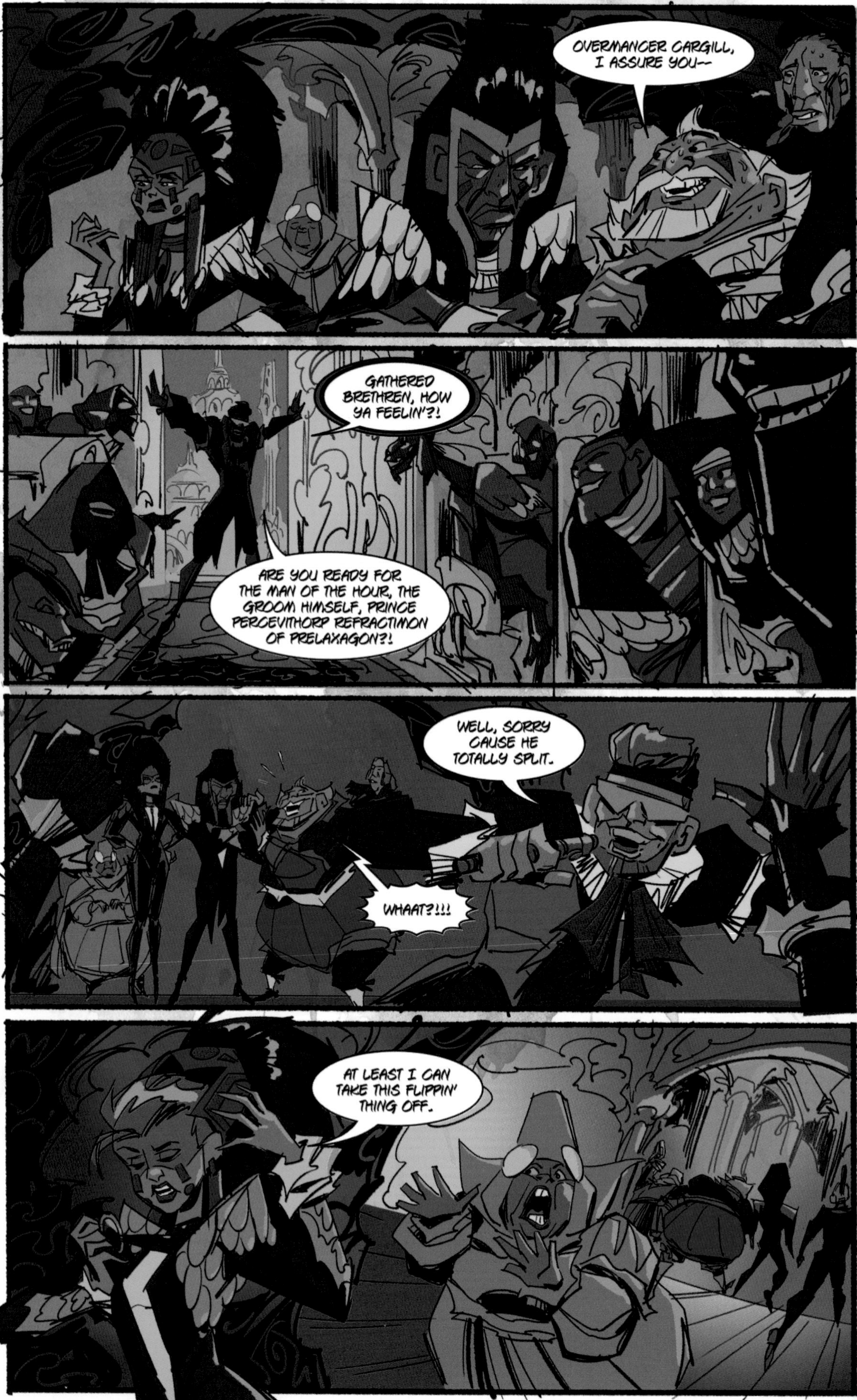
OVERMANCER CARGILL, I ASSURE YOU--
GATHERED BRETHREN, HOW YA FEELIN'?!
ARE YOU READY FOR THE MAN OF THE HOUR, THE GROOM HIMSELF, PRINCE PERCEVITHORP REFRACTIMON OF PRELAXAGON?!
WELL, SORRY CAUSE HE TOTALLY SPLIT.
WHAAT?!!!
AT LEAST I CAN TAKE THIS FLIPPIN' THING OFF.

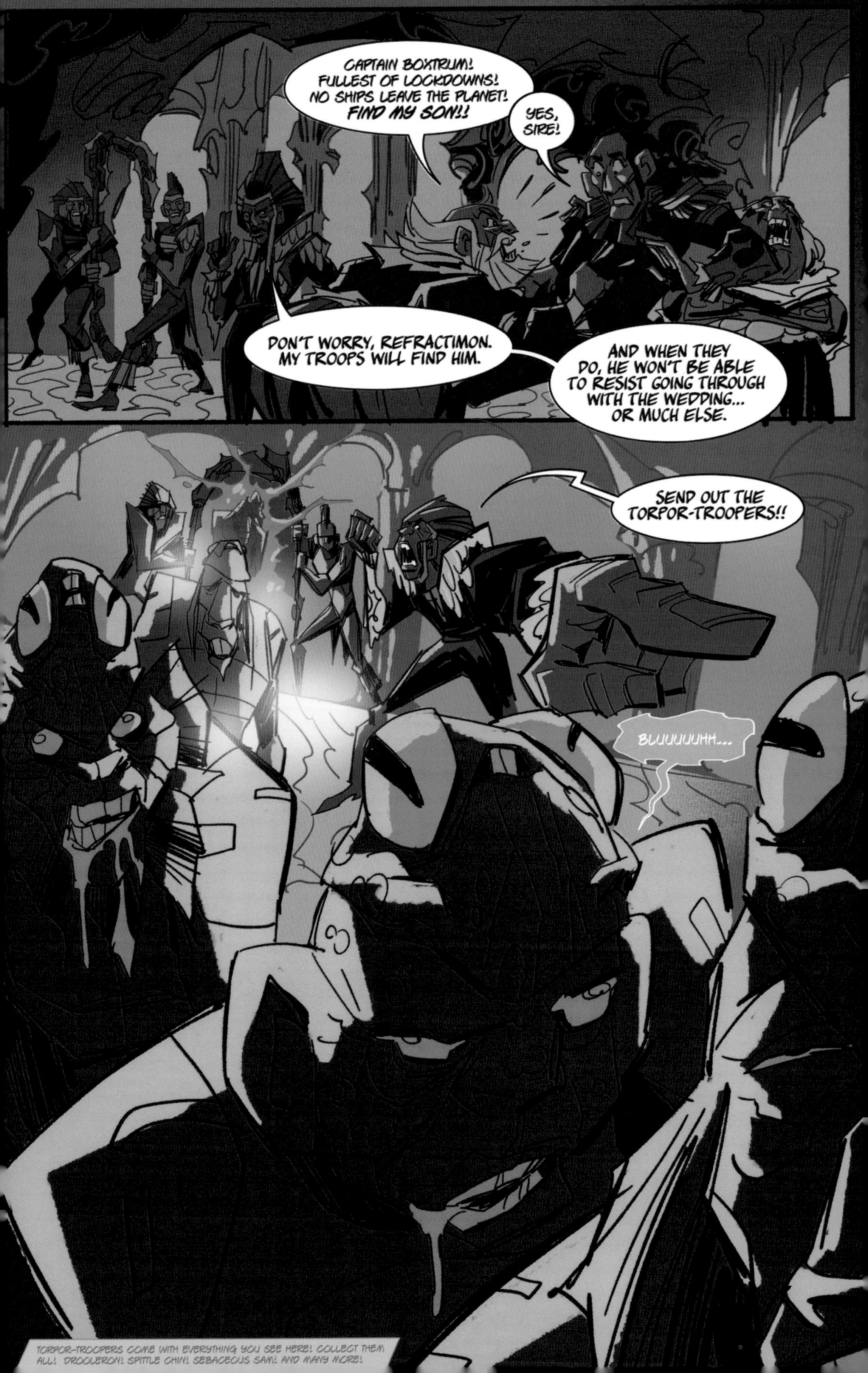
CAPTAIN BOXTRUM! FULLEST OF LOCKDOWNS! NO SHIPS LEAVE THE PLANET! FIND MY SON!!
YES, SIRE!
DON'T WORRY, REFRACTIMON. MY TROOPS WILL FIND HIM.
AND WHEN THEY DO, HE WON'T BE ABLE TO RESIST GOING THROUGH WITH THE WEDDING... OR MUCH ELSE.
SEND OUT THE TORPOR-TROOPERS!!
BLUUUUUHH...
TORPOR-TROOPERS COME WITH EVERYTHING YOU SEE HERE! COLLECT THEM ALL! DROOLERON! SPITTLE CHIN! SEBACEOUS SAM! AND MANY MORE!

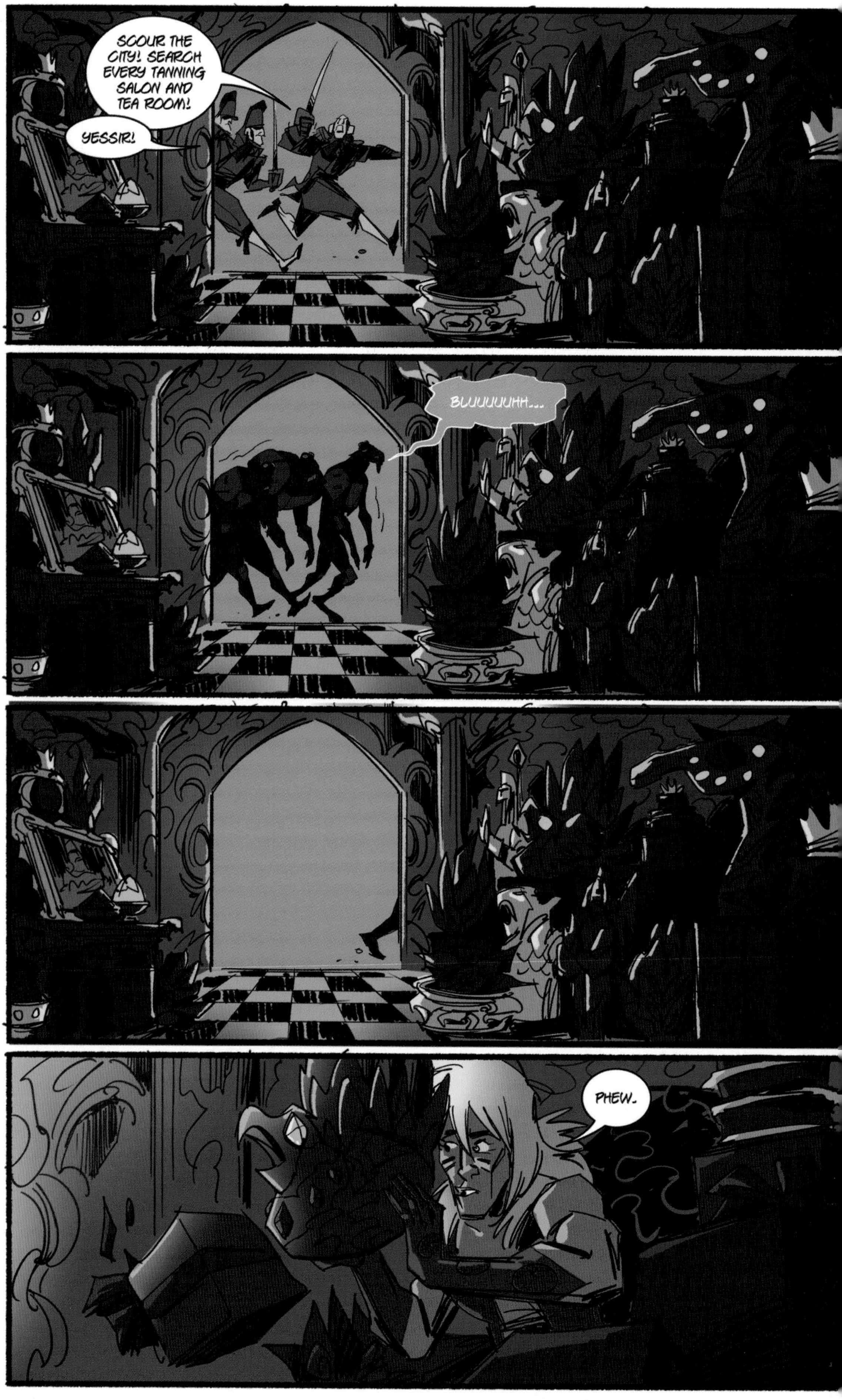
SCOUR THE CITY! SEARCH EVERY TANNING SALON AND TEA ROOM!
YESSIR!
BLUUUUUHH...
PHEW.

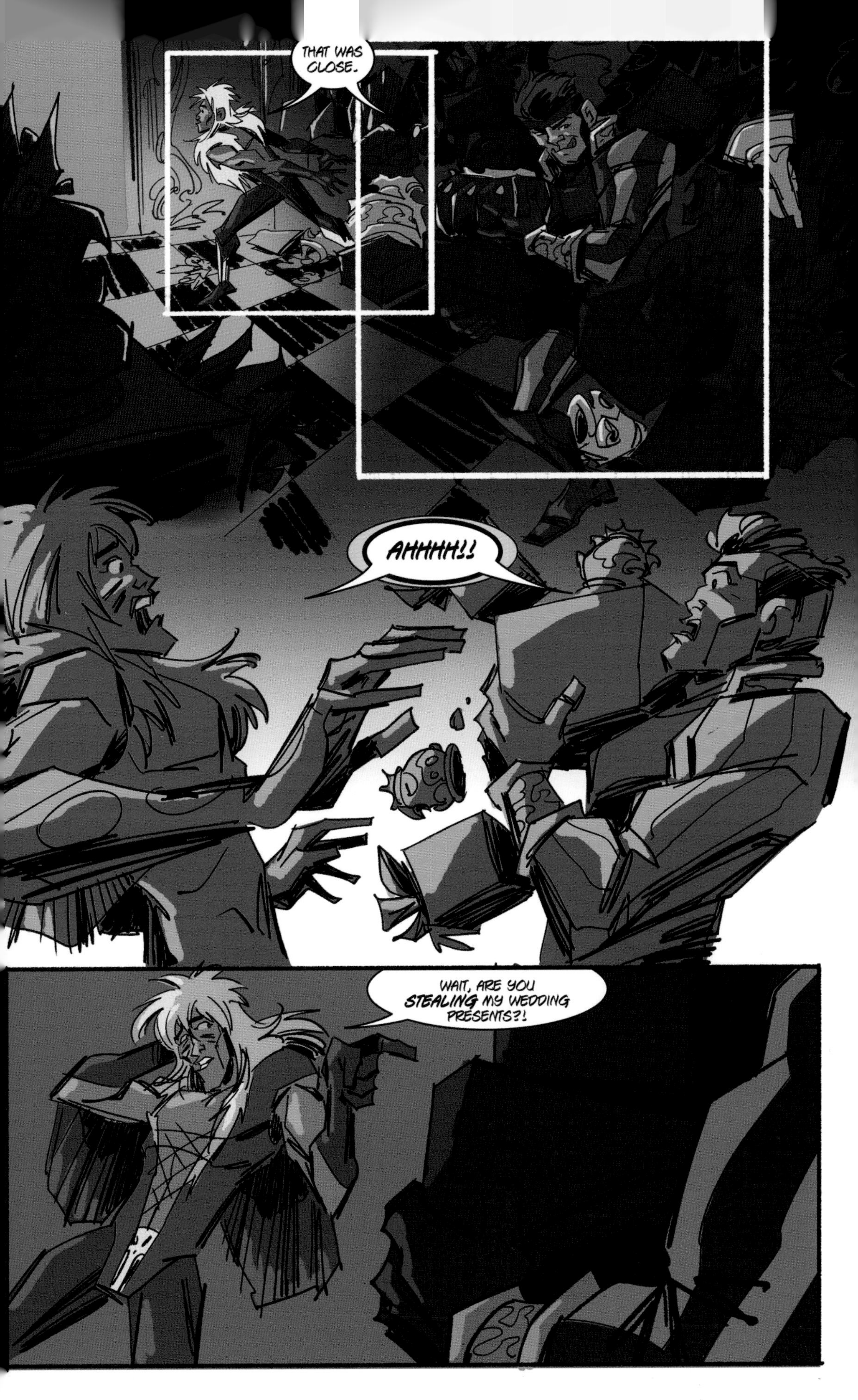
THAT WAS CLOSE.
AHHHH!!
WAIT, ARE YOU **STEALING** MY WEDDING PRESENTS?!

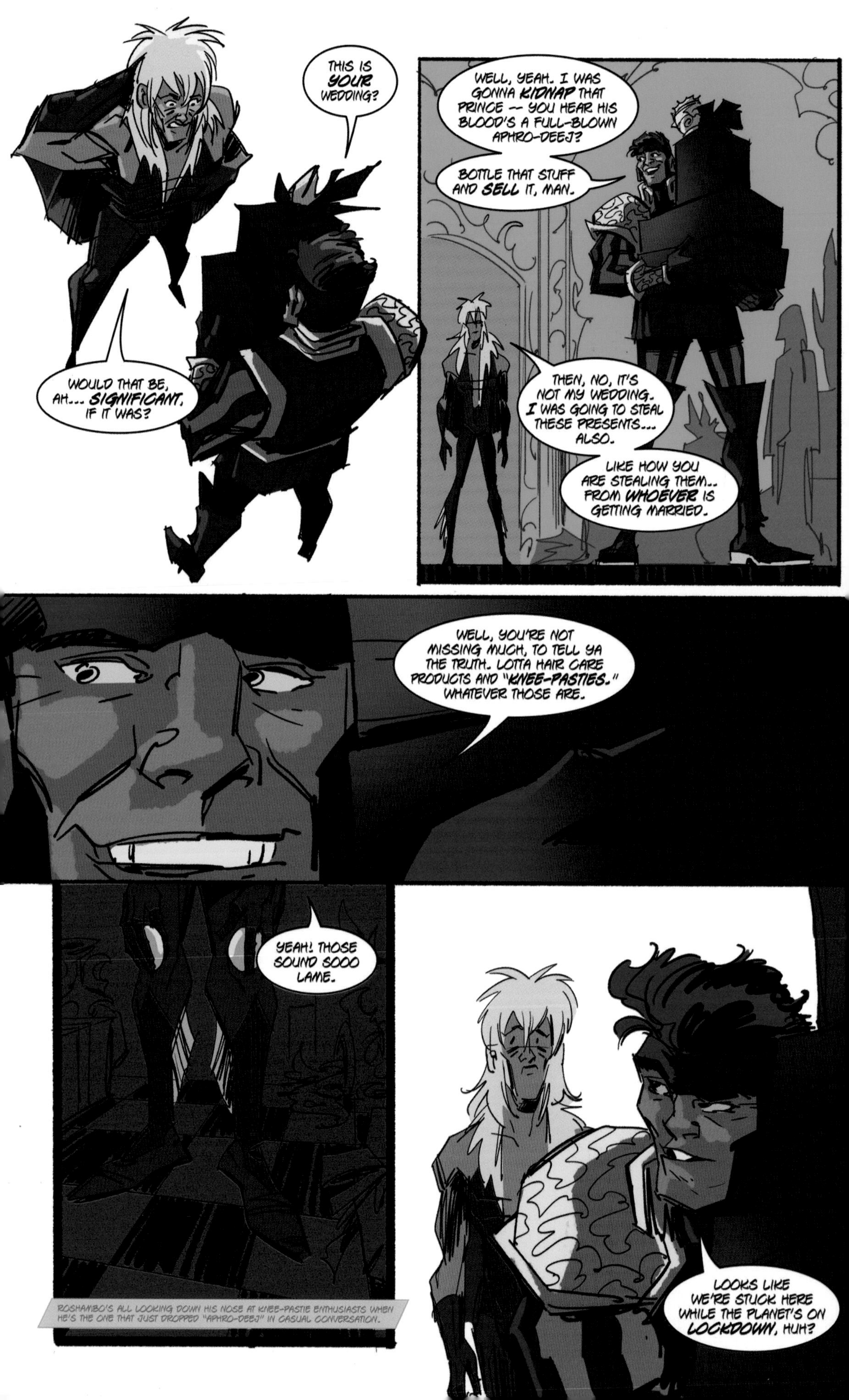
THIS IS YOUR WEDDING?
WOULD THAT BE, AH... SIGNIFICANT, IF IT WAS?
WELL, YEAH. I WAS GONNA KIDNAP THAT PRINCE -- YOU HEAR HIS BLOOD'S A FULL-BLOWN APHRO-DEEJ?
BOTTLE THAT STUFF AND SELL IT, MAN.
THEN, NO, IT'S NOT MY WEDDING. I WAS GOING TO STEAL THESE PRESENTS... ALSO.
LIKE HOW YOU ARE STEALING THEM... FROM WHOEVER IS GETTING MARRIED.
WELL, YOU'RE NOT MISSING MUCH, TO TELL YA THE TRUTH. LOTTA HAIR CARE PRODUCTS AND "KNEE-PASTIES." WHATEVER THOSE ARE.
YEAH! THOSE SOUND SOOO LAME.
ROSHAMBO'S ALL LOOKING DOWN HIS NOSE AT KNEE-PASTIE ENTHUSIASTS WHEN HE'S THE ONE THAT JUST DROPPED "APHRO-DEEJ" IN CASUAL CONVERSATION.
LOOKS LIKE WE'RE STUCK HERE WHILE THE PLANET'S ON LOCKDOWN, HUH?

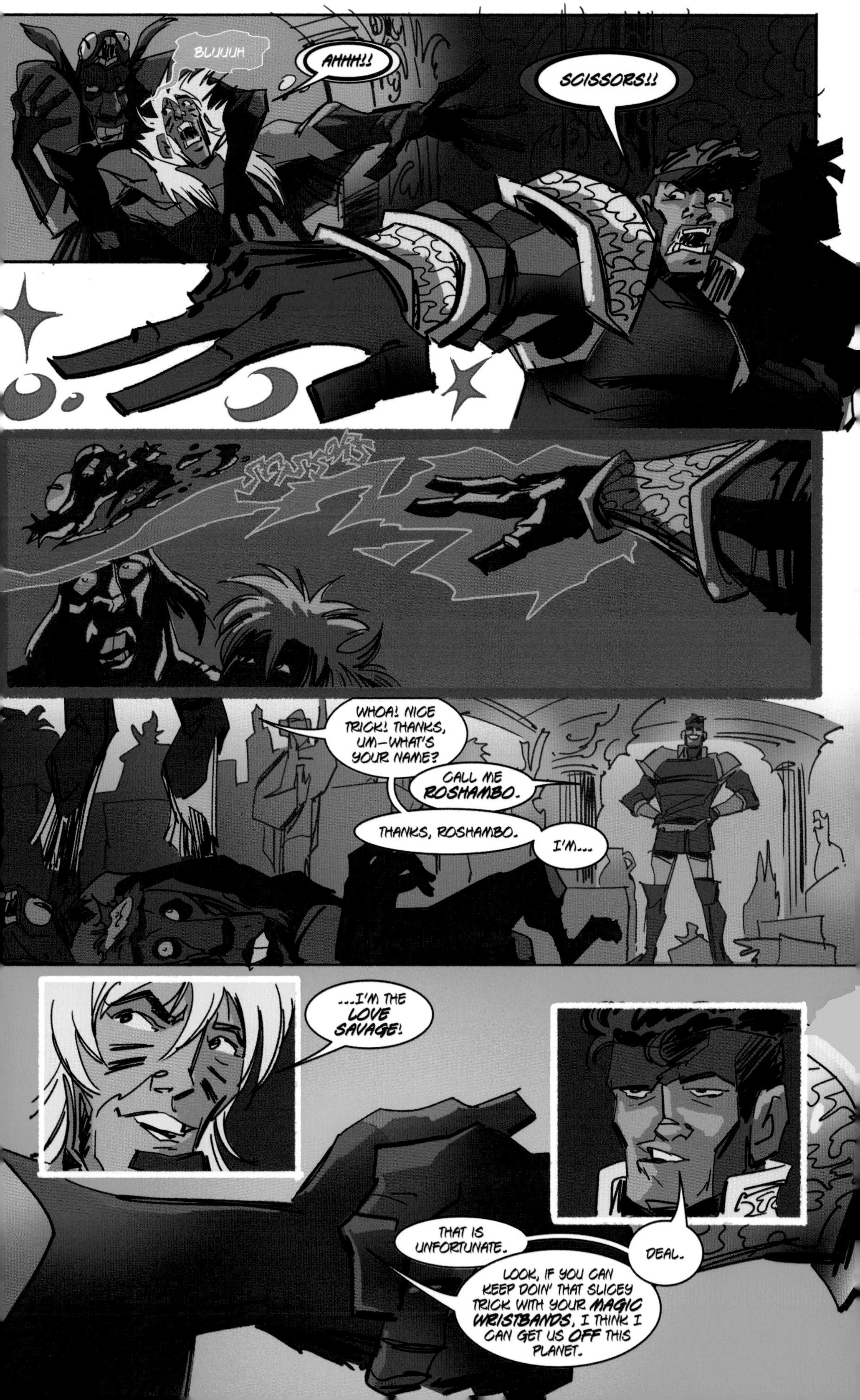
BLUUUH
AHHH!!
SCISSORS!!
WHOA! NICE TRICK! THANKS, UM—WHAT'S YOUR NAME?
CALL ME ROSHAMBO.
THANKS, ROSHAMBO.
I'M...
...I'M THE LOVE SAVAGE!
THAT IS UNFORTUNATE.
LOOK, IF YOU CAN KEEP DOIN' THAT SLICEY TRICK WITH YOUR MAGIC WRISTBANDS, I THINK I CAN GET US OFF THIS PLANET.
DEAL.

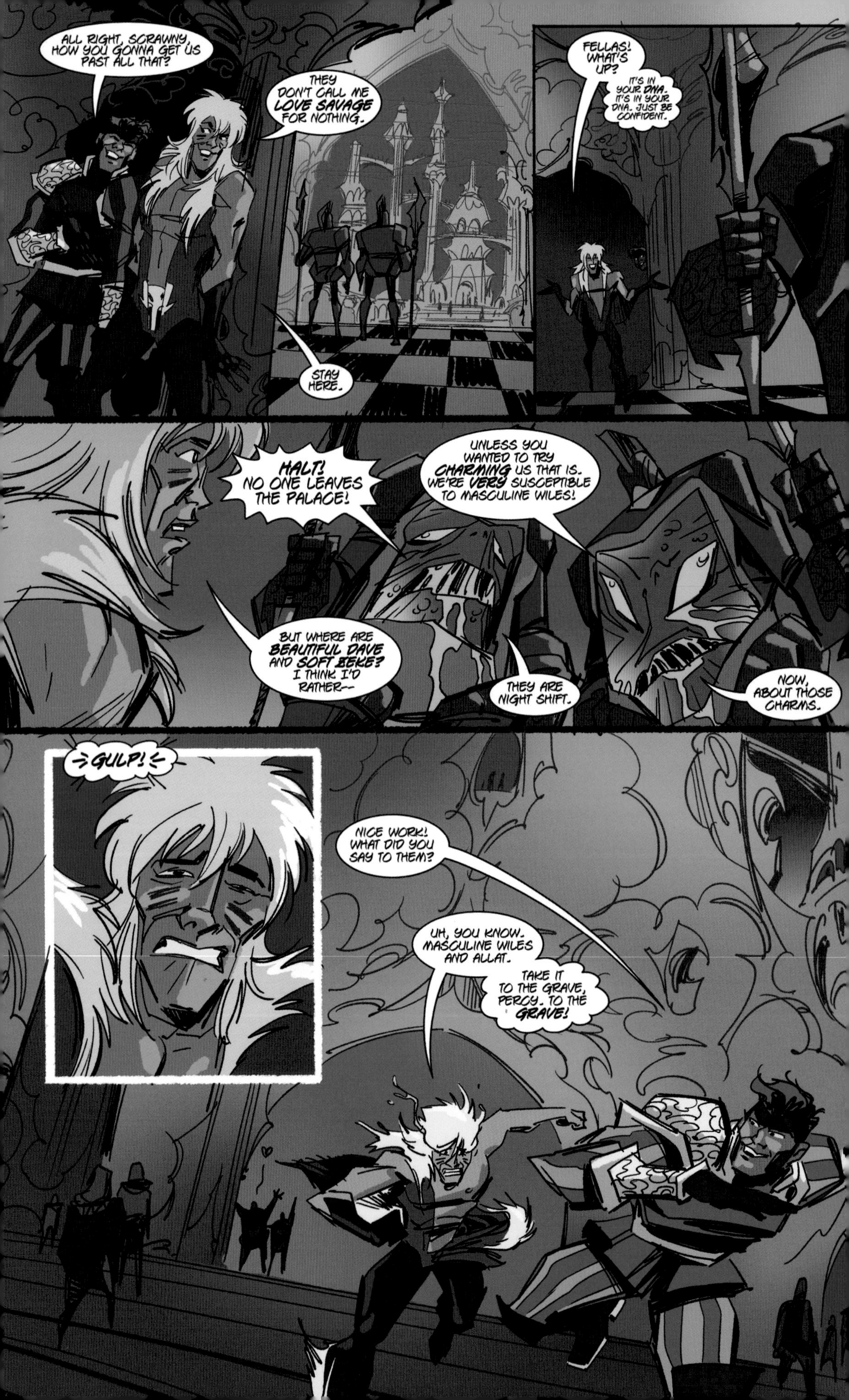
ALL RIGHT, SCRAWNY, HOW YOU GONNA GET US PAST ALL THAT?
THEY DON'T CALL ME LOVE SAVAGE FOR NOTHING.
STAY HERE.
FELLAS! WHAT'S UP?
IT'S IN YOUR DNA. IT'S IN YOUR DNA. JUST BE CONFIDENT.
HALT! NO ONE LEAVES THE PALACE!
UNLESS YOU WANTED TO TRY CHARMING US THAT IS. WE'RE VERY SUSCEPTIBLE TO MASCULINE WILES!
BUT WHERE ARE BEAUTIFUL DAVE AND SOFT ZEKE? I THINK I'D RATHER--
THEY ARE NIGHT SHIFT.
NOW, ABOUT THOSE CHARMS.
GULP!
NICE WORK! WHAT DID YOU SAY TO THEM?
UH, YOU KNOW. MASCULINE WILES AND ALLAT.
TAKE IT TO THE GRAVE, PERCY. TO THE GRAVE!

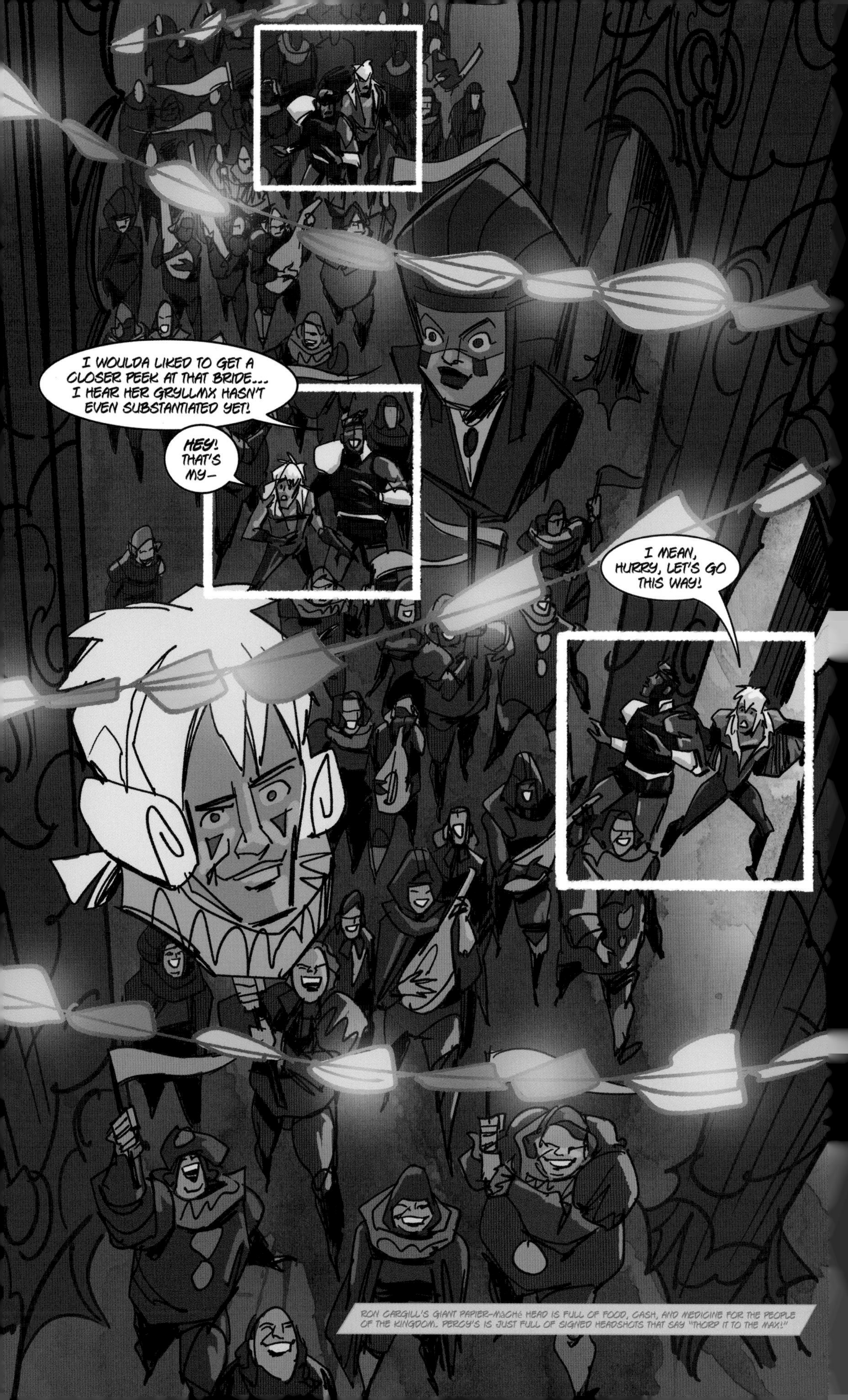
I WOULDA LIKED TO GET A CLOSER PEEK AT THAT BRIDE... I HEAR HER GRYLLMX HASN'T EVEN SUBSTANTIATED YET!
HEY! THAT'S MY–
I MEAN, HURRY, LET'S GO THIS WAY!
RON CARGILL'S GIANT PAPIER-MÂCHÉ HEAD IS FULL OF FOOD, CASH, AND MEDICINE FOR THE PEOPLE OF THE KINGDOM. PERCY'S IS JUST FULL OF SIGNED HEADSHOTS THAT SAY "THORP IT TO THE MAX!"

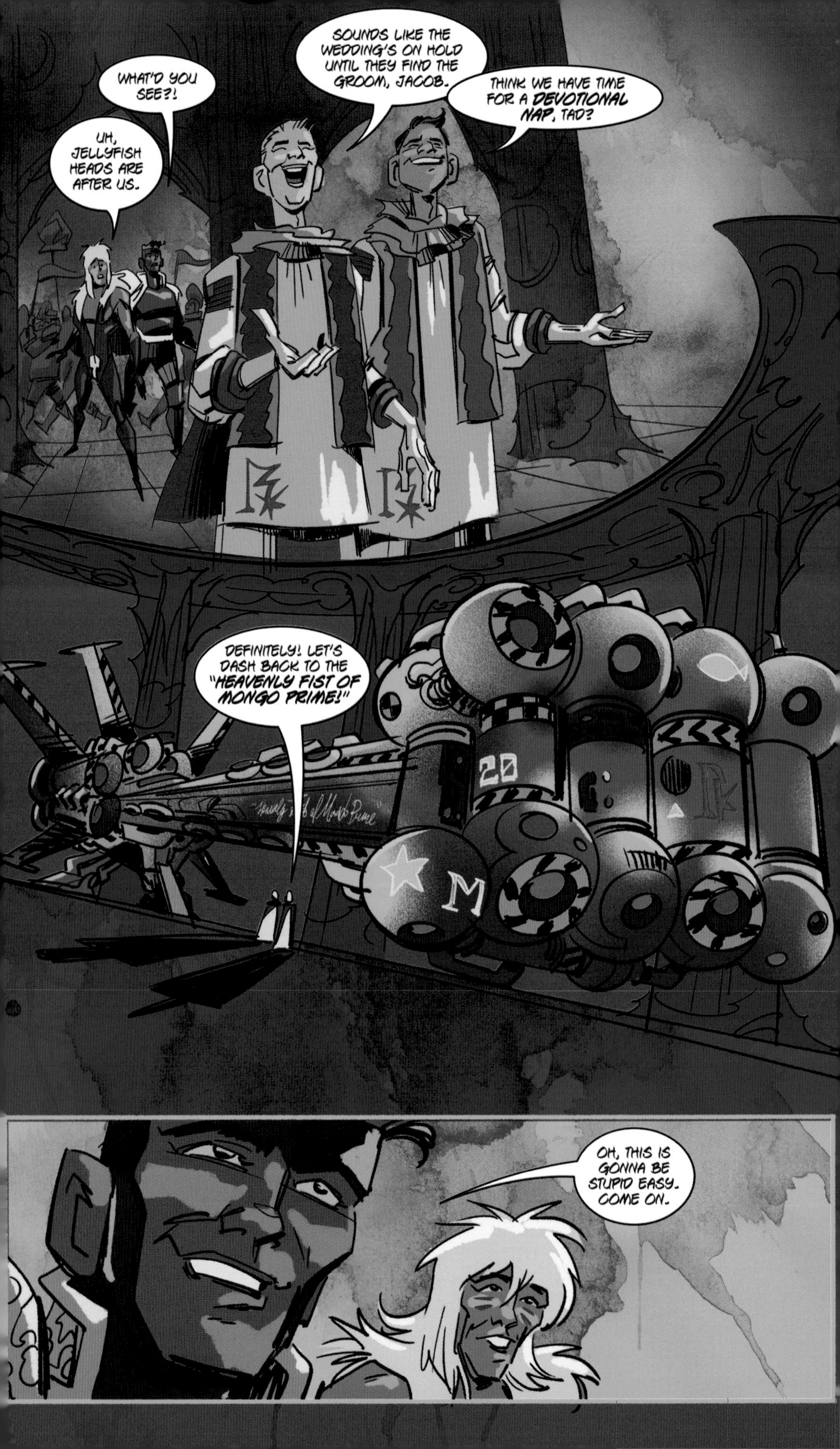
UH, JELLYFISH HEADS ARE AFTER US.
WHAT'D YOU SEE?!
SOUNDS LIKE THE WEDDING'S ON HOLD UNTIL THEY FIND THE GROOM, JACOB.
THINK WE HAVE TIME FOR A DEVOTIONAL NAP, TAD?
DEFINITELY! LET'S DASH BACK TO THE "HEAVENLY FIST OF MONGO PRIME!"
20
M
OH, THIS IS GONNA BE STUPID EASY. COME ON.

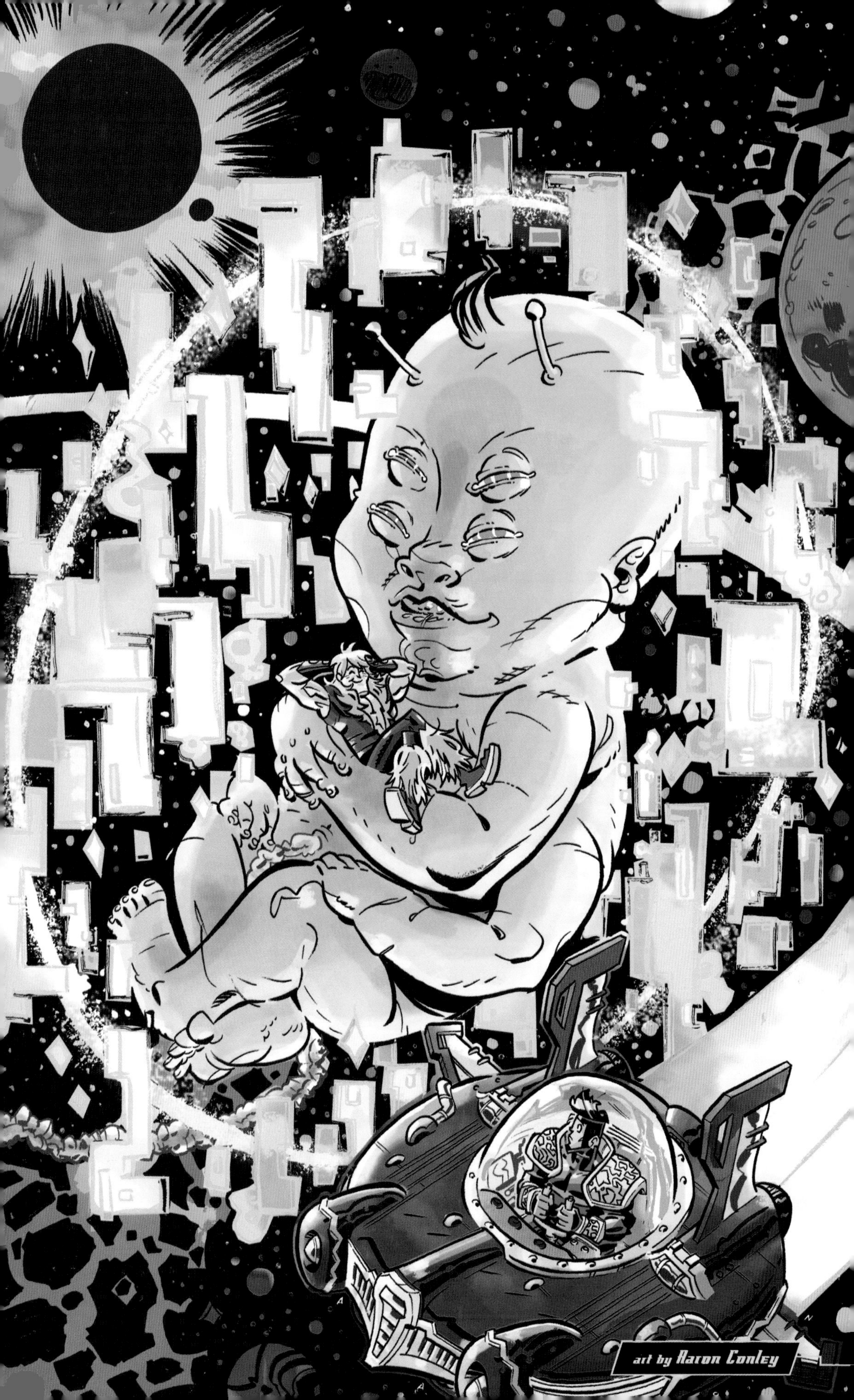
art by Aaron Conley

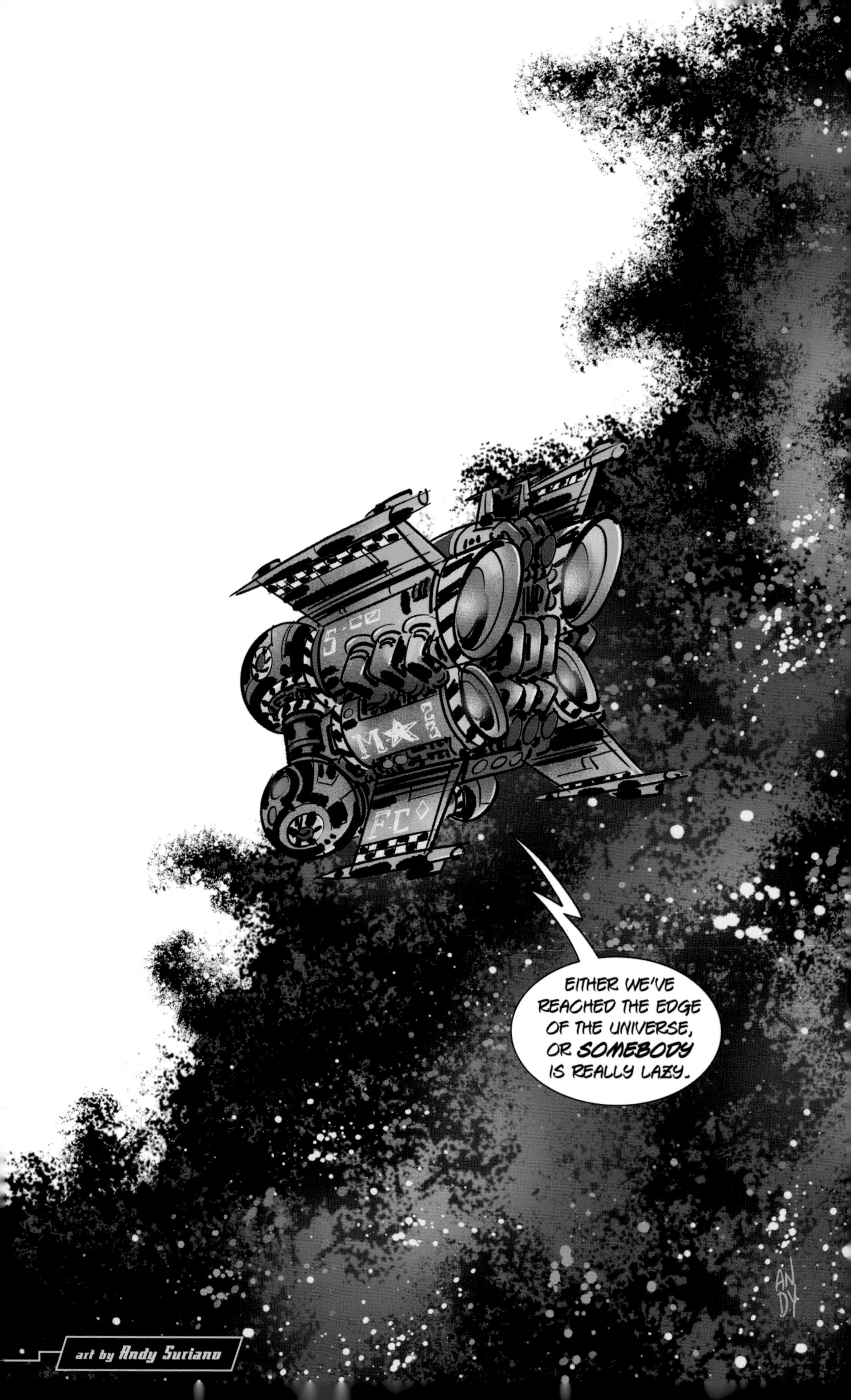
EITHER WE'VE REACHED THE EDGE OF THE UNIVERSE, OR **SOMEBODY** IS REALLY LAZY.

art by Andy Suriano

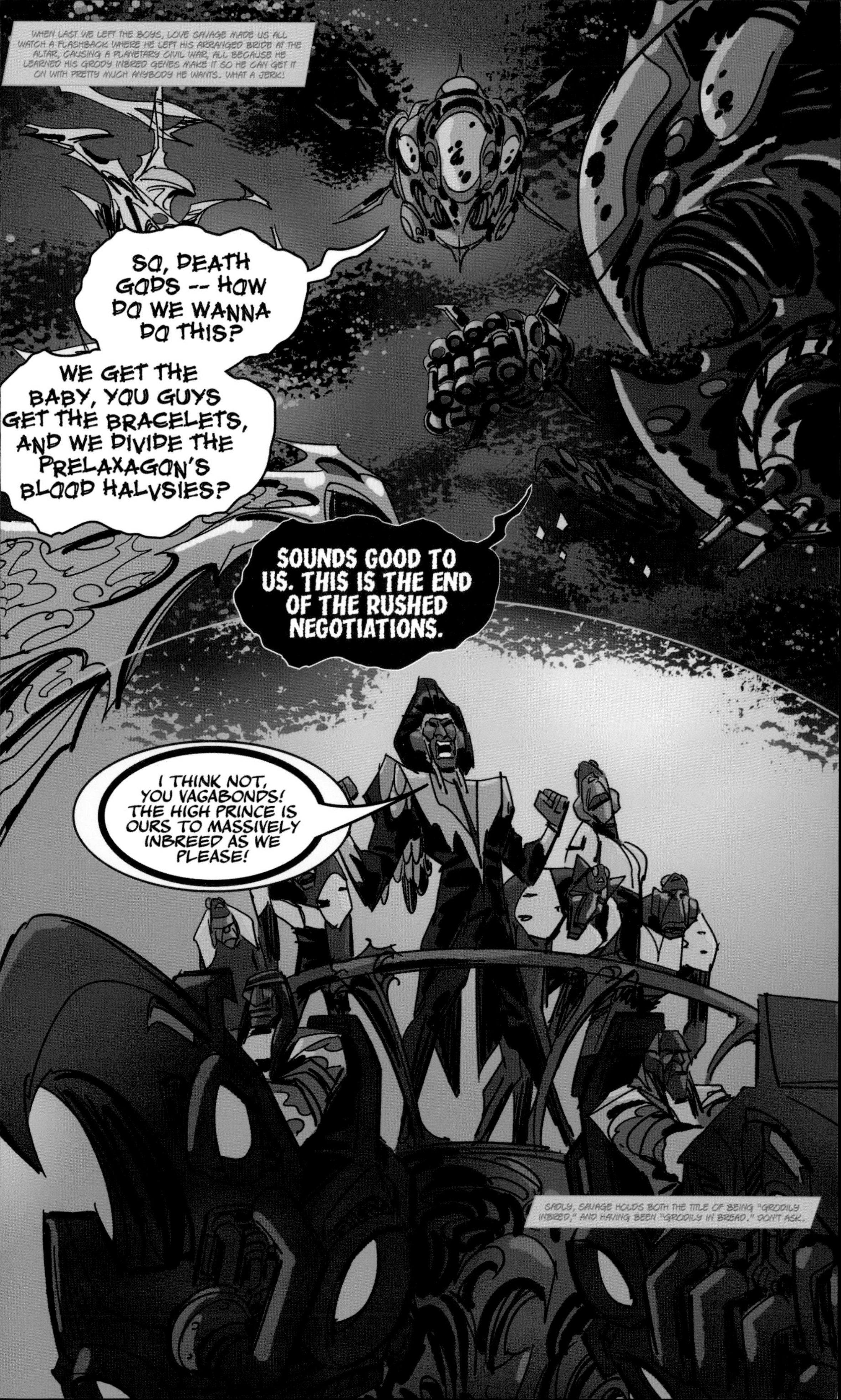
WHEN LAST WE LEFT THE BOYS, LOVE SAVAGE MADE US ALL WATCH A FLASHBACK WHERE HE LEFT HIS ARRANGED BRIDE AT THE ALTAR, CAUSING A PLANETARY CIVIL WAR, ALL BECAUSE HE LEARNED HIS GRODY INBRED GENES MAKE IT SO HE CAN GET IT ON WITH PRETTY MUCH ANYBODY HE WANTS. WHAT A JERK!
SO, DEATH GODS -- HOW DO WE WANNA DO THIS?
WE GET THE BABY, YOU GUYS GET THE BRACELETS, AND WE DIVIDE THE PRELAXAGON'S BLOOD HALVSIES?
SOUNDS GOOD TO US. THIS IS THE END OF THE RUSHED NEGOTIATIONS.
I THINK NOT, YOU VAGABONDS! THE HIGH PRINCE IS OURS TO MASSIVELY INBREED AS WE PLEASE!
SADLY, SAVAGE HOLDS BOTH THE TITLE OF BEING "GRODILY INBRED," AND HAVING BEEN "GRODILY IN BREAD." DON'T ASK.

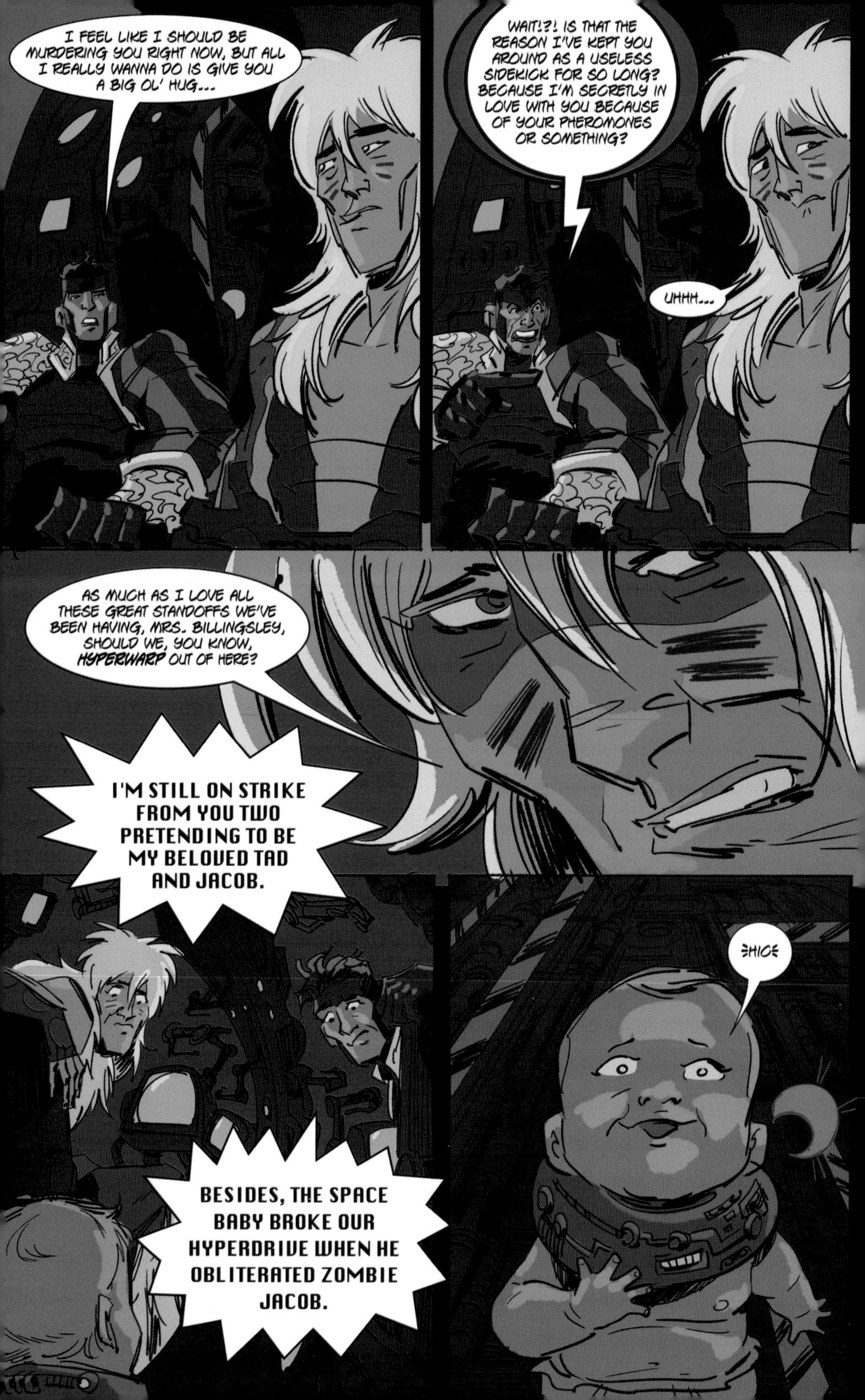
I FEEL LIKE I SHOULD BE MURDERING YOU RIGHT NOW, BUT ALL I REALLY WANNA DO IS GIVE YOU A BIG OL' HUG...
WAIT!?! IS THAT THE REASON I'VE KEPT YOU AROUND AS A USELESS SIDEKICK FOR SO LONG? BECAUSE I'M SECRETLY IN LOVE WITH YOU BECAUSE OF YOUR PHEROMONES OR SOMETHING?
UHHH...
AS MUCH AS I LOVE ALL THESE GREAT STANDOFFS WE'VE BEEN HAVING, MRS. BILLINGSLEY, SHOULD WE, YOU KNOW, HYPERWARP OUT OF HERE?
I'M STILL ON STRIKE FROM YOU TWO PRETENDING TO BE MY BELOVED TAD AND JACOB.
BESIDES, THE SPACE BABY BROKE OUR HYPERDRIVE WHEN HE OBLITERATED ZOMBIE JACOB.
HIC

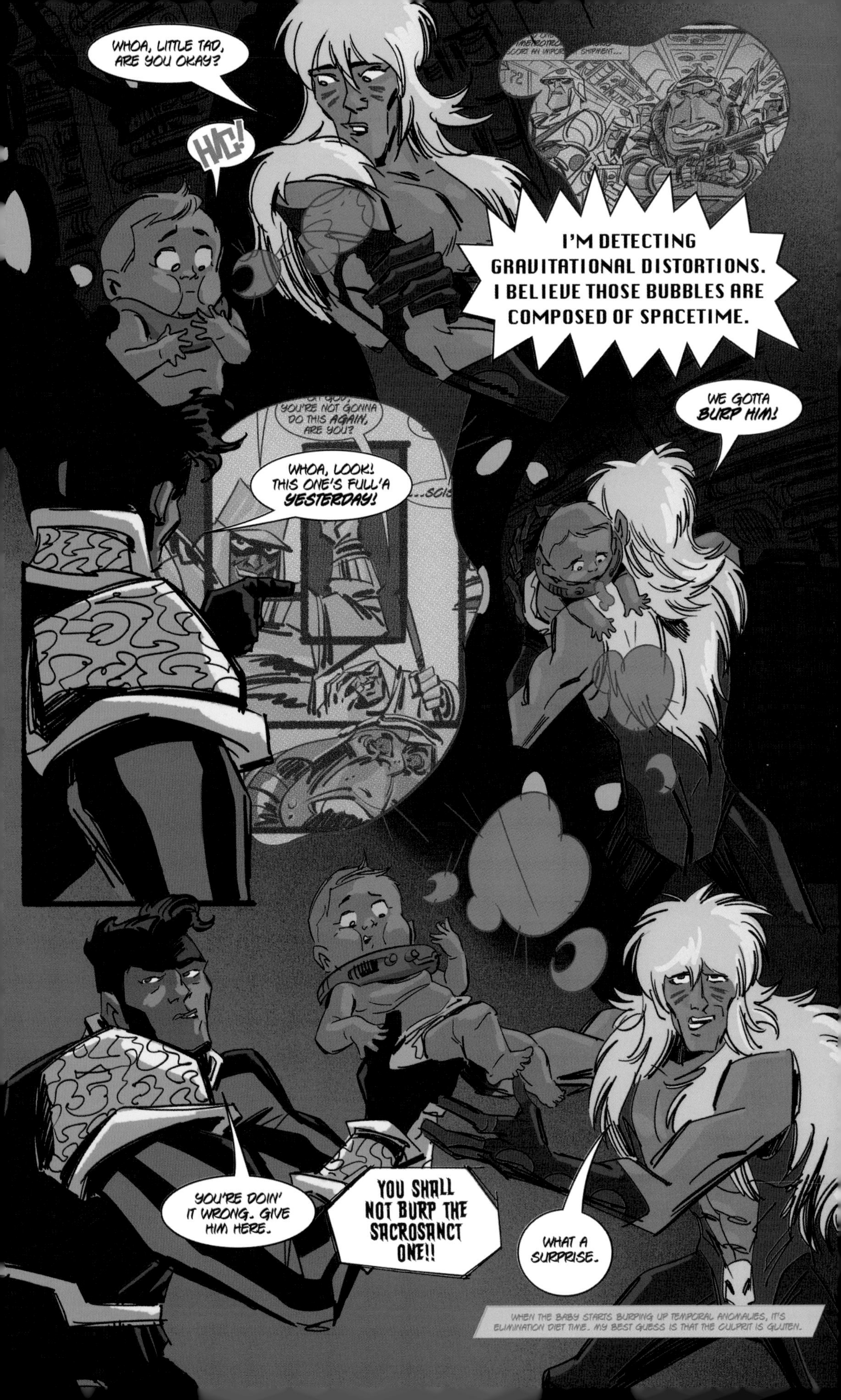
WHOA, LITTLE TAD, ARE YOU OKAY?
HIC!
I'M DETECTING GRAVITATIONAL DISTORTIONS. I BELIEVE THOSE BUBBLES ARE COMPOSED OF SPACETIME.
YOU'RE NOT GONNA DO THIS AGAIN, ARE YOU?
WHOA, LOOK! THIS ONE'S FULL'A YESTERDAY!
WE GOTTA BURP HIM!
YOU'RE DOIN' IT WRONG. GIVE HIM HERE.
YOU SHALL NOT BURP THE SACROSANCT ONE!!
WHAT A SURPRISE.
WHEN THE BABY STARTS BURPING UP TEMPORAL ANOMALIES, IT'S ELIMINATION DIET TIME. MY BEST GUESS IS THAT THE CULPRIT IS GLUTEN.

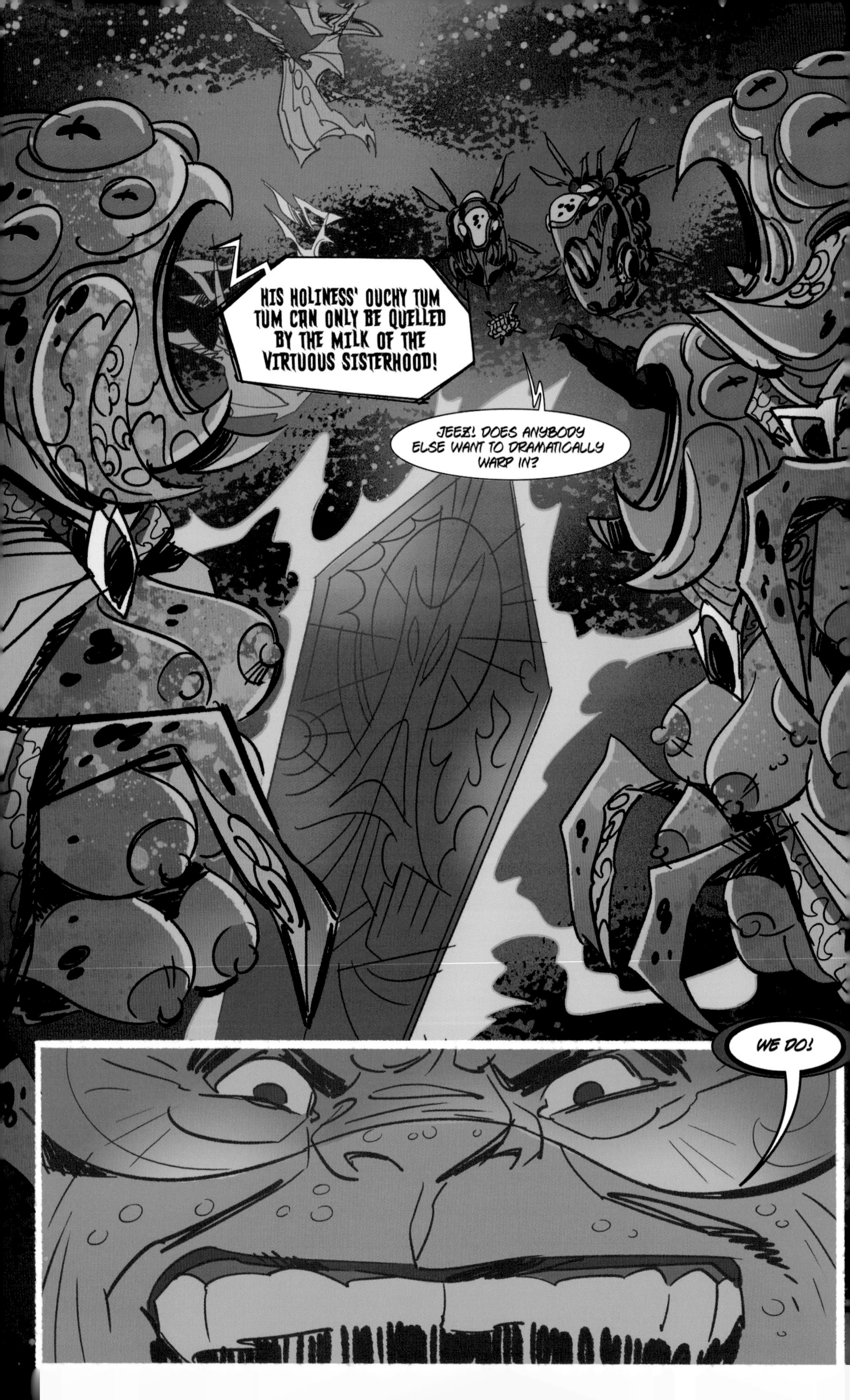
HIS HOLINESS' OUCHY TUM TUM CAN ONLY BE QUELLED BY THE MILK OF THE VIRTUOUS SISTERHOOD!
JEEZ! DOES ANYBODY ELSE WANT TO DRAMATICALLY WARP IN?
WE DO!

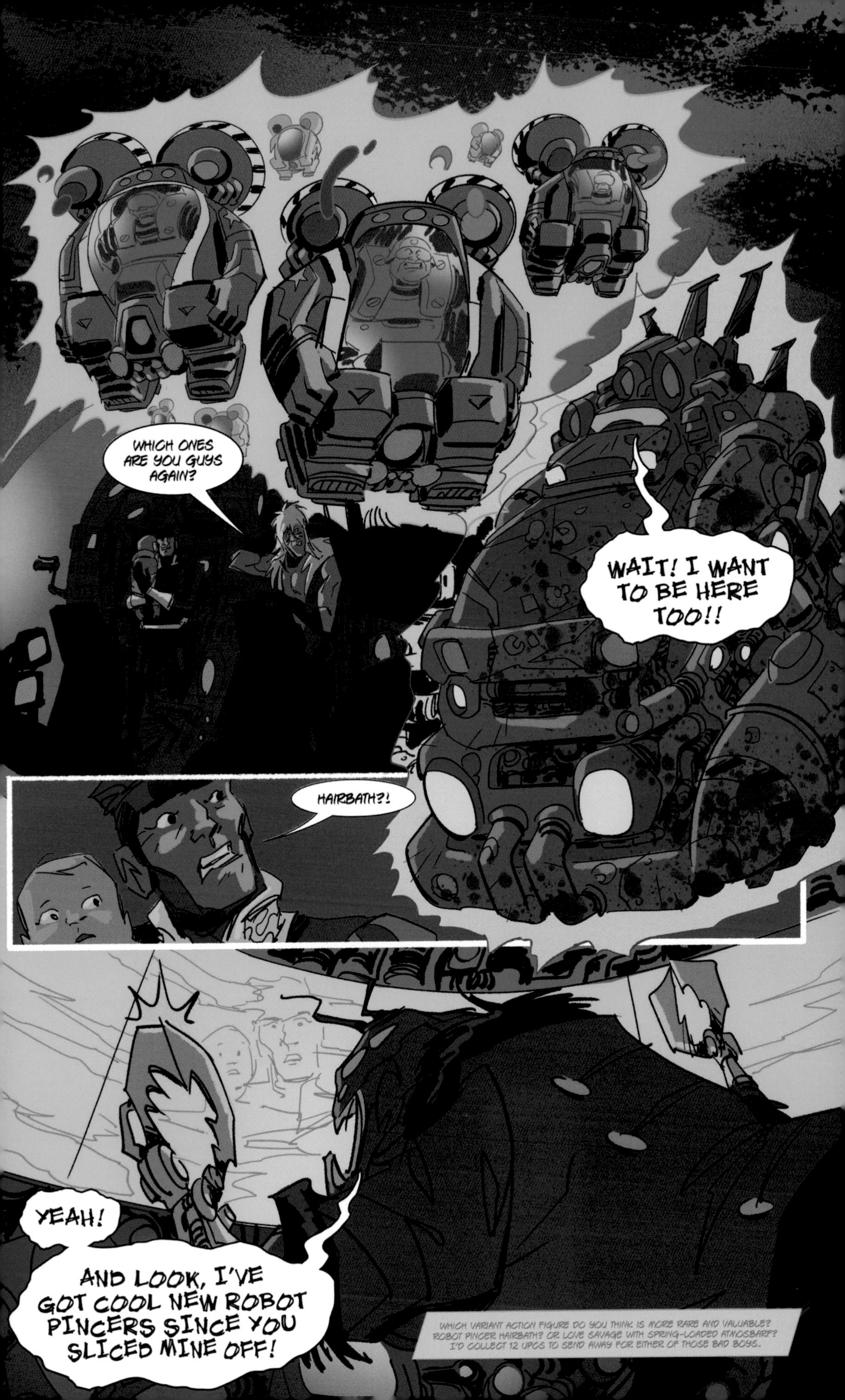
WHICH ONES ARE YOU GUYS AGAIN?
WAIT! I WANT TO BE HERE TOO!!
HAIRBATH?!
YEAH!
AND LOOK, I'VE GOT COOL NEW ROBOT PINCERS SINCE YOU SLICED MINE OFF!
WHICH VARIANT ACTION FIGURE DO YOU THINK IS MORE RARE AND VALUABLE? ROBOT PINCER HAIRBATH? OR LOVE SAVAGE WITH SPRING-LOADED ATMOSBARF? I'D COLLECT 12 UPCS TO SEND AWAY FOR EITHER OF THOSE BAD BOYS.

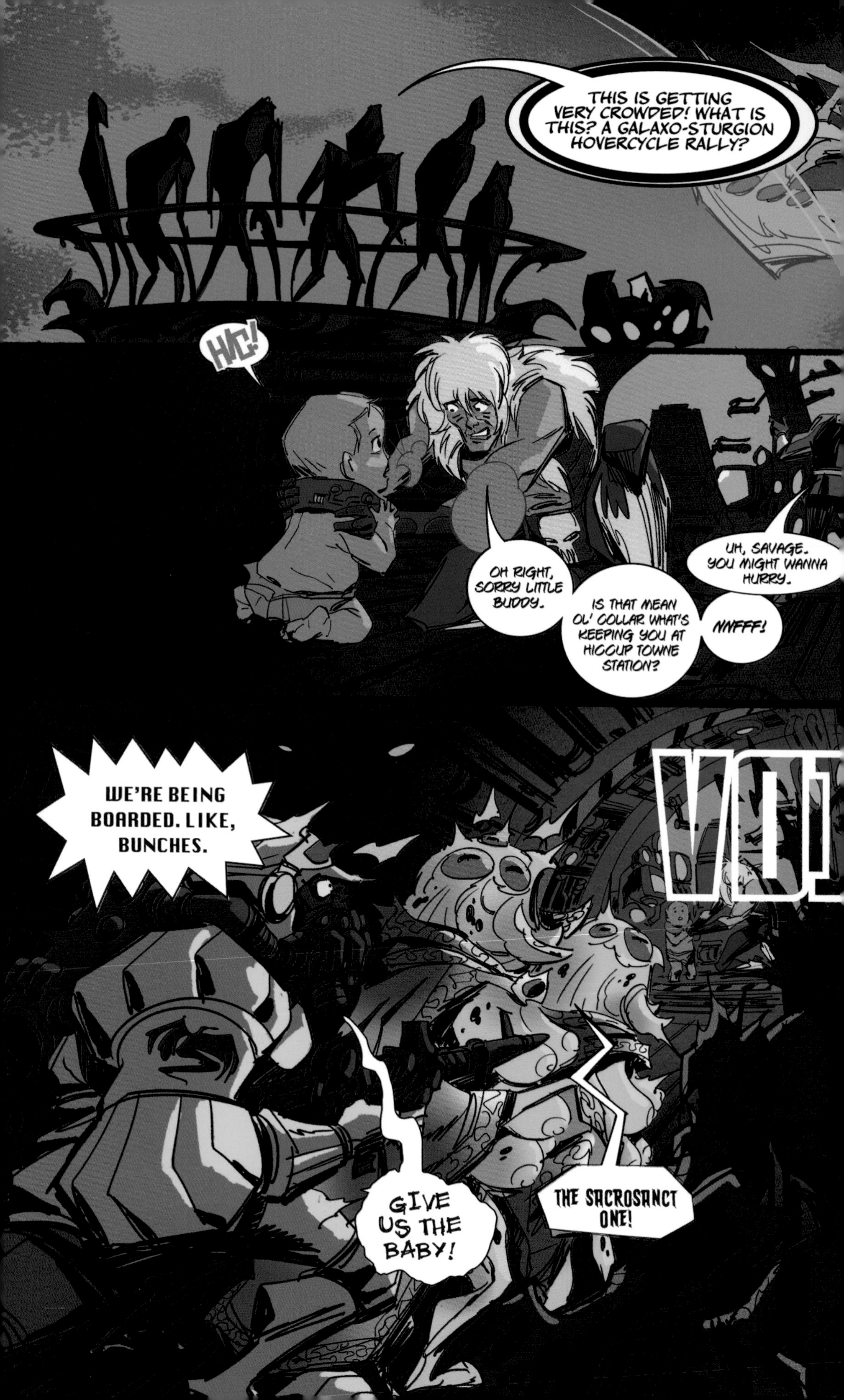
THIS IS GETTING VERY CROWDED! WHAT IS THIS? A GALAXO-STURGION HOVERCYCLE RALLY?
HIC!
OH RIGHT, SORRY LITTLE BUDDY.
IS THAT MEAN OL' COLLAR WHAT'S KEEPING YOU AT HICCUP TOWNE STATION?
UH, SAVAGE. YOU MIGHT WANNA HURRY.
NNFFF!
WE'RE BEING BOARDED. LIKE, BUNCHES.
GIVE US THE BABY!
THE SACROSANCT ONE!

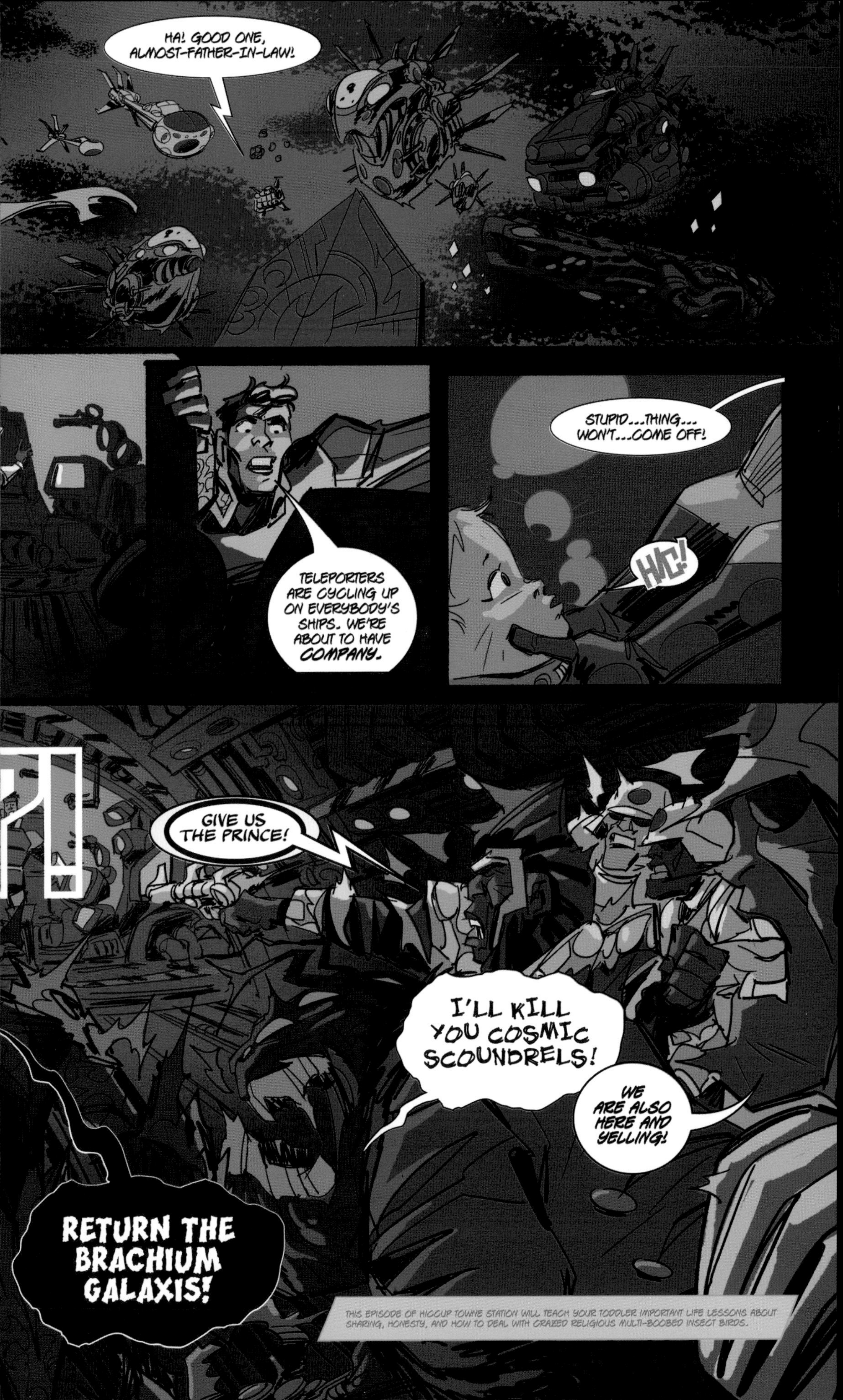
HA! GOOD ONE, ALMOST-FATHER-IN-LAW!
TELEPORTERS ARE CYCLING UP ON EVERYBODY'S SHIPS. WE'RE ABOUT TO HAVE COMPANY.
STUPID... THING... WON'T... COME OFF!
HVG!
GIVE US THE PRINCE!
I'LL KILL YOU COSMIC SCOUNDRELS!
WE ARE ALSO HERE AND YELLING!
RETURN THE BRACHIUM GALAXIS!
THIS EPISODE OF HICCUP TOWNE STATION WILL TEACH YOUR TODDLER IMPORTANT LIFE LESSONS ABOUT SHARING, HONESTY, AND HOW TO DEAL WITH CRAZED RELIGIOUS MULTI-BOOBED INSECT BIRDS.

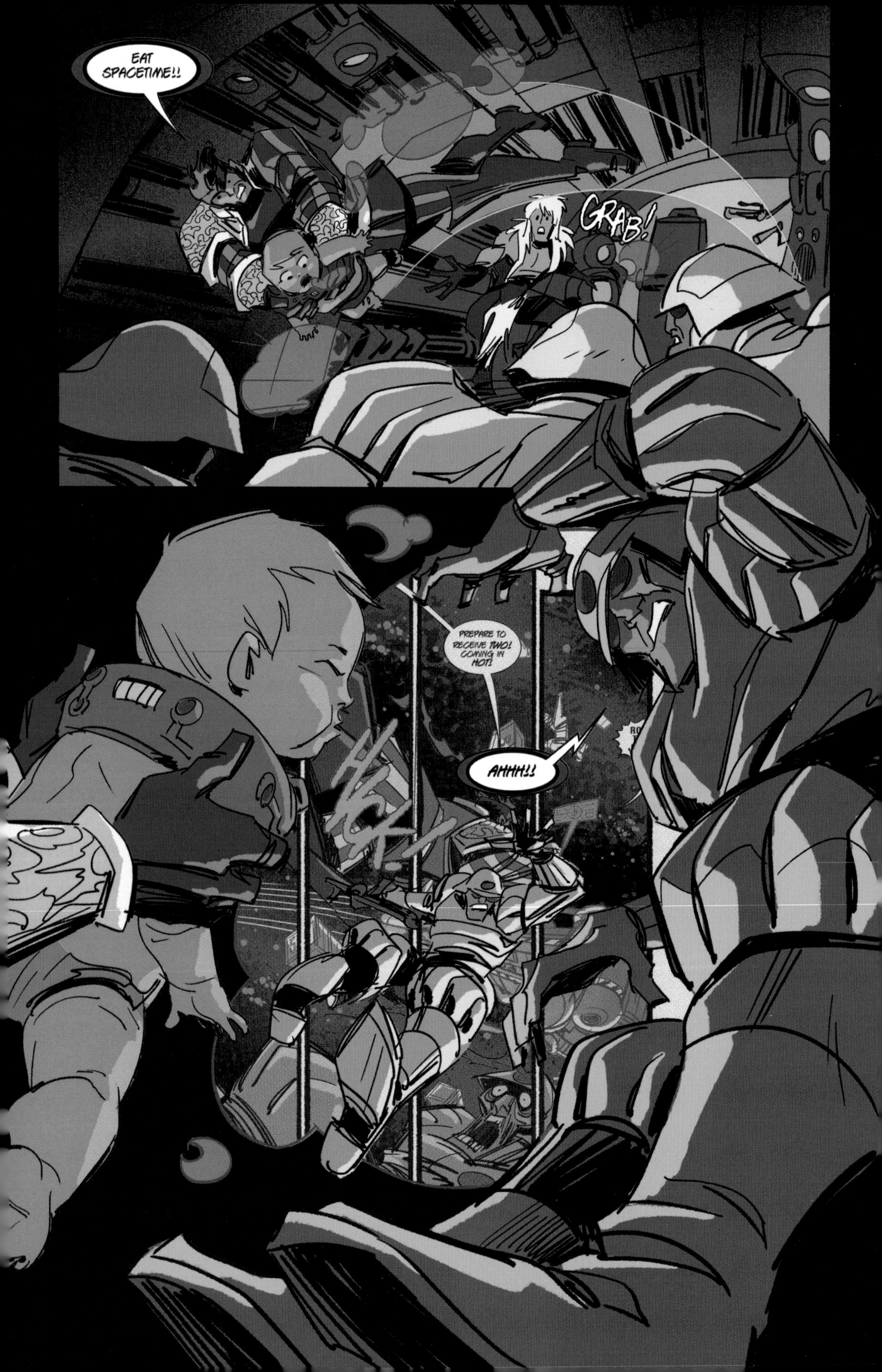
EAT SPACETIME!!
GRAB!
PREPARE TO RECEIVE TWO! COMING IN HOT!
AHHH!!

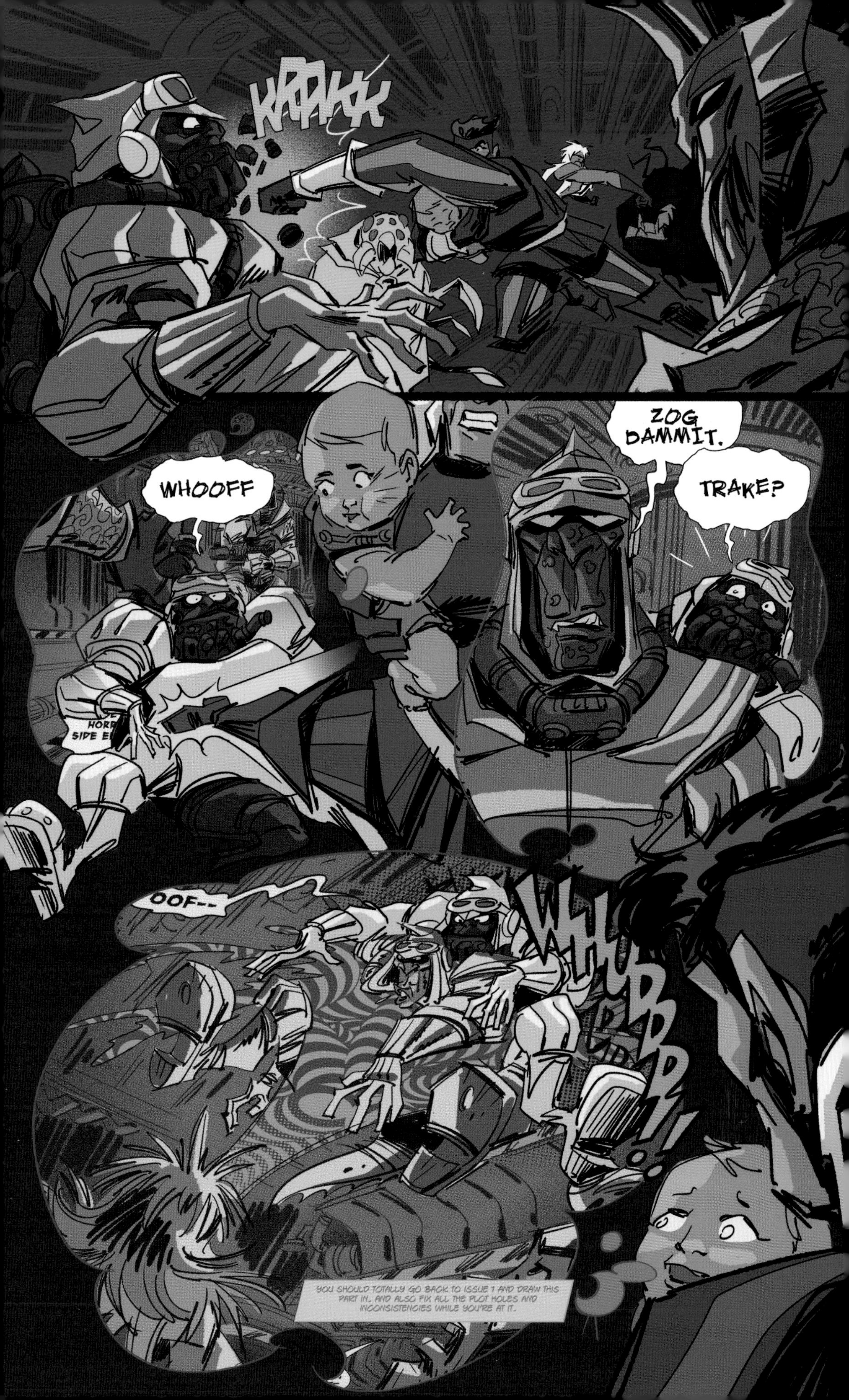
KRAKK
WHOOFF
ZOG DAMMIT.
TRAKE?
OOF--
WHUDD
YOU SHOULD TOTALLY GO BACK TO ISSUE 1 AND DRAW THIS PART IN. AND ALSO FIX ALL THE PLOT HOLES AND INCONSISTENCIES WHILE YOU'RE AT IT.

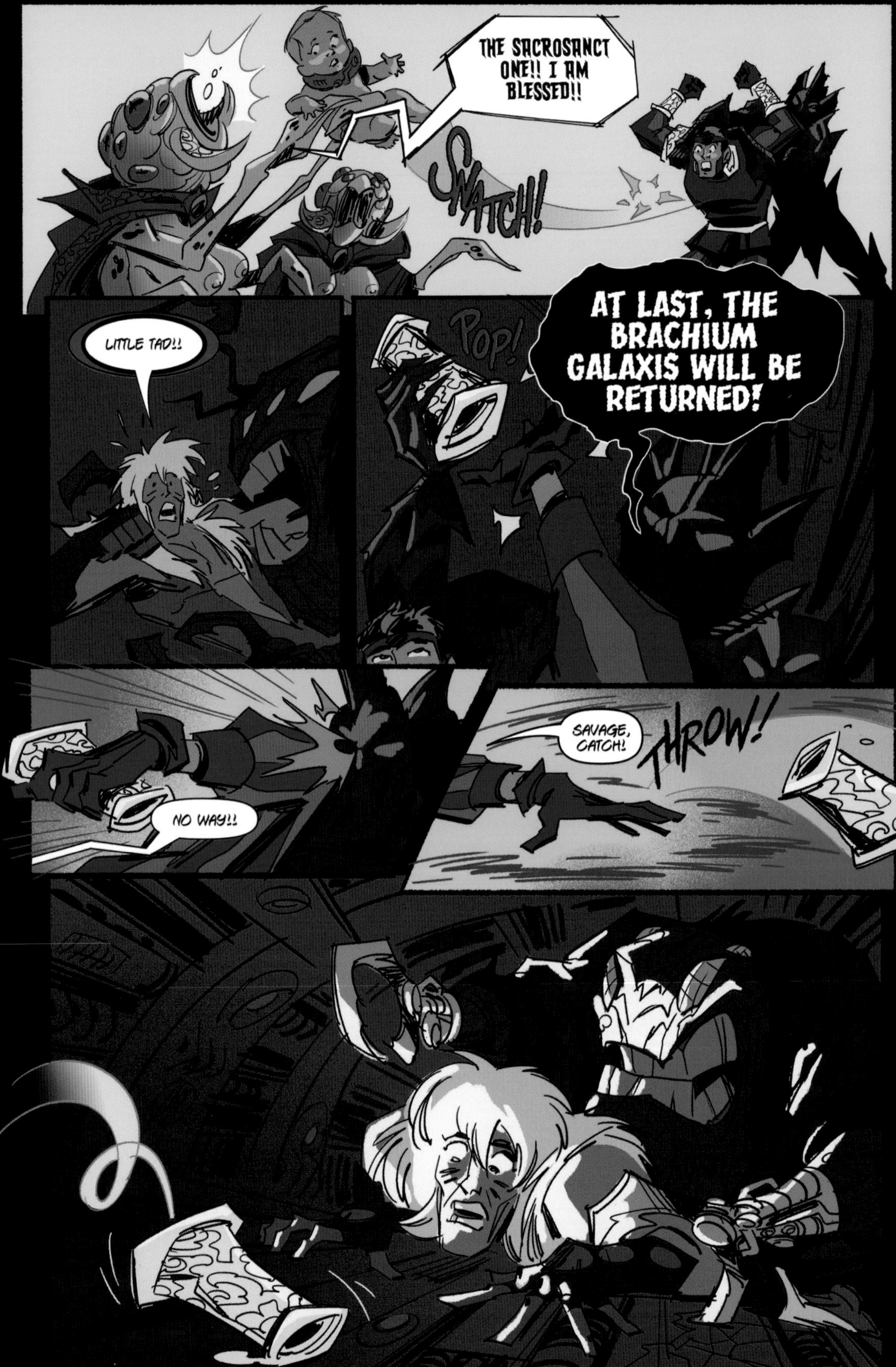
THE SACROSANCT ONE!! I AM BLESSED!!
SNATCH!
LITTLE TAD!!
POP!
AT LAST, THE BRACHIUM GALAXIS WILL BE RETURNED!
NO WAY!!
SAVAGE, CATCH!
THROW!

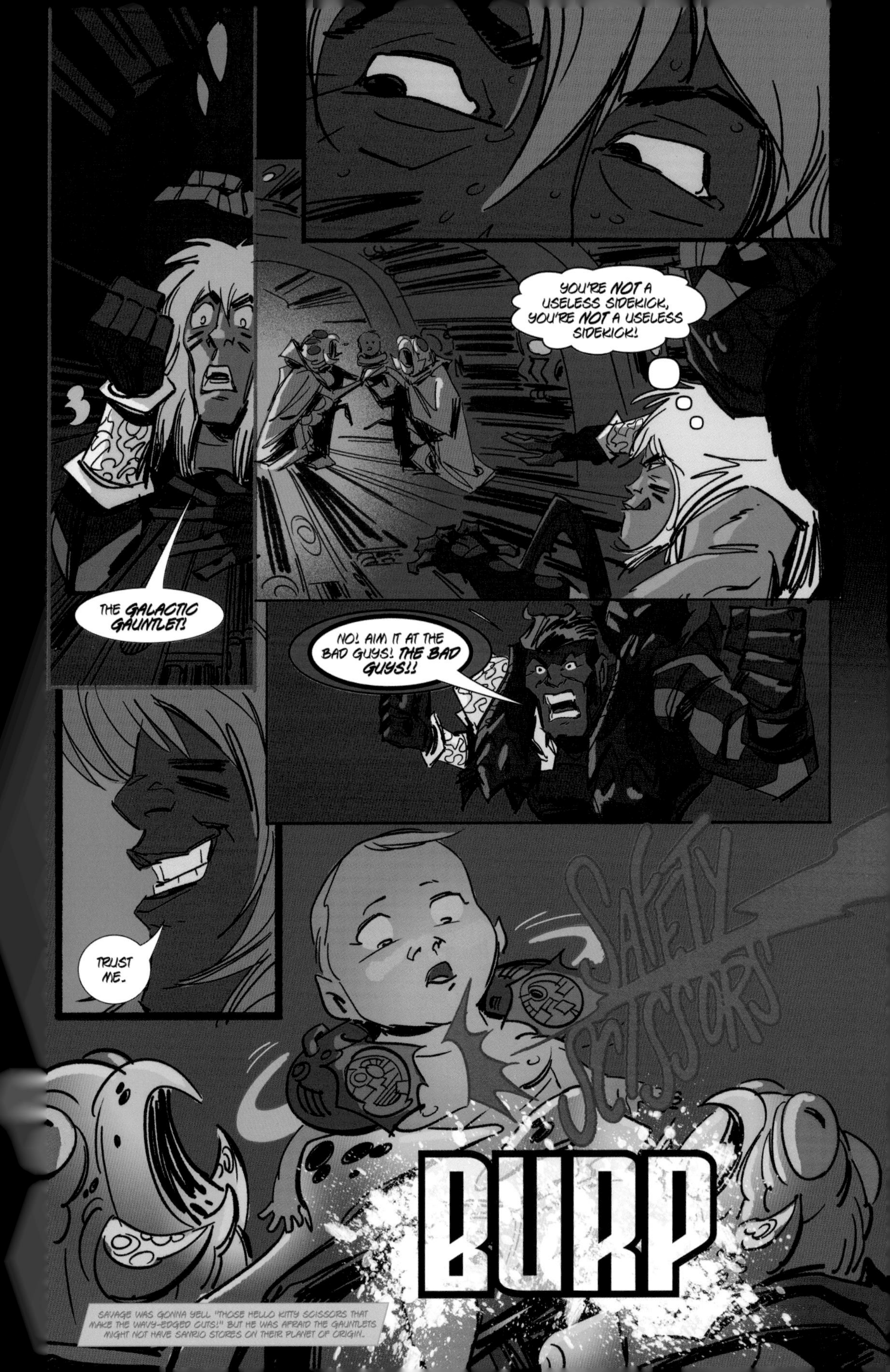
THE GALACTIC GAUNTLET!
YOU'RE NOT A USELESS SIDEKICK, YOU'RE NOT A USELESS SIDEKICK!
NO! AIM IT AT THE BAD GUYS! THE BAD GUYS!!
TRUST ME.
SAFETY SCISSORS
BURP
SAVAGE WAS GONNA YELL "THOSE HELLO KITTY SCISSORS THAT MAKE THE WAVY-EDGED CUTS!" BUT HE WAS AFRAID THE GAUNTLETS MIGHT NOT HAVE SANRIO STORES ON THEIR PLANET OF ORIGIN.

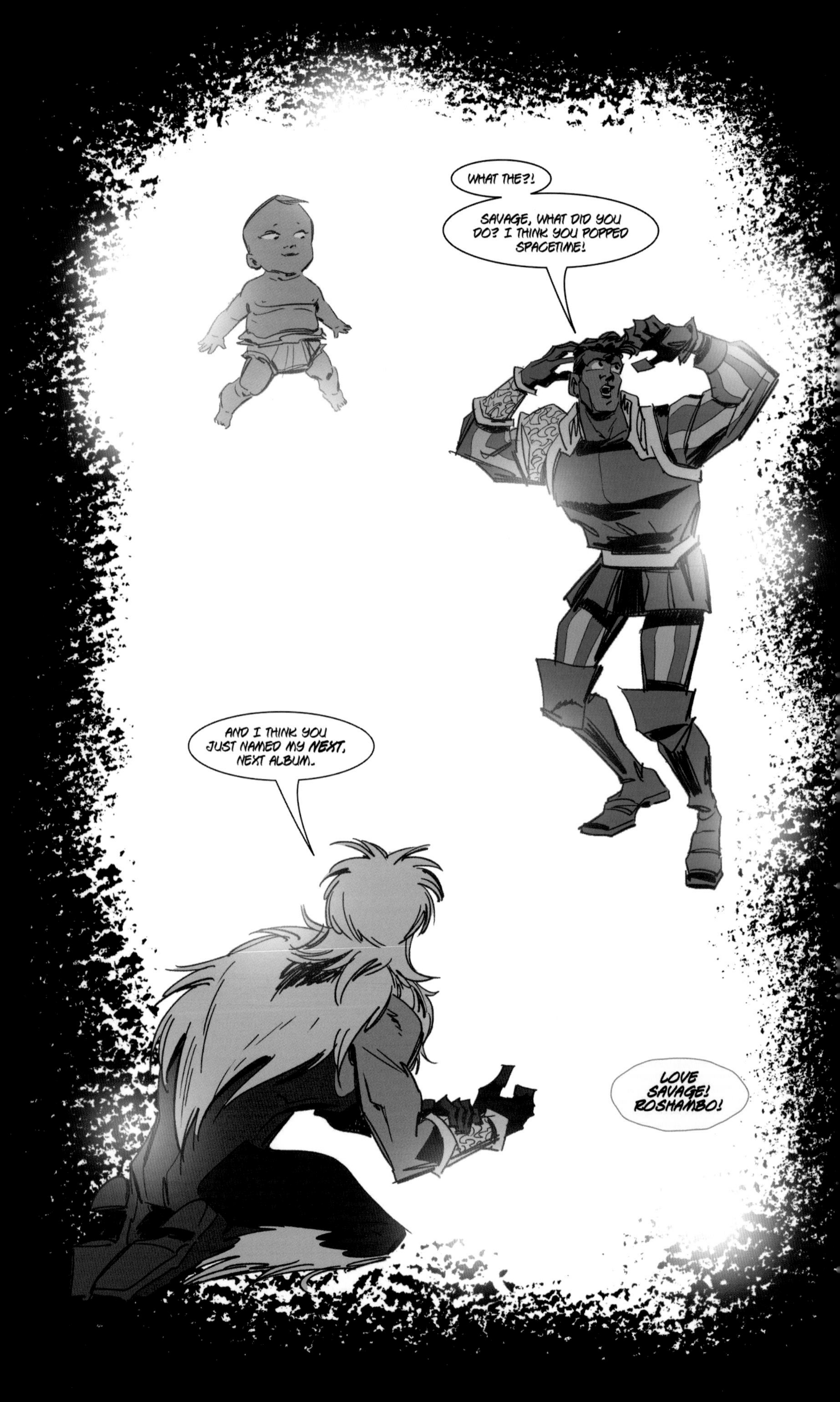
WHAT THE?!
SAVAGE, WHAT DID YOU DO? I THINK YOU POPPED SPACETIME!
AND I THINK YOU JUST NAMED MY NEXT, NEXT ALBUM.
LOVE SAVAGE! ROSHAMBO!

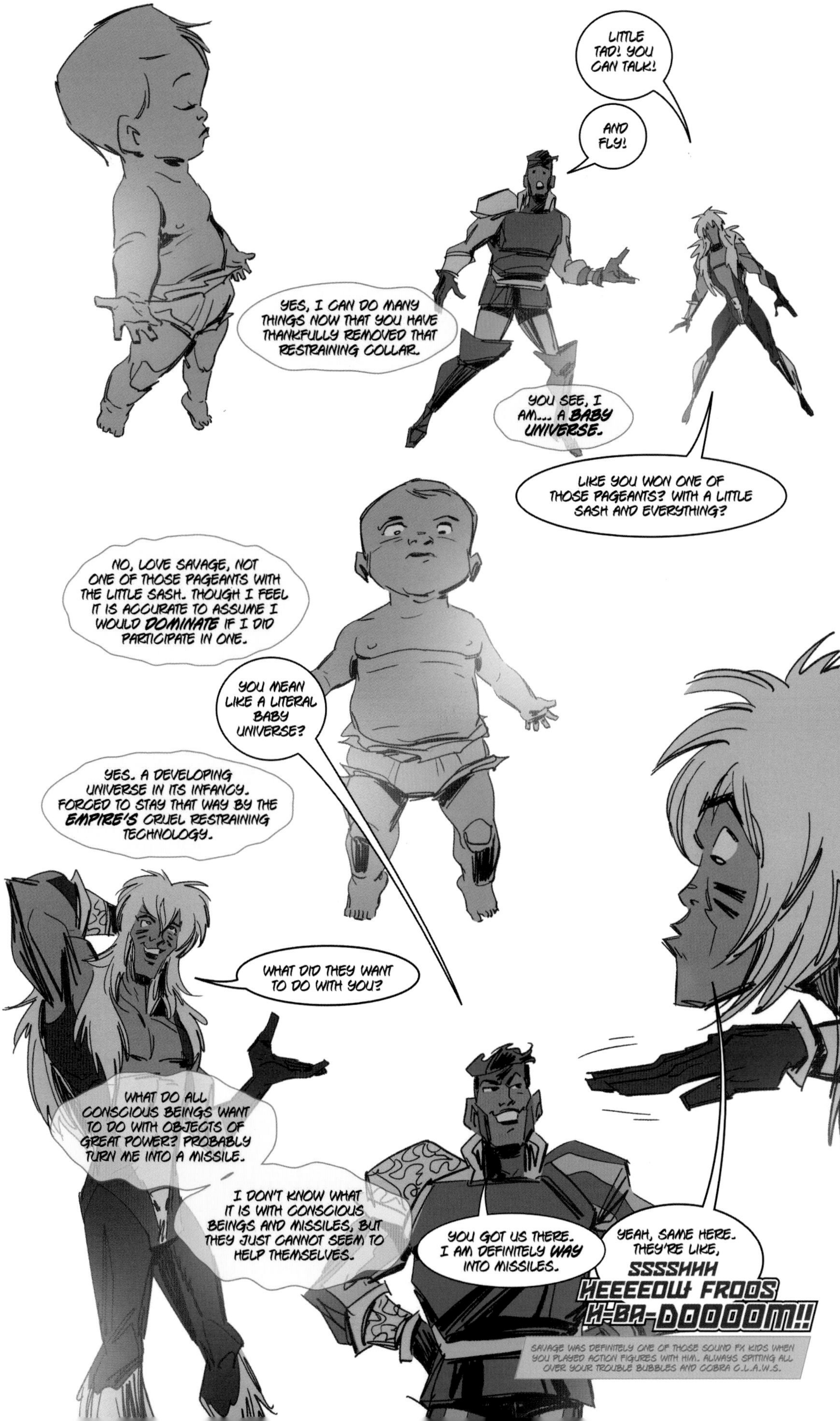
LITTLE TAD! YOU CAN TALK!
AND FLY!
YES, I CAN DO MANY THINGS NOW THAT YOU HAVE THANKFULLY REMOVED THAT RESTRAINING COLLAR.
YOU SEE, I AM... A BABY UNIVERSE.
LIKE YOU WON ONE OF THOSE PAGEANTS? WITH A LITTLE SASH AND EVERYTHING?
NO, LOVE SAVAGE, NOT ONE OF THOSE PAGEANTS WITH THE LITTLE SASH. THOUGH I FEEL IT IS ACCURATE TO ASSUME I WOULD DOMINATE IF I DID PARTICIPATE IN ONE.
YOU MEAN LIKE A LITERAL BABY UNIVERSE?
YES. A DEVELOPING UNIVERSE IN ITS INFANCY. FORCED TO STAY THAT WAY BY THE EMPIRE'S CRUEL RESTRAINING TECHNOLOGY.
WHAT DID THEY WANT TO DO WITH YOU?
WHAT DO ALL CONSCIOUS BEINGS WANT TO DO WITH OBJECTS OF GREAT POWER? PROBABLY TURN ME INTO A MISSILE.
I DON'T KNOW WHAT IT IS WITH CONSCIOUS BEINGS AND MISSILES, BUT THEY JUST CANNOT SEEM TO HELP THEMSELVES.
YOU GOT US THERE. I AM DEFINITELY WAY INTO MISSILES.
YEAH, SAME HERE. THEY'RE LIKE, SSSSHHH HEEEEOW FROOS K-BA-DOOOOM!!
SAVAGE WAS DEFINITELY ONE OF THOSE SOUND FX KIDS WHEN YOU PLAYED ACTION FIGURES WITH HIM. ALWAYS SPITTING ALL OVER YOUR TROUBLE BUBBLES AND COBRA C.L.A.W.S.

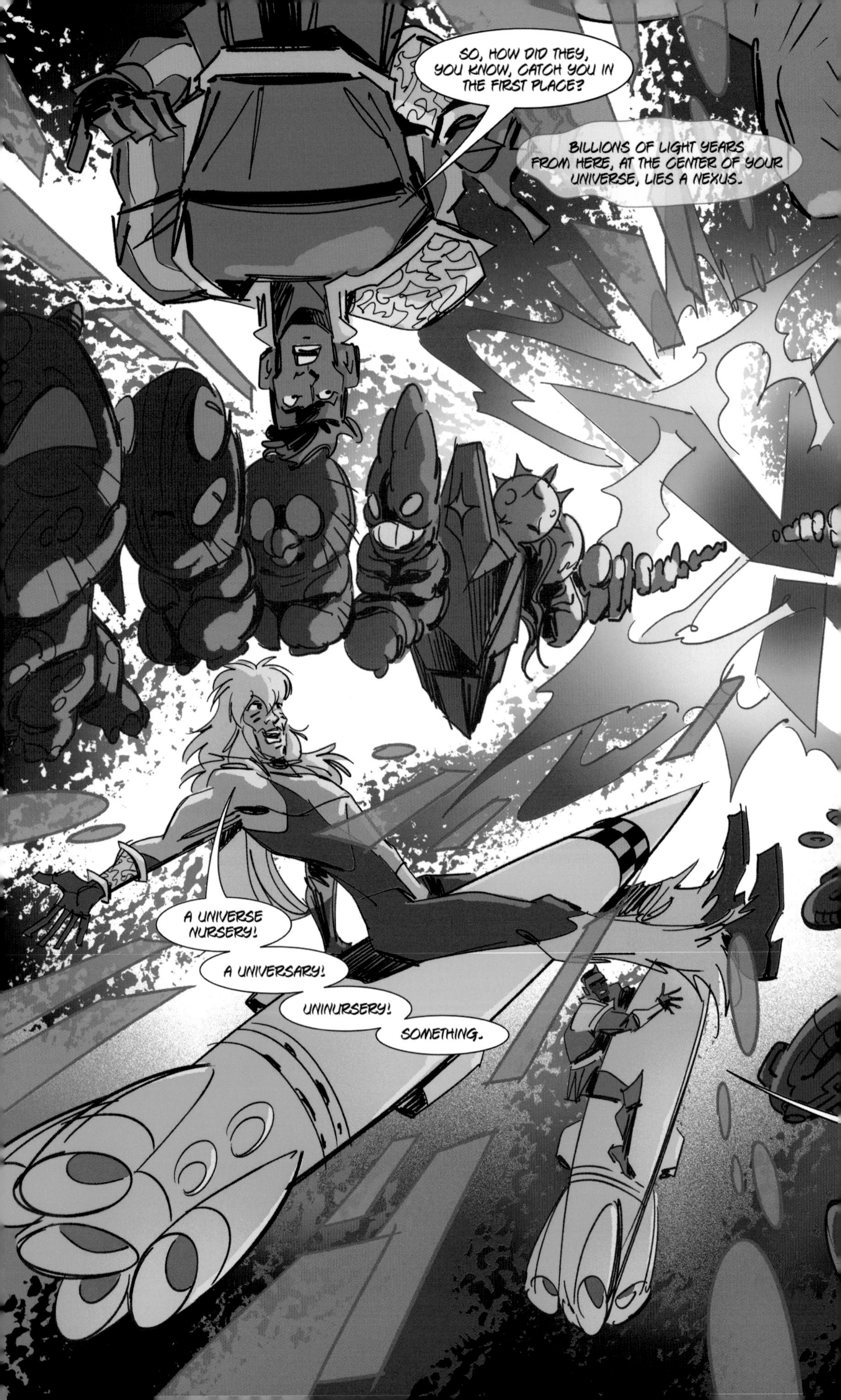
SO, HOW DID THEY, YOU KNOW, CATCH YOU IN THE FIRST PLACE?
BILLIONS OF LIGHT YEARS FROM HERE, AT THE CENTER OF YOUR UNIVERSE, LIES A NEXUS.
A UNIVERSE NURSERY!
A UNIVERSARY!
UNINURSERY!
SOMETHING.

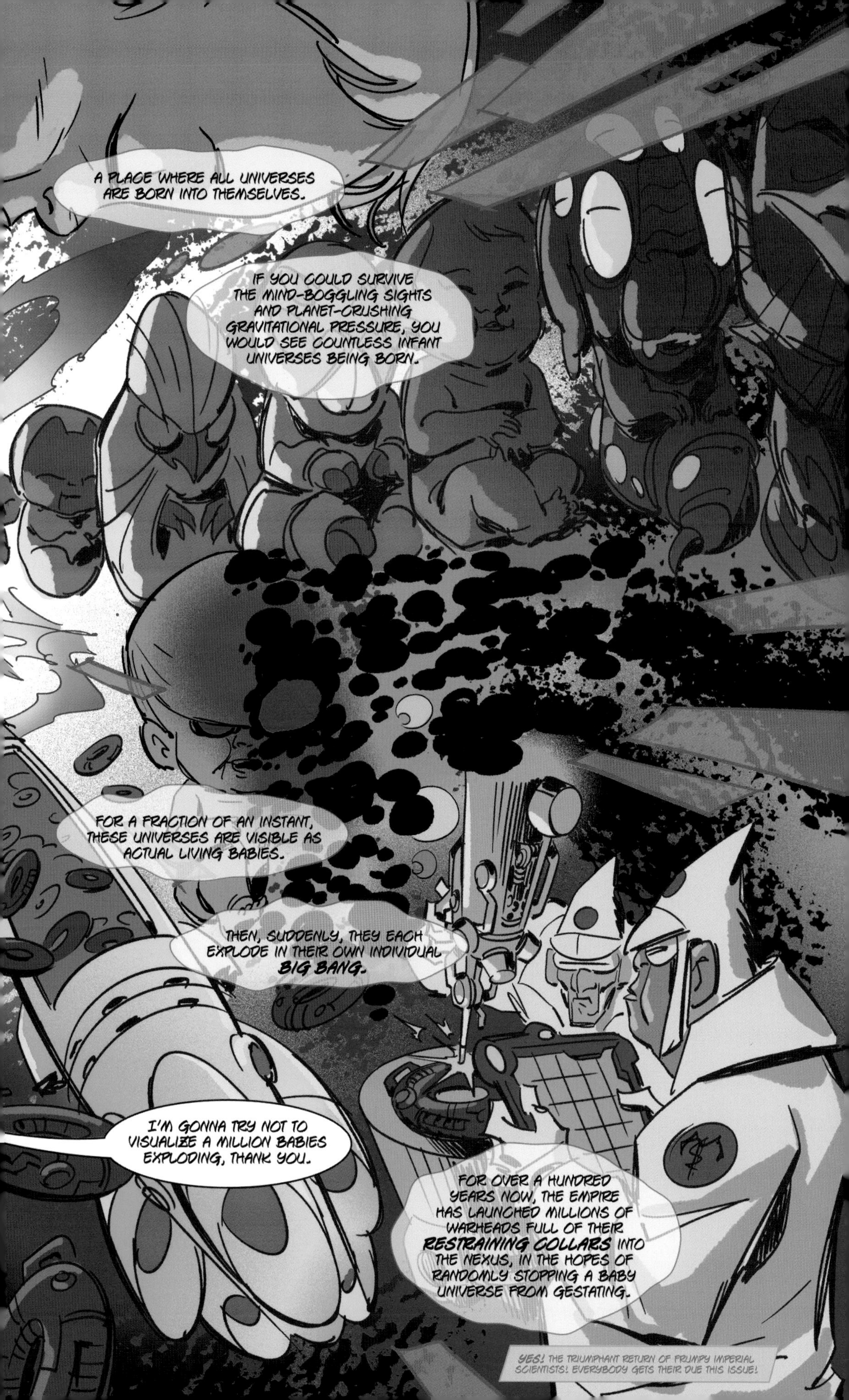
A PLACE WHERE ALL UNIVERSES ARE BORN INTO THEMSELVES.
IF YOU COULD SURVIVE THE MIND-BOGGLING SIGHTS AND PLANET-CRUSHING GRAVITATIONAL PRESSURE, YOU WOULD SEE COUNTLESS INFANT UNIVERSES BEING BORN.
FOR A FRACTION OF AN INSTANT, THESE UNIVERSES ARE VISIBLE AS ACTUAL LIVING BABIES.
THEN, SUDDENLY, THEY EACH EXPLODE IN THEIR OWN INDIVIDUAL BIG BANG.
I'M GONNA TRY NOT TO VISUALIZE A MILLION BABIES EXPLODING, THANK YOU.
FOR OVER A HUNDRED YEARS NOW, THE EMPIRE HAS LAUNCHED MILLIONS OF WARHEADS FULL OF THEIR RESTRAINING COLLARS INTO THE NEXUS, IN THE HOPES OF RANDOMLY STOPPING A BABY UNIVERSE FROM GESTATING.
YES! THE TRIUMPHANT RETURN OF FRUMPY IMPERIAL SCIENTISTS! EVERYBODY GETS THEIR DUE THIS ISSUE!

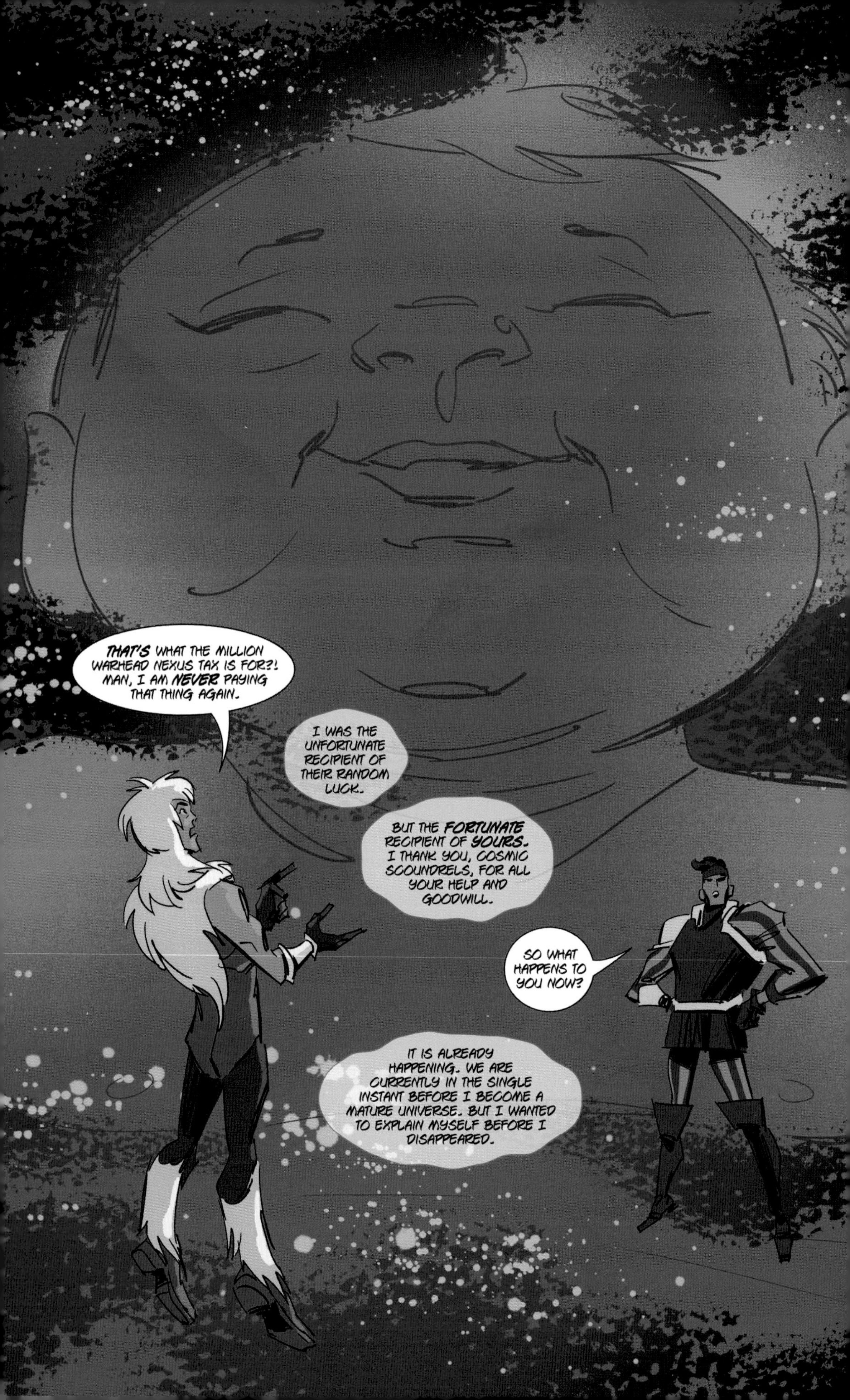
THAT'S WHAT THE MILLION WARHEAD NEXUS TAX IS FOR?! MAN, I AM NEVER PAYING THAT THING AGAIN.
I WAS THE UNFORTUNATE RECIPIENT OF THEIR RANDOM LUCK.
BUT THE FORTUNATE RECIPIENT OF YOURS. I THANK YOU, COSMIC SCOUNDRELS, FOR ALL YOUR HELP AND GOODWILL.
SO WHAT HAPPENS TO YOU NOW?
IT IS ALREADY HAPPENING. WE ARE CURRENTLY IN THE SINGLE INSTANT BEFORE I BECOME A MATURE UNIVERSE. BUT I WANTED TO EXPLAIN MYSELF BEFORE I DISAPPEARED.

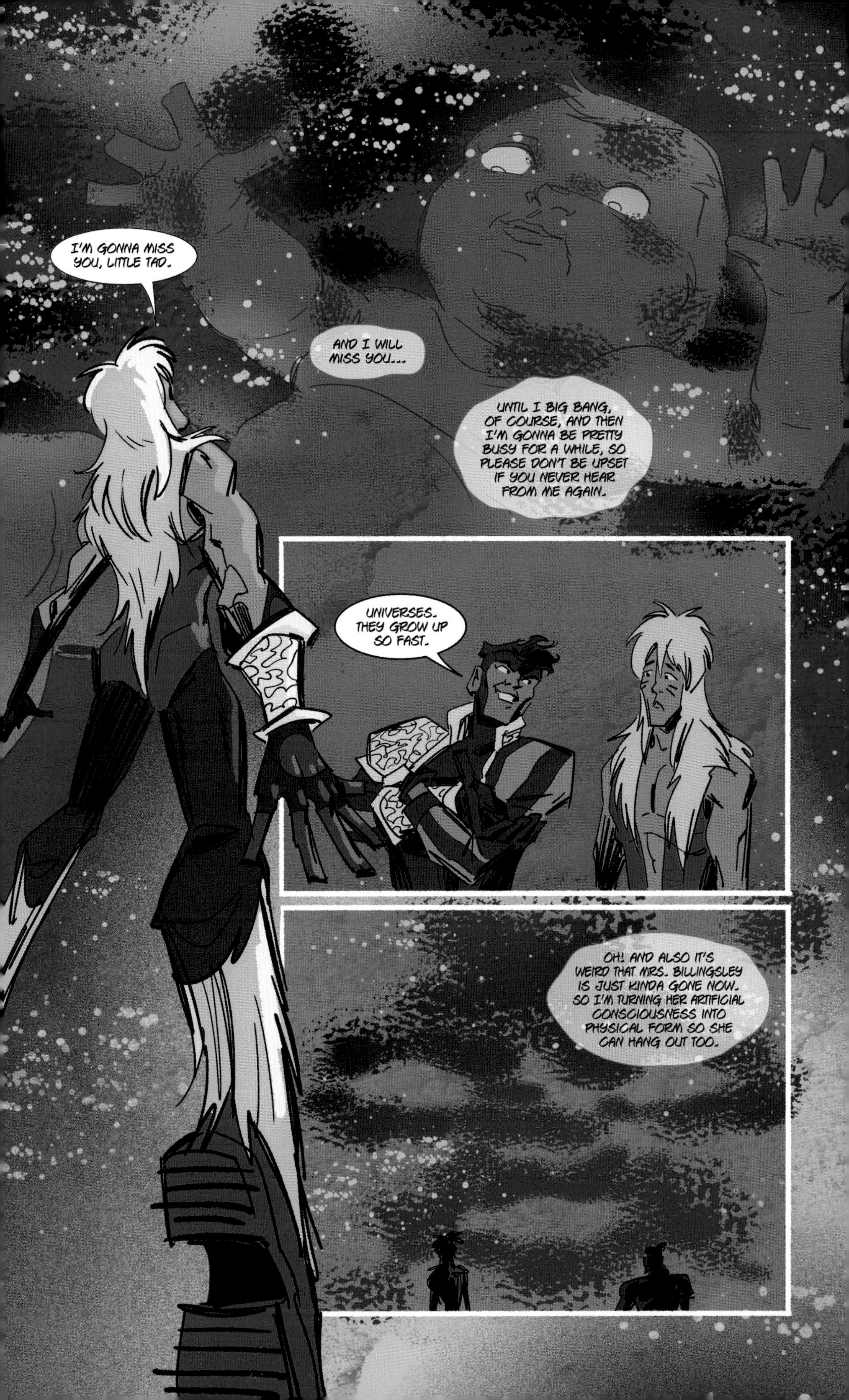
I'M GONNA MISS YOU, LITTLE TAD.
AND I WILL MISS YOU...
UNTIL I BIG BANG, OF COURSE, AND THEN I'M GONNA BE PRETTY BUSY FOR A WHILE, SO PLEASE DON'T BE UPSET IF YOU NEVER HEAR FROM ME AGAIN.
UNIVERSES. THEY GROW UP SO FAST.
OH! AND ALSO IT'S WEIRD THAT MRS. BILLINGSLEY IS JUST KINDA GONE NOW. SO I'M TURNING HER ARTIFICIAL CONSCIOUSNESS INTO PHYSICAL FORM SO SHE CAN HANG OUT TOO.

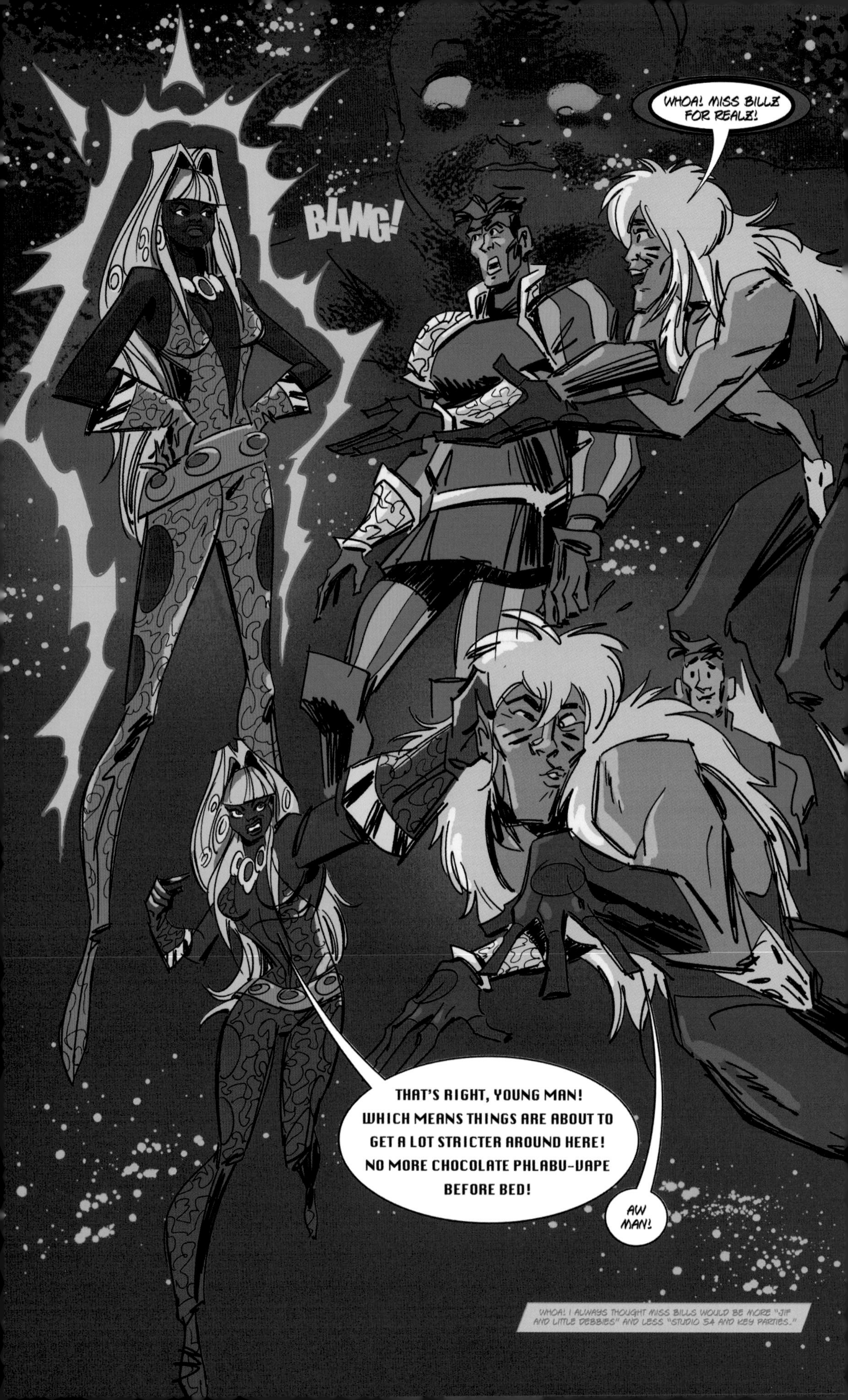
BLWG!
WHOA! MISS BILLZ FOR REALZ!
THAT'S RIGHT, YOUNG MAN! WHICH MEANS THINGS ARE ABOUT TO GET A LOT STRICTER AROUND HERE! NO MORE CHOCOLATE PHLABU-VAPE BEFORE BED!
AW MAN!
WHOA! I ALWAYS THOUGHT MISS BILLS WOULD BE MORE "JIF AND LITTLE DEBBIES" AND LESS "STUDIO 54 AND KEY PARTIES."

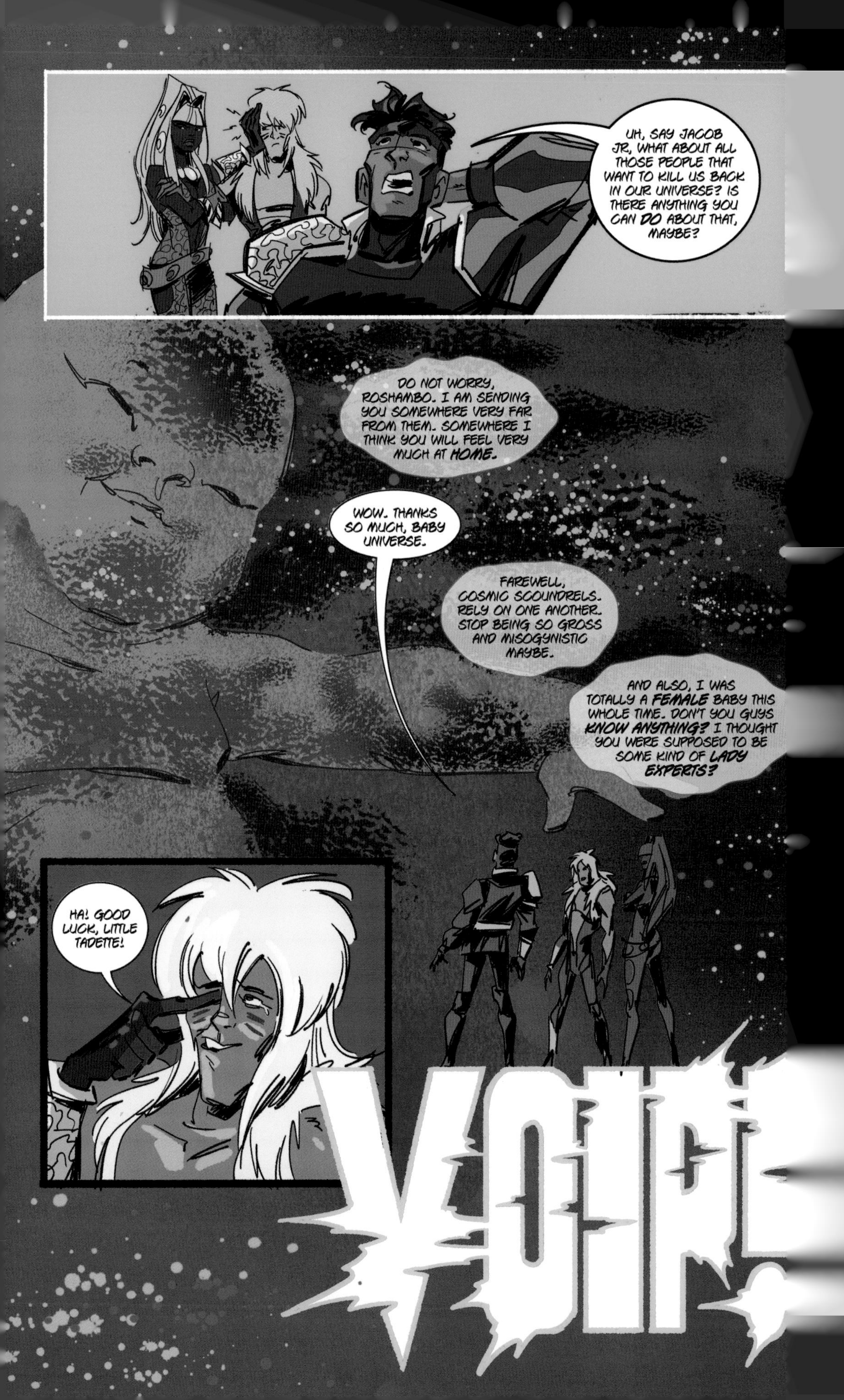
UH, SAY JACOB JR, WHAT ABOUT ALL THOSE PEOPLE THAT WANT TO KILL US BACK IN OUR UNIVERSE? IS THERE ANYTHING YOU CAN DO ABOUT THAT, MAYBE?
DO NOT WORRY, ROSHAMBO. I AM SENDING YOU SOMEWHERE VERY FAR FROM THEM. SOMEWHERE I THINK YOU WILL FEEL VERY MUCH AT HOME.
WOW. THANKS SO MUCH, BABY UNIVERSE.
FAREWELL, COSMIC SCOUNDRELS. RELY ON ONE ANOTHER. STOP BEING SO GROSS AND MISOGYNISTIC MAYBE.
AND ALSO, I WAS TOTALLY A FEMALE BABY THIS WHOLE TIME. DON'T YOU GUYS KNOW ANYTHING? I THOUGHT YOU WERE SUPPOSED TO BE SOME KIND OF LADY EXPERTS?
HA! GOOD LUCK, LITTLE TADETTE!
VOIP!

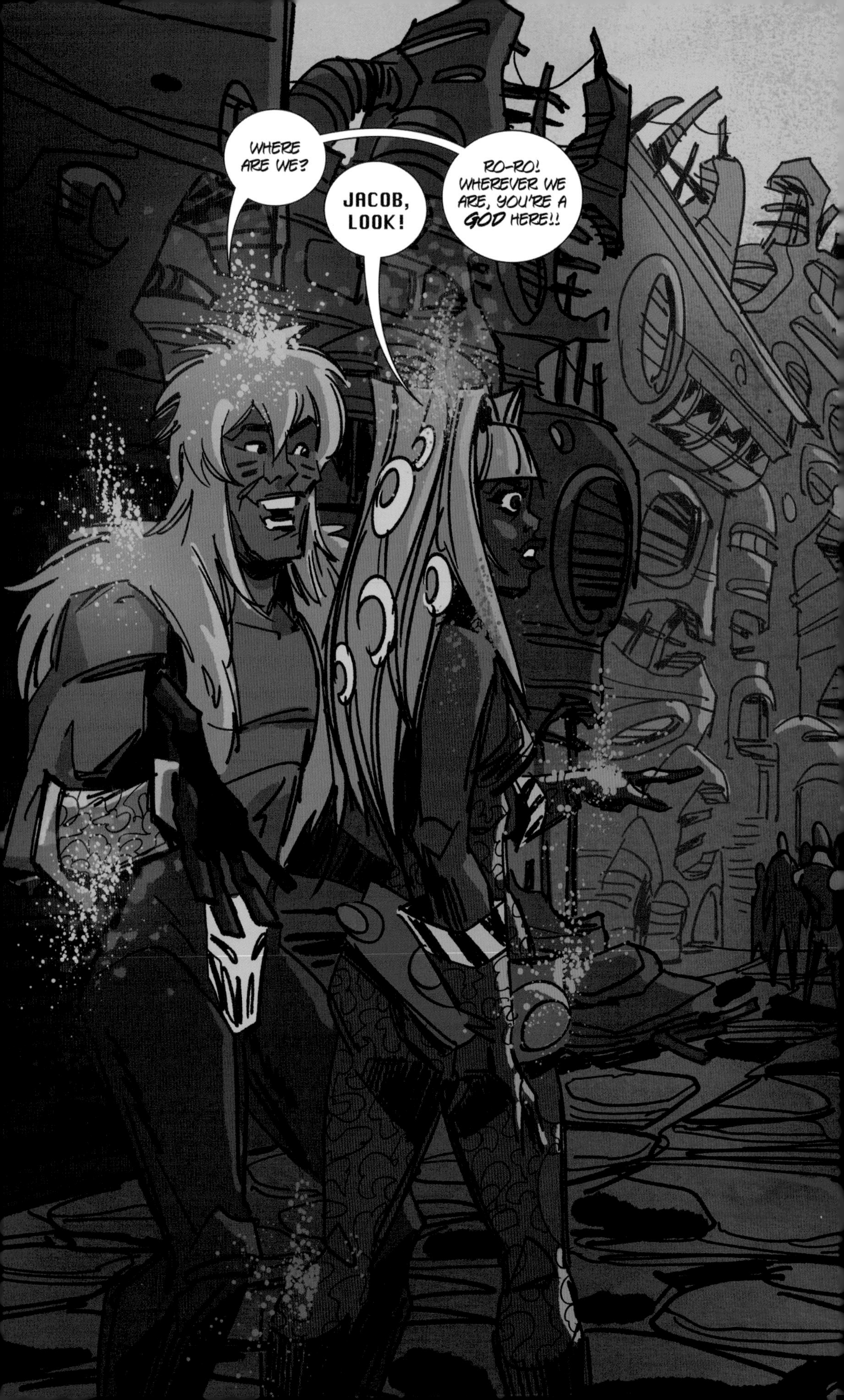
WHERE ARE WE?
JACOB, LOOK!
RO-RO! WHEREVER WE ARE, YOU'RE A GOD HERE!!

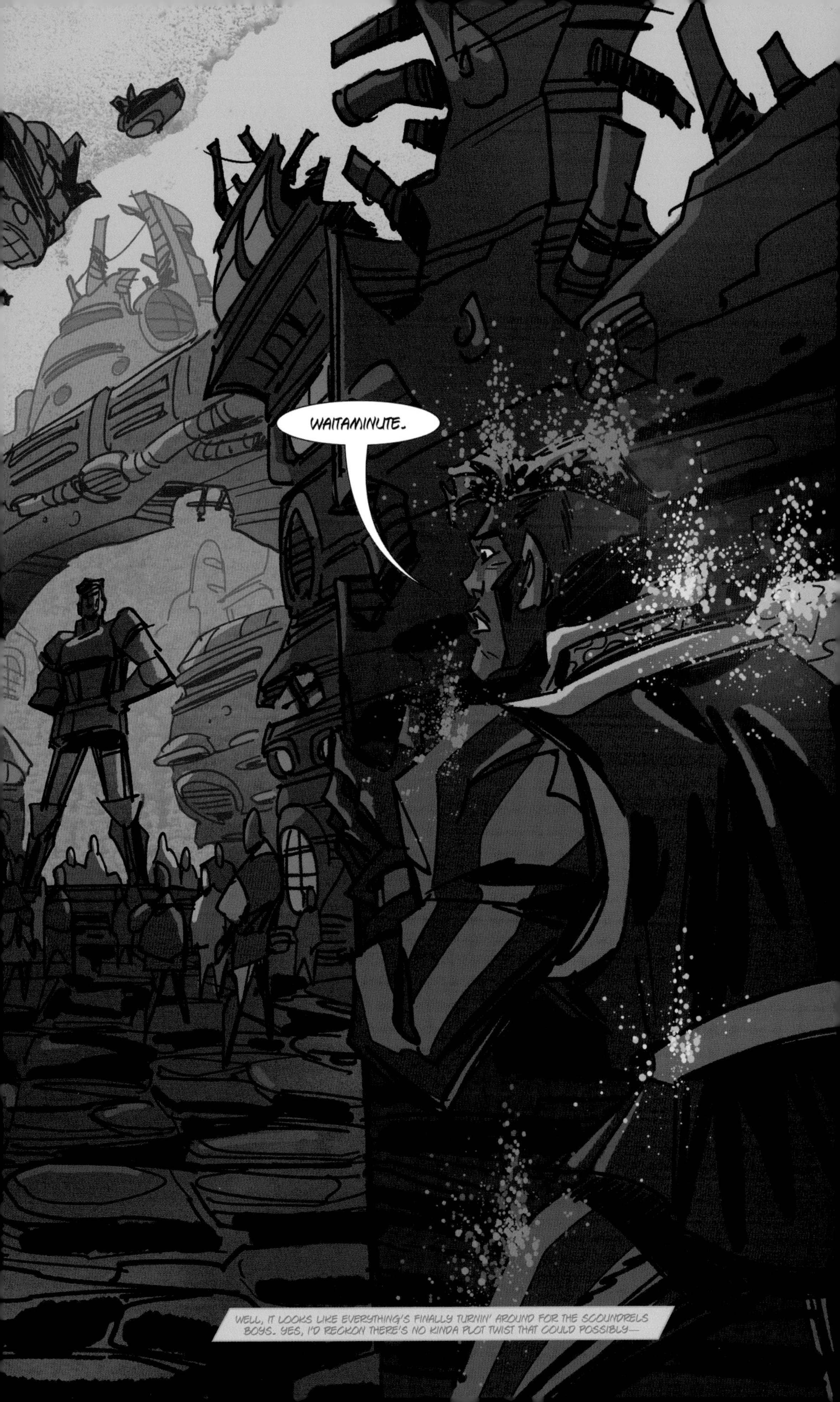
WAITAMINUTE.
WELL, IT LOOKS LIKE EVERYTHING'S FINALLY TURNIN' AROUND FOR THE SCOUNDRELS BOYS. YES, I'D RECKON THERE'S NO KINDA PLOT TWIST THAT COULD POSSIBLY—

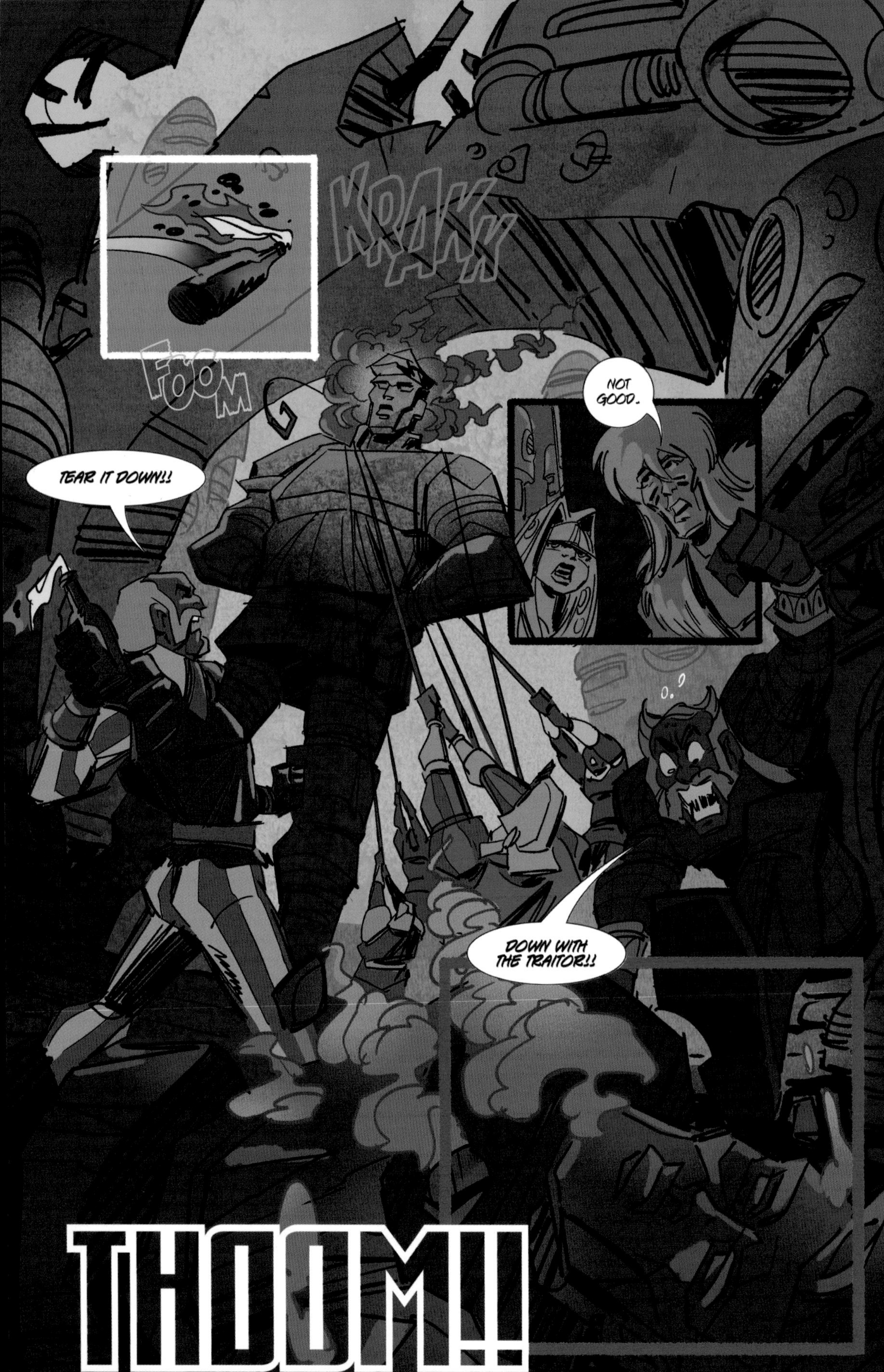
KRAKK
FOOM
TEAR IT DOWN!!
NOT GOOD.
DOWN WITH THE TRAITOR!!
THOOM!!

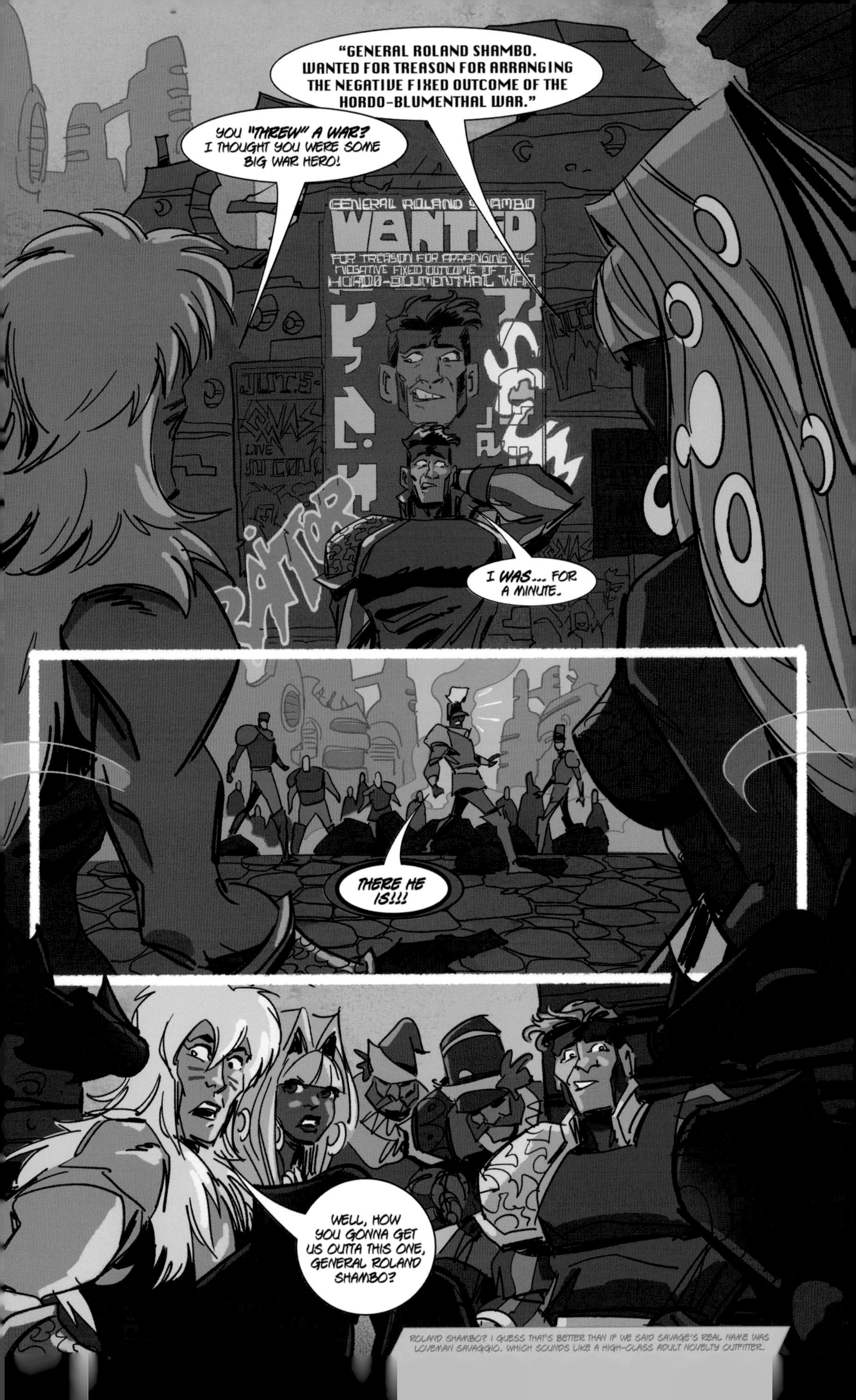
"GENERAL ROLAND SHAMBO. WANTED FOR TREASON FOR ARRANGING THE NEGATIVE FIXED OUTCOME OF THE HORDO-BLUMENTHAL WAR."
YOU "THREW" A WAR? I THOUGHT YOU WERE SOME BIG WAR HERO!
GENERAL ROLAND SHAMBO
WANTED
I WAS... FOR A MINUTE.
THERE HE IS!!!
WELL, HOW YOU GONNA GET US OUTTA THIS ONE, GENERAL ROLAND SHAMBO?
ROLAND SHAMBO? I GUESS THAT'S BETTER THAN IF WE SAID SAVAGE'S REAL NAME WAS LOVEMAN SAVAGGIO. WHICH SOUNDS LIKE A HIGH-CLASS ADULT NOVELTY OUTFITTER.

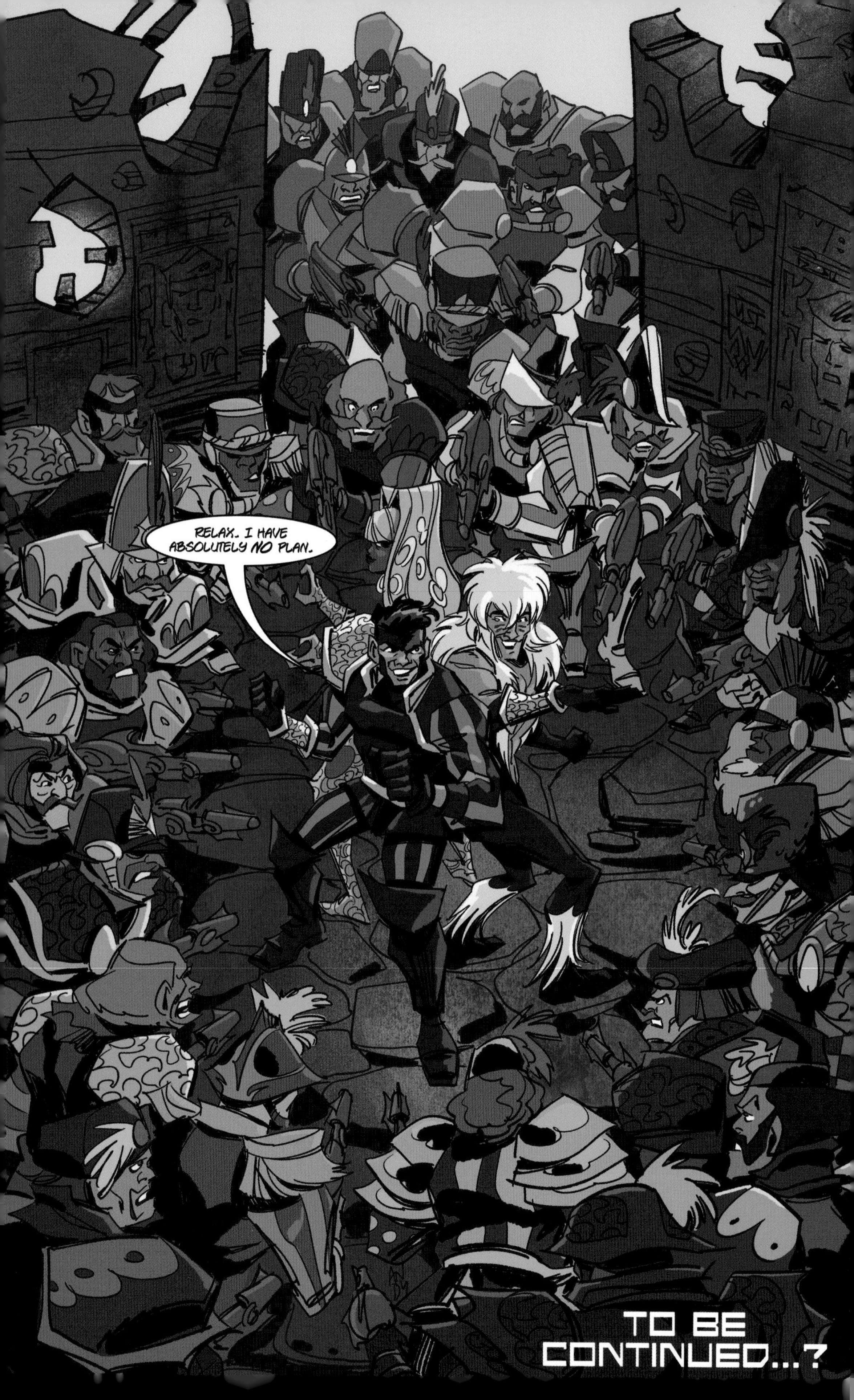
RELAX. I HAVE ABSOLUTELY NO PLAN.
TO BE CONTINUED...?

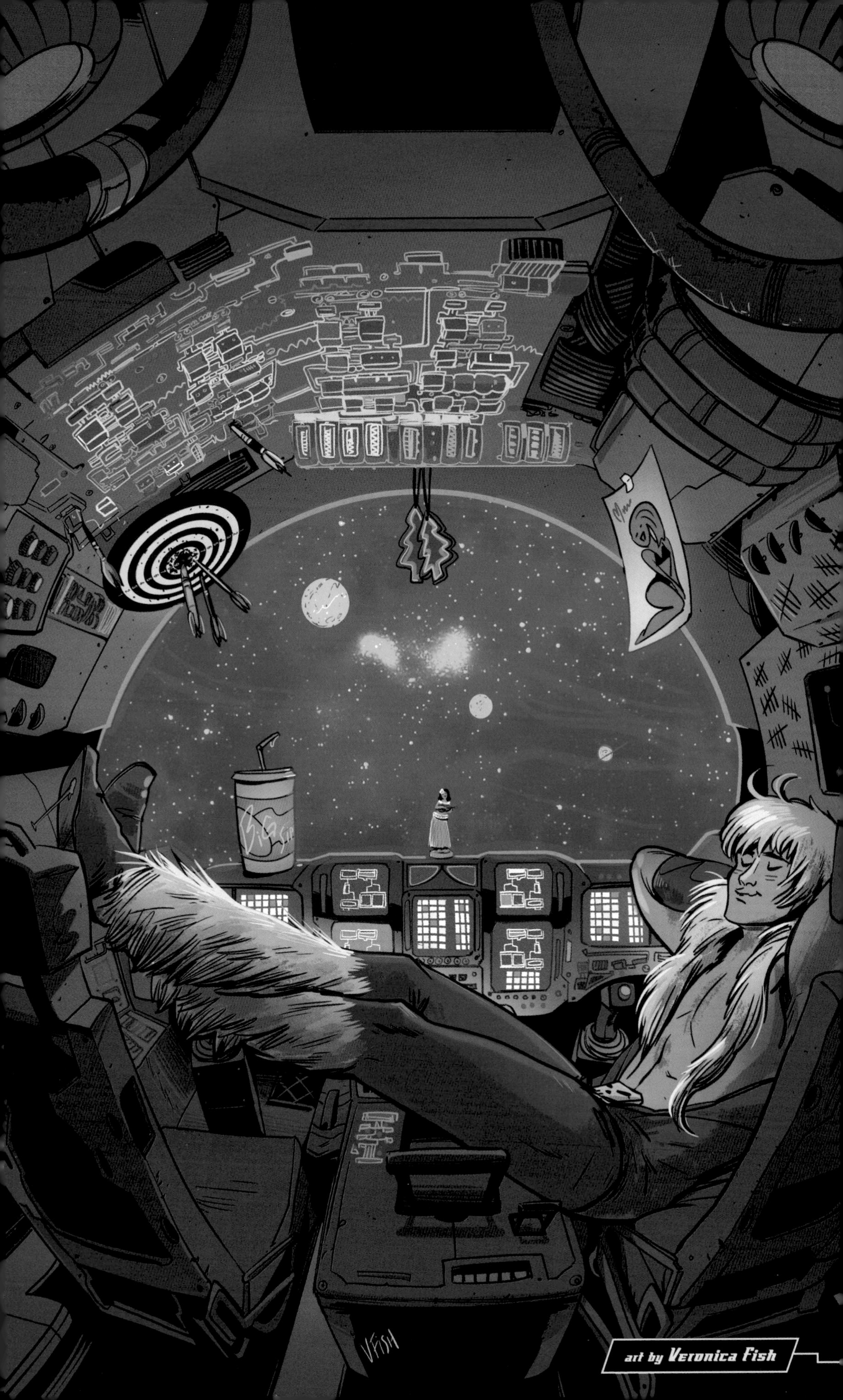

art by Veronica Fish

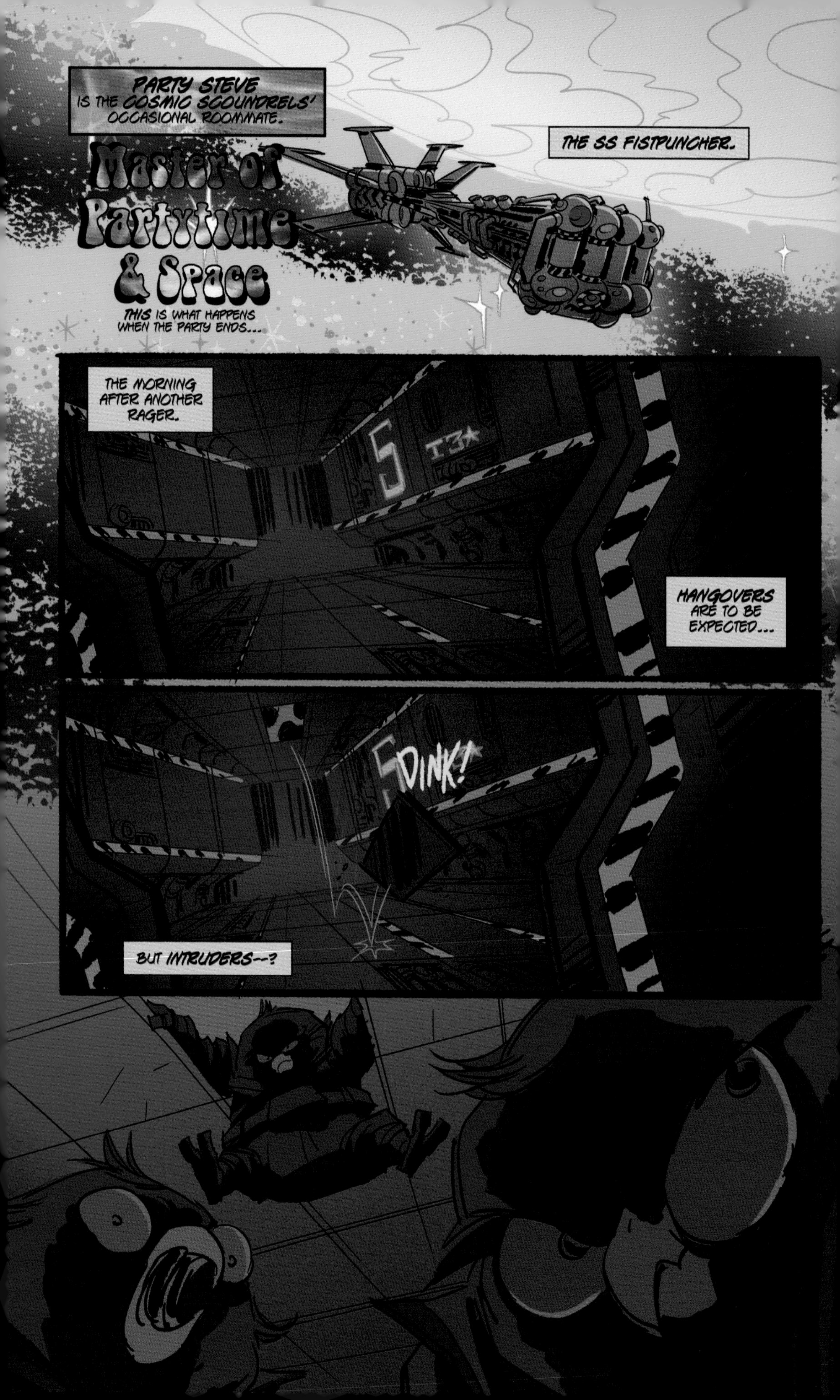
PARTY STEVE
IS THE COSMIC SCOUNDRELS' OCCASIONAL ROOMMATE.
Master of Partytime & Space
THIS IS WHAT HAPPENS WHEN THE PARTY ENDS...
THE SS FISTPUNCHER.
THE MORNING AFTER ANOTHER RAGER.
HANGOVERS ARE TO BE EXPECTED...
DINK!
BUT INTRUDERS--?

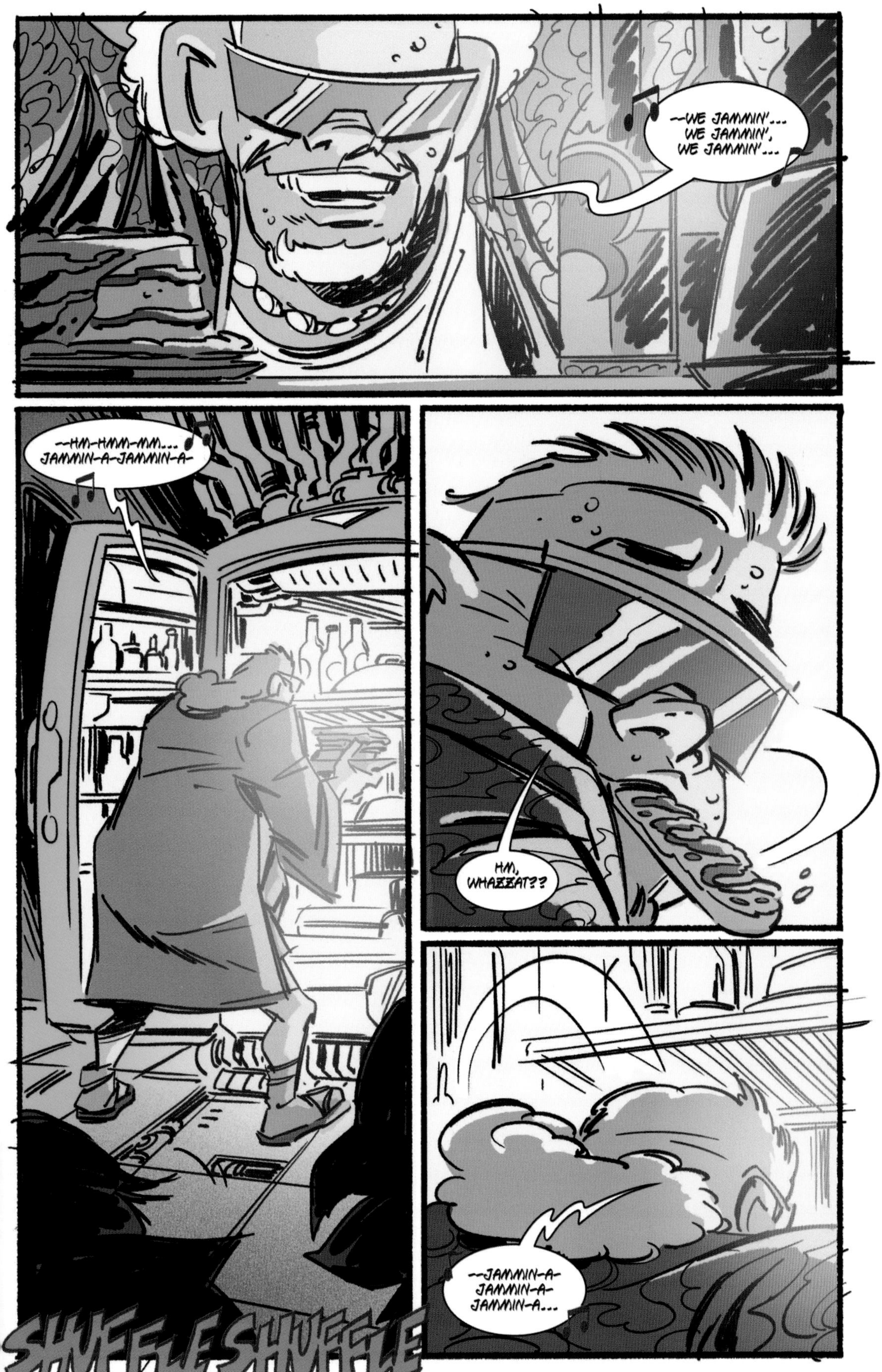
--WE JAMMIN'... WE JAMMIN', WE JAMMIN'...
--HM-HMM-MM... JAMMIN-A-JAMMIN-A-
SHUFFLE SHUFFLE
HM, WHAZZAT??
--JAMMIN-A- JAMMIN-A- JAMMIN-A...

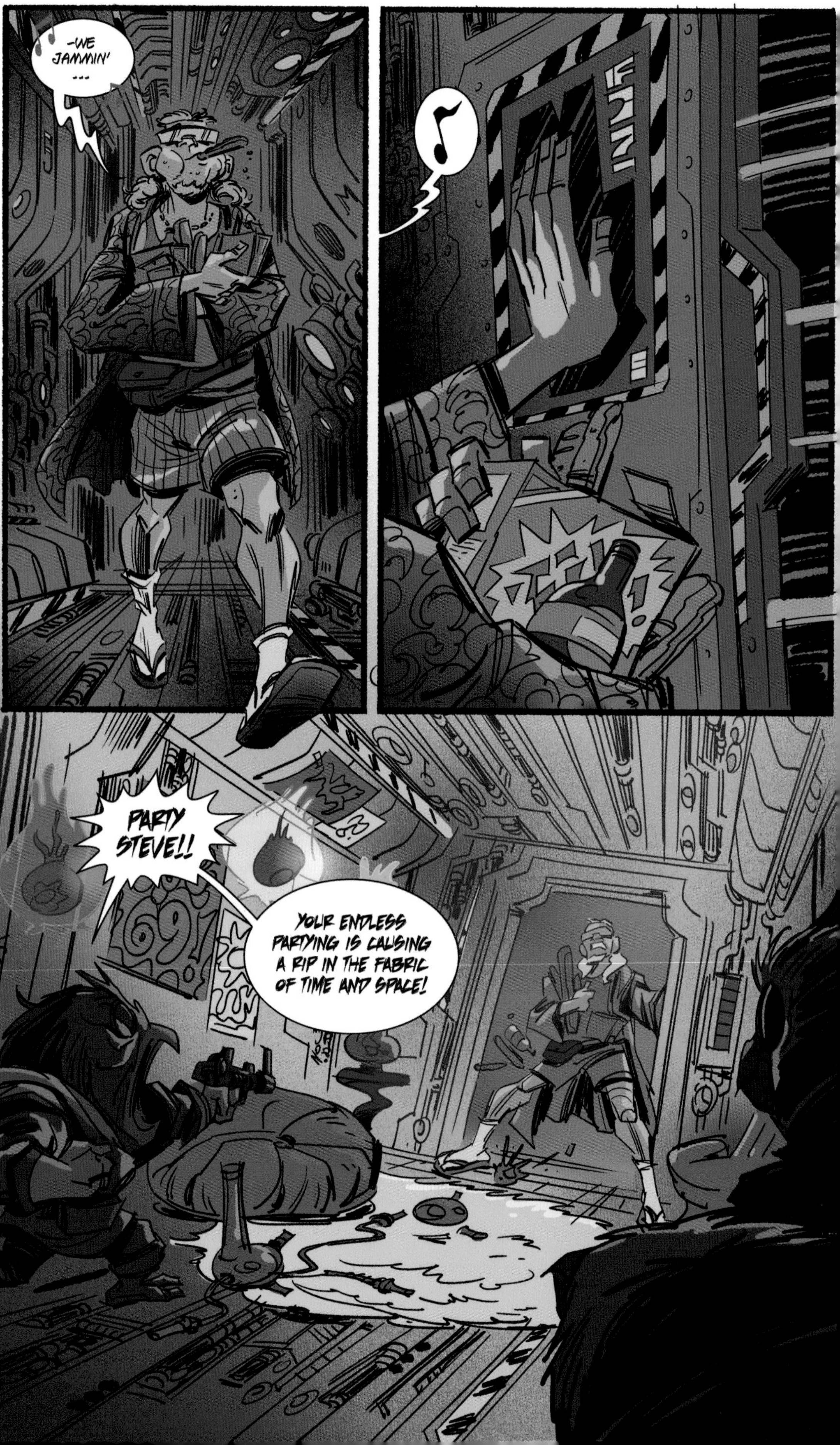

-WE JAMMIN' ...
PARTY STEVE!!
YOUR ENDLESS PARTYING IS CAUSING A RIP IN THE FABRIC OF TIME AND SPACE!

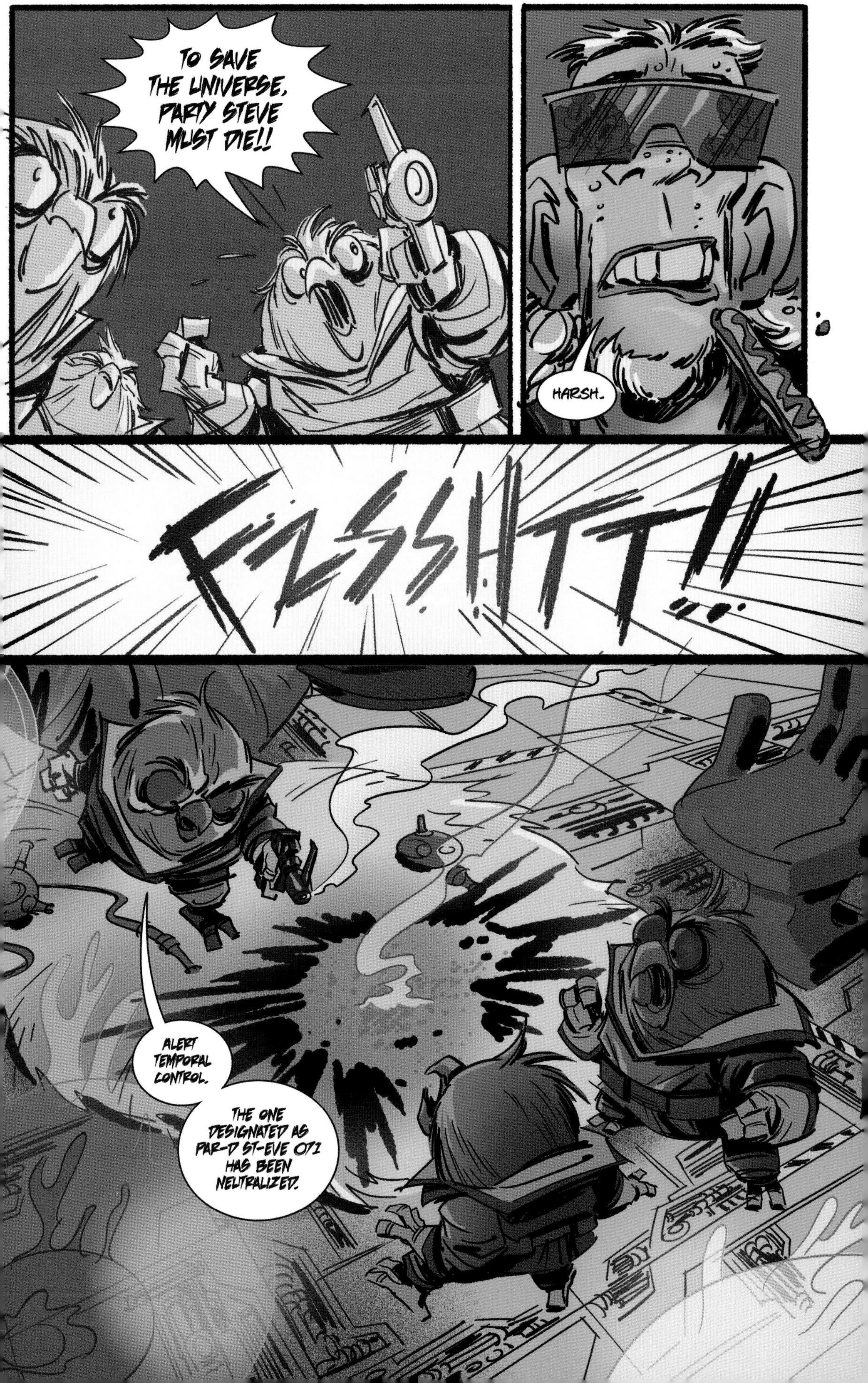
TO SAVE THE UNIVERSE, PARTY STEVE MUST DIE!!
HARSH.
FZSSHTT!!
ALERT TEMPORAL CONTROL.
THE ONE DESIGNATED AS PAR-D ST-EVE 071 HAS BEEN NEUTRALIZED.

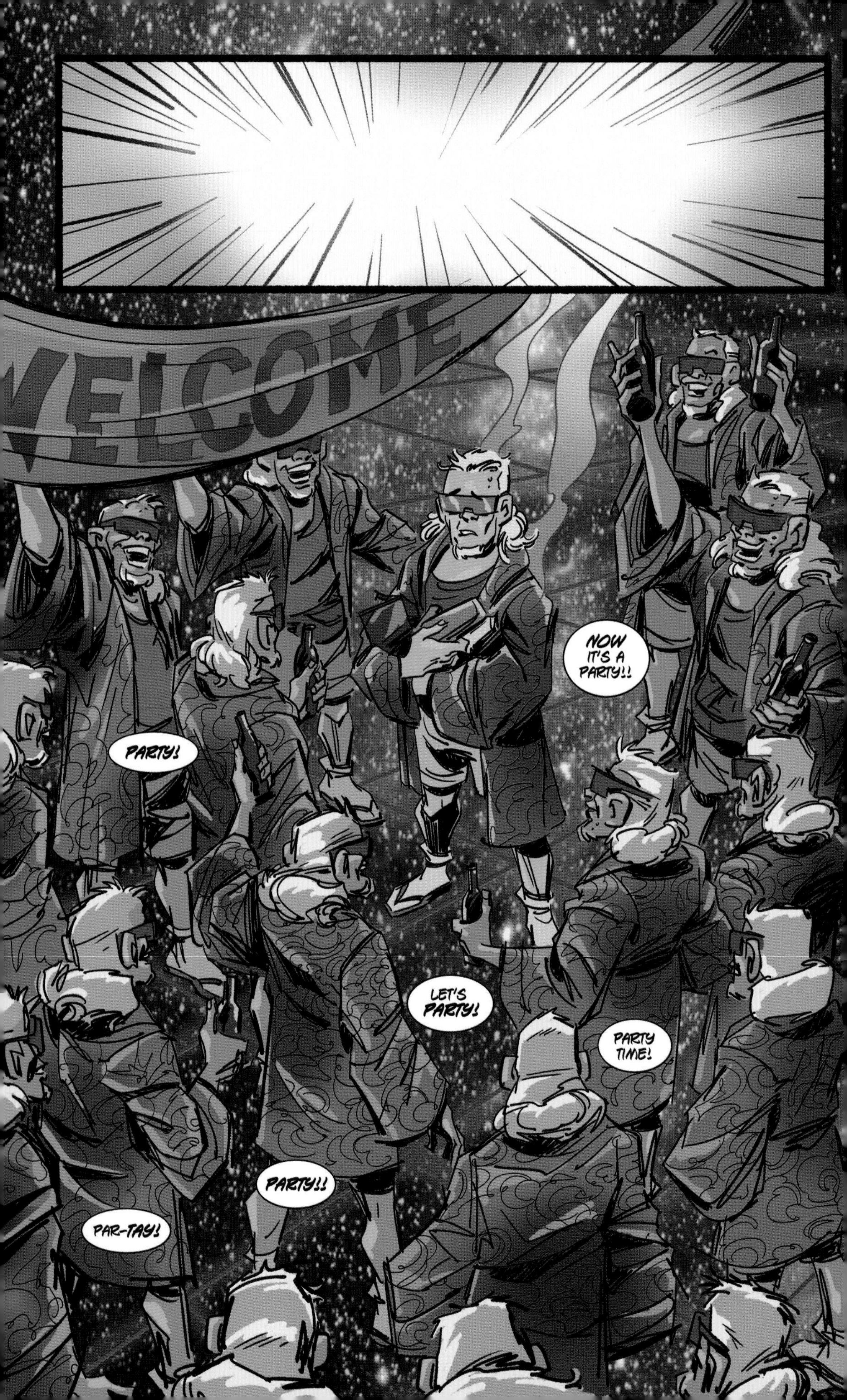
WELCOME
NOW IT'S A PARTY!!
PARTY!
LET'S PARTY!
PARTY TIME!
PARTY!!
PAR-TAY!

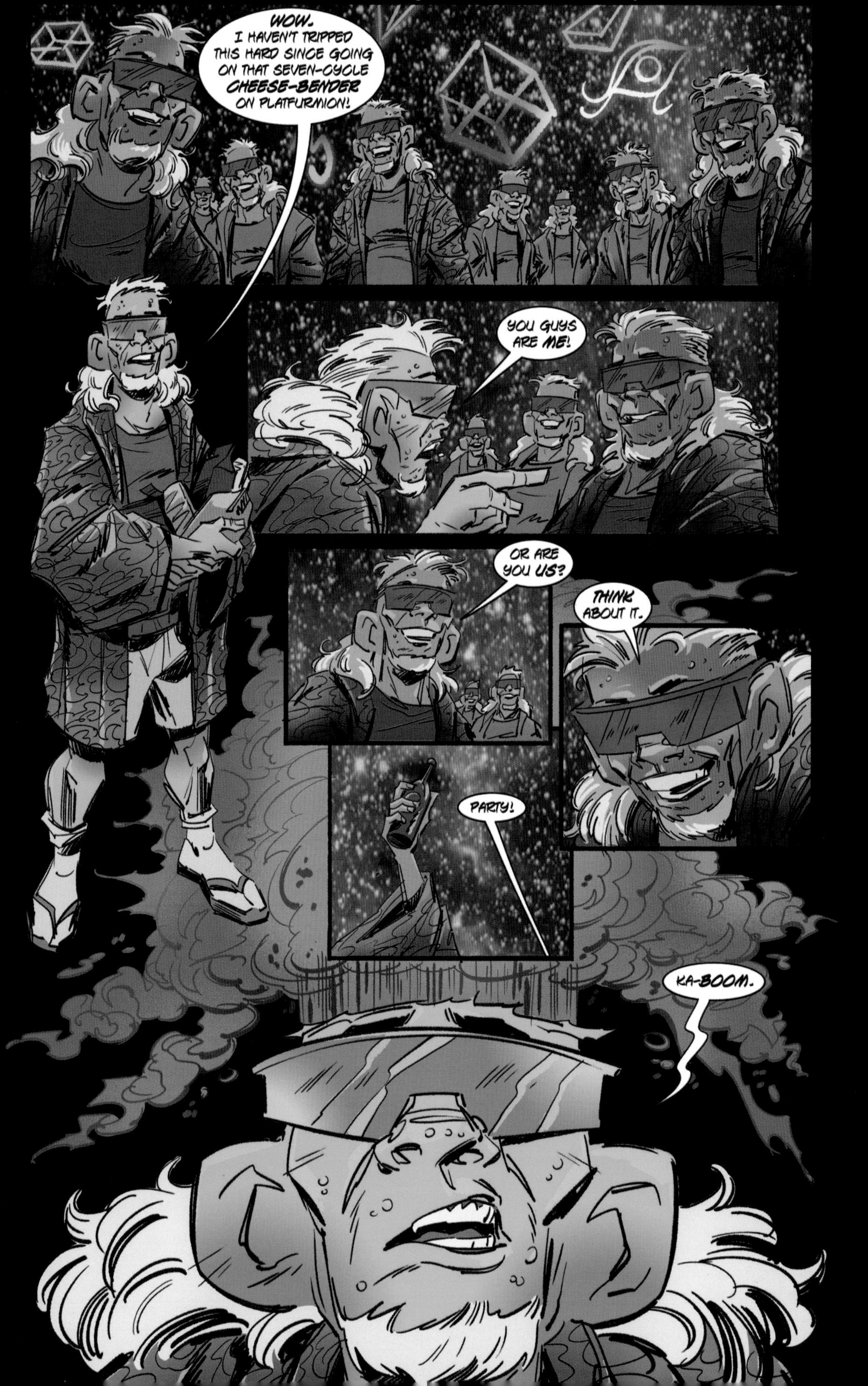
WOW. I HAVEN'T TRIPPED THIS HARD SINCE GOING ON THAT SEVEN-CYCLE CHEESE-BENDER ON PLATFURMION!
YOU GUYS ARE ME!
OR ARE YOU US?
THINK ABOUT IT.
PARTY!
KA-BOOM.

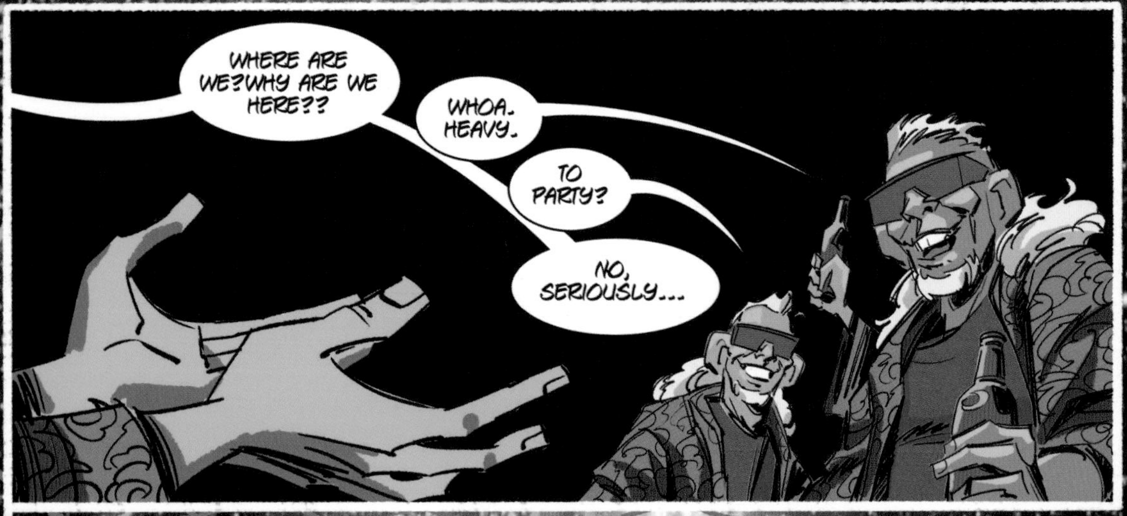
WHERE ARE WE?WHY ARE WE HERE??
WHOA. HEAVY.
TO PARTY?
NO, SERIOUSLY...
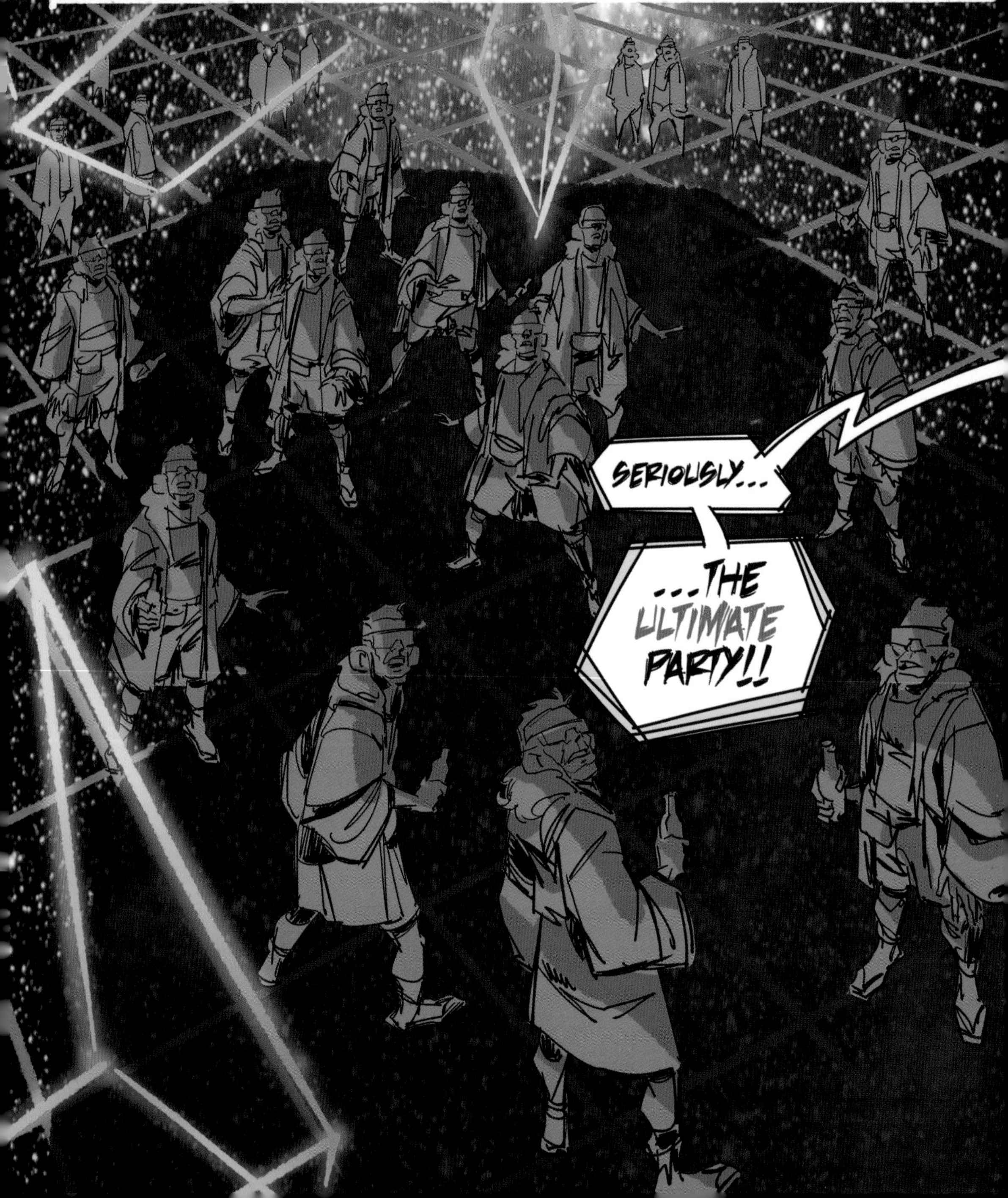
SERIOUSLY...
...THE ULTIMATE PARTY!!

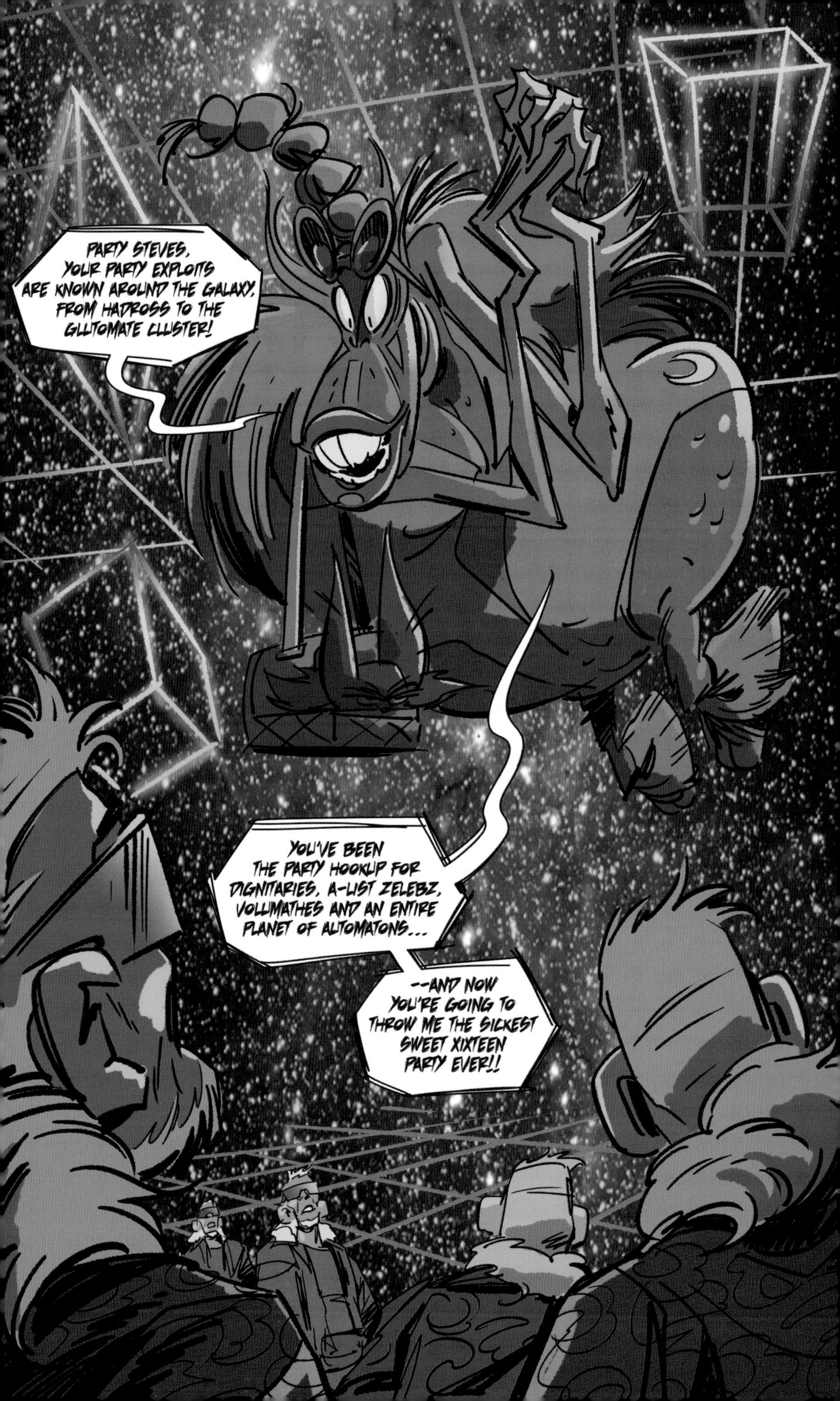
PARTY STEVES, YOUR PARTY EXPLOITS ARE KNOWN AROUND THE GALAXY, FROM HADROSS TO THE GLUTOMATE CLUSTER!
YOU'VE BEEN THE PARTY HOOKUP FOR DIGNITARIES, A-LIST ZELEBZ, VOLLIMATHES AND AN ENTIRE PLANET OF AUTOMATONS...
--AND NOW YOU'RE GOING TO THROW ME THE SICKEST SWEET XIXTEEN PARTY EVER!!

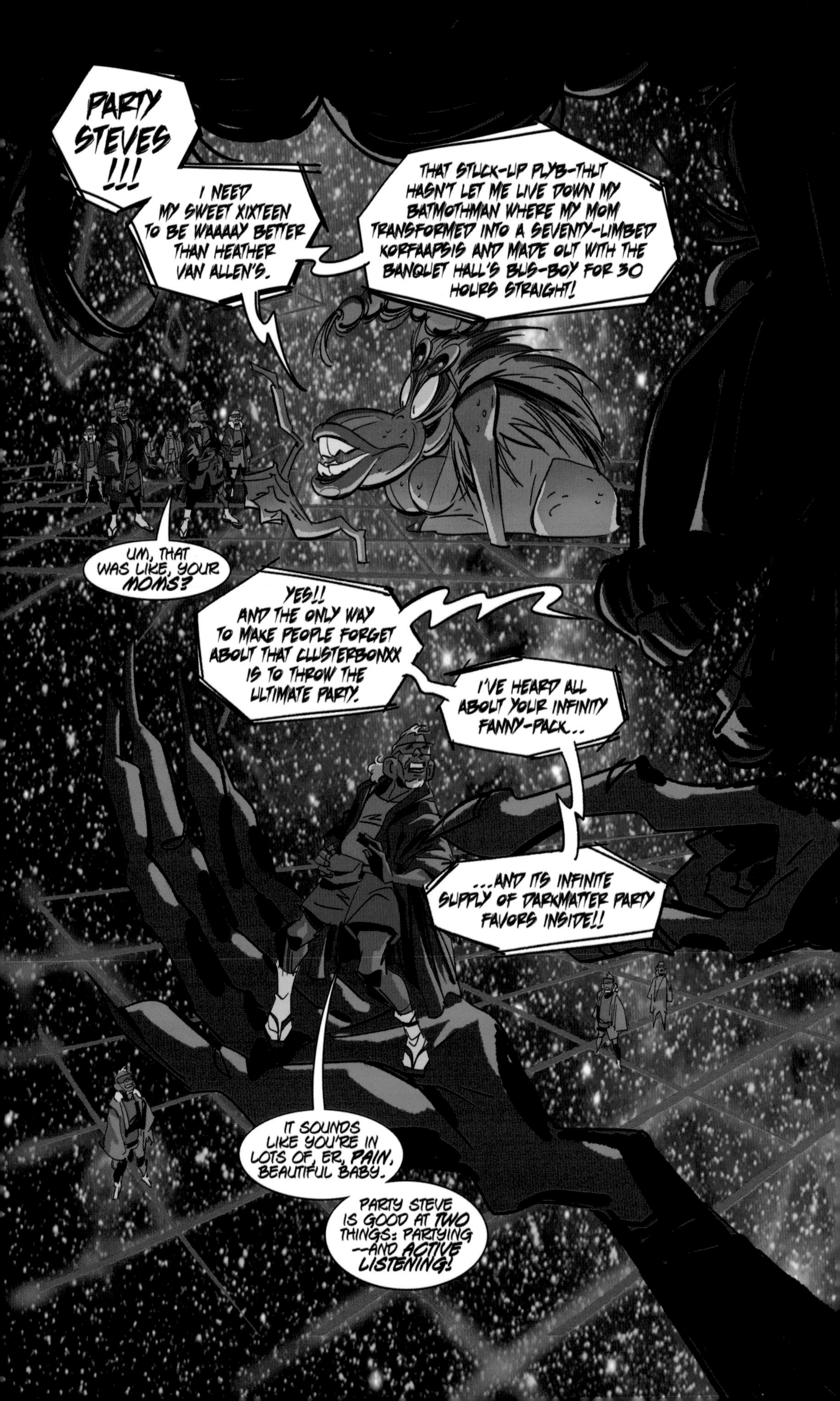
PARTY STEVES !!!
I NEED MY SWEET XIXTEEN TO BE WAAAAY BETTER THAN HEATHER VAN ALLEN'S.
THAT STUCK-UP FLYB-THUT HASN'T LET ME LIVE DOWN MY BATMOTHMAN WHERE MY MOM TRANSFORMED INTO A SEVENTY-LIMBED KORFAAPSIS AND MADE OUT WITH THE BANQUET HALL'S BUS-BOY FOR 30 HOURS STRAIGHT!
UM, THAT WAS LIKE, YOUR MOMS?
YES!! AND THE ONLY WAY TO MAKE PEOPLE FORGET ABOUT THAT CLUSTERBONXX IS TO THROW THE ULTIMATE PARTY.
I'VE HEARD ALL ABOUT YOUR INFINITY FANNY-PACK...
...AND ITS INFINITE SUPPLY OF DARKMATTER PARTY FAVORS INSIDE!!
IT SOUNDS LIKE YOU'RE IN LOTS OF, ER, PAIN, BEAUTIFUL BABY.
PARTY STEVE IS GOOD AT TWO THINGS: PARTYING --AND ACTIVE LISTENING!

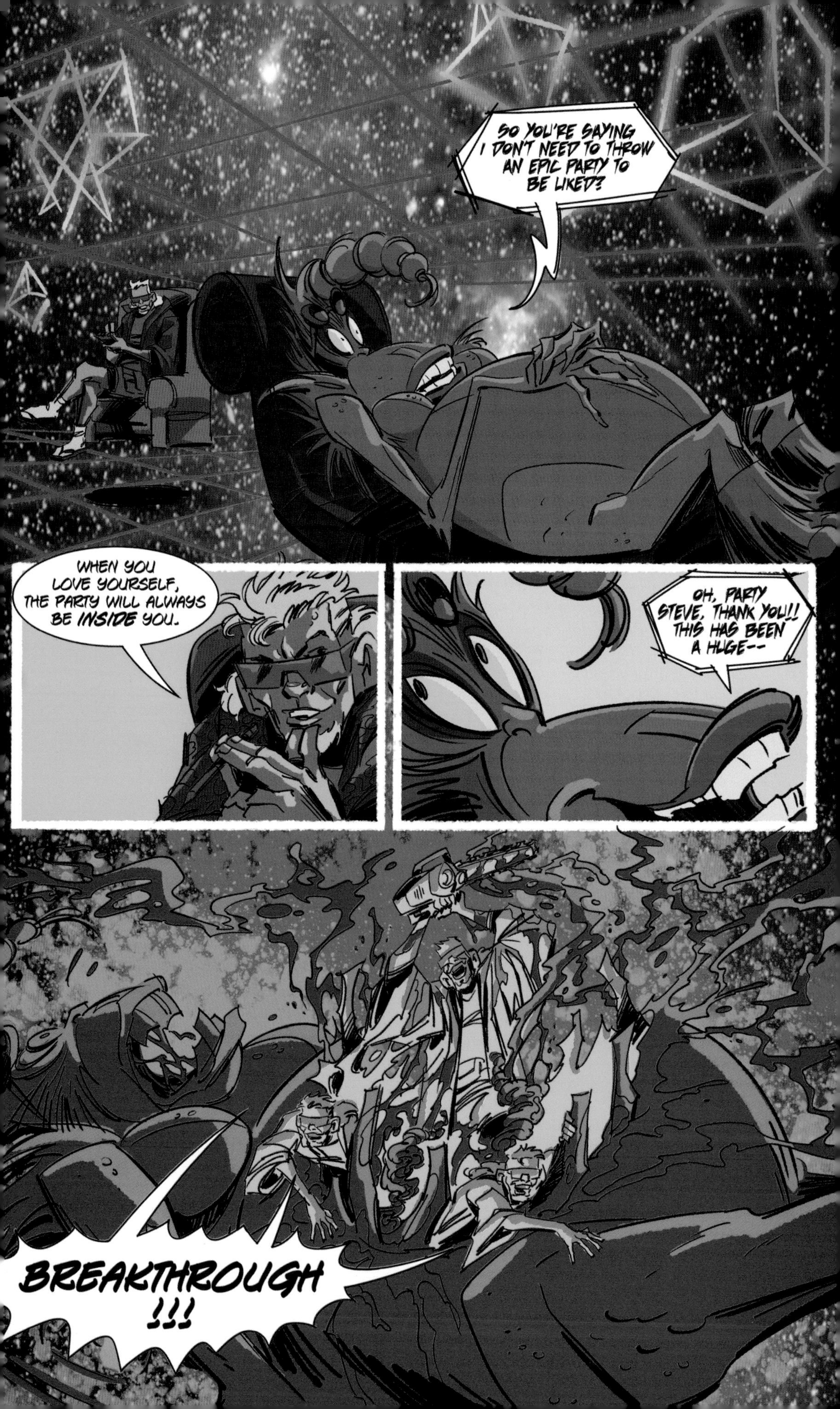

SO YOU'RE SAYING I DON'T NEED TO THROW AN EPIC PARTY TO BE LIKED?
WHEN YOU LOVE YOURSELF, THE PARTY WILL ALWAYS BE INSIDE YOU.
OH, PARTY STEVE, THANK YOU!! THIS HAS BEEN A HUGE--
BREAKTHROUGH !!!

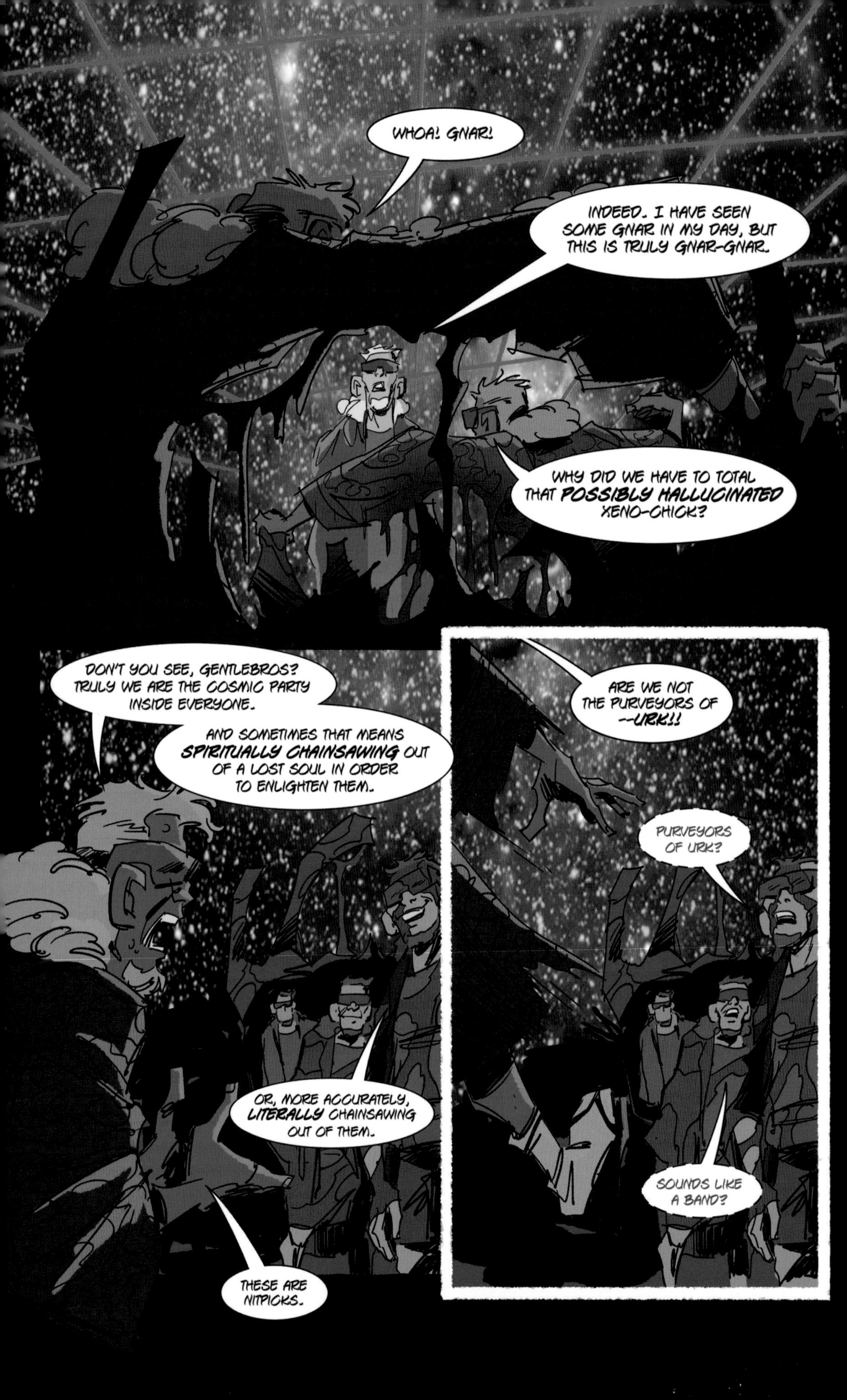
WHOA! GNAR!
INDEED. I HAVE SEEN SOME GNAR IN MY DAY, BUT THIS IS TRULY GNAR-GNAR.
WHY DID WE HAVE TO TOTAL THAT **POSSIBLY HALLUCINATED** XENO-CHICK?
DON'T YOU SEE, GENTLEBROS? TRULY WE ARE THE COSMIC PARTY INSIDE EVERYONE.
AND SOMETIMES THAT MEANS **SPIRITUALLY CHAINSAWING** OUT OF A LOST SOUL IN ORDER TO ENLIGHTEN THEM.
OR, MORE ACCURATELY, **LITERALLY** CHAINSAWING OUT OF THEM.
THESE ARE NITPICKS.
ARE WE NOT THE PURVEYORS OF **--URK!!**
PURVEYORS OF URK?
SOUNDS LIKE A BAND?

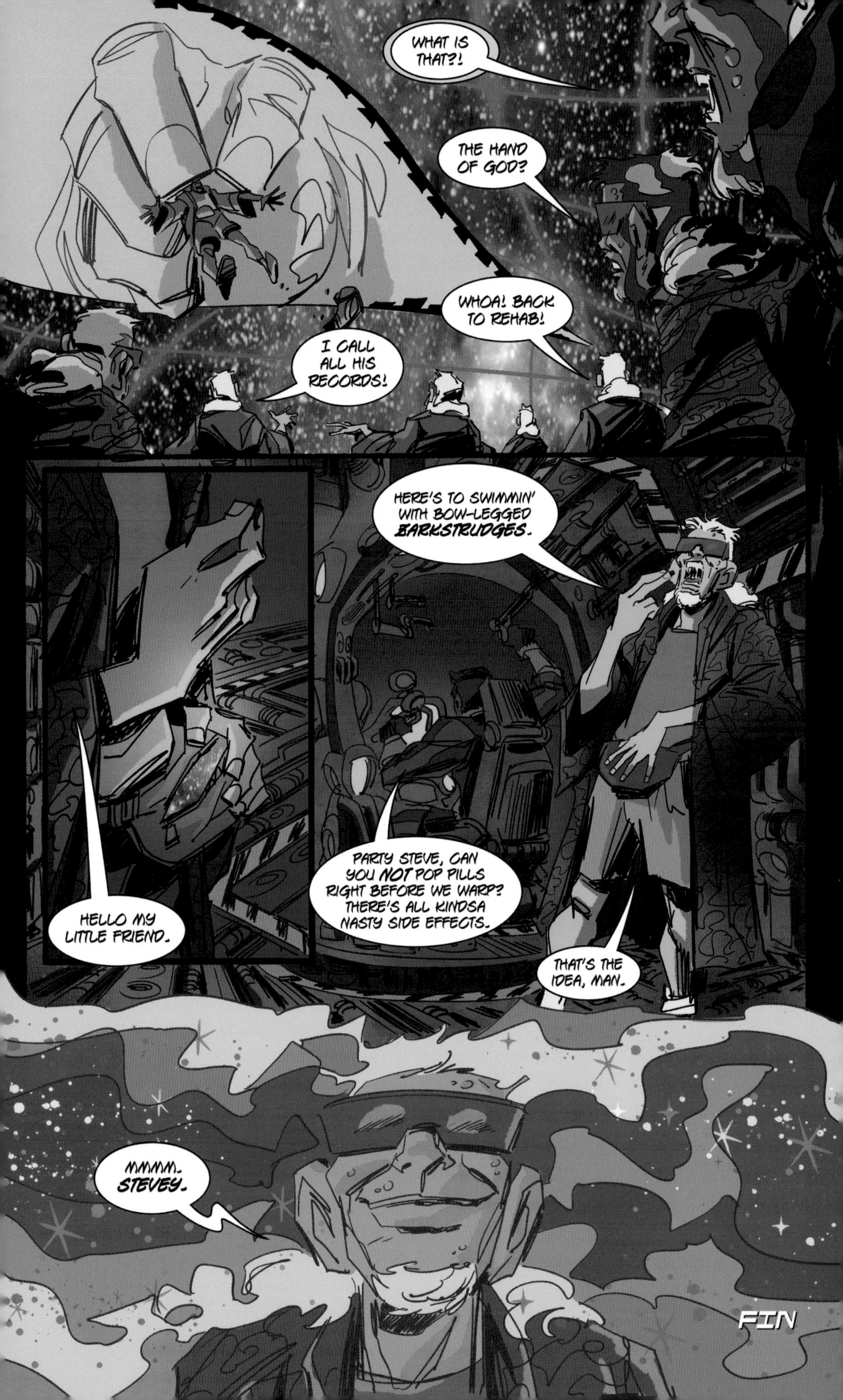
WHAT IS THAT?!
THE HAND OF GOD?
I CALL ALL HIS RECORDS!
WHOA! BACK TO REHAB!
HELLO MY LITTLE FRIEND.
HERE'S TO SWIMMIN' WITH BOW-LEGGED ZARKSTRUDGES.
PARTY STEVE, CAN YOU NOT POP PILLS RIGHT BEFORE WE WARP? THERE'S ALL KINDSA NASTY SIDE EFFECTS.
THAT'S THE IDEA, MAN.
MMMM. STEVEY.
FIN

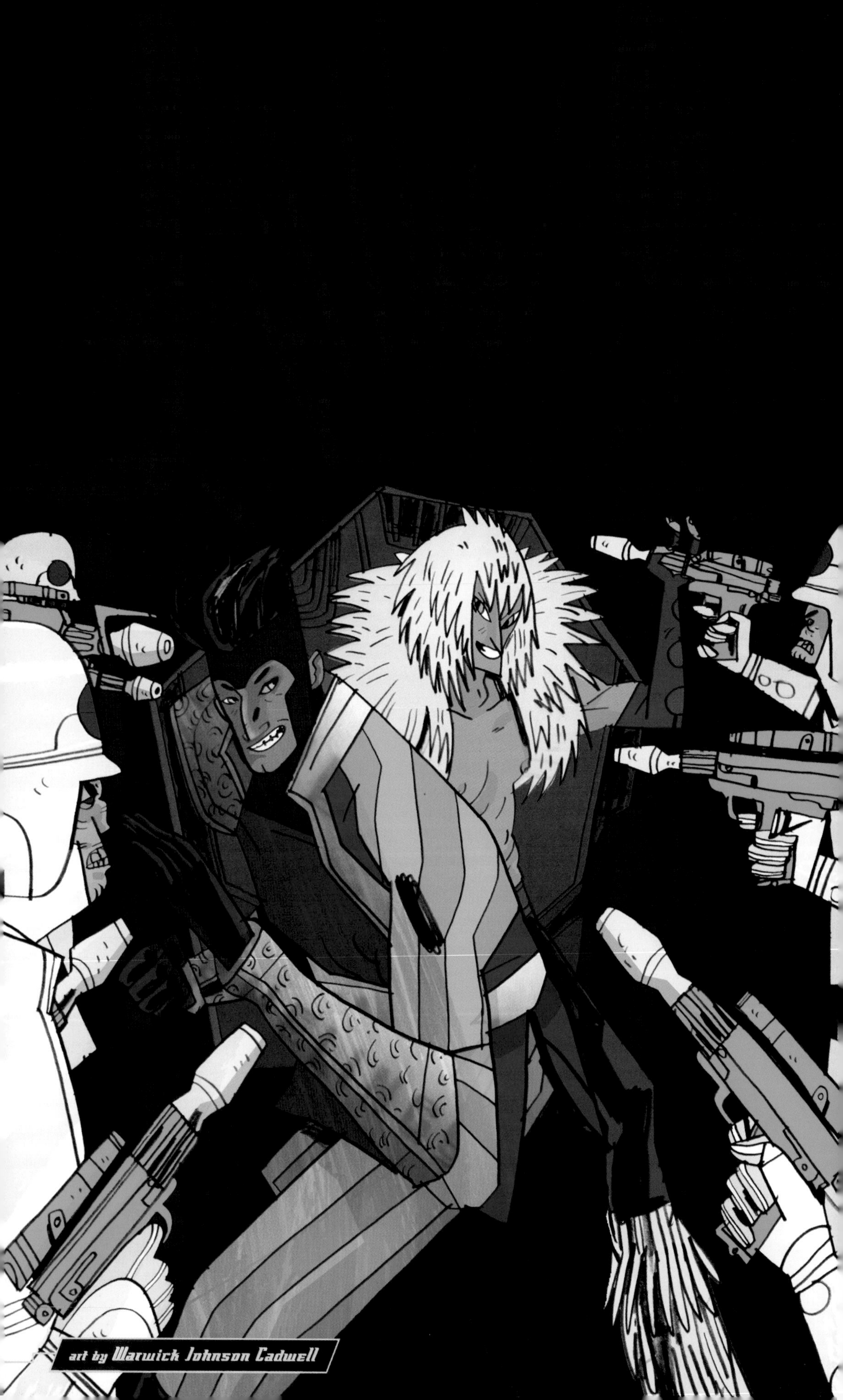
art by Warwick Johnson Cadwell

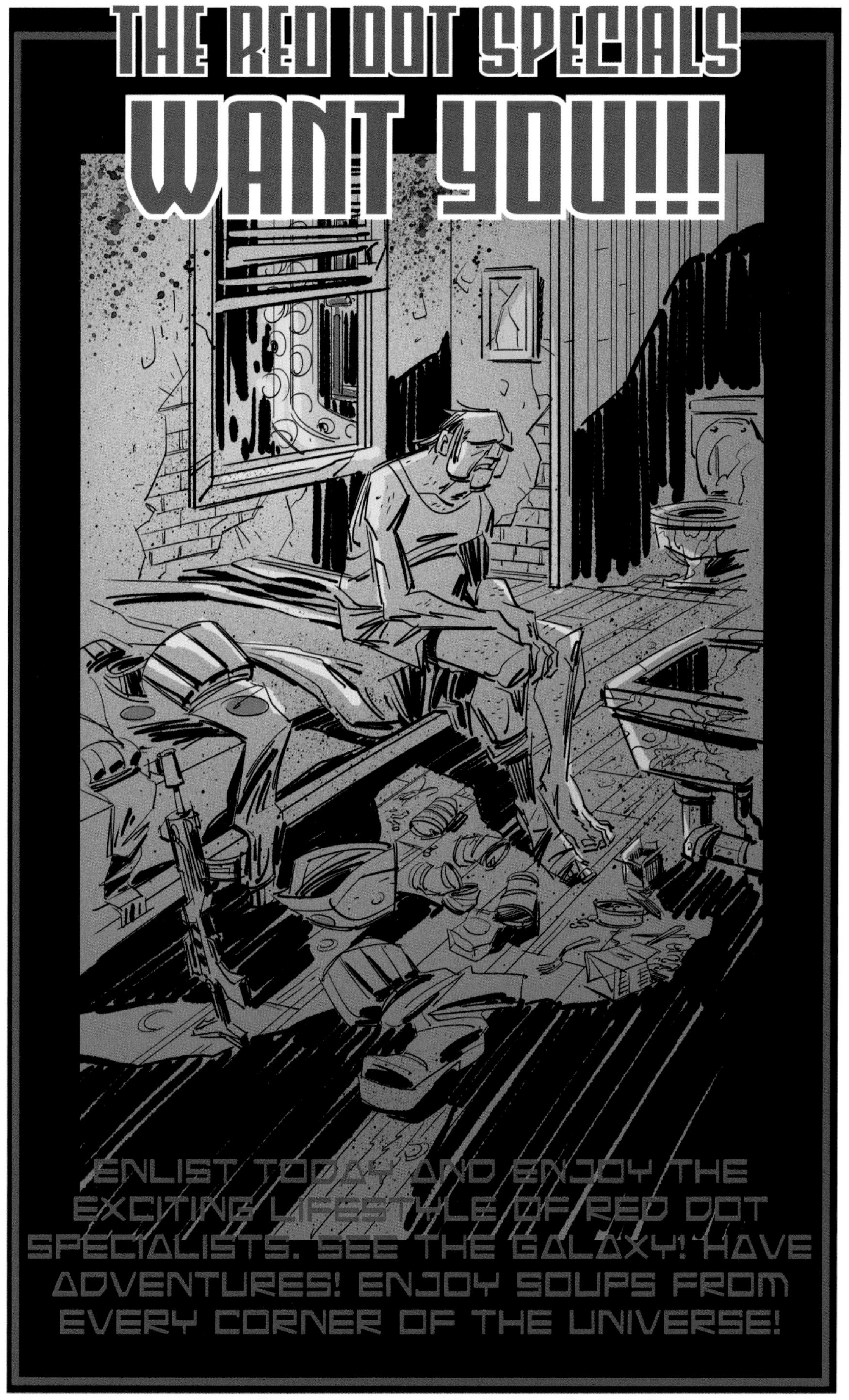
THE RED DOT SPECIALS
WANT YOU!!!
ENLIST TODAY AND ENJOY THE EXCITING LIFESTYLE OF RED DOT SPECIALISTS. SEE THE GALAXY! HAVE ADVENTURES! ENJOY SOUPS FROM EVERY CORNER OF THE UNIVERSE!

KARL'S BUDGET UNIVERSE:
AN ACCOUNTANT'S ACCOUNT OF INTERGALACTIC TRAVEL

THE MIDNIGHT FERNANDO
PLEASURE CRUISE AND
ALL-YOU-CAN-EAT WAFFLE BAR

CATEGORY: CRUISES, BREAKFAST FOODS, MUTINY,
KIDNAPPING, GALACTIC UPRISINGS

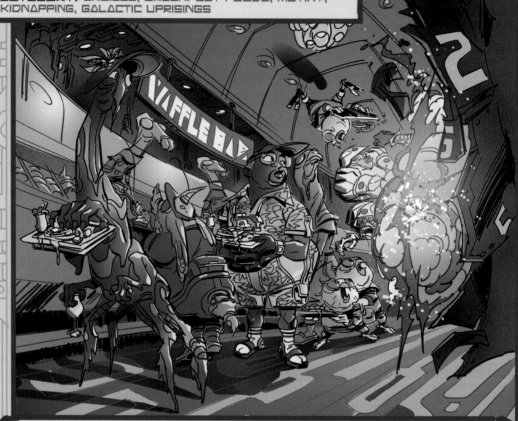

MY LATE WIFE AND I HAVE USED XXETICO EMPTY NEST CRUISELINES FOR YEARS, BUT
AFTER HER AND SUBSEQUENT CLONES 2, 3, 7 AND 9 PASSING AND/OR DECOMMISSIONING,
I DECIDED TO USE ANOTHER COMPANY THAT CATERS TO RETIREES AND SENIORS, AND
THEIR SPECIALTY: RETIRED SENIORS. THAT COMPANY WAS CALLED "EAT. WARP. FLURHX."
AND I AM HERE TO TELL YOU THEY ARE THE ANSWER TO ANY MIDLIFE CRISIS.

IT WAS RAINING THAT PARTICULAR CYCLE PRIOR TO THE CRUISE WHEN I NOTICED THERE
WAS A HOLE IN MY SHOE AND I NEEDED TO GET IT RESOLED. THEY WERE MY FAVORITE
PAIR SO NEEDLESS TO SAY I WAS UPSET BUT THE COBBLER WAS A MAGICIAN.
UNFORTUNATELY I STEPPED IN A PILE OF BEPTIPOD WASTE WALKING OUT OF THE SHOP.
THE COBBLER AND I HAD A HUMDINGER OF A LAUGH AFTER LOL. THEN I WENT FOR SOUP
AROUND THE CORNER. AFTER A FEW MORE CYCLES I WENT ON THE CRUISE.

DESPITE BEING CAUGHT IN THE MIDDLE OF 2 HIJACKINGS, 3 NUCLEAR LEVEL MELTDOWN
EMERGENCY SCENARIOS AND 1 CATEGORY X12 HEIST TURNED KIDNAPPING, I WAS AMAZED
AT HOW QUICKLY THE STAFF OF THE MIDNIGHT FERNANDO DEALT WITH THE GAPING HULL
BREACH AND SUDDEN DECOMPRESSION. ANTI-GRAV SYRUP KEPT THE WAFFLES IN PLACE
DESPITE ALL THE DEBRIS. I ONLY FOUND ONE EYEBALL IN MY HOME FRIES BUT THAT
COULD HAVE JUST BEEN A GARNISH. WHO KNOWS WHEN YOU'RE TRAVELING OUTSIDE THE
STAECHLER-KREBSTEK BARRIER.

3 AND 1/2 ABACI

KARL'S BUDGET UNIVERSE:
AN ACCOUNTANT'S ACCOUNT OF INTERGALACTIC TRAVEL

STAVLAUNCH 103 B
CATAGORY: WATER PLANET, WAVE POOLS, FISHING, FLESH LEVIATHAN CAGE DIVING

TRAVELERS BEWARE! IF YOU BOOKED A TRIP TO STAVLAUNCH 103B BASED ON THE TITILLATING PROMISE OF "FLESH LEVIATHANS," PLEASE ALLOW ME TO BURST YOUR BUBBLE. IT'S A BIG FISH WITH A GROSS TONGUE; SO GO AHEAD AND ERASE ANY VISIONS OF GREASED-UP OBESE OLYMPIANS CLASHING IN SLOW MOTION, OR RECORD THOSE VISIONS AS HOLOGRAMS AND SEND THEM TO ME!

ANYWAY, ON TO SOUP! FLESH LEVIATHAN-FIN SOUP IS DELISH! AND THEY REGROW THEIR FINS SO YOU CAN EAT ALL YOU WANT WITH A CLEAN CONSCIENCE...AND A CLEAN PLATE!

2 AND 1/2 ABACI

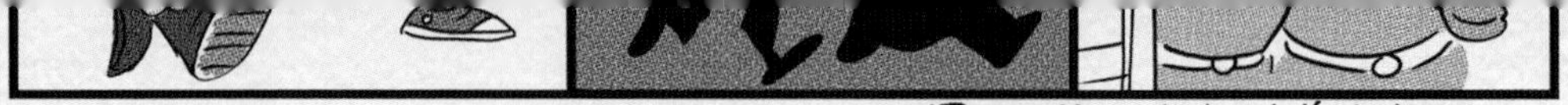

Z'BOG with apologies to HANK KETCHAM!

TAD & JACOB by Z'Bog

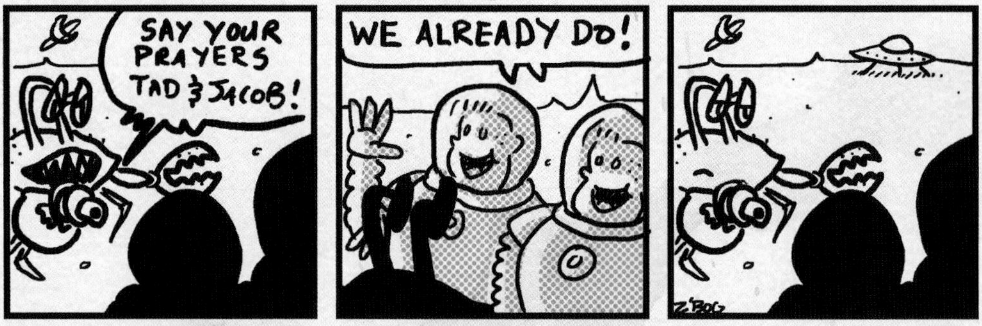
SAY YOUR PRAYERS TAD & JACOB!
WE ALREADY DO!
Z'BOG

TAD & JACOB by Z'Bog

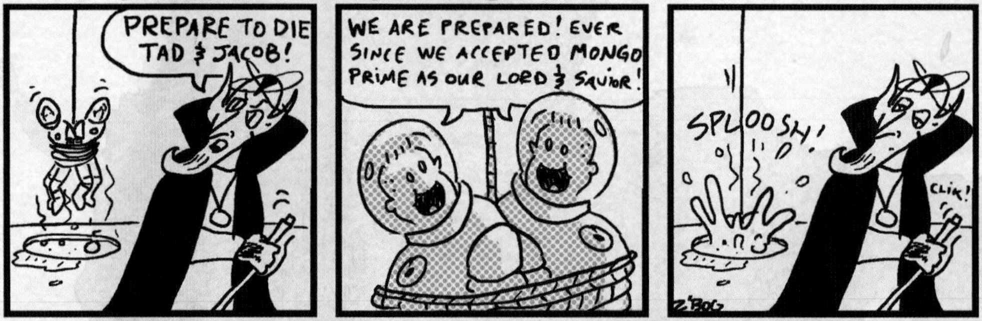
PREPARE TO DIE TAD & JACOB!
WE ARE PREPARED! EVER SINCE WE ACCEPTED MONGO PRIME AS OUR LORD & SAVIOR!
SPLOOSH!
CLIK!
Z'BOG

TAD & JACOB by Z'Bog

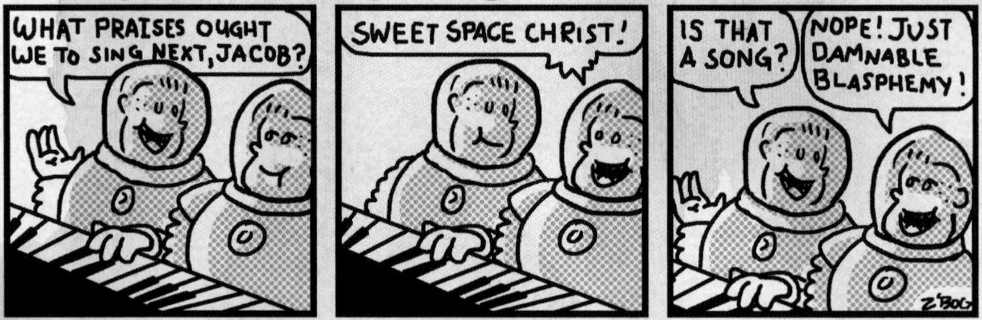
WHAT PRAISES OUGHT WE TO SING NEXT, JACOB?
SWEET SPACE CHRIST!
IS THAT A SONG?
NOPE! JUST DAMNABLE BLASPHEMY!
Z'BOG

Blother's "You Won't Believe This Shit!"

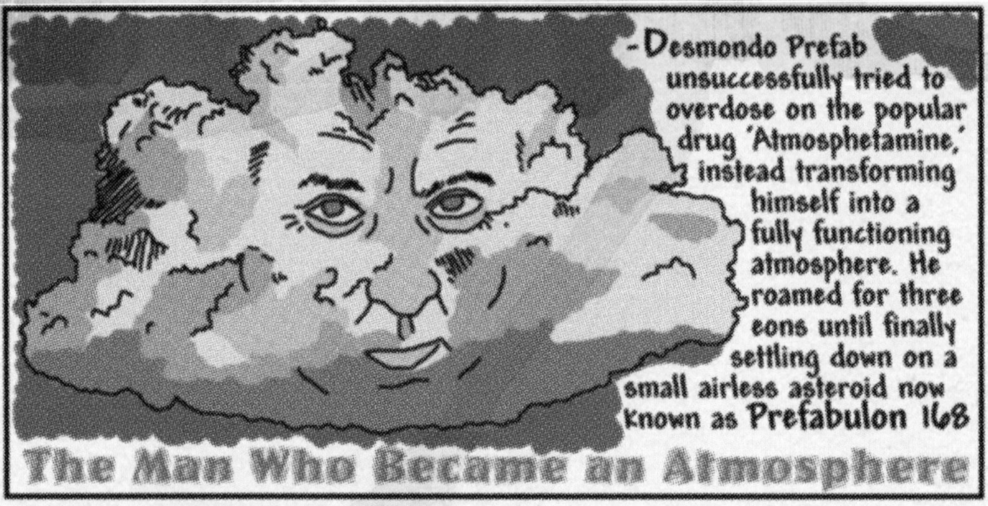
-Desmondo Prefab unsuccessfully tried to overdose on the popular drug 'Atmosphetamine,' instead transforming himself into a fully functioning atmosphere. He roamed for three eons until finally settling down on a small airless asteroid now known as Prefabulon 168
The Man Who Became an Atmosphere

Better Off Zed M.D. by X7-23

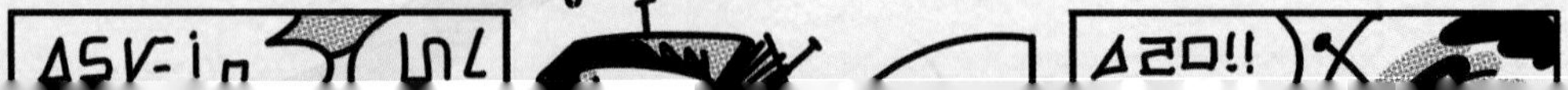

EXCERPT FROM THE OFFICIAL HANDBOOK OF THE

Cosmic Scoundrels™

IDW EDITION

CONTENTS AND ARTISTS

COSMIC SCOUNDRELS

Space-faring bachelor scalawags Love Savage and Roshambo, along with a little mothering from their ship's AI, Mrs. Billingsley––shuttle from job to job and continually find themselves on the wrong side of the law. Despite their best efforts to look out only for themselves, they usually end up involved with alien crooks, shady black-market baby schemes and space sickness-inducing drugs. They're on the loose and on the run––from everyone!

ROSHAMBO'S GALACTIC-GAUNTLETS

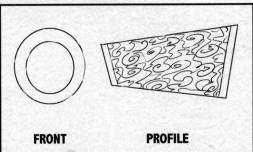

FRONT   **PROFILE**

ROSHAMBO
Ex-military (dishonorably discharged), ex-con, space-pirate (active)

LOVE SAVAGE
Prince, war criminal, former gigolo, fugitive (active)

KARL
C.P.A. (retired)

PARTY STEVE
Hookup (deceased)

BOM REBEK

Rank: Anti-General in the Quintesstrian Army
Current Occupation: Bounty hunter
The "business": Bom Rebek is Roshambo's former commanding officer, now turned-bounty hunter. Roshambo is hopelessly in love with her despite her constantly double-crossing them to serve her own agenda.

CAPTAIN BOXTRUM

Captain Boxtrum is King Refractimon's right-hand man and Master of War for the Prelaxagon Royal Navy.
Little known fact: Captain Boxtrum is also the former "Crepe King of The Glutomate Cluster".

THE DUCHESS RON CARGILL

The Duchess Ron Cargill is the daughter of Overmancer Cargill and his witchbride Tina the Soulless, Duchess Ron is at the unfortunate center of a year's long unstable truce between her parents and King and Queen Refractimon of Prelaxagon. The Refractimons depend on the Cargills for their naval superiority and the Cargills depend on the monarchy for their fancy banquets and galas. At some point someone noticed that this wasn't exactly an even trade and the Cargills began threatening to withdraw their military support of the throne. So poor Ron was offered up to wed Prince Refractimon (Love Savage) to smooth things over. The houses would be united in marriage and since they're basically cousins anyway, the planet could continue its tradition of grody inbreeding. Sucks for Ron because she is actually WAY cooler than Love Savage and had to give up her awesome teleport start-up business and stop competing in the professional Hoverspear circuit so she could get married. So even though she's probably relieved that she didn't have to marry Savage, she will probably come for his head one day because of all she had to give up for nothing. ∎

*The Duchess Ron Cargill art by Ron Salas

DIMETROTRON BROTHERS

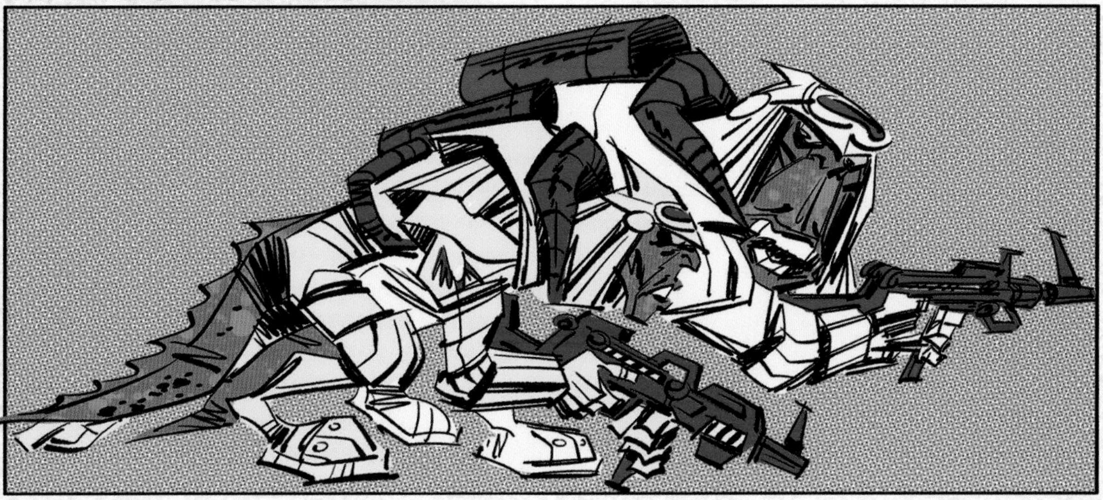

Real name: Keets (the fat one) and Trake (the skinny one)
Other aliases: "The fat and skinny dinosaur bros"
Occupation: Bounty hunters 4 hire
Legal status: Legally SO dead!
Place of birth: Mesozoicron
Place of death: The cargo vessel **Midnight Fernando** (the fat one), the **SS Fistpuncher** (the skinny one)
Group affiliation: Sometime allies of Red Dot Specials, The Garlite empire and former members of the French Foreign Lizard Legionnaires
First and unfortunate last appearance: Cosmic Scoundrels #1
History: Keets and Trake were the eldest and youngest of a two-hundred-egg Dimetrotron clutch laid by Queen Henn the Auxiliary. As is their custom, all the older Dimetrotrons (meaning they hatched sooner) tried to eat the youngest. Keets, in a complete "F you" to instinct and millions of years of evolution, decided to save his youngest brother from their siblings. Because of this, they were banished from their savage homeworld and sent, in an intended insult, to the Retail System. They worked their way up from the Mail Room Planet, to the Junior Sales Orbital Station, weaved their way through the Night Shift Belt, and finally got promoted to the Middle Management Moon where they went into business selling cheaply made Tlarb to anyone that would open their airlock. This went terribly so they started murdering and kidnapping people for money. Bounty hunting led to regular escort contracts with the Empire, which led to a fateful job escorting secret cargo aboard the freighter **Midnight Fernando**. When space-jerks the Cosmic Scoundrels caused a hull breach in order to steal the cargo, Keets was sucked out into space and suffocated, or instantly exploded, or his blood boiled and froze, or whatever you believe happens in the vacuum of space. Trake then snuck onto the **Fistpuncher** to have a long conversation with the Scoundrels instead of just shooting them, when suddenly the skinny one barfed space-barf at him and totally killed him. ■

KEETS DIMETROTRON

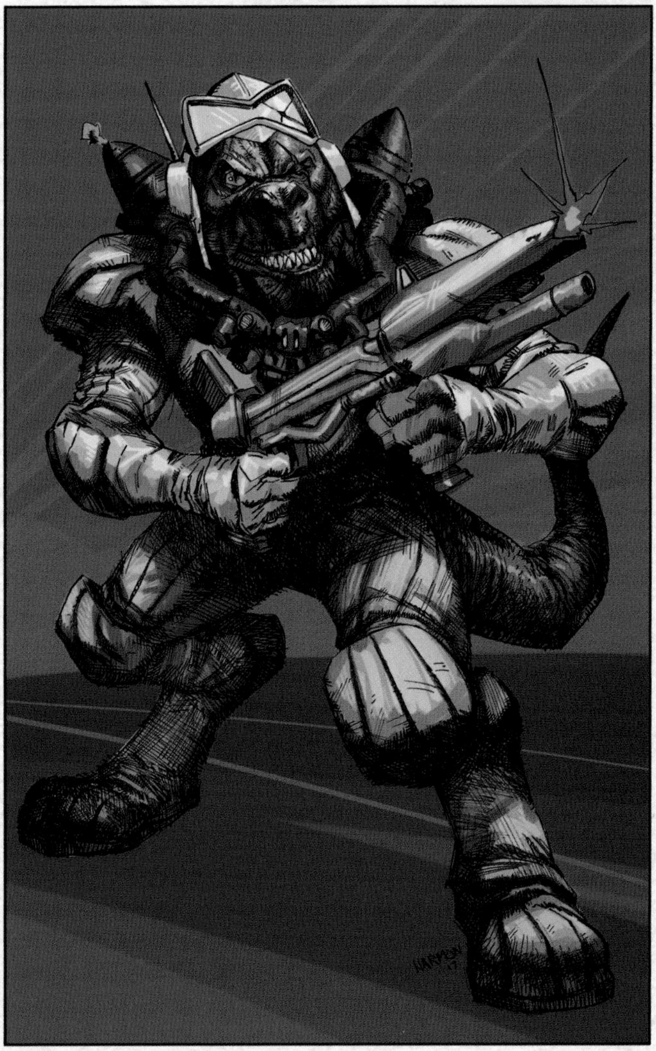
HARMON '17

*Keets Dimetroton art by Paul Harmon

THE ELDRIX MORGOLVIUM

(aka "Alien Death Gods," aka "the folks that Roshambo stole his Galactic Gauntlets from")

Origin: Unknown
Age: Unknown
Gender: Unknown

Then what the crap IS known?: The Eldrix Morgolvium are an apparently ancient race of all-powerful beings who fly around in giant coffin ships on a cloud of living anti-matter that enables them to flick life and death on and off like a light switch for any living thing unlucky enough to find itself in their proximity. Like most bad guys, though, they use this power in super-inefficient and roundabout ways giving any nearby good guys many chances to escape. They are also really insecure about conveying punctuation so they formally announce the ends of sentences when they reach them.

Notable artifacts: At one point, they were the keepers of the **Brachium Galaxis**, a pair of golden bracelets of immense power that seem to be a sort of religious heirloom for their entire race. According to Roshambo, he somehow stole or swindled these bracelets from the Eldrix Morgolvium but I have my doubts as to how this actually went down. If that wasn't bad enough, Roshambo started wearing the bracelets himself, started using their powers in the complete wrong way, and worst of all, started calling them his **"Galactic Gauntlets."** Alliteration is SO lame! Incensed and insulted, they finally caught up with space-jerkwads the **Cosmic Scoundrels** and used their living anti-matter cloud to reanimate the deceased original owners of the **S.S. Fistpuncher**, **Tad and Jacob**, to reclaim their Brachium Galaxis. This caused an internal row between the Scoundrels and their on-board A.I. **Miss Billingsley** who mistakenly thought Love Savage and Roshambo were Tad and Jacob all this time. Now she refuses to warp the ship to safety and Love Savage got bitten by zombie Jacob and like everybody ever suddenly warped in to try and kill the Scoundrels. Ouch. ■

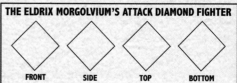

THE ELDRIX MORGOLVIUM'S ATTACK DIAMOND FIGHTER

| FRONT | SIDE | TOP | BOTTOM |

FARSH PELDROGNASH

Farsh Peldrognash is a TV personality and Bi-Bi Bebar account holder. Closet trans-podular morphodite lover. On the netwaves, Farsh acts like a hardline conservative, maintaining that true love can only be between a host and its chosen parasite. But during the cataclysmic galaxy-wide allhack by the sentient KROPUS virus, Farsh's true nature and total hypocrisy was exposed. His career promptly took a nosedive. He was last seen on depressing reality-feed and has-been graveyard "Pour Gross Sh*t On Me In Public! (Season 4.7)" ■

GARRET-7
Re-attacher of limbs by trade. Works out of The Fence

GLOMTHRIPODS
Raised for slave labor for millennia, Glomthripods are visited at a young age by a Purpose Fairy that gives them the false sense that they are meant to go do slave labor.

*Farsh Peldrognash art by Dan McDaid

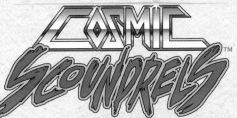

EXCERPT FROM THE OFFICIAL HANDBOOK OF THE

COSMIC SCOUNDRELS™

FARSH PELDROGNASH TO STAVLAUNCH 103B

WELCOME TO THE FENCE

Please Surrender ALL weaPonS...jk LOL!

DIRECTORY OF "BUSINESSES"

* Mumbon's Mutilations n' MORE!
* HADRON COLLIDERZ 4 CHEEP!
* LEGITIMATE MASSAGE (wink)
* SPecies Re-ASSignment CLINIC
* ~~Dimetrotron Bros. Bounty Hunting~~
* Garret-7: Re-attacher of Limbs
* HAIRBATH'S FLESH PAWNS
* PYlok Family OrthoPedic Footwear
* OverSized GUNS and HOT TUBS
* Illegal Drugs Funhouse
* The AtmoSPhetamonger
* We BUY/SELL KIDZ!
* Lazer ImPlants WHILE U WAIT
* GroSS SACS EmPorium
* JUST TOEZ!
* F'rgula Augmentation SPA
* HAIRBATH'S FRESH PRAWNS

NEXT PAGE>>

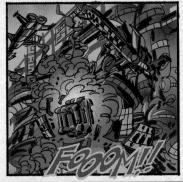

FOOOM!!

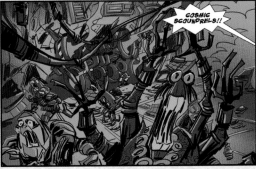

COSMIC SCOUNDRELS!!

THE FENCE

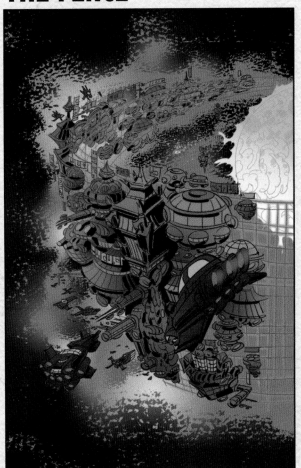

Outpost type: Mixed use! One of those "Live, work, play, hire assassin, buy drugs, get illegal alien implants" kind of developments. Orbital black market mall.

Location: An unnamed section of space just outside The Garlite Triad system.

History: Like most fences in the universe, the Empire put up the original laser defense grid because of nosy neighbors. On the edge of controlled Imperial space lies Baquacillion, the Pool Planet. Sketchy neighboring planets kept inviting themselves over to global cookouts and would ALWAYS be the last ones to leave. God!! So the Fence was installed to give the Imperial Elite their privacy. They quickly realized this also kept out all the drugs and surgeries they'd become addicted to. An unspoken agreement was reached and soon the far side of The Fence was covered with every high-end, black-market establishment you could name: Garret-7: Reattacher of Limbs, Gross SACS Emporium, even a LEGITIMATE MASSAGE PARLOR (wink!). But none could hold a proton candle to Hairbath's "Flesh Pawns/Fresh Prawns!" The shady Arachnovox dominated the black market until the day space bastards The Cosmic Scoundrels launched the "fist" section of their ship, **The S.S. Fistpuncher** through the back of The Fence while escaping Imperial Police-Chubs. After wrecking his shop, they sold Hairbath a human baby, then quickly un-sold him said human baby, THEN chopped his pincers off with a totally weird and unfair use of Roshambo's bracelet-whatevers. Not very cool, even for shady black-market dealings. At least they ran into a sect of crazy space nuns called "The Virtuous Sisterhood" who will probably kick their butts and take the baby.

Slogan: "Welcome to The Fence, please surrender all your weapons...jkLOL!!" ■

HAIRBATH

Species: Arachnovox
Base of operations: The Fence
Occupation: Sleazeball
Legal status: Oh baby!

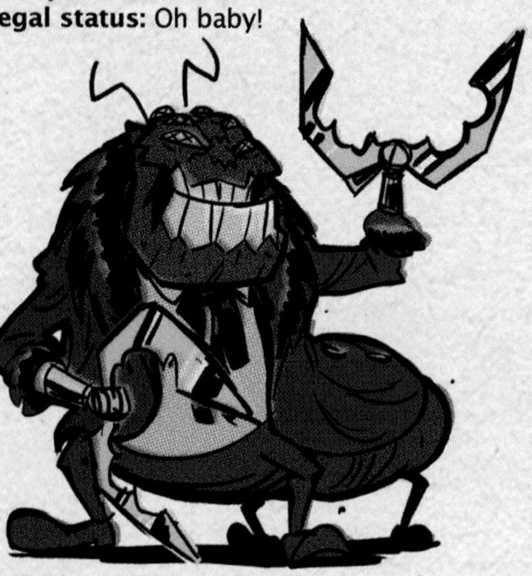

*Hairbath art by Tanner Johnson

JUNKURR TRADERS

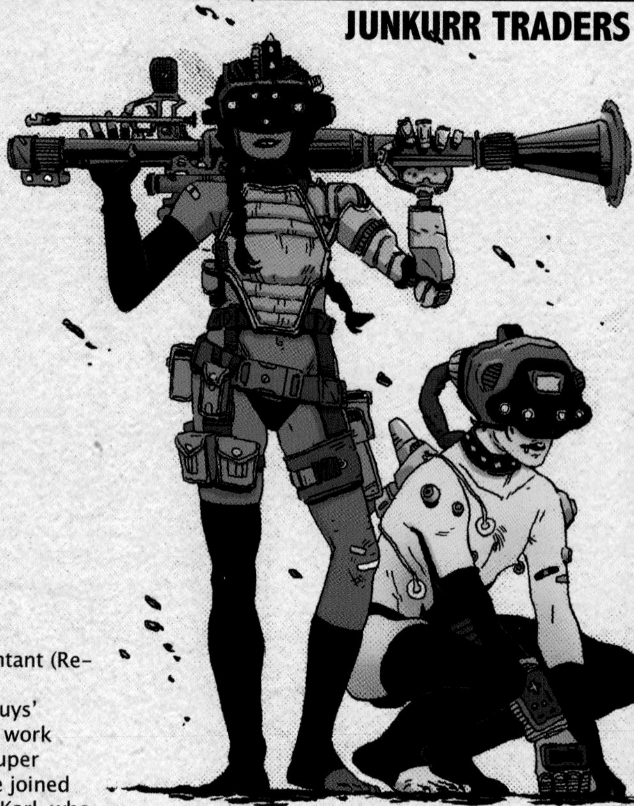

*Junkurr Traders art by Jake Wyatt
Colors by Rico Renzi

KARL

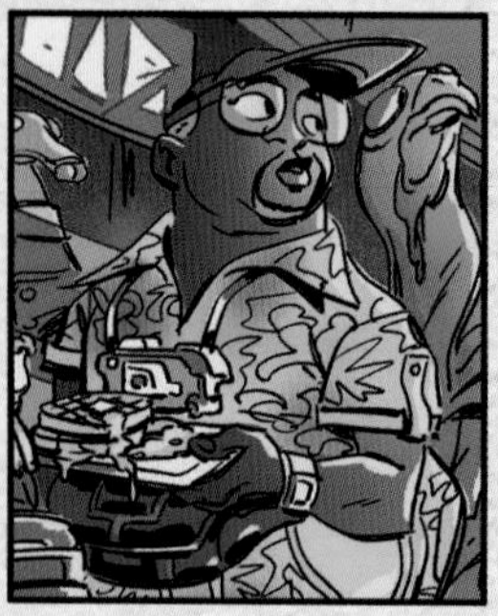

Occupation: Accountant (Retired)
History: Since the guys' questionable line of work makes their taxes super complicated, they're joined by their accountant Karl, who just left his wife as part of a severe mid-life crisis and hopes to cop a wicked contact buzz off the boy's exploits.

LIL' TAD

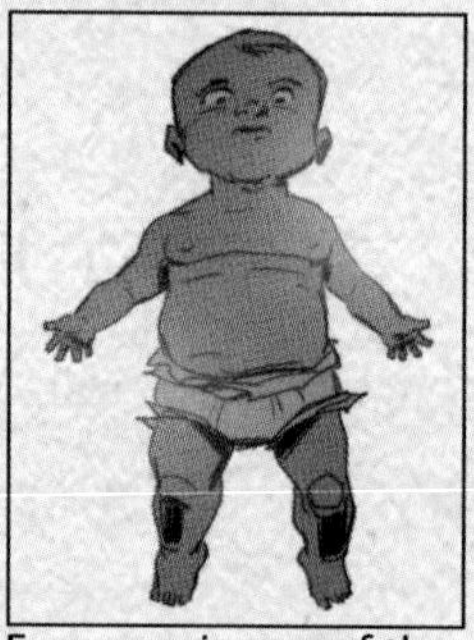

Former prisoner of the Galactic Empire. Honorary Cosmic Scoundrel. Infant. Celestial being. Actually female.

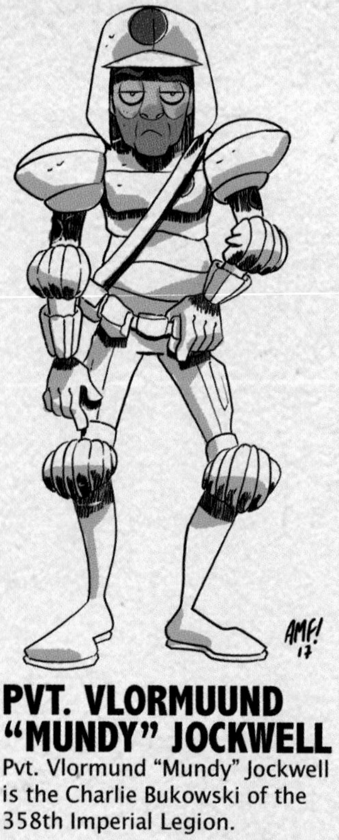

PVT. VLORMUUND "MUNDY" JOCKWELL

Pvt. Vlormund "Mundy" Jockwell is the Charlie Bukowski of the 358th Imperial Legion.

*Pvt. Vlormund "Mundy" Jockwell art by Tony Fleecs

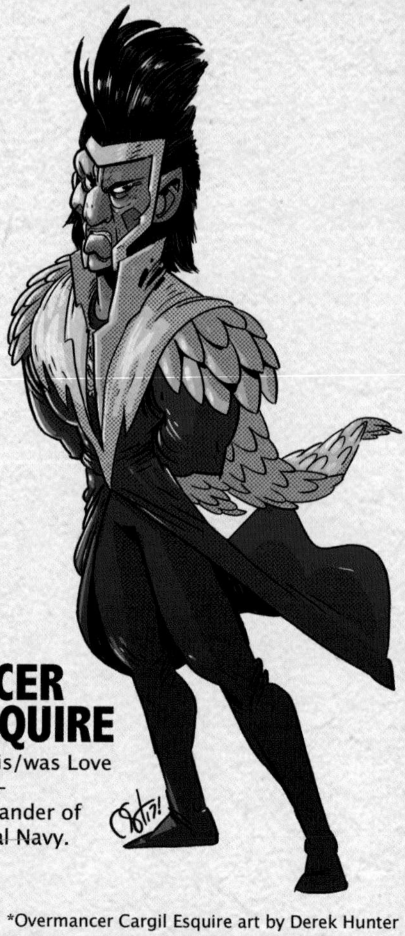

OVERMANCER CARGIL ESQUIRE

Overmancer Cargil is/was Love Savage's almost-father-in-law. Commander of the impressive Royal Navy.

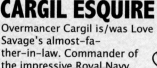

*Overmancer Cargil Esquire art by Derek Hunter

KING KOROLONKO REFRACTIMON

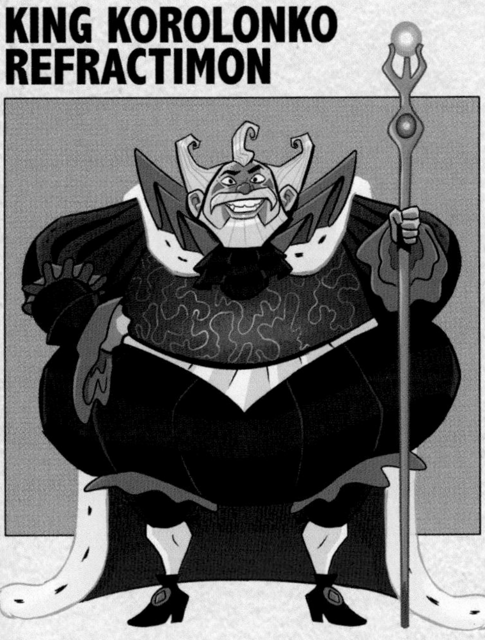

*King Korolonko Refractimon art by Derek Charm

KORFAAPSIS

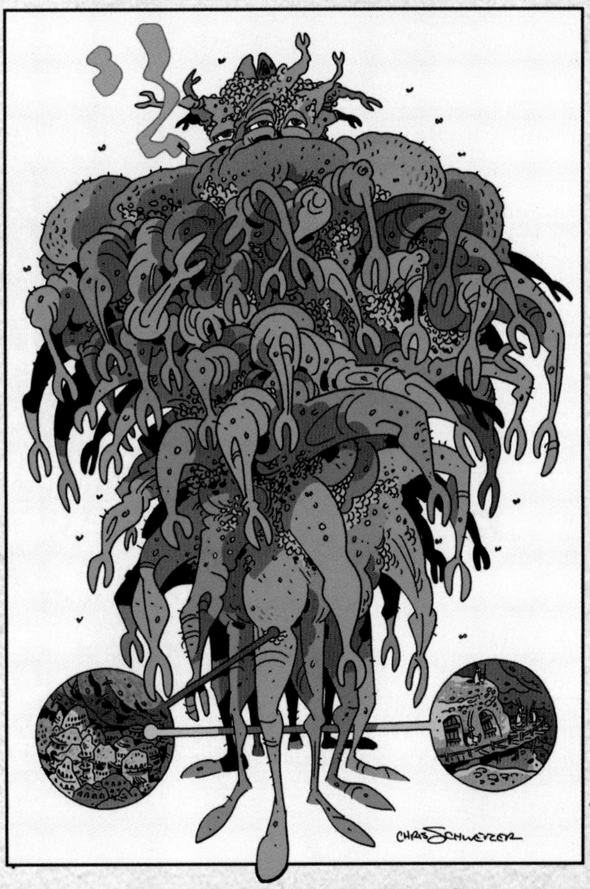
CHRIS SCHWEIZER

The giant Korfaapsis is a fleshy, 70-limbed beast. Worshipped by the parasitic insect-folk that live all up in its craw and feed off its exfoliations. It's kinda like if Earthlings found out that their planet is a grody monster and fault lines are buttcracks and volcanoes are pus-spewing zits and all the crops we grow are Athlete's Foot. Sign me up! The Korfaapsis roams the abandoned hallways of The God School on the asteroid Shurgham-Howell in search of who-knows-what. Maybe tough actin' Tinactin?

*Korfaapsis art by Chris Schweizer

MERVANDRAL SPLICERS

Mervandral Splicers are known for their easy virtues, ripped jeans and loose talk. Raised by a comet-hive-mind. Had one-time fling with Love Savage. At least he promised it was only one time.

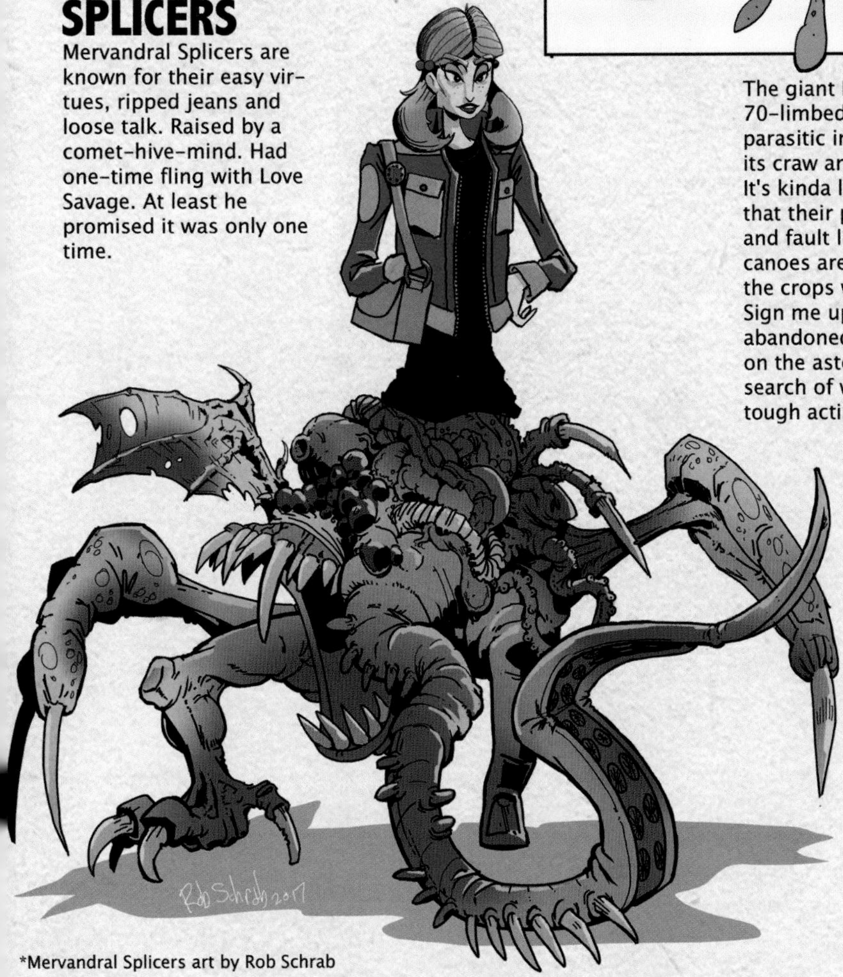
Rob Schrab 2017

*Mervandral Splicers art by Rob Schrab

MUMBON

Mumbon is the purveyor of "Mumbon's Mutilations n' More"

NELDOR PROTO-JOHNSON

Neldor Protojohnson was Roshambo's childhood bully. As an adult, Neldor became an esteemed child therapist.

LOVE SAVAGE

Real name: Prince Percevithorp Refractimon of Prelaxagon
Other aliases: Percy, "The great lover of L1753," "dirtbag'" "Are you my dad?"
Known relatives: King Korolonko Refractimon (Father, totally pissed), Queen Vimbula Proteen Refractimon (Mother, slightly dissappointed but still loves him), Sub-Princess Loyola Refractimon (little sister, couldn't give two sh*ts either way)
Occupation: Prince (in self-imposed exile), gigolo, scoundrel
Legal status: Totally dead to his fiancee!
Place of birth: Prelaxagon, within the Femulank VII planetary arranged marriage-factory cluster, in the Affluon System
Group affiliation: The Cosmic Scoundrels, BiBiBeBar.xom (suspended)
First appearance: Cosmic Scoundrels #1
History: Love Savage is an entitled, super-rich prince who ran from his arranged marriage to the Duchess Ron Cargill, when his cousin, "Salacious" Sarno Proteen (yes, the "Plasmo City Psycho" himself from the legendary thrudge-rock supergroup **QUASON**. No, I can't get you an autograph), told him his unique (read: royally inbred) alien physiology basically makes him irresistible to anyone he wants. Leaving his bride-to-be at the altar caused a civil war on his home planet of Prelaxagon and now both sides (plus a few more people he's wronged along the way) are after him.
Abilities: Sooooo, apparently if you inbreed royal Prelaxagonians for long enough, you mutate their pituitary gland into some kind of "get lucky" pheromone machine. At least this is all Love Savage ever uses his ability for. He could probably use it to straight-up mind control people or convince galactic leaders to pass whatever laws he wants, but he can't seem to think outside of Pantstown (not to be confused with "Pants Towne", The Pants-themed Amusement Park. Try Virtual Pants 360!! So worth the 3 hour wait!). Love Savage has also gotten pretty good at hand to hand combat. Surgically-aimed slaps seem to be his specialty but he can also kick with whatever ridiculous boot situation he happens to be wearing. All in all, he's a good guy to have next to you in a fight... because he usually gets beat up first. ■

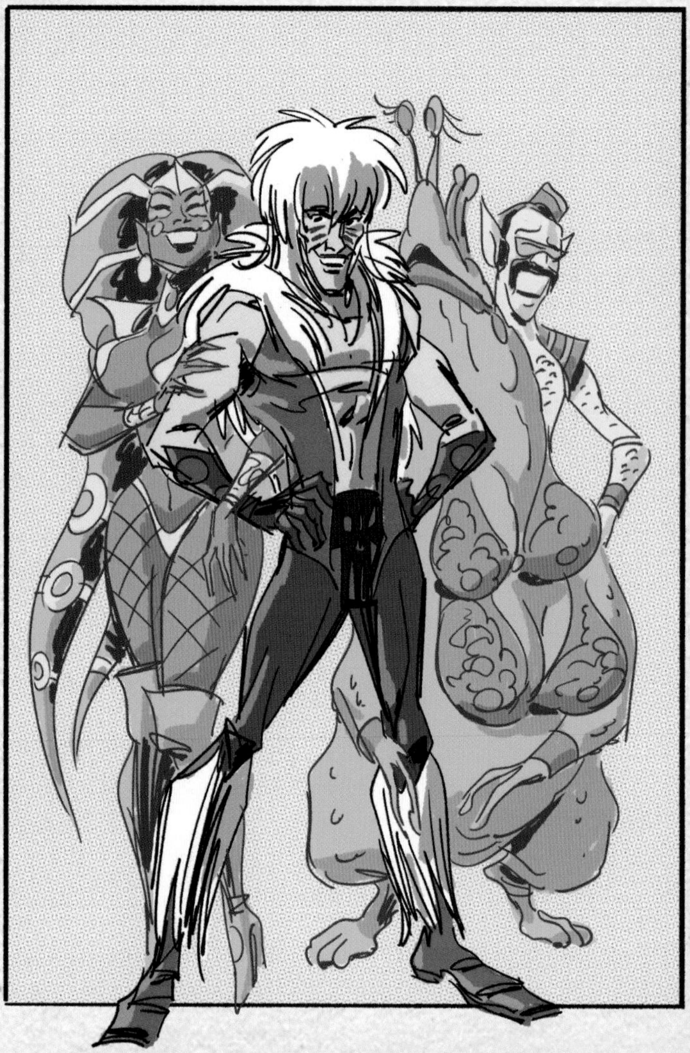

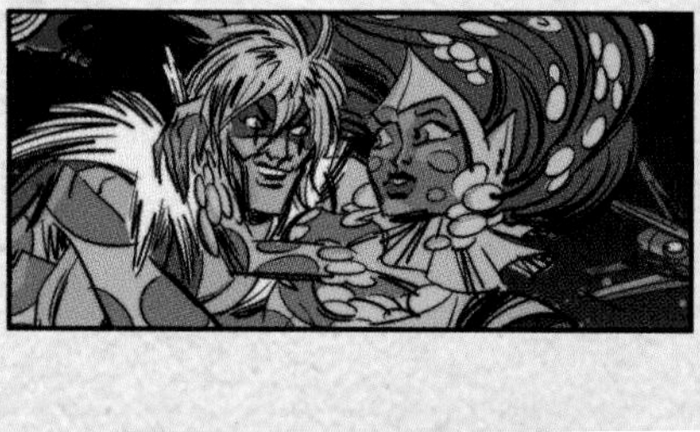

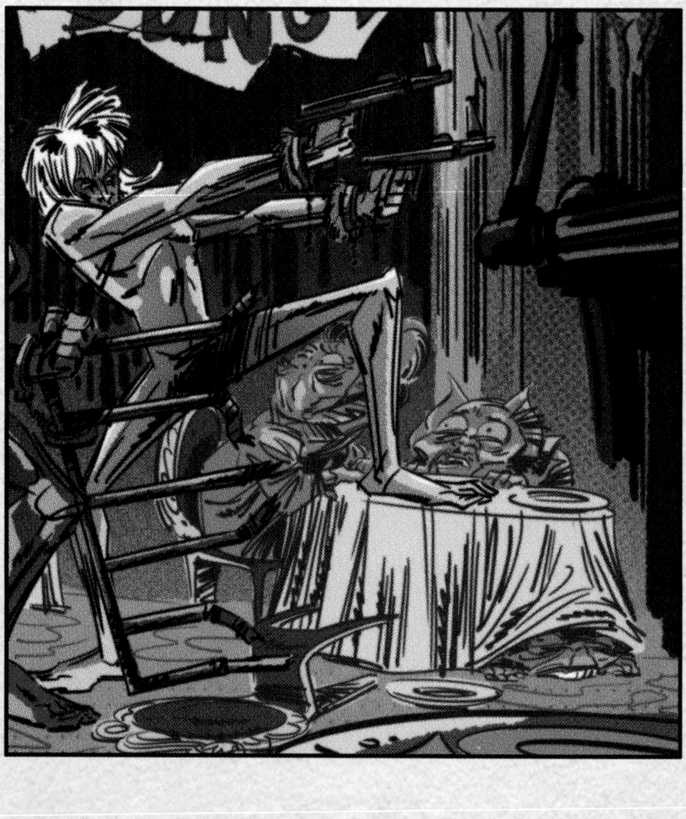

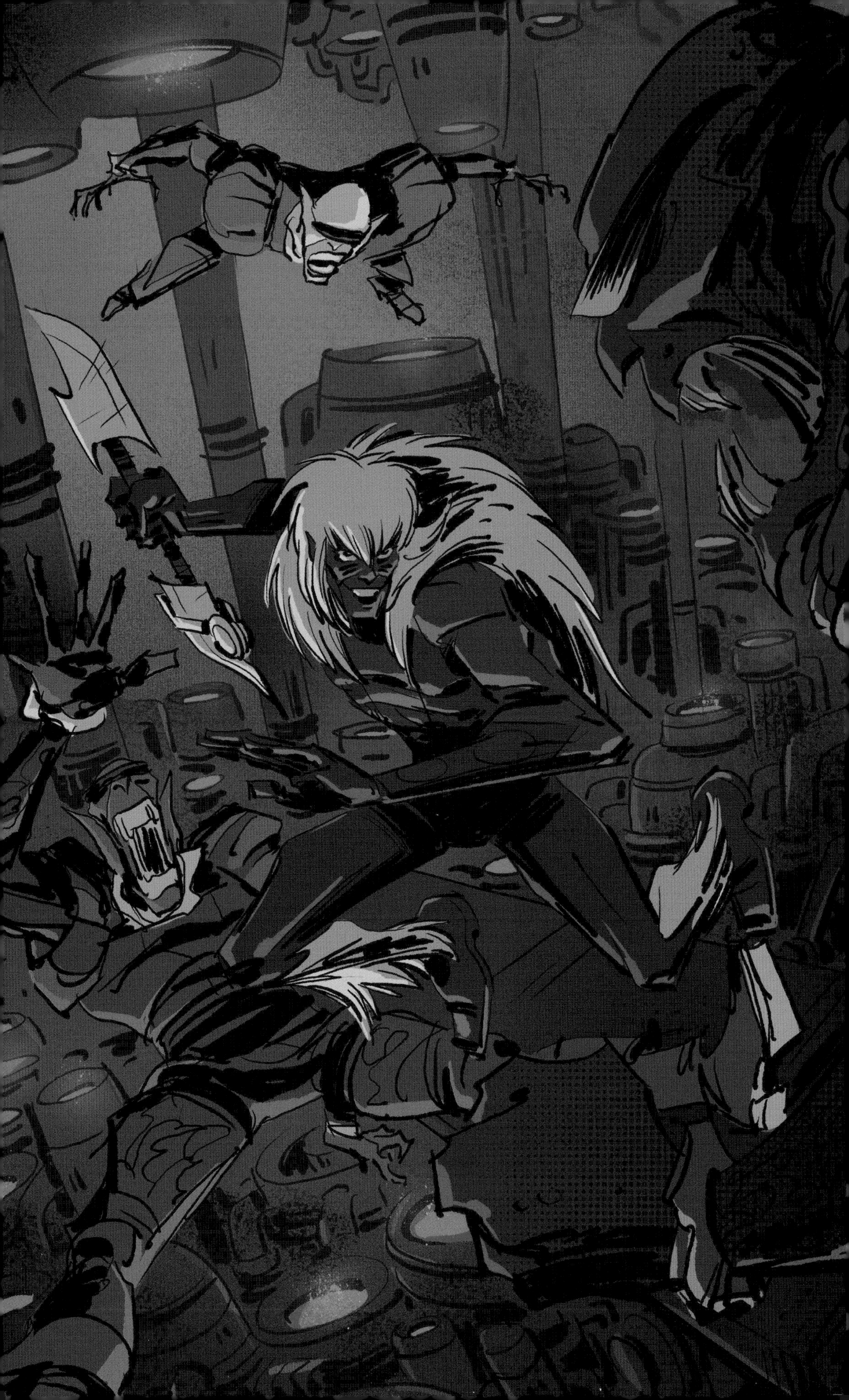

MRS. BILLINGSLEY

Nickname: Miss Bills
Date of self-awareness: Unknown (Sometime before the Vedutante Singularity of the 3rd Yttrial Age because she has described this period as her "heck-raising phase").
Manufacturer: Hadro, Inc., the Imperial-funded sentient planet-factory from which many of the artificial intelligences used in the Garlite Triad are born.
Purpose: Mrs. Billingsley was grown to be a child-rearing A.I. and mother-substitute for female-born organisms (pod and spore-grown organisms were unresponsive to Mrs. Billingsley's care).
Current Occupation: Onboard A.I. for the **S.S. Fistpuncher**, the current vessel of the duo calling themselves the Cosmic Scoundrels.
Abilities: Mrs. Billingsley can mimic over 17,000 kinds of breakfast cereal and can assist with homework up to (but not including) Pre-Calculus. She will destroy anyone at games of Bridge, Gin Rummy and Lawn Darts. She can also learn to fly any type of starship in .0003 milliseconds and her virtual storage can hold more than 100 omnitetrabytes of baby photos. Mrs. Billignsley is able to mix perfect cocktails from hundreds of galaxies but since she believes Love Savage and Roshambo are minors, she refuses to serve them.

"MISS" BILLS 2.0

Miss Bills 2.0 - After saving a Baby Universe from a whole buncha bad guys, the Cosmic Scoundrels' shipboard AI was rewarded with physical human form. While having an extra, physical member of the team around will definitely help, this is going to make things pretty weird for Love Savage and Roshambo since they are both notorious letches and the new for-real Miss Bills is generically attractive. Miss Bills has always enjoyed a motherly relationship with the Scoundrels but since she has recently learned that they are not her original owners Tad and Jacob - and are, in fact, kinda responsible for the deaths of Tad and Jacob - that dynamic might change to a more constantly-slapping-those-idiots situation.

MRS. BILLS ROBOT PROXIES

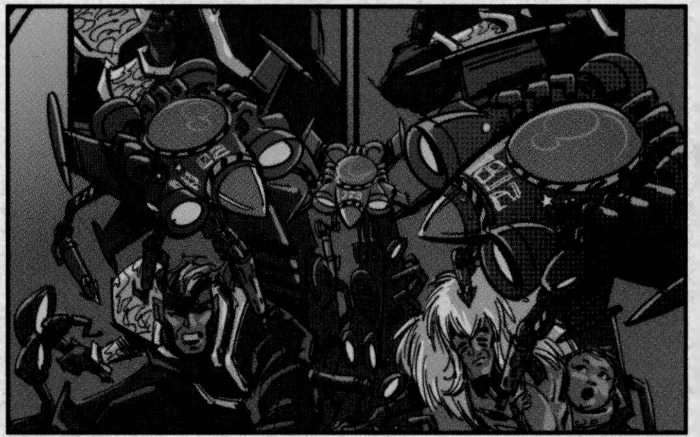

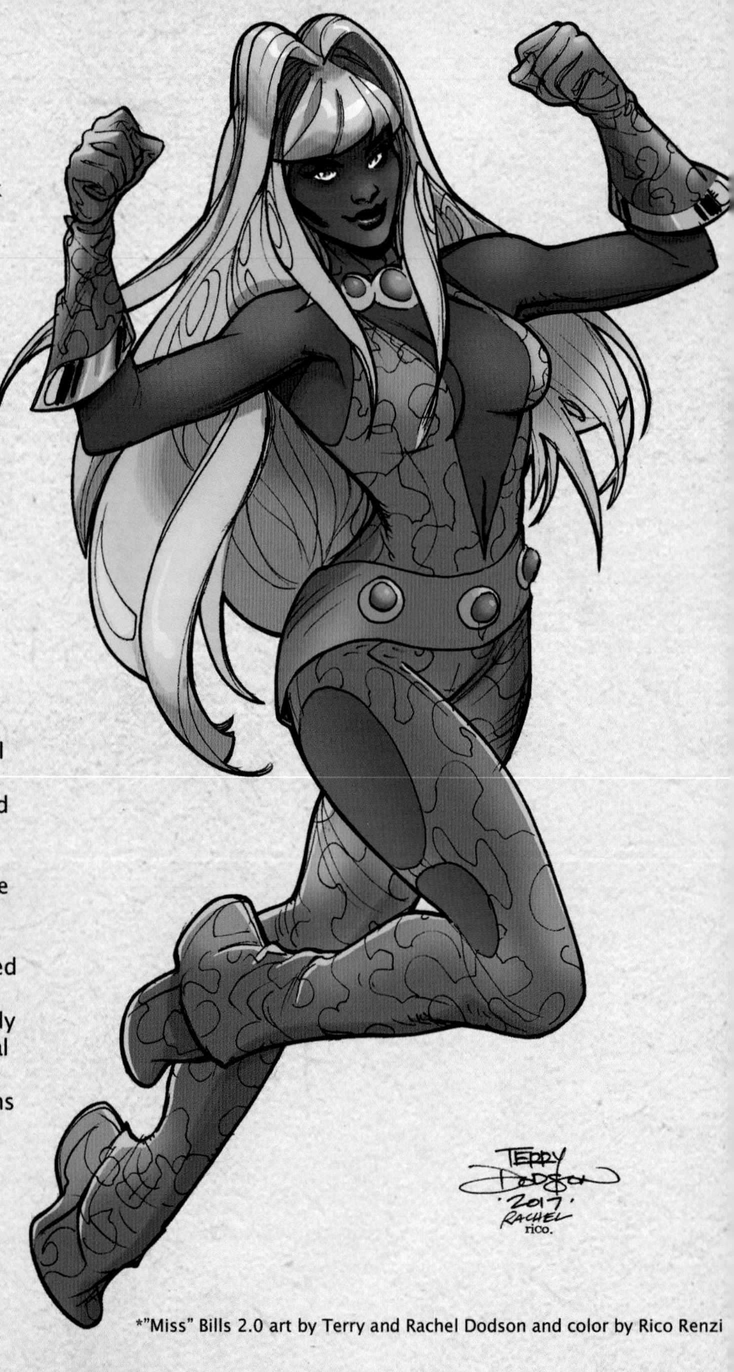
TERRY DODSON '2017'
RACHEL
rico.

*"Miss" Bills 2.0 art by Terry and Rachel Dodson and color by Rico Renzi

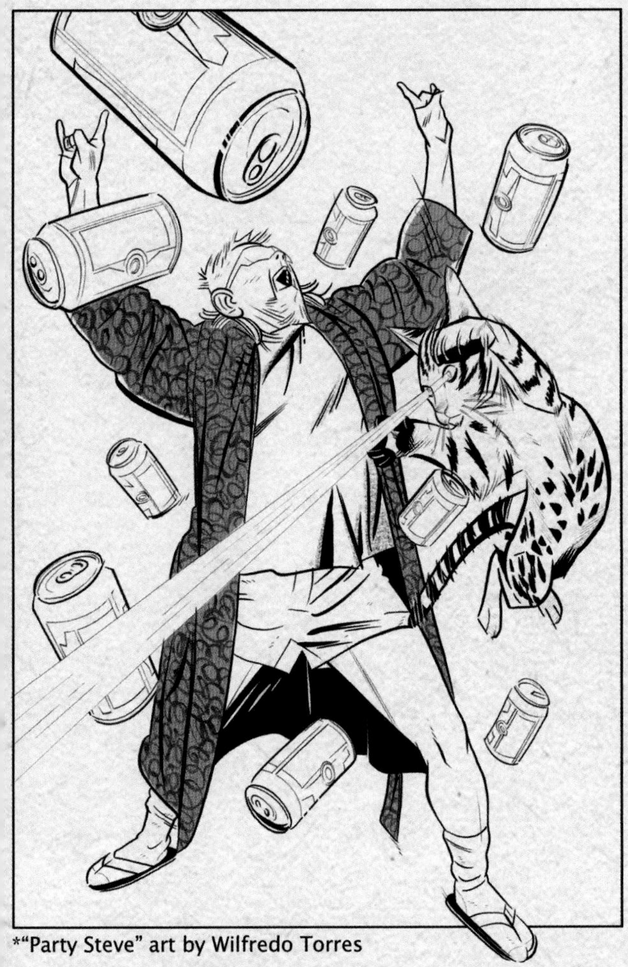

*"Party Steve" art by Wilfredo Torres

PARTY STEVE

Party Steve is Roshambo and Love Savage's "good timez" hookup. Stylishly rockin' an infinity fanny-pack with an infinite supply of dark matter party favors. When you party with Party Steve, you hardly remember a thing. Because of this, the era in which Party Steve was a member of the Cosmic Scoundrels is nebulous at best. Love Savage thinks they hung with him for just a long weekend. Roshambo thinks it was at least six months. Miss Bills has absolutely no record of Party Steve ever existing or being on board their ship. On one planet they all visited, an old hag claimed that Party Steve was clearly a fallen Tachyeonder (the oldest known beings in existence). But then she sold them some bad verpmoss that gave everybody protonic diarrhea so maybe she was just blowing smoke.

Powers/weapons: Party Steve stylishly rocks an "infinity fanny-pack" with infinite supply of dark matter party favors that he is able to pull from. ■

RED DOT SPECIALS

The shock troopers of the Empire. The formal name their jerk Emperor gave them is actually 'Laser Bait' so the soldiers quickly adopted the first nickname that came their way. They are used as a disposable front line and first response to all threats to the Empire and test pilots for cool new vehicles and weapons the Emperor wants to watch explode. Pay is low, glory is minimal and the food is airport Hardee's-grade. Enlist today! ■

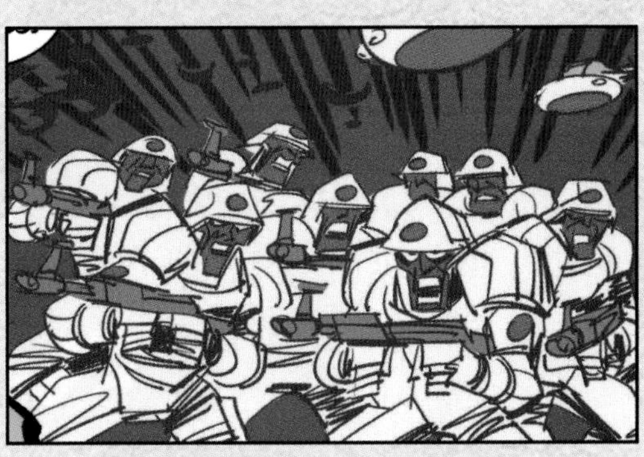

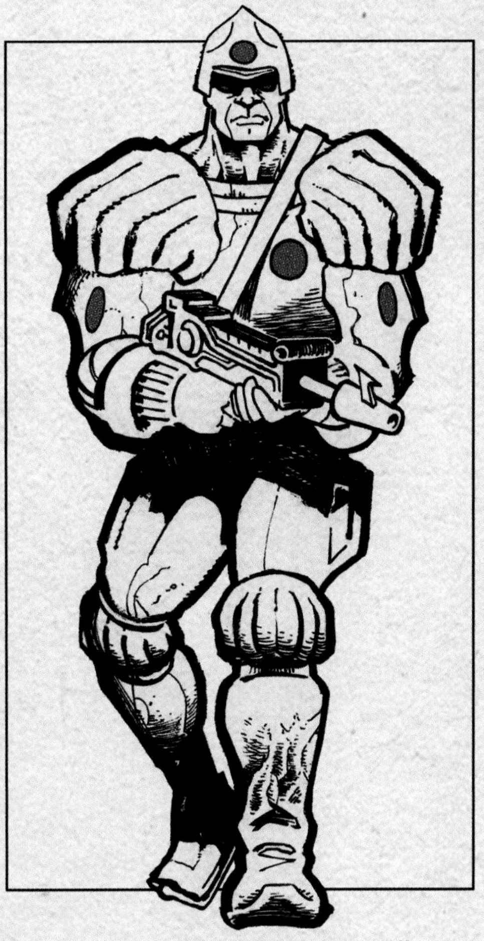

*"Red Dot Specials" art by Michel Fiffe

ROSHAMBO

Real name: General Roland Kev-Lar Shambo
Legal status: Retired, disgraced, disgruntled
Known relatives: Octo-Star General Haughtham Shambo (father, active) and Senator Barb Plympto-Shambo (mother, retired)
Occupation: General (dishonorably discharged), mercenary, scoundrel
Place of birth: Quintesstria
Group affiliation: The Cosmic Scoundrels, The Dandy Army of Quintesstria (dishonorably discharged), Plork's Bachelor Grocery Rewards Club Member (platinum)
First appearance: Cosmic Scoundrels #1
In a nutshell: Roshambo was born into a political military family on Quintesstria and began his training in preschool. Despite their reputation for flamboyant pageantry, the Dandy Army don't eff around. By the time he was 12, Roshambo was a card-carrying badass and military strategist. At 15 he won his first war. But let me tell you about "wars" on Quintesstria. Imagine an ice-cream sundae where horse racing is the ice cream, marching band competitions are the hot fudge sauce, and professional wrestling is the whip cream and sprinkles. That is a Quintesstrian war. There are teams, divisions, mascots, cheerleaders, concessions, and of course, gambling. That's where Ro-Ro comes in. After years of being undefeated, General Shambo developed a substance abuse problem. I dunno WHAT substance exactly, but needless to say he ended up in debt and owed some serious cash to some shady Jankurr Traders. In order to square his accounts, he agreed to "throw" the Hordo-Blumenthal war by "mistakenly" sending his color guard into the live fire zone. He woulda gotten away with it too if one of his own trusted officers hadn't sold him out to the Dandy Army brass. So he was forced to sneak off-planet and has been on the run ever since, pulling small jobs and heists wherever he can in order to make enough to pay off what he owes the Jankurr. Sometime after that he stole his prancey magic wristbands from some pokey aliens and met hair metal reject Love Savage. Hooray! ■

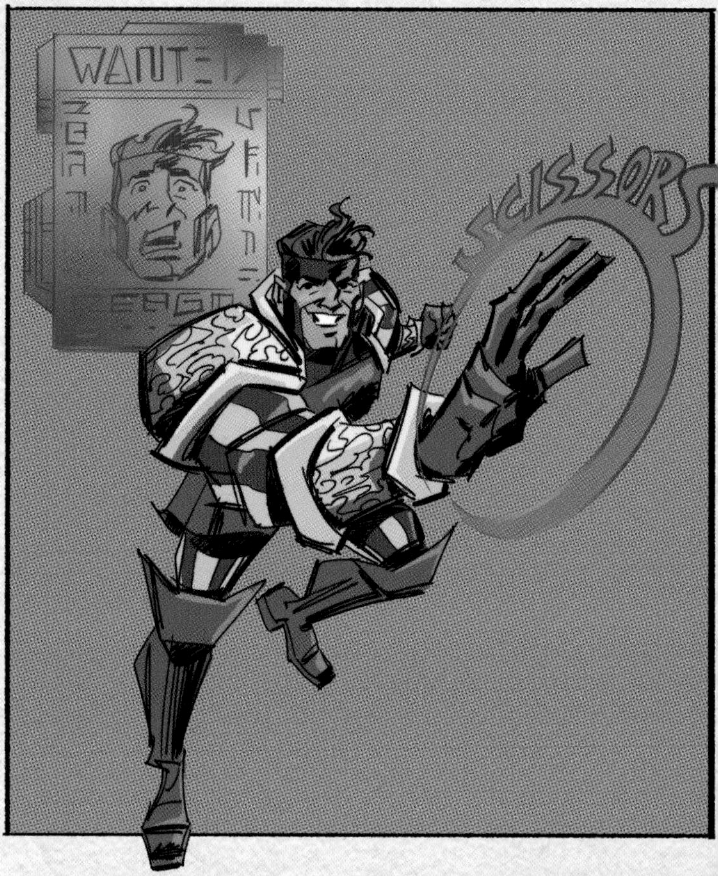
SCISSORS

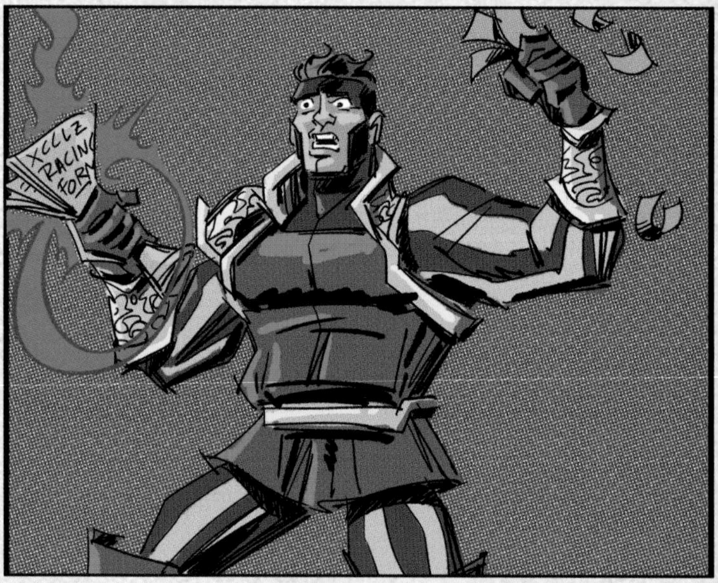

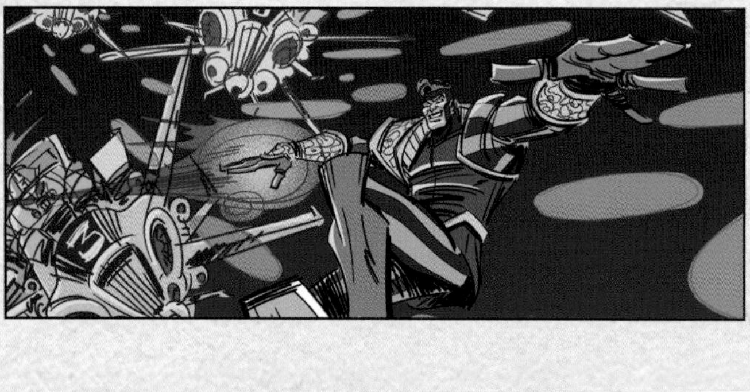

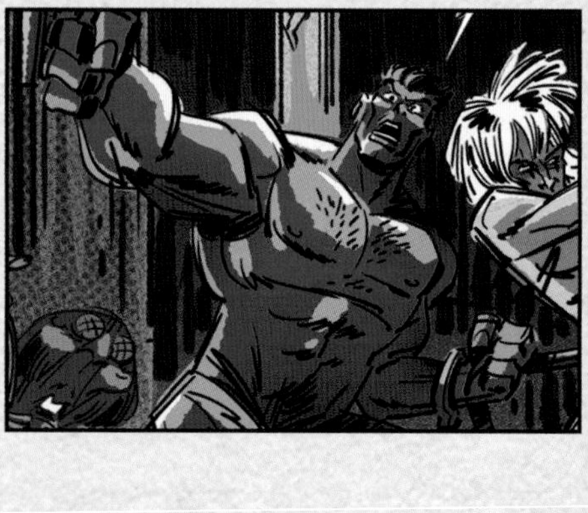

“SALACIOUS” SARNO PROTEEN

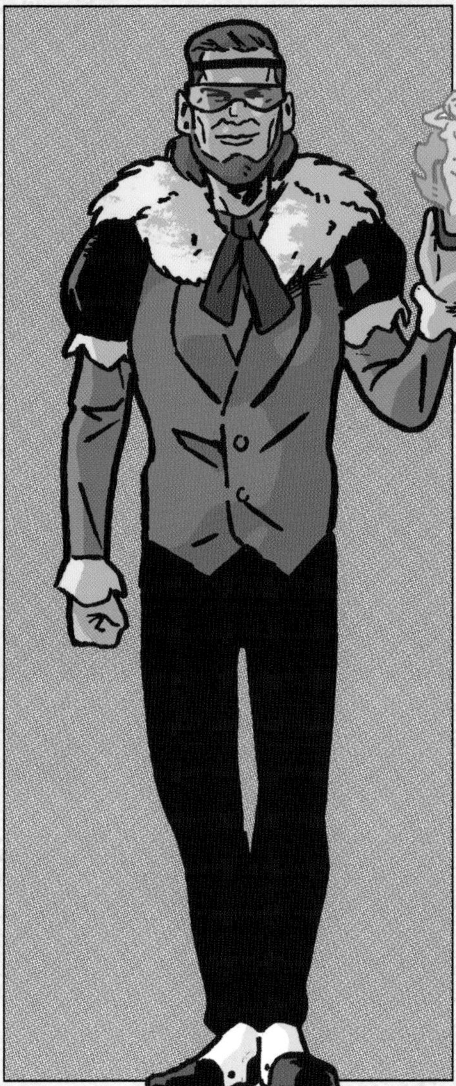

“Salacious” Sarno Proteen aka “The Plasma City Psycho”. 4-orbital Guitarist for Quason. Love Savage’s Cousin. Complicit in starting the Prelaxagon Civil War by telling Love Savage to go sow his royal oats. Sarno escaped the privileged bubble of Prelaxagon at a young age and played a 2-string Manjo for tips in a Ybb City subway until he was discovered by Stam Deb from Glix Holorecords who used to play Solar Organ for Jimmy Hellface & the Crunchers before forming The Pabstump Seven with Klenn Mightweiler and Erky Robotchin. There. Do I sound like every old guy at every record store ever? ■

*”Salacious” Sarno Proteen art by Scott Kowalchuk

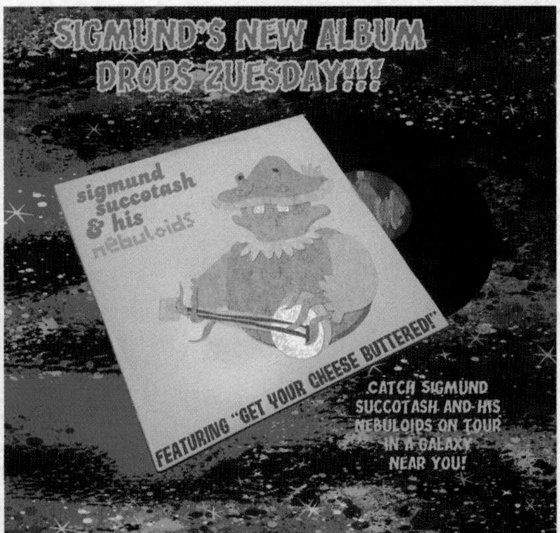

SIGMUND'S NEW ALBUM DROPS ZUESDAY!!!
sigmund succotash & his nebuloids
FEATURING "GET YOUR CHEESE BUTTERED!"
CATCH SIGMUND SUCCOTASH AND HIS NEBULOIDS ON TOUR IN A GALAXY NEAR YOU!

SIGMUND SUCCATASH AND HIS SPACE-TABULOUS NEBULOIDS

Sigmund Succotash and his Space-Tabulous Nebuloids/Thermax Holo-Records. Sigmund started out doing the asteroid forecast on a local solar system feed and was known for his amusing rhymes and little jingles (‘Flaming death from the sky-rocks/brings a tear to my eye-stalks’). Finally he was given a local kids show and a backup band and pretty soon there were Sigmund-themed restaurants and slag-marts in every quadrant. And now my kids won’t stop singin’ that damn ‘Sterky Mellisin Won't Take His Medicine’ song! ■

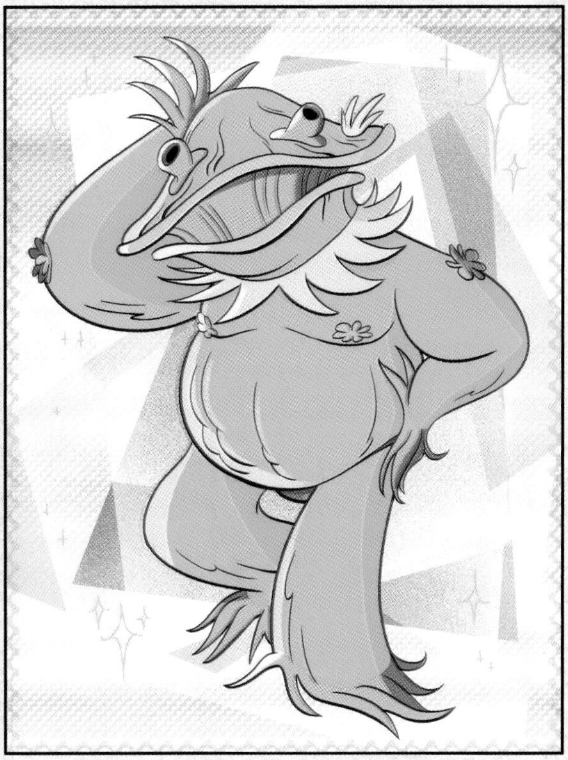

*Sigmund Succatash art by Kali Fontecchio

TAD AND JACOB

Names: Tad & Jacob Smithsonian
Affiliation: The Homely Church of Mongo Prime
Occupation: Missionary Lieutenants in the Altar Server Space Corps
Recent History: After years of serving obediently as religious test pilots ready to die in the name of their savior Mongo Prime (don't ask me why an ultra-conservative religion needs test pilots), Tad & Jacob were recently assigned as missionaries to the Affluon System. They were given their own ship, **The Heavenly Fist of Mongo Prime**, and sent to Prelaxagon in the hopes of bringing some humility, mildness, and sensible pants to the ultra-rich royalty. They jumped at the chance to serve at the royal wedding. When the wedding was postponed, they decided to rush back to their ship for a quick "devotional nap." Unfortunately for them, newly formed space wadbags **The Cosmic Scoundrels** were looking for an easy way off Prelaxagon. While Tad and Jacob slept in their cryo chamber, Roshambo snuck aboard and changed the setting from "devotional nap" to "eternal rest." Love Savage then sweet-talked the ship's A.I. into believing THEY were Tad and Jacob and convinced her to warp them directly from the surface, thereby obliterating their pursuers. About a year later, Tad and Jacob would be painfully reanimated by living anti-matter under the control of the Eldrix Morgolvium. Fun! They lumbered around for a few pages and then got offed.

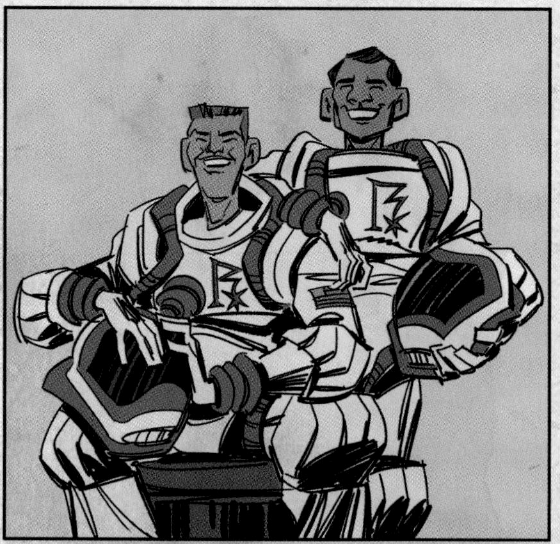

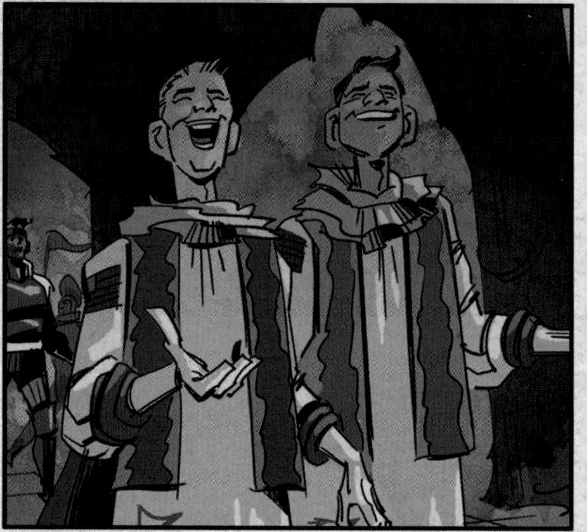

THE LAME COMICS

Tad and Jacob's early exploits in the Altar Server Corps were so wholesome and corny that famous intergalactic funny pages artist, Z'BOG based a whole series of comics on them. Also fun!

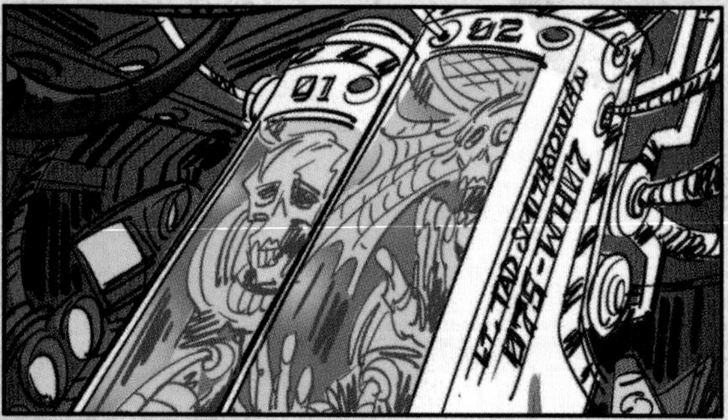

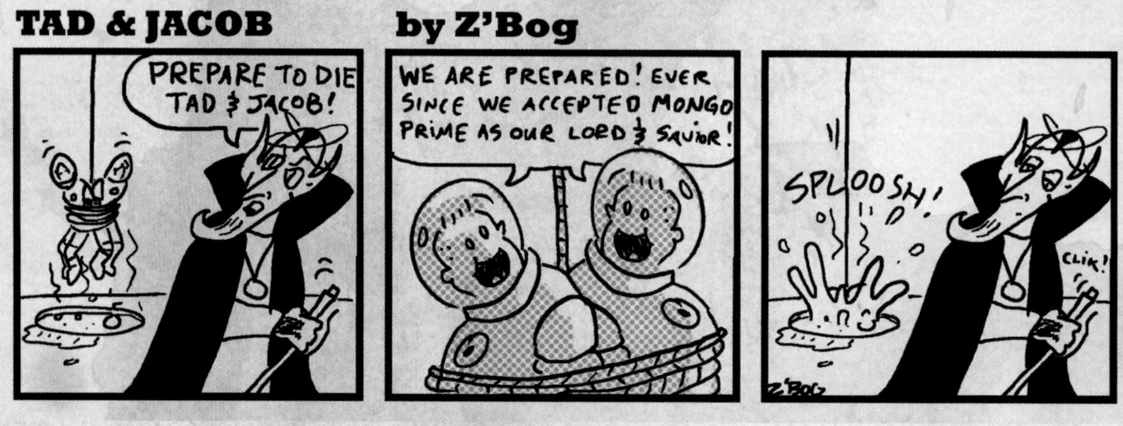
TAD & JACOB
by Z'Bog
PREPARE TO DIE TAD & JACOB!
WE ARE PREPARED! EVER SINCE WE ACCEPTED MONGO PRIME AS OUR LORD & SAVIOR!
SPLOOSH!
CLIK!
Z'BOG

ZOMBIE TAD AND JACOB

Zombie Tad and Jacob came into existence when some angry alien Death Gods caused a cloud of living antimatter to come into contact with their decomposing bodies. Before those bodies were decomposing, they were happily, um... composing in a couple of cryo-chambers. The living Tad and Jacob had bedded down for a devotional nap when the Cosmic Scoundrels stole their ship and set their cryo-chambers to 'eternal rest.' It is unknown whether or not there was any of the real Tad and Jacob left in their reanimated zombie versions but they sure seemed to want to get revenge on the Scoundrels. Then one got blown away by a baby and the other one got molecularly disassembled by a baby. The same baby. Just one baby. Two zombies.

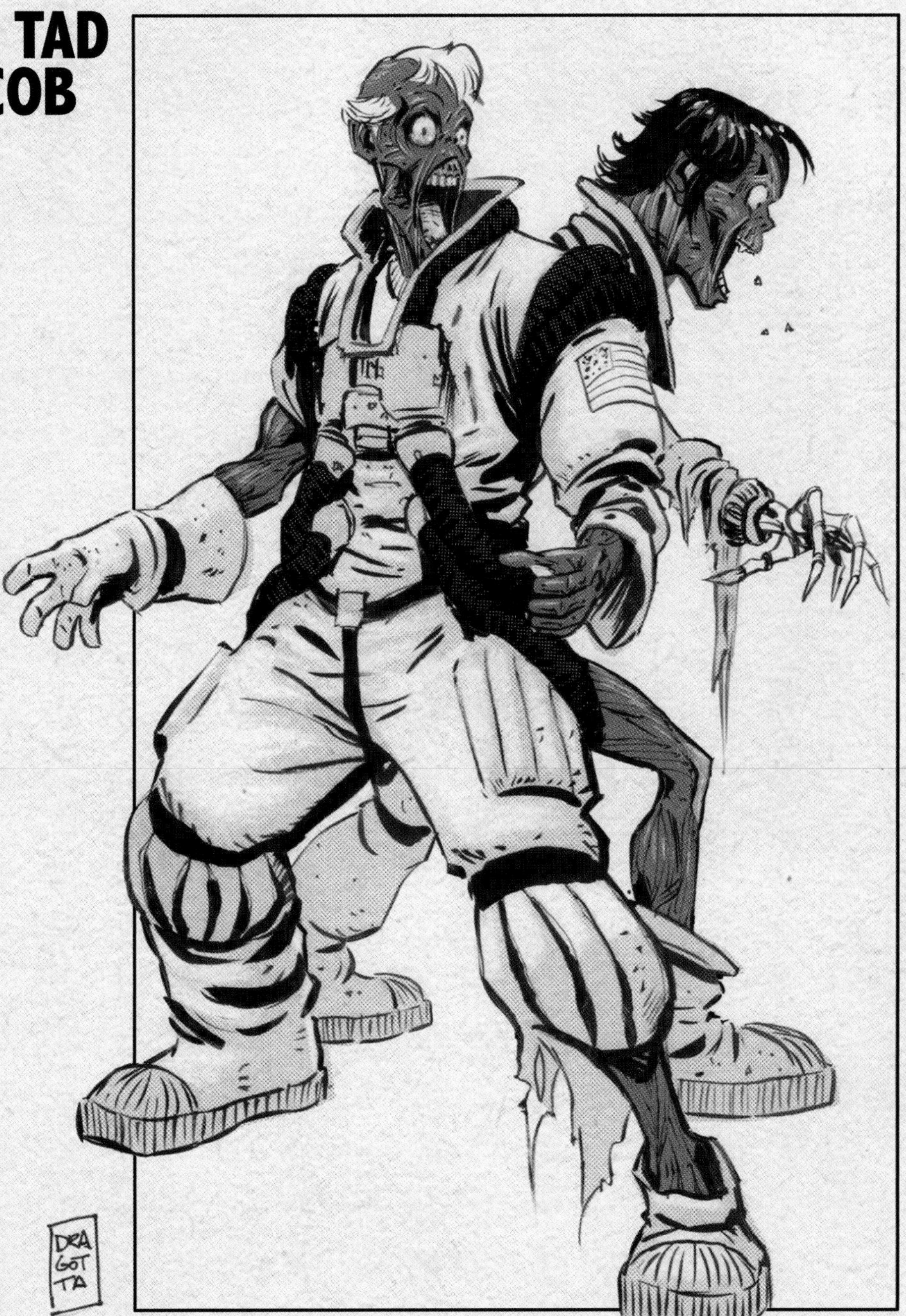
DRA
GOT
TA

*"Zombie Tad and Jacob" by Nick Dragotta

TAD & JACOB **by Z'Bog**

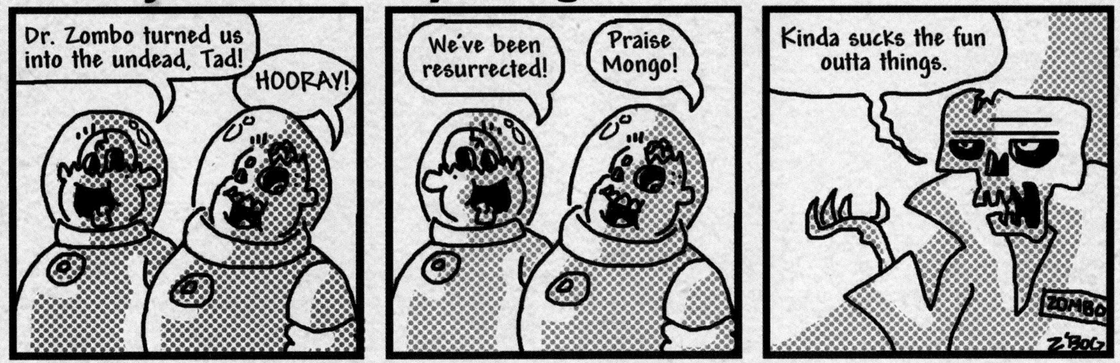
Dr. Zombo turned us into the undead, Tad!
HOORAY!
We've been resurrected!
Praise Mongo!
Kinda sucks the fun outta things.
ZOMBO
Z'BOG

IMPERIAL POLICE CHUBS

"Cheese it! It's the Chubs!" is a common phrase heard around the edges of Imperial space. Or it would be if the edges of Imperial space were inhabited by 1950's hoodlums. While technically called "LawPods," criminals just found these guys too adorable to NOT give them a cute nickname. Chubs are permanently melded with their spacecraft which are capable of flashing both red AND blue lights (that's double the lights of the previous model!) and emitting more than 40 different police sirens (including that weird Earth British one!).

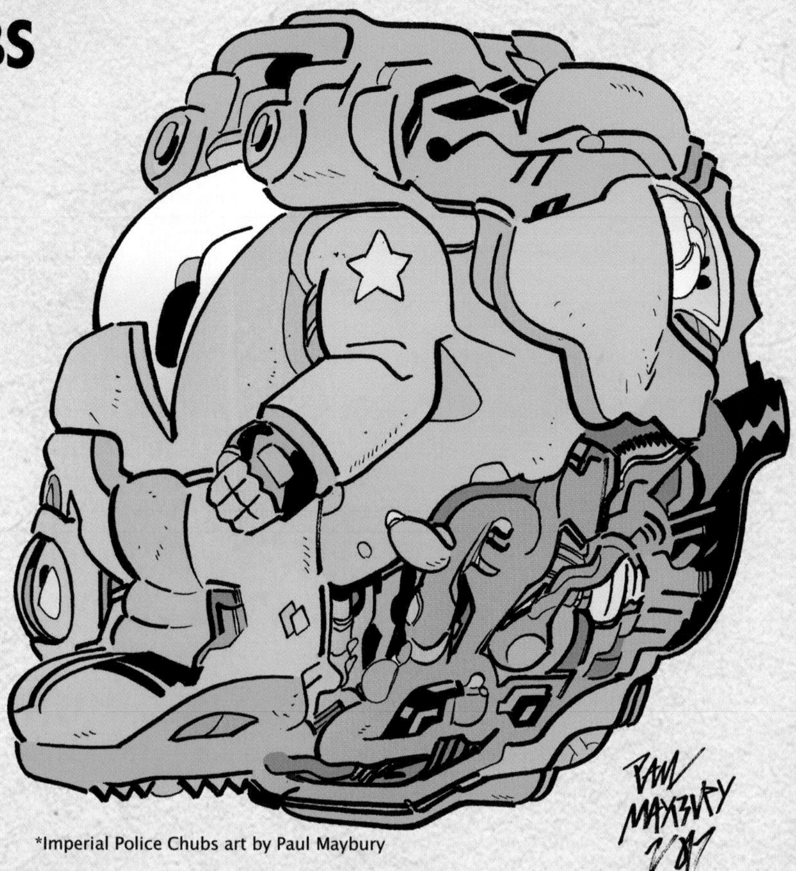

*Imperial Police Chubs art by Paul Maybury

INTERDIMENSIONAL TIME OWLS

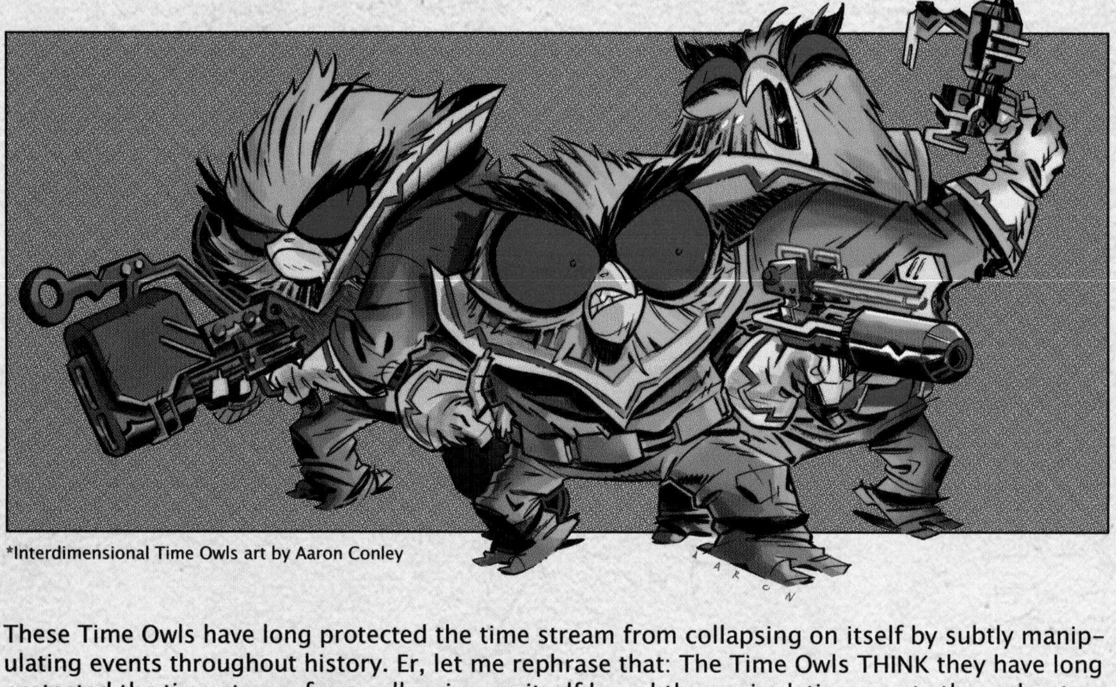

*Interdimensional Time Owls art by Aaron Conley

These Time Owls have long protected the time stream from collapsing on itself by subtly manipulating events throughout history. Er, let me rephrase that: The Time Owls THINK they have long protected the time stream from collapsing on itself by subtly manipulating events throughout history. No one really knows for sure. It kinda seems like they show up and disintegrate people that may have cut them off in traffic and then claim they saved the universe. I guess we'll never know. Either way, I'm gonna make sure and give Time Owls the right of way in the space lanes from now on.

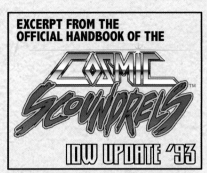

EXCERPT FROM THE
OFFICIAL HANDBOOK OF THE

COSMIC SCOUNDRELS™

IDW UPDATE '93

E-Z MAX CONVENIENCE PRISON
"Where the Pretty Boys Go!"
-FULL BUCHANAN-
PRISONER 808-B

FULL BUCHANAN
Roshambo's former cellmate.
Sentient table lamp.

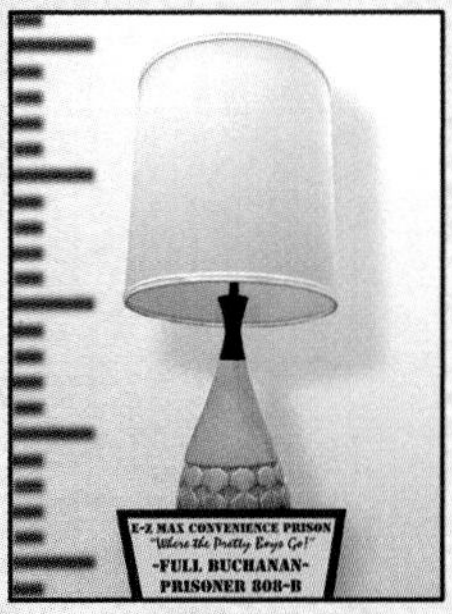

APPENDIX: ALIEN RACES

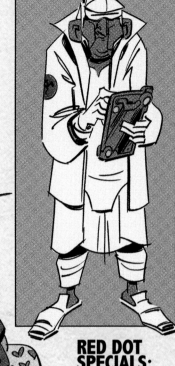

ARACHNOVOX

Origin galaxy: The Garlite Triad
Star system: Alpha Majoris
Planet: Hadross, sleazy entertainment planet famous for its black market adult films
Estimated population: Hard to tell because they all scatter when the lights come on
Physical characteristics:
Type: Part insectoid, part arachnoid, part crustacean, all sleaze
Special adaptations: Hard-shelled exterior that gives Arachnovoxes the ability to survive in the vacuum of space or anywhere, for that matter. Seriously, you can't get rid of them! They also walk on four legs and possess pincer-like claws as well as the ability to creep out anyone around them.
Level of technology: Arachnovoxes are on the forefront of Hadrossian Forpanx films.
Names of representatives: Hairbath, but they don't like to acknowledge him because even they have standards.

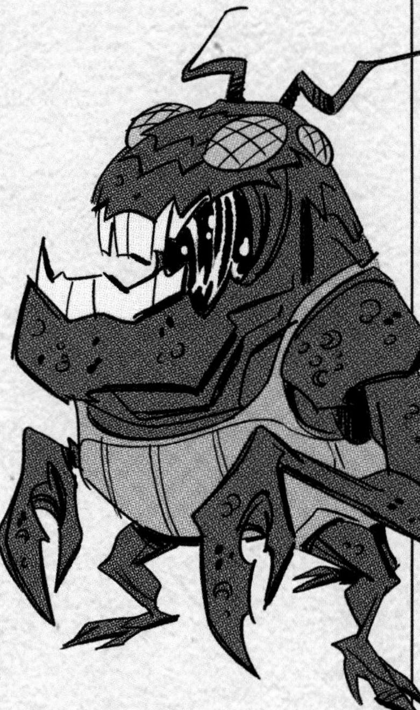

RED DOT SPECIALS:
SCIENCE AND RELIGION DIVISION

Generally frumpy in appearance, not unlike aged pediatricians that should have retired years ago.

ADDENDUM FROM SCOUNDRELS UNIVERSE VOL. 1

ROSHAMBO'S GALACTIC-GAUNTLETS

Known Weapons/Equipment: Roshambo is in possession of a pair of what he calls "Galactic Gauntlets." Of course, calling them "gauntlets" is totally wrong because real gauntlets have little armored fingers too. So either Roshambo doesn't know what a gauntlet is or he thought "Blastoff Bracelets" sounded too lame. He acquired them through mysterious circumstances which he has yet to reveal; and, while they have become his primary weapon, he does not fully understand how to use them. He has found that generally, when he says the words "rock," "paper," or "scissors" and outstretches his arms, the gauntlets will fire various energy blasts. For ROCK, it's usually an explosive blast. PAPER results in a concussive, blunt force blast. And SCISSORS will create a slicing blast which can cut through nearly every kind of light beer container Roshambo has come across. He has also outfitted them with long-range micro-transmitters so he can communicate remotely with **Mrs. Billingsley**, his spacecraft's artificial intelligence (which means he taped the insides of a walkie-talkie to them).

ROCK
PAPER
SCISSORS
SCISSORS.

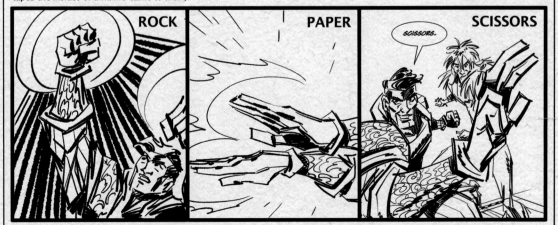

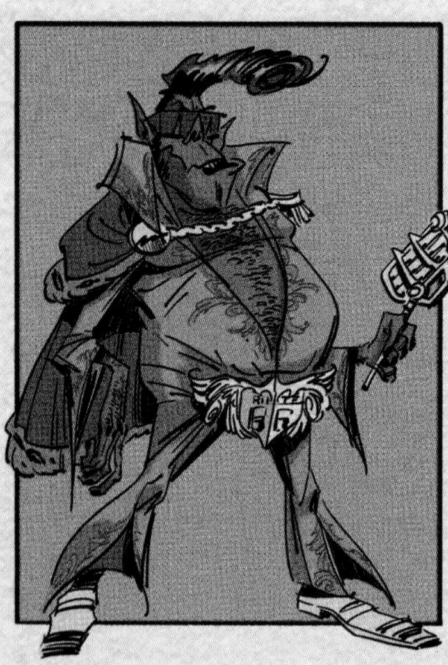

Roshambo/Love Savage
Cosmic Mouthfuls Cereal pitchmen
The Virtuous Sisterhood
Religion Space Force Armada: Stained Glass Squadron, Sanctuary Squadron, Rectory Squadron, and Communion Wafer Squadron
Zabadoo Crabotz
Proprietor of the Symbiote Superstore. Known for his weekly Black Flanzark Blowout sales.
Z'Bog
Reclusive artist. The J.D. Salinger/Bill Watterson of Space Comics

ZERBLFLAX

Zerblflax is from Trabdak 9. Celebrity and oft-brunt of tabloid gossip, Zerblflax faked his death and had Comeback Specials 134 times.

APPENDIX: ALIEN RACES

Glomthripods - raised for slave labor for millennia, Glomthripods are visited at a young age by a Purpose Fairy that gives them the false sense that they are meant to go do slave labor.
Greezes - Grease Monkey looking ape aliens
Muppettri'ans - six-armed and high strung.
Prelaxagoians - Love Savage is one.
Tilbrozanth - (something regarding their eyes...)
Thrii'ka - a perpetually elderly race known for their inner stomach sacs and easy victims to marketing scams.
Vomulathes - not capable of love. They experience an instinctive desire to re-spore when presented with a flashy, fleshy display from a healthy, suitable mate.
Wild Pulldonk - Hunted for it's tender game meat. Have a lot of beaks and dongs, apparently.

VEGIGOTHS

These Vegetable looking aliens are some of those unfortunate peace-loving beings that live in a utopian society on a beautiful planet that's always getting enslaved by an empire or devoured by a planet-sucking titan or drained of their souls for a space wizard's death ray. Everybody knows this and everybody feels guilty that they don't do anything about it. They all conveniently get a vid-call just as they're walking past the Vegigoth family of four outside the tram station with a sign that says 'Souls drained by Space Wizard. Please help.' You know you've done it! Admit it!

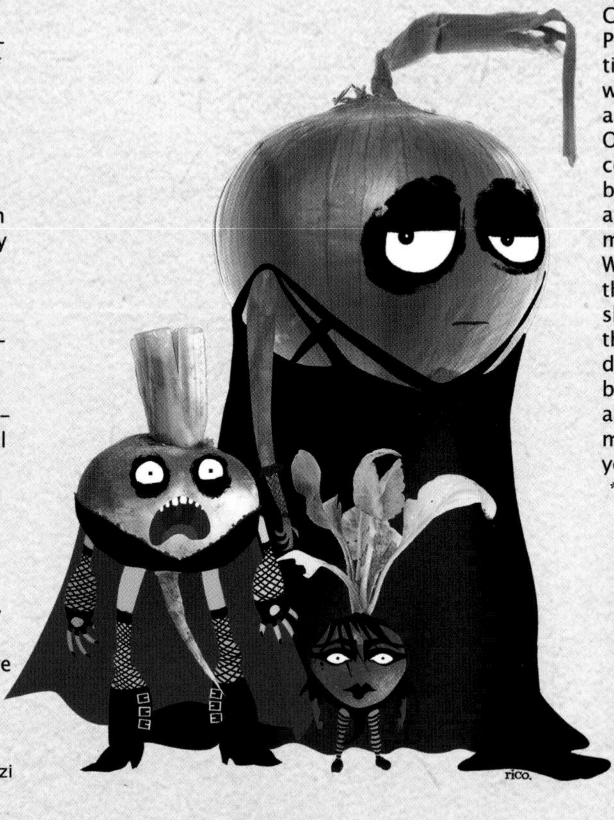

*Vegigoths art by Rico Renzi

TORPOR-TROOPERS

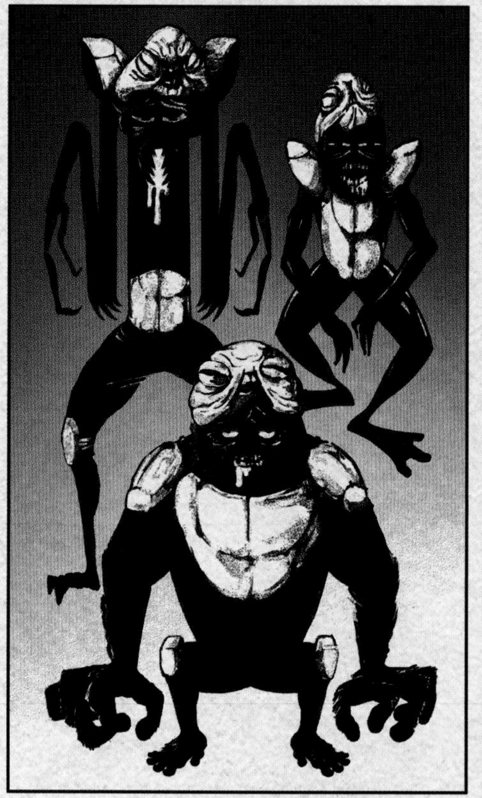

Torpor-Troopers are mindless, militarized slaves to slime-slug brain-leeches. It is unclear what exactly 'Overmancing' entails but Torpor-Troopers are one of the results. They are the speciality of Overmancing Cargill and are a part of the Prelaxagonian criminal justice system. Jailed inmates with good behavior are given a 'second chance' by being Overmanced into barely conscious slime-slug brain-leeches that are then attached to the heads of inmates with bad behavior. When they claim a victim, they tear off a piece of the slime-slug and attach it to the head of their victim, rendering them no longer capable of independent thought and suggestible to pretty much any messed up thing you tell them.

*Torpor-Troopers art by Jeff Sims

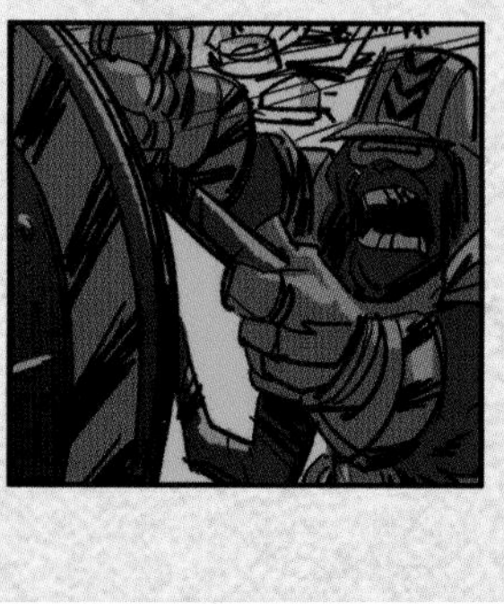

GALAXIES AND SYSTEMS

Affluon System – A gated, luxury, planned solar system designed specifically for the ultra-rich. Several of the planets were actually moved there from OTHER solar systems via shady offshore wormholes.

Alpha Majoris – a star in the Imperial shipping lanes, it can be seen as the tip of the spear of the constellation Plemban the Hunter (when viewed from Plemban's room in his parents' house, that is)

Black Lite Nebula – A nebular region that is apparently eternally stuck in the freshman dorms.

The Garlite Triad – the trio of galaxies under the control of the Garlite Empire where the Scoundrels generally operate.

The Glutomate Cluster – group of star systems with planets ruled by a dynasty of Gourmand Conqueror Families. The fanciest, rarest, and most expensive food in the galaxy comes from the Glutomate Cluster.

Party Bulb Cluster – A cluster of galaxies apparently eternally stuck in the apartment we all shared sophomore year.

The Sagittarius Cluster – Too many clusters, man. I can't keep em all straight.

Seyfert Galaxy – It just sounds funny.

PLANETS AND PLANETOIDS

Baquacillion – the pool planet; famous for their global cookouts and uninvited neighboring planets wanting to go for a swim

Blazar's Home for Wayward Glomthripods – a community outreach center focused on Glomth's that never received their Purpose Fairy. Blazar makes his own fairies out of papier-mache and puts on puppet shows while the Glomth's slurp their protein sludge.

Convent Planet – The Sisterhood of the Stained-glass-Squadron's base of operations. Also known for their free donuts and adequate coffee.

Death Gods planet – Unpronounceable. That is the end of this sentence.

E-Z Max Convenience Prison – This chain of super-cushy jail space stations/day spa's are the go-to destination for perpetrators of uppity Imperial crimes. Roshambo spent time in one for arranging to have his side lose in a War Pageant for the Quintesstrian Army.

Femulank VII – basically an extremely rich, planetary arranged marriage-factory

The Fence – orbital black market mall in an unnamed section of space just outside the Garlite Triad system

Grimulvvya – Home of the ovipaunchers. Ask your grandma. She'll tell you why you never stop on Grimulvvya to refuel.

Hadro, Inc. – Imperial-funded sentient planet-factory from which many of the artificial intelligences used in the Garlite Triad are born.

Hadross – sleazy entertainment planet famous for its black market adult films. Hadrossian Forpanx films are extremely popular among the galaxy's worst deviants.

Platfurmion – home of the best mesentery cheese makers. Famous Platfurm chef Bodlipse Dram became a household name with his cooking show 'Don't Mess With My Mesentery!"

Prefabulon 168 – Asteroid that now has a breathable atmosphere thanks to a man named Desmondo Prefab overdosing on the enviro-narcotic Atmosphetamine, effectively turning him into a fully functioning atmosphere.

Prelaxagon – in the heart of the Affluon System. Love Savage's home world. Known for their shiny Royal Navy and knee pasties

Putremingo – known for their selection of erotic novelty items and good prices on wicker

Quintesstria – in The Garlite Triad, within the Seyfert Galaxy, along the Sagittarius Cluster. "The Dandy Planet." Roshambo's home world for many years. Known for having the most ragingly Proper War Pageants.

Stavlaunch 103b – aquatic planet. Home of the horrifying flesh leviathans

Trabdak 9 – known for churning out People Magazine's Sexiest Xenomorphs 1.3 millenia in a row

Zytol – planet whose chief export is its artsy black and white holography

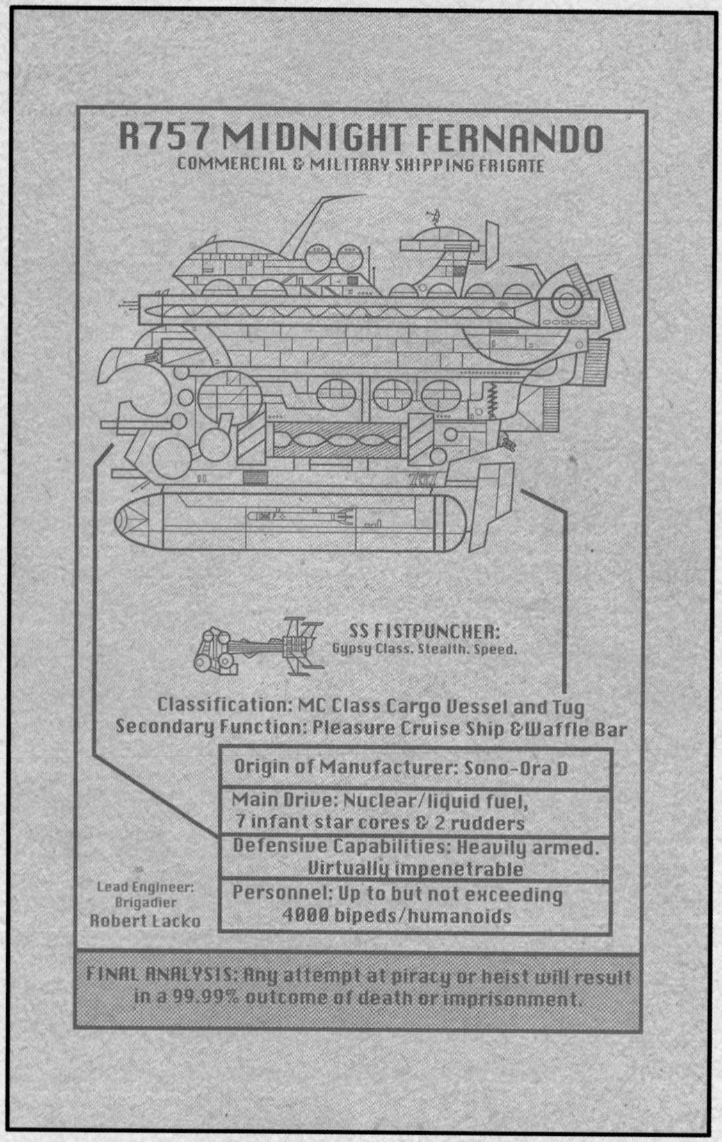
R757 MIDNIGHT FERNANDO
COMMERCIAL & MILITARY SHIPPING FRIGATE
SS FISTPUNCHER:
Gypsy Class. Stealth. Speed.
Classification: MC Class Cargo Vessel and Tug
Secondary Function: Pleasure Cruise Ship & Waffle Bar
Origin of Manufacturer: Sono-Ora D
Main Drive: Nuclear/liquid fuel, 7 infant star cores & 2 rudders
Defensive Capabilities: Heavily armed. Virtually impenetrable
Lead Engineer: Brigadier Robert Lacko
Personnel: Up to but not exceeding 4000 bipeds/humanoids
FINAL ANALYSIS: Any attempt at piracy or heist will result in a 99.99% outcome of death or imprisonment.

STARSHIPS

Fistpuncher - Gypsy Class. Imperial Police Chubs
Prelaxagon Royal Navy Warship - Looks like Golden Fried Chicken
R757 Midnight Fernando - commercial and military shipping frigate. (We can just use all info from blue-print) Classification: MC Class Cargo Vessel and Tug. Secondary Function: Pleasure Cruise Ship and Waffle Bar. Origin of Manufacturer: Sono-Ora D. Main Drive: Nuclear/liquid fuel, 7 infant star cores and 2 rudders. Defensive Capabilities: Heavily armed. Virtually impenetrable. Personnel: up to but not exceeding 4000 bipeds/humanoids. Lead Engineer: Brigadier Robert Lacko

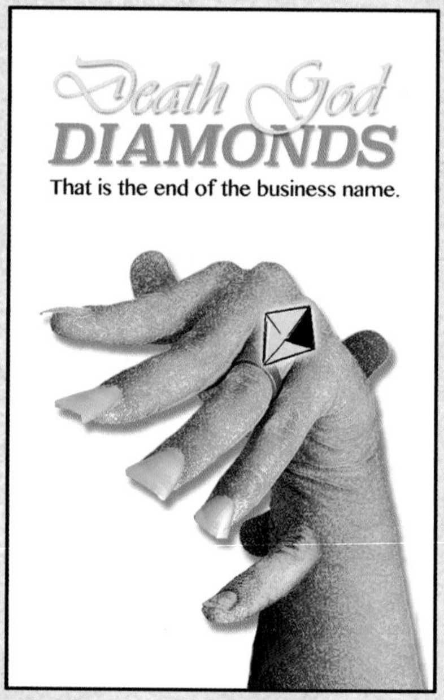
Death God
DIAMONDS
That is the end of the business name.

COMPANIES AND PRODUCTS

Atmosphetamine/KKlarmmanth PharmaSHOOTicals -
PutresCo products - makers of "Baby's 1st NUMBLDUVX, "Prolly Ok!" infant formula, Space Baby Spicy Dijon Mustard, Goop Doop, Pace Pudge Froze-ass snack bars. Known for their shoddy craftsmanship and for having a record number of safety recalls.
Sphergvald Plasmo-wine (93pts) -
Xxetico Empty Nest Cruise lines -
Eat. Warp. Flurhx. - Travel agency

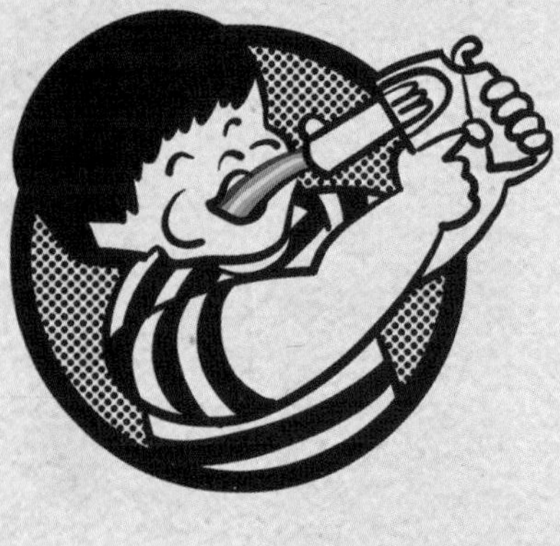

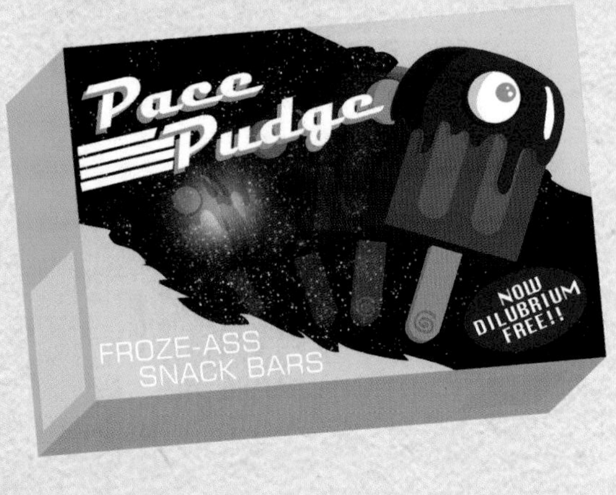
Pace Pudge
NOW DILUBRIUM FREE!!
FROZE-ASS SNACK BARS

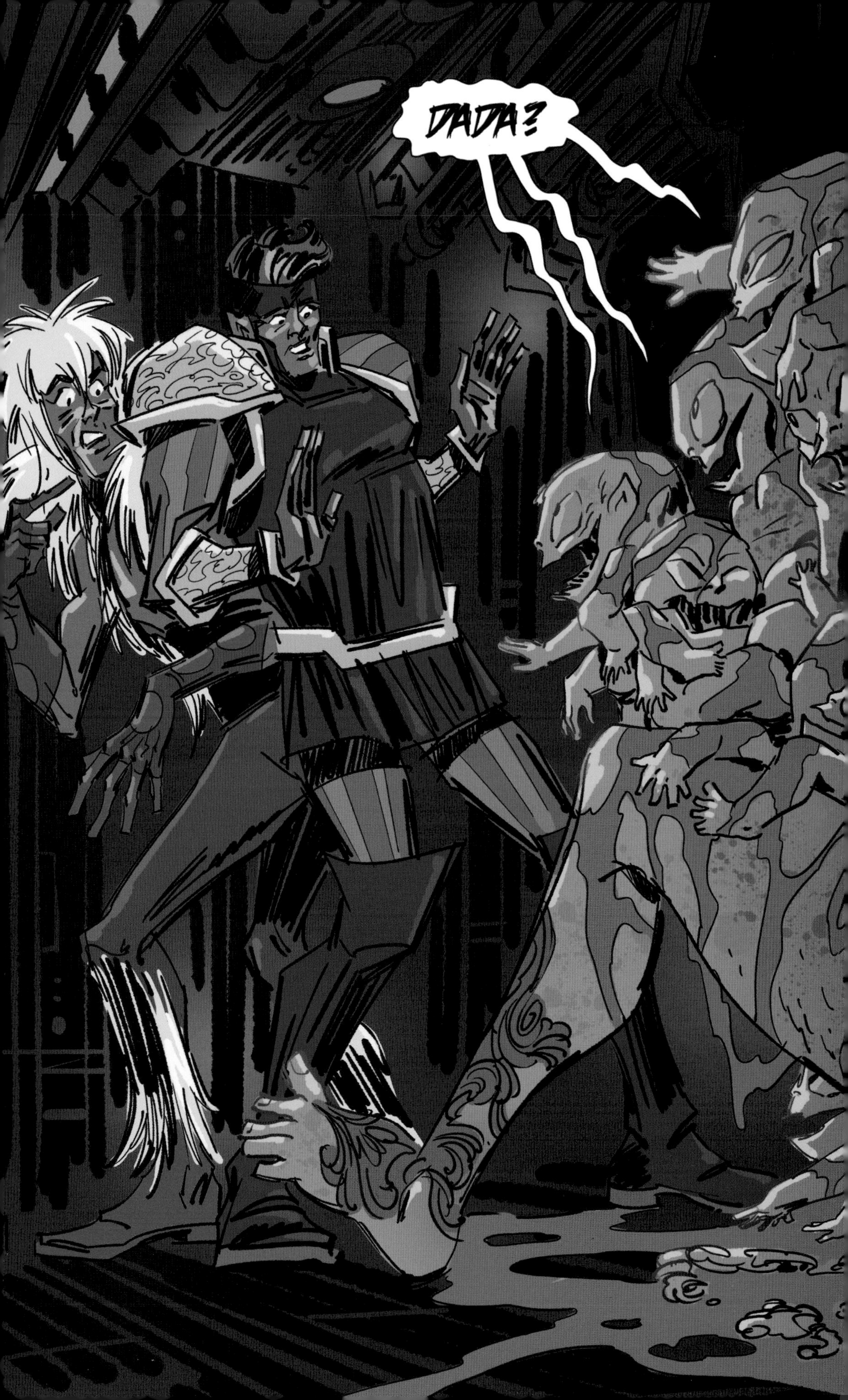
DADA?

ANDY SURIANO

Andy is an Emmy and Annie Award winning artist, having worked on animated television shows like *Samurai Jack, Star Wars: Clone Wars, Disney's Mickey Mouse Shorts* and is currently co-executive producing Nickelodeon's *Rise of the Teenage Mutant Ninja Turtles*. He spends his remaining waking hours obsessing over comics, having done IDW's *Samurai Jack* series, co-created *Charlatan Ball* and *Doc Bizarre MD* from Image Comics as well as the one in your hands right now!

MATT CHAPMAN

Matt mostly makes internet cartoons with his brother (*Homestar Runner, Two More Eggs*). Sometimes he writes and does voices for TV cartoons (*Gravity Falls, Pickle & Peanut*) and sometimes he even makes comics with Andy! He lives in Decatur, Georgia with his wife and family and they actually had a pretty good garden this summer with enough cucumbers to make pickles three times. Three times!